Power, Passions, and Purpose

Power, Passions, and Purpose
Prospects for North-South Negotiations

edited by
Jagdish N. Bhagwati
and
John Gerard Ruggie

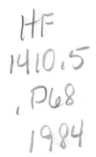

The MIT Press
Cambridge, Massachusetts
London, England

Second printing, 1985

This book was set in Palatino
by The MIT Press Computergraphics Department
and printed and bound by The Murray Printing Co.
in the United States of America.

Library of Congress Cataloging in Publication Data

Main entry under title:

Power, passions, and purpose.

   Papers presented at the Conference on Global Negotiations, held in New Delhi,
January 1983, sponsored by the Indian Council for Research in International Eco-
nomic Relations and the International Economics Research Center of Columbia
University.

   Includes bibliographies and index.
   1. International economic relations—Congresses.
I. Bhagwati, Jagdish N., 1934– . II. Ruggie, John Gerard, 1944– . III. Conference on
Global Negotiations (1983 : New Delhi, India).   IV. Indian Council for Research on
International Economic Relations. V. Columbia University. International Economics
Research Center.
HF1410.5.P68   1984   337   83–24843
ISBN 0–262–02201–X
ISBN 0–262–52091–5 (pbk.)

This book was prepared under the auspices of the International Economics Research
Center at Columbia University in New York.

Contents

Preface

In January 1983 the Indian Council for Research in International Economic Relations (ICRIER) and the International Economics Research Center (IERC) of Columbia University jointly held a Conference on Global Negotiations in New Delhi. The conference, attended by several policy makers and by academics from different countries, was inaugurated by India's finance minister. Its objective was to consider the stalled Global Negotiations at the United Nations and to seek ways to revitalize efforts at promoting North-South international economic cooperation.

The conference was a considerable success. In addition to the main invited papers, which are published in this volume, the participants had the benefit of several prepared documents and statements by distinguished speakers who held diverse points of view.

The present volume is not the only publication to emerge from the New Delhi conference. The ICRIER issued a pamphlet, *Global Negotiations: A Pragmatic Approach*, written by S. Guhan and M. R. Shroff, which splendidly summarized the discussions and indicated forcefully the actions that the Southern leadership might take in North-South matters. The IERC issued a statement, drafted by Carlos Díaz-Alejandro and Jagdish Bhagwati and signed by several academics and policy makers from countries in both North and South, that also urged the South (and the North) to take specific steps to break the logjam in Global Negotiations. The statement, along with other documentation, was published as a policy paper by the IERC in February 1983. The ICRIER and IERC publications were both released in time for the meeting of the nonaligned nations at New Delhi in March 1983, and may have played some part in influencing the shift toward more pragmatic negotiating positions that emerged from that meeting.

The conference could not have been organized without the tireless efforts of K. B. Lall, the dynamic chairman of the ICRIER, and Vijay Pande, the deputy director of the Ford Foundation in New Delhi. They not only provided excellent facilities but also managed to procure the attendance of many distinguished policy makers. The brilliant young economists at the ICRIER, and the supporting staff there and at the Ford Foundation, must also be thanked for their organizational work.

We also thank the Ford Foundation, especially Enid Schoettle and Vijay Pande, for providing the financial support without which we could not have translated our plan for this conference into reality.

In conclusion, we record our thanks to the late S. V. Purushottam, deputy representative of the Indian mission at the United Nations. He was widely known and respected for his considerable grasp of the North-South negotiations, for his grace and wit, and for his unceasing willingness to listen to new ideas. His deep interest in our efforts, both during and after the conference, was of enormous value to us. His untimely death shortly after his return to New York from the nonaligned countries' meeting in New Delhi has deprived the Group of 77 of one of its most dynamic and effective leaders and the intellectual community of an invaluable bridge to the ongoing Southern diplomatic initiatives on North-South questions.

Jagdish N. Bhagwati
John Gerard Ruggie

Power, Passions, and Purpose

1 Introduction

Jagdish N. Bhagwati

Sudden changes in style and substance have afflicted the North-South dialogue since the 1960s. The tortuous twists are traceable to the fact that the North-South debate and negotiations have reflected shifting realities and perceptions (which are not necessarily rooted in realities) of the configuration of power within and between these two political entities. In the postwar period, there have been sharp and discontinuous shifts as a result of dramatic changes (such as the rise of OPEC) and gradual ones in response to underlying trends (such as the increasing integration of the Southern nations into the world economy).

The style of the dialogue has therefore shifted from a civilized, bourgeois conversation during periods of undoubted Northern power and tentative Southern probing in the early postwar years, to the passionate Southern voice of solidarity and confrontation in the immediate aftermath of OPEC, and then to a frustrated Southern monologue ever since as the early post-OPEC Northern perception of Southern strength yielded to reality.

The substance, in turn, has shifted equally from "minimalist" ameliorative demands for changes in the international economic management structure devised at Bretton Woods, to "maximalist" demands for a major "restructuring" of this edifice, and then back to seeking "immediate measures" to confront (in the Brandt Commission's words) the common crisis.

The changing substance has reflected underlying philosophical differences in the way North-South interactions (and hence the optimal global institutional design and objectives) are conceived. It has also embraced what appear superficially to be matters of mere form but are matters of certain import: the question as to where the North-South negotiations should take place and the related issue of whether these negotiations must be comprehensive or global in format rather than sectoral and addressed only to segmented issues at a time.

The volatility of the perceptions of power configurations and the complexity of the interaction among these perceptions and negotiating positions and processes have contributed to the malaise that afflicts the current state of the North-South dialogue. As is argued in this volume (in the chapters by Bhagwati and Bressand, in particular), a substantial disjunction arose in the late 1970s, and even more in the early 1980s, between the ambitious negotiating style and stances adopted by the Southern leadership and the objectively weak negotiating power of the South (which was further recognized as such by the North). The Global Negotiations on North-South issues, which the South had sought at the United Nations since 1979, presupposed a power configuration that obtained fleetingly in the first flush of OPEC's success; they were incongruent with the power configuration that soon followed. The power had vanished; the passions had not subsided; the grand purpose still endured.

My objective at the New Delhi conference in January 1983 that led to this volume was to illuminate this disjunction between power and purpose and to explore its consequences. In particular, this question had to be asked: Should the South persist in trying to launch these negotiations, or is a different approach to North-South negotiations called for? The answer would have to confront realistically the prevailing power configuration and judgments as to its stability. It would also have to address both the forum for and the substance of the negotiations that would be advocated.

These issues are variously addressed by the authors in this volume. However, their thoughts need to be synthesized with one another and put into a coherent historical and analytical perspective. This chapter seeks to do that by exploring alternative views (each of which is historically relevant to some segment of the postwar period) of the power configuration characterizing the North and the South and the consequences of these views for the issues at hand.

Power Configurations and Consequences for North-South Negotiations

If for the present we set aside the issues raised by intra-South and intra-North power distribution and concentrate on the North-South power configuration,[1] we can distinguish four different sets of such configurations. Each of them has led to divergent views about what kinds of North-South dialogue and relations can be expected to materialize and evolve.[2] Because reform proposals (except when proposed as utopias) must reflect implicit assumptions of feasibility, these in turn have varied according to the implicit views concerning the North-South power configuration.

Virtual Dominance of the North

At one end of the spectrum, the South has no bargaining power at all. This was possibly true of the 1950s, when countries were still emerging into independent nationhood or struggling with the manifold problems attendant thereon.

In this situation the South can be expected to go along with the international economic management structure devised by the North—in this instance, Bretton Woods—reflecting the North's economic, philosophical, and ideological conception of what the world order should be like. With the United States dominant at the end of World War II, the economic ideology was naturally what I earlier described (Bhagwati 1977) as one of "benign neglect" within a Benthamite framework, extending to the international arena the viewpoint held equally at the national level. Alternatively, this order has been described as the Liberal International Economic Order (LIEO) and as *Pax Americana* in view of U.S. dominance (or hegemony, in the Gramscian sense as adapted by the political scientist Cox and discussed immediately below).[3]

Evidently, no real negotiations between North and South can be expected if this view is held, and indeed none were expected in the postwar period through much of the 1950s. The South was simply supposed to fit into the LIEO and (in views made more explicit by the Reagan administration ideologues recently) to gain like everyone else from the LIEO framework. The World Bank extended a small hand to the private sector in the Southern nations. Aid programs were beginning, but they were largely altruistic, not the result of demands from a strong South that had to be accommodated.

Northern Hegemony and the Voice of the Southern Nonhegemons

The Gramsci-Cox version of the postwar period of "benign neglect" or the LIEO, however, goes one step further toward endowing the South with some voice. In this view, the North's dominating position implied a hegemonic role. A hegemon is a stability-seeking power that recognizes that its dominant ideology and the attendant institutional structure cannot endure for long unless the nonhegemonic members of that structure accept its legitimacy. This legitimacy is secured through incrementalist, gradualist, marginalist accommodation of nonhegemonic discontent. The voice of the nonhegemons therefore does matter, for it can be stilled only at a price. The South is therefore not entirely powerless.[4] Probed deeper, this thesis is perhaps only a variant of the "enlightened self-interest" doctrine that keeps reemerging, especially in the service of social democrats. Moreover, although *ex ante* the hegemonic distribution of accommodationist largesse in search of legitimacy seems sensible, *ex post* realities may be wholly unexpected; for example, such accommodation may destabilize rather than co-opt.

There may be something in the hegemonic view, however, if we think of North-South relations through the late 1950s and the 1960s. As I note in my chapter, and as Ruggie also observes in his,[5] several of the changes the Bretton Woods international economic management structure undertook, such as the enactment of part IV at the General Agreement on Tariffs and Trade (GATT) and the start of the Compensatory Finance Facility at the International Monetary Fund (IMF), responded to Southern, nonhegemonic discontent without compromising the central thrust of the LIEO as devised by a hegemonic United States and its willing quasi-hegemonic allies in Western Europe.

That Southern dissent and discontent were growing through this period is beyond doubt. Several nonhegemons certainly did not subscribe wholeheartedly to the "benign neglect" philosophy underlying the LIEO, and the hegemonic consensus over the LIEO was beginning to fray at the periphery as what I have described elsewhere (Bhagwati 1977) as the "malign neglect" and "malign intent" views of how the LIEO operates with respect to the South came into vogue and competed for attention. Moreover, these were the years when a growing number of Southern nations came to be politically conscious of the fact that they did not have much say in the creation of the Bretton Woods institutions, nor (owing to weighted voting) were they influential in their operation. Accommodation in some respects was therefore prudent. In some respects it was not even expensive, as in the granting of exemptions from most-favored-nation (MFN) obligations and reciprocity requirements at the GATT, which, given the low interdependency in trade at the time, could be safely conceded without serious damage to the North's own interests.[6]

Consistent with the presumed lack of strength on the part of the nonhegemonic South, these accommodations were made on a single-issue basis at the specialized international agencies: the International Monetary Fund (IMF), the International Bank for Reconstruction and Development (IBRD), and the GATT.[7] The United Nations Conference on Trade and Development (UNCTAD) was indeed created in 1964, over initial U.S. hesitation. However, while it did evolve into an institution that increasingly adopted positions reflecting Southern aspirations and demands, it did not play an executive, negotiating, and implementing role in regard to any of the substantive matters falling traditionally within the jurisdiction of the Bretton Woods agencies. The action was still at those agencies, where hegemonic dominance was ensured.

North-South Interdependence and Mutual Gains

If the hegemonic paradigm argues that the South has an element of strength simply because the hegemon seeks legitimacy, the "interdependence" school endows the South with a somewhat greater and more effective voice by suggesting that the world economy offers, in view of the multifarious interactions among the nations of the North and the South, several opportunities for creative "partnership."[8] Seizing these opportunities provides the rationale for international cooperation; failure to do so implies an opportunity cost in terms of benefits forgone. Indeed, failure to cooperate in certain areas, such as the human environment, may imply a positive harm to all.

This is indeed a "super-functionalist" view of North-South relations, and it stands, in my judgment, in contrast to the Cox-eyed hegemonic conception, which implies that the North ideologically opts for the LIEO and then modifies its institutional structure marginally to accommodate the South simply to secure legitimacy. On the other hand, the super-functionalist view implies that the LIEO, while constructed to everyone's advantage, has to be modified and supplemented through institutional changes that benefit all.[9] The contrast between the two viewpoints is evident if one considers foreign aid and institutions dispensing it. The hegemonic thesis would view such aid as a pacification device, a bribe to buy stability. The super-functionalists, if they do not wish to regard it as an altruistic phenomenon, as they well might (in contrast to the Coxian conception), will be inclined to look for a broader range of nonideological arguments that show the North to have an indirect self-interest in parting with funds such that mutual gain follows. A classic example is provided by the Brandt Commission's first report, issued in 1979, which proposed that aid would generate demand for Northern goods and hence redound to Northern advantage. This was, of course, the economists' counterpart of the political argument advanced during the 1950s and later by several aid proponents that aid, in addition to being altruistic and a moral obligation, would promote democracy and social harmony in the South by accelerating development and would thereby serve the political interests of the democratic Western nations.

However, while the advocates of redistributive programs, with their essential zero-sum-game thrust, have often tried to pull them out of the altruistic arena, the "interdependence" thesis is in its most natural habitat when rather more direct and plausible "mutual gain," or non-zero-sum-game, opportunities are detected and institutions plus programs suggested for seizing them. Since economists have been trained to recognize mutual-gain situations ever since the invisible hand was seen by Adam Smith, it may be inevitable that they have been in the forefront of the proponents of this approach. These proponents include Richard Cooper (1977) and me (1977), and they also have influential converts, such as the Brandt commissioners.

Super-functionalists are not necessarily gradualists or incrementalists, whether in relation to the LIEO philosophy or in regard to the magnitude and nature of institutional reform. Thus, they have occasionally argued that the North and the South can find mutual advantage in instituting commodity schemes; if so, this leads to the Common Fund and certainly a departure from the vulgar, purist version of the LIEO philosophy. Again, I have argued that there are now both moral and mutual-gain arguments for filling the institutional vacuum in regard to international migration, via a code of conduct and possibly through the creation of an agency (similar to the UNCTAD) to oversee and review developments comprehensively in this field.[10]

Yet another fallacy that needs to be laid to rest is that super-functionalist mutual-gain proposals promise certain progress in North-South negotiations. What is valid, and what has really been the assertion of the super-functionalists, is rather that mutual-gain schemes are more likely to be accepted than zero-sum-gain redistributive proposals—unless the South is strong (as was fleetingly thought during the mid-1970s). I believe that this assertion is unimpeachable. The progress in acceptance of most mutual-gain schemes is, however, likely to be slow, simply because such mutual gains have to be perceived as such by the parties, and they have to be seen as substantial enough relative to alternative arrangements over which they have greater control for governments to undertake the process of institutional change or innovation. The problem is further compounded by the unending dissensions among economists themselves on the consequences (and hence the merits) of alternate proposals such as commodity schemes, and by the fact that different countries within the broad groups such as the South and the North are often differently affected by specific changes of policies and institutions so that coalition forming can become an arduous and often an insuperable process. Telling evidence of the former difficulty is the deep division among eminent economists on the merits of commodity schemes aimed at price or revenue stabilization and the volatility of opinion on the subject by the same economists.[11] A distressing example of the latter difficulty is the question of debt relief in the mid-1970s. Proposals for granting generalized debt relief to the developing countries, as against treating them case by case, eventually divided the poorest developing countries from the newly industrialized countries (NICs), which had massively entered the post-OPEC financial market and did not wish to see their access to these sources of funds jeopardized by talk of generalized debt relief.

In fact, the mutual-gain approach, while capable of being pursued on a single-issue negotiating track, has provided some momentum instead to a many-issue, comprehensive-bargaining approach for precisely this coalition-forming reason, and not simply because, from a theoretical viewpoint, simultaneous bargains on many fronts can lead to greater payoffs than segmented bargains on single issues.[12]

At the same time, however, the all-embracing bargaining approach has been pursued largely in the context of a militant posture of Southern strength that stressed maximalist, zero-sum-game-type demands or restructuring. It is difficult, therefore, to judge whether the approach has yielded few results because of maximalist demands or because of the difficulties inherent in such an ambitious bargaining approach (for reasons such as those explored by Zartman and Sewell in this volume from the theoretical perspectives of negotiating theory and the practical perspectives of several recent multilateral negotiations). These difficulties are, primarily, that the negotiations would become excessively cumbersome; that coalition forming among the 117 members of the Group of 77 (G-77), which speaks for the South, is too impractical in scope; and that the pluralistic, democratic countries of the North have bureaucratic structures and single-issue political lobbies that make it difficult to contemplate the governments' sacrificing on one issue to gain on another in an overall, grand North-South bargain. Partial derivatives are, unfortunately, difficult to take in the analysis of such phenomena.

Southern Strength: Commodity Power, NIEO, and Global Negotiations

Without doubt, a contributory factor in the stalemate on North-South negotiations to date has been that the immediate post-OPEC-success years, especially 1973 and 1974, witnessed the emergence of the perception that the South, in conjunction with the "newly emancipated" OPEC countries, had significant political strength in relation to the North. OPEC signified a role model for several other commodities exported by the South; unilateral cartelization would lay the importing North open to unavoidable redistribution of income. Besides, such redistribution would be accompanied by sovereign capacity to use the redistributed resources, whereas aid entails restrictions and performance criteria.

The notion of "commodity power" plus OPEC's political support of the developing countries (evidently with a view to legitimating their cartel to minimize the risks inherent in the exercise of such dramatic economic power in conjunction with total military impotence with respect to the North) combined with the North's immediate perception of economic vulnerability to produce a fleeting but significant period when the South's negotiating ability was remarkably enhanced.[13]

The result was that the sound level of the North-South dialogue, which hitherto had variously reflected elements of the three paradigms I have just outlined, went up several decibels. The militancy of style was matched by a shift in the negotiating substance toward increased emphasis on redistributive programs such as producers' cartels, the Special Drawing Rights (SDR)-link proposal, increased aid flows, and a managed shift of industries from the North to the South to conform to definite targets. A New International Economic Order (NIEO)—no less—was the objective.

It may have been inevitable that such objectives would require negotiating everything together. If the South were to set ambitious targets, it had to stick together in solidarity; the bargains to be struck therefore would have to be to everyone's advantage, and hence the issues could not be taken up in isolation. Moreover, restructuring the LIEO into an NIEO also meant taking a comprehensive view. It was also, perhaps, inevitable that eventually the South would consider the United Nations the ideal place to strike the grand bargain; that is where the South had the voting strength, not in the specialized agencies.[14] Part of the grand bargain would then also be the simultaneous, ongoing shift of the foci of control and operation of international economic management away from the specialized agencies to the United Nations.

A Requiem and a New Beginning?

None of this, however, made political sense once commodity power was seen to be ephemeral. And, as I note in my chapter, once OPEC itself began its slide as the world slumped, the negotiating strength of the South waned. The ambitious substance and the all-embracing nature of the Global Negotiations sought by the South therefore lost their raison d'être. The failure to get the North to launch the negotiations since 1980 was easily understood once one saw clearly the sharp disjunction between Southern demands and Southern strength.

If the Global Negotiations are not in conformity with the North-South power configuration that obtains and is likely to endure, then a quite requiem is appropriate. This is what many—including Bressand, Gwin, and me—suggest in the present volume. Temporarily suspending the Global Negotiations, or bypassing them, is the agreeable version of this prescription; it may also be the wise one in view of the potential for disrupting the South's political solidarity that an excessive influx of reality might pose.[15] Ruggie reinforces this viewpoint by underlining that restructuring cannot take place without power. It is remarkable that, although this position aroused controversy at the time of the conference in January 1983, it had won wide acceptance by the time of the nonaligned nations' meeting in March 1983, at which the Global Negotiations were put on the back burner for a year.

If the Global Negotiations are to be effectively suspended, what prescriptions follow at the constructive level? One long-term remedy from the power-configuration analysis is that the South ought to build up its bargaining strength. Economic relations with the centrally planned economies and within the South have often been considered in this light. This volume explores these possibilities.

Desai's chapter offers little comfort to those who would look to the South-CPE arena toward this end. The Soviet Union rejects multilateral obligations of the kind envisaged under the North-South negotiating umbrella, preferring to stick wholly to what Desai christens as the philosophy of *quid pro quo* bilateralism. The South therefore gets little in the way of formal commitments to its advantage. At the same time, the Soviet Union and the other centrally planned economies have become competitors with the South for credits in the world's financial markets. Their technology, principally in the heavy sector, is also no longer appropriate; the NICs have moved on to sophisticated know-how from the North, whereas the newly developing countries at the bottom of the scale embrace developmental programs that require agricultural, educational, and other technologies where the Soviet comparative and absolute advantages are minuscule. A faltering economic partnership with the Soviet bloc is in prospect.

South-South economic prospects are more promising, and Sanjaya Lall's chapter helps to put them into perspective. While he touches lightly on technology flows within the South, it is evident that these are emerging between the NICs and other developing countries, as would be expected from the fact that the NICs have achieved a degree of industrialization and attendant technological sophistication that puts them ahead of the lesser developing countries. However limited they are to date, these flows constitute an improvement in the Southern capacity for better bargains in some cases in a highly imperfect technology market. An interesting example is provided, in fact, by Desai in the Soviet context: The Nigerians used Indian design engineering capacity, partly assisted originally by Soviet training programs for Soviet-aided steel plants at Bhillai and Bokaro, to evaluate Soviet plans for a steel mill in Nigeria. Southern technology also has diversified somewhat the range of technological choice open to other developing countries. Trade in goods has also witnessed a surge, reflecting again a nascent and growing NIC comparative advantage with respect to the less industrialized developing countries in skill-intensive goods. Perhaps this momentum will sustain itself. I imagine that the outcome will depend ultimately on whether more developing countries will learn to operate relatively open trading systems. The lesson of the postwar period has been that remarkable growth in world trade is feasible as long as access to markets is preserved under the "rule of law" as was more or less managed under GATT. By contrast, planning trade by quantities, under managed systems, tends to undercut trade expansion, since bureaucrats simply cannot perceive and seize trade opportunities that a multitude of profit-seeking entrepreneurs can under ensured market access. As long as developing countries fail to ease restrictions on access to their markets, it is not likely that significant South-South trade expansion can be sustained in the long run.[16]

Therefore, although in specific instances and areas the CPE-South and South-South economic interactions are certain to be useful in themselves and may even at times contribute to better bargaining ability vis-à-vis the North, they are not an alternative to North-South relations. Nor can they be expected to serve as a method of securing general concessions from the North.

Can we nonetheless derive greater optimism concerning Southern bargaining ability via the interdependence and mutual-gain route? The super-functionalists can point to two phenomena that have intensified North-South linkages. On the trade side, 40 percent of U.S. exports are to developing countries now. More compelling is the world debt situation, which links Southern financial solvency, and hence Southern economic prosperity, directly with Northern bankers' health and hence with Northern economic prosperity.

However, the former linkage via trade does not quite translate into effective power for several reasons. That this linkage implies that the North would benefit from Southern prosperity does not mean that the South has power, any more than such linkage means that the North has power; the vulgar fallacy of dependency should apply symmetrically if at all. Moreover, as Ruggie notes, the enhanced linkage is only with a very small group of developing countries, the NICs. As it happens, many of these NICs, such as Brazil, Taiwan, and Singapore, are not even members of the nonaligned movement and often are unsympathetic to G-77 opinions on North-South issues.

The latter linkage, via the explosive debt situation, is far more of a useful linkage than trade provides, for it does pull into the game more of the influential Northern pressure groups (in the shape of banks) than trade ever does (since, for reasons that economists interested in political economy have begun to explore systematically, the exporting pressure groups are far less effective than import-competing lobbies).[17] But again the efficacy of this linkage in improving the Southern bargaining capacity is limited by several facts. For one thing, the Southern countries deeply affected by the debts are the NICs. Their general inclination is likely to be cautious, precisely because they would like to continue borrowing, for the political survivability of their governments is a function of their continued borrowing. Moreover, many of the NICs, such as Brazil, Singapore, and Taiwan, are not exactly enthusiastic supporters of Southern positions in North-South issues; not only are the prosperous developing countries under both internal and external psychological and political pressure to be co-opted into Northern postures, but a combination of political circumstances has made it more costly for them to take more militant positions against the North, especially the United States. Nonetheless, the debt position does imply a certain bargaining advantage. The possible nature of this advantage is discussed by Díaz-Alejandro in his chapter:

> How much pressure can LDCs exercise in international financial bargaining? Can Southern debts be aggregated into one powerful bargaining chip? One is skeptical: Mexico is unlikely to want its debt lumped with that of Bolivia or even Brazil for bargaining purposes. One may recall that during the December 1933 Pan American conference held in Montevideo, the Mexican delegation proposed a general moratorium on external debts, an initiative promptly shot down by the distinguished Argentine Foreign Minister, Dr. Saavedra Lamas. . . . Yet demonstration effects among debtors could occur during a severe international crisis, leading them to sequentially suspend normal debt service, as during the early 1930s. This may be enough to give at least some LDCs a bit of influence to press for reexamination of international monetary and financial arrangements, perhaps in the context of a "new Bretton Woods."

Recognizing this possible bargaining advantage, I propose in my chapter that the Southern leadership ought to seek a movement in the stalled North-South relations by asking for an international monetary conference, stressing for diplomatic reasons that the original idea was put forth by U.S. Secretary of the Treasury Donald Regan. Such a conference would not merely provide a forum for dealing with the debt situation by examination and possible negotiation of one of the many schemes currently canvased by prominent proponents;[18] it also would provide a means to underline the critical relationship between holding protectionism in the North at bay and ensuring the solvency of the debtors who must sell to repay and borrow. Such market access can be provided by negotiating for a protectionist "standstill"—for example, while the world works its way out of the Reaganomics-caused world slump.

Since the NICs are the ones who are most affected by potential protectionism, the linkage of the debt-management solution to the ensuring of market access is of interest, and hence of negotiating value, to the same Southern countries that are endowed with the bargaining "strength" by the debt situation. It can therefore be confidently expected that such Southern concerns in trade matters would find their way onto the agenda of such a proposed conference. At the same time, the NICs can fully expect the North to raise the issue of "graduation," such that the NICs wind up "losing" their nonreciprocity and preferential-entry privileges under the GATT (as amended to permit the developing countries to be granted such privileges). This is a difficult issue for the NICs, but it must be confronted sometime. As both Wolf and Behrman emphasize in their chapters, the advantages of an open trading system have by now been sufficiently demonstrated, not just theoretically by the theorists of international trade[19] but also by the contrasting postwar experience of the developing countries that adhered too long to the import-substitution strategy and those that moved rapidly onto an export-promoting and outward-oriented posture.[20]

If such advantages do occur, and if the advantages from preferential-entry schemes have been both small and negligible compared to those derived from nondiscriminatory access to the markets of the North, as Wolf also stresses, then the case is indeed rather strong for dispensing with the protectionist structure that many developing countries (especially the NICs) still embrace. It is not clear that the willingness to graduate can be translated into firmer market access at the bargaining table where the NICs would face the North, but it is certainly a card that will need to be played soon. Besides, as Wolf notes, the NICs' ability to argue plausibly for a protectionist standstill and for continued, ensured access to Northern markets cannot be expected to carry weight as long as the NICs refuse to accept some form of market-access obligations themselves, despite their new status in the world markets.

Where does all this leave the developing countries that have neither substantial debt-related bargaining power nor market-access interests that can be linked to it? For such Southern countries (and there are many) there is really no effective bargaining power except that which emerges from bilateral, political considerations (for example, the strategic importance of the Central American countries gives them some bargaining power with the United States), as indeed does occur in some instances for the NICs as well (as in the case of Brazil, Argentina, and Mexico with respect to the United States). There is really no such consideration that yields effective bargaining power to the bulk of the developing countries, however. Yet these are among the majority of the Southern countries. What are their concerns? Can they be fitted into the NICs' concerns somehow at an international conference of the type proposed in my chapter?

The most compelling questions for these developing countries relate to their export earnings, which are heavily dependent on primary exports, and to their need for official assistance. Both problems have been extremely serious during the recent world depression. The cyclical aspect of the former problem has led to a renewed demand for commodity schemes aimed at price or revenue stabilization, including at the Belgrade UNCTAD meeting in June 1983. Unfortunately, such schemes typically tend to come apart, even when successfully launched, since the producers tend to lose interest when prices are rising and the consumers when they are falling. But there is also a theoretical reason to prefer a different, two-policy-instrument approach. Revenue destabilization over the cycle may be alleged to create two different problems. One is in the foreign exchange market, where liquidity problems can arise from such exchange earning fluctuations; the other is an internal problem of shifting incentives for producers and instability for consumers. If these are indeed problems, then the Tinbergen theory that the number of necessary instruments should generally equal the number of targets implies that it would be necessary, and more efficient, to use two instruments in the present problem rather than one. Commodity schemes to use international buffer stocks to stabilize earnings represent the use of one instrument to solve both problems. On the other hand, the use of two instruments—say, the Compensatory Financing Facility (CFF), suitably augmented, to address the international liquidity problem, and national buffer stocks to address the domestic producer and consumer effects if they are considered detrimental—would seem to be a more efficient solution. The answer to the problem of the cyclical instability of the developing countries' primary exports earnings therefore lies, in terms of international implications, in the area of the CFF and its reform and augmentation. The details of this are discussed by Díaz-Alejandro in the context of the overall cyclical instability of the world economy and its effects on the downside of the business cycle in the present age of heavy financial integration and indebtedness in the world economy.[21]

Since, then, the primary export earnings problem of the developing countries itself embraces reform and expansion in international monetary facilities such as the CFF, it is evident that the proposed international monetary conference can readily be extended to address the chief concerns of not merely the NICs but also the rest of the developing countries.

An international monetary conference, therefore, provides both an appropriate format and the possibility of a realistic and useful agenda for seeking negotiable changes in the international regime in the present power configuration. By contrast, the pursuit of Global Negotiations at this stage could prove to be a distraction—indeed a wasteful and counterproductive diversion—with no rationale in the current power configuration. These conclusions are stark and must sound like a betrayal to the faithful, but Southern interests and aspirations are ill served by politically irrelevant rhetoric that is aimed at the unnegotiable; they are advanced, rather, by realistic analysis and prescription.

It is interesting, therefore, that the New Delhi summit of the non-aligned countries decided to put the Global Negotiations on the back burner for at least one year and embraced the objective of an international monetary conference. Both of these proposals had been advanced during the deliberations by the contributors to this book two months earlier in New Delhi.

These initiatives, which will need Southern leadership to be translated into effective action, need to be supplemented by a further set of actions concerning what Díaz-Alejandro and I (in a statement issued before the nonaligned summit and annexed to this book) have called "medium-term reform": first, further changes within the specialized agencies such as the IMF and the World Bank to give greater voice to the South without compromising (and indeed often improving) the efficiency of their operation, as extensively argued by Gwin in her chapter; second, a serious examination of the working of the United Nations to restructure it such that it can play a role where a comprehensive view of the world economy and its functioning and implications for institutional action can be provided,[22] with the negotiations for institutional changes being undertaken at the specialized agencies; third, the filling of institutional lacunae to deal with new international economic problems such as international migration. There is indeed much here to keep the North-South diplomats and negotiators productively occupied. The radicals in the South will fear that this means abandoning the grand design and purpose of yesteryear, but did not Mao Tse-Tung say that even a long journey starts with a small step?

Notes

1. Strictly speaking, this is not always a valid procedure. If Algeria was dominant within the South and the South was strong vis-à-vis the North, the North-South power configuration would be very different from what it would be if Algeria was replaced by Taiwan or Brazil.

2. Each has had relevance to some part of the postwar period, and my description and analysis of each therefore will be intertwined with that historical experience.

3. Evidently I mean "liberal" in the Manchester School sense rather than the U.S. sense, where "liberals" have been more akin to European social democrats.

4. Evidently the USSR and the Soviet bloc do not fit this mold; here legitimacy is hard to get and power must come from the end of the barrel.

5. See Bhagwati 1977 and Ruggie 1982 for earlier, extended analyses of this period.

6. It is arguable, however, that it may have damaged the South's interests to have conceded the South's demands for such exemptions, as suggested by Wolf in his chapter.

7. The specialized international agencies referred to here are not what the phrase stands for in UN bureaucratic jargon, where they refer rather to FAO, WHO, and similar agencies. Also, while I and many authors include the GATT as part of the liberal Bretton Woods superstructure, it was not created at the Bretton Woods Conference.

8. This was the key concept in the Report of the Pearson Commission, the body that preceded the recent Brandt Commission.

9. I call this a "super-functionalist" rather than simply a functionalist view because, while the "structure and function" approach introduced into social anthropology by Radcliffe Brown was general in its scope, some political scientists have used the word *functionalism* in a much narrower sense. See, for example, Jacobson 1979.

10. Cf. my letter to *New York Times*, February 13, 1983, and an Associated Press interview, *New Haven Register*, March 1, 1983.

11. Thus, for example, Johnson (in Bhagwati 1977) was far more critical of these schemes than in his earlier writing (1967) on the subject for the Brookings Institution.

12. If each party in a two-agent, two-issue game loses on one issue but gains on another, there could well be no bargain struck although there is net gain from striking a bargain on each issue, whereas a simultaneous bargain on both issues could leave each party better off and hence make a deal feasible. The Law of the Sea negotiations are perhaps a telling example of how a many-issue negotiation, balancing commercial and military interests, made a treaty possible that otherwise would have been nonnegotiable. The eventual objections by the new Reagan administration were almost wholly ideological.

13. A detailed exploration of this theme is provided in Bhagwati 1977. The argumentation is carried to the present date in my chapter in this book.

14. Yet another contributing factor in the desired shift to the United Nations appears to have been the fear of the weaker Southern countries that their interests would be inadequately served if only a few of their Group of 77 members were participating in any negotiations. Global participation, as at the United Nations, would give them direct voice.

15. While politics puts a premium on compromise and therefore suspension rather than abandonment of Global Negotiations appears to offer an advantageous option, it is equally true that forceful leadership may be able to go

further. My own assessment, which is consonant with later events, is that the ideological diversity within the nonaligned movement is so great that compromise is the only diplomatic option.

16. This pessimism is equally applicable to the prospects for CPE trade. While CPEs are indeed capable of dramatic deals, their capacity to build up exports is severely limited by their inability to free up their system to perceive and exploit trading opportunities. Their denial of market access rights to developing countries, as indeed to all others, in turn dampens seriously the prospects for CPE-South trade, as Desai concludes in her chapter.

17. For a useful survey of this literature, see the essay by Robert Baldwin in Bhagwati 1982.

18. These are the "structural" reforms schemes such as the one proposed by Kenen, for example, which require going beyond the simple augmentation of the IMF quotas and SDR allocations, and the provision of funds under the General Agreement to Borrow (GAB). However, the willingness of the U.S. administration to consider such schemes is not currently noteworthy; in fact, the conversion of this administration to the view that GAB is not GRAB by the debtors was a relatively slow business. But the situation is volatile, and one cannot rule out further conversion of the administration to an acceptable structural reform plan at a monetary conference.

19. See, in particular, the arguments in the theoretical works of Bhagwati, Johnson and Meade, and other theorists cited by Martin Wolf.

20. For a survey of this literature, see my 1978 review with T. N. Srinivasan, "Trade Policy and Development." Several eminent economists at the start of the postwar period had raised the question of the appropriate strategies in this regard, among them Ragnar Nurkse, Gottfried Haberler, Jacob Viner, and Raul Prebisch. The younger generation of economists who have illuminated this area includes Bela Balassa (who has conducted several studies for the World Bank), Ian Little, Tibor Scitovsky and Maurice Scott (who conducted major studies for the OECD), and Anne Krueger (who codirected an ambitious project with me for the NBER). For a recent assessment by a group of political scientists, see Ruggie (1983).

21. Admittedly this solution does not extend to the desire to have commodity schemes that aim not just at revenue stabilization but also at increasing the trend price in favor of the developing countries. Quite aside from whether such schemes can be effectively implemented, there is the problem that these schemes are not what one can put on a North-South agenda any more than the OPEC oil price hikes were a matter of negotiation rather than unilateral acts that had to face the test of economic and political survivability.

22. The London Economist, June 11, 1983, p. 14, suggested such a role on North-South issues for UNCTAD. The respective roles of the UN Secretariat in New York and the UNCTAD in Geneva in these matters would also need to be clarified as part of the examination I propose. The Office of the Director General for Development and International Economic Cooperation in New York was

originally conceived to play a role that could have provided the comprehensive-view function I suggest.

References

Bhagwati, Jagdish N. 1977. *The New International Economic Order: The North-South Debate*. Cambridge: MIT Press.

———— and T. N. Srinivasan. 1978. "Trade Policy and Development." In R. Dornbusch and Jacob Frenkel, *International Economic Policy: Theory and Evidence*. Baltimore: Johns Hopkins University Press.

————, ed. 1982. *Import Competition and Response*. Chicago: University of Chicago Press.

Cooper, Richard. 1977. "A New International Economic Order for Mutual Gain." *Foreign Policy* (Spring).

Cox, Robert. 1980. "The Crisis of World Order and the Problem of International Organization in the 1980s." *International Journal* 35.

Jacobson, Harold K. 1979. *Networks of Interdependence: International Organizations and the Global Political System*. New York: Knopf.

Johnson, Harry G. 1967. *Economic Policies toward Less Developed Countries*. New York: Praeger.

Ruggie, John Gerard. 1982. "International Regimes, Transactions, and Change." *International Organization* 36.

————, ed. 1983. *The Antinomies of Interdependence*, New York: Columbia University Press.

I

The "Global Negotiations"

2

Rethinking Global Negotiations

Jagdish N. Bhagwati

The Global Negotiations at the United Nations have been stalemated ever since the UN General Assembly resolved at the 34th Session in 1979 to launch them in 1980 at a special session. The continued frustration of the South over this stalled situation and the bitterness generated by the sense that the North has been intransigent inject a sorry note into the ongoing North-South dialogue that traces back at least to the 1964 UNCTAD Conference. As attempts are currently being made to seek yet again a successful launching of the Global Negotiations during 1983, it is important to assess the underlying objectives that the South aspires to, and indeed to ask whether the Global Negotiations are the ideal, or possibly even a feasible, way to achieve these objectives.

A Historical Overview: Oil and All That

The story of North-South relations, and the dialogue concerning them, could be written in oil. In fact, the present state of Global Negotiations and the constraints and prospects that it presents in the evolving North-South situation cannot be meaningfully understood unless the key role played by oil is appreciated. Before oil entered the picture, North-South issues were already on the international scene, but they were to be transformed with the triumph of OPEC. A backward glance at that transformation is most illuminating.

Phase I: LIEO, Pax Americana, and the pre-OPEC Era

The postwar period was indeed the era of the Liberal International Economic Order (LIEO) par excellence. Under US leadership, which was tantamount to *Pax Americana*, the international institutions founded at the end of the war (IMF, IBRD, and GATT) provided the institutional umbrella under which trade, investments, and growth prospered. Unprecedented growth rates characterized the 1950s and 1960s, a Golden Age that has sadly vanished. But already the seeds of Southern unhappiness were sprouting during this period. Two, in particular, need to be noted.

First, the process of decolonization created many of the new nations of the South. In consequence, they played no role in shaping the specialized international agencies that defined the LIEO: Many of these nations simply did not exist at the time of this creation! This meant that they had little weight in the voting patterns; they were skeptical that their interests would be properly accounted for in the deliberations of these agencies; and even if they stood to gain from the workings of these agencies, perhaps the division of the gains was skewed against them. Politically, therefore, this translated into the familiar position which divides the South from the North: a preference for the one-nation one-vote approach, which in turn implies a preference for negotiations at the United Nations rather than at the international agencies with their traditionally weighted voting procedures.

Second, the dominant ideological position embodied in the LIEO was not fully shared by the new countries. And it could not be, especially in matters dealing with the classical choice between protection and freer trade. Historically, few countries have embraced free trade when they were behind. Moreover, export pessimism was fairly rampant in various guises during the 1950s, when several developing countries opted for import-substituting (IS) industrialization. But if views diverged on this fundamental issue, they were to grow apart on several others too. The LIEO reflects the traditional, mutual-gain approach under which benign neglect, with the right Benthamite framework, leads to the improvement of all. But as developing countries struggled with their problems and the early optimism about aid-assisted takeoffs gave way, and aid programs withered with the decline of the Cold War, rival philosophies appeared, accentuating the differences in perceptions, prejudices, and principles. In particular, the benign neglect school had now to compete with the malign neglect school—recall the famous aphorism: "Integration into the world economy leads to disintegration of the national economy"—and, in certain influential radical critiques, with the malign intent school as typified by the view that aid was an extension of the imperialist arm that sought to suffocate the new countries in a neocolonial embrace.[1] *Rashomon* is rooted in reality; and only an ideologue would deny these harsh possibilities altogether. So the ideological picture became increasingly blurred, with the South often not quite in harmony with the dominant ideological position of the North on the LIEO.

The period up to 1973 was therefore characterized by a growing, but still manageable, ideological and political disharmony between the politically influential countries of the South and the North. The postwar institutional structure, and its basic underlying rationale, were not yet subject to any radical onslaught. In fact, the developed countries had already made some accommodating responses by modifying the specialized agencies to reflect the Southern desires and concerns—introducing Part IV in GATT in 1964 and clearing the grant of GSP through waiver of Article I of GATT for ten years in the area of trade; instituting new low-conditionality facilities at the IMF to benefit Southern nations, the Compensatory Financing Facility in 1963 and the Buffer Stock Facility in 1969;[2] and creating at the IBRD the International Finance Corporation in 1956 and the International Development Association in 1960. Even the creation of UNCTAD in 1964 to oversee the manifold developmental problems of the developing countries, although a result of their aspirations and efforts at the UN, must also be viewed in this light, despite UNCTAD's later identification with Southern positions and the resulting tensions with specialized agencies such as GATT, and hence the disfavor it has subsequently incurred in the North.

Phase II: The Rise of OPEC and NIEO

The mildly accommodationist status quo of the postwar international regime was sharply interrupted by the success of OPEC, beginning in 1971. Four aspects of the resulting shift in the tone and content of the North-South dialogue must be emphasized.

First, the example of OPEC suggested to the developing countries that other commodities could be cartelized to extract resources unilaterally from the North. Hence reliance on commodity exports, which had always been thought of as a sign of dependence and the necessity for industrialization, was now considered a source of strengh! The economic concept of "commodity power" was born. The use of the 1973 oil embargo also suggested the political concept of commodity power: the North might be dependent on the South for commodities if the South could take unified positions and threaten interrupted supplies of commodities.

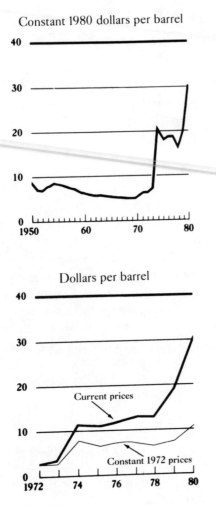

Constant 1980 dollars per barrel

Dollars per barrel

Current prices

Constant 1972 prices

Figure 2.1
Petroleum prices, 1950–1980 and 1972–1980 (annual averages).

Hence, the early 1970s witnessed a definite shift of gears. The South entered, with a perception of new strength, the negotiations phase, for negotiations cannot occur meaningfully between grossly unequal partners.

Second, and this is a critical point, the South's perception of new power was largely shared by the North at the time. OPEC's demonstrated strength made commodity power seem credible; and it was also directly pitted alongside the South in mutually supportive legitimation roles. Western Europe, feeling particularly vulnerable to OPEC and by and large also intellectually less antipathetic to Southern positions than the United States, played a major role in the conciliatory Northern response, which also led to the Conference on International Economic Cooperation (CIEC) at Paris during 1975–77.

Third, the key role of OPEC and commodity power in this equation made emphasis on commodities in the new situation inevitable. Just as GSP had become the symbol of the New Delhi UNCTAD II in 1968, commodity schemes were the symbol of the early 1970s and indeed at the Nairobi UNCTAD IV in 1976 where the negotiations on the integrated Program for Commodities were agreed upon.

Fourth, this key focus on commodities went hand in hand with the stance that the entire range of international economic issues—trade, money, aid, energy, raw materials, etc.—be negotiated together. This was partly a negotiating ploy, to prevent energy being negotiated in isolation to the North's advantage. But it also reflected the view, embodied in the New International Economic Order proclaimed at the 1973 Algiers Non-Aligned Conference and embraced at the UN General Assembly's 1974 Sixth Special Session, that the postwar LIEO institutional structure had to be reorganized to reflect the South's aspirations and interests. This approach was followed also at the CIEC in Paris.

Phase III: Déjà Vu and Regress

The euphoria that attended OPEC's success, however, soon vanished. The 1976–79 period was therefore characterized by a sense of déjà vu and frustration for the South.

First, OPEC itself gradually dimmed as a threat once the first oil shock (especially the quadrupling of oil prices during 1973) was absorbed, oil prices stabilized in subsequent years and conservation programs got hesitantly under way. Second, commodity power was soon realized to be illusory; oil was seen to have been a special case. The desired commodity schemes were therefore de facto transformed from unilateral OPEC-type producer cartels into joint arrangements between producers and consumers, thus destroying their original raison dêtre for superstellar status in North-South negotiations. Therefore, the Northern sense of vulnerability diminished during this period, and the urgency of reaching an accommodation with the South in a global negotiation, either at CIEC or elsewhere in the UN, vanished quickly from the scene.

Third, from the South itself, this tendency was reinforced in a paradoxical fashion. The successful recycling of petrodollars to several of the more developed of the developing countries meant that these were now being integrated into the current international regime. Their capacity to adopt militant, radical-reformist positions with respect to the North was thus increasingly undermined, making Southern solidarity somewhat less of a reality.

The result was regress in the North-South negotiations, with the South unable to exert effective pressure for its demands but still wedded to them. The North basically played along, conversing but making no real concessions. While the Northern lack of response was generally premised on the belated perception of lack of Southern power, it was also reinforced, in my view, by the paradoxical fact that OPEC's success, while whetting the South's demands politically, had also weakened significantly the Northern leaders' macroeconomic situation and hence their political and financial capacity to respond constructively, especially in regard to redistributive measures such as foreign aid flows. Thus, even the Carter Administration, despite its early professions of commitment to Third World causes, failed to deliver. A *Guardian* cartoon at the time captured this latter point rather well by showing Carter, Schmidt, et al. on the beach, busy reading a book on how to swim, while the Third World is drowning in the ocean. The caption read: "Hang in there; we will come out and get you as soon as we have learnt how to swim."

Phase IV: Return to Strong Posture: The Global Negotiations

During 1978–80, the 6 percent cut in world supply triggered by the Iranian Revolution led to the second set of sharp increases in the real price of oil: this time by 80 percent. This turn of events was the catalyst for a new lease of life for the notion of negotiating from strength.

At the Manila UNCTAD Conference in 1979, several developing countries had raised afresh the question of a special energy deal for the South. This was taken up at other Southern meetings throughout the succeeding months. The dramatic rise in oil prices that preceded the 1979 Havana Conference of the Non-Aligned Nations seems to have prompted Algeria to resurrect in Havana the NIEO approach it had launched in 1973 and to move these nations into resolving that comprehensive, global negotiations should be launched on North-South issues. This approach again found favor both with OPEC, which sought to defuse the Southern demands by linking energy to nonenergy issues, and with the North that again was reacting to the energy situation with renewed concern. As with Algiers, the Havana consensus was followed up at the UN General Assembly in its 34th Session where it was resolved that, at its 1980 special session, a round of global negotiations on international economic cooperation for development would be launched. These Global Negotiations, as a legacy from the unsuccessful CIEC attempt during 1975–77, would simultaneously embrace a whole range of issues: trade, finance, aid, energy, raw materials, etc. And the venue would be the UN, with the Committee of the Whole of the General Assembly acting as the preparatory body for these negotiations.

Phase V: The World Recession and Its Aftermath

But the consensus for launching Global Negotiations has been followed by inaction. Why?

The most compelling reason is that the oil card is currently played out. The success of conservation played a minor role. But ultimately the world recession, following on the tight-money policies of the Federal Reserve combined with the expansionary budget deficits and the resulting phenomenal rise in US interest rates, delivered the coup de grâce. In a sagging world oil market, as OPEC is increasingly in public view as a cartel in distress, the Global Negotiations have lost their political rationale once again. OPEC has nothing to offer, nothing to threaten: no quid pro quo therefore can be demanded from the North. Negotiations from strength, therefore, are simply unrealistic once again. And, hanging over the entire issue is the ideological orientation of the Reagan administration which has shifted the United States from the traditional, sympathetic, and accommodating role to a rather unabashed "rejectionist" one, as evidenced most dramatically in the refusal to sign the Law of the Sea treaty in Jamaica.[3] We are therefore back to regress on the Global Negotiations. Where should we then turn?

What Should We Do?

If the current capacity of the South to negotiate from strength, to extract concessions from the North, is virtually negligible, it is imperative that the Global Negotiations be reexamined realistically.

A principal lesson seems to be the futility of persisting with the Global Negotiations at this juncture, if at all. The most attractive option from the viewpoint of the South seems therefore to be an adjournment—at least until further notice. Or, if this sounds too drastic, a time limit for formally returning to efforts at launching them could be negotiated: a period of one year might be best, since it would broadly coincide with the beginning of a new presidential term in the United States and also with the anticipated recovery of the world economy. Given the South's political investment in the Global Negotiations, this step, in either of the two forms suggested, would naturally be preferable to abandonment of the talks altogether.

But this step, while disappointing to those wedded to the Global Negotiations, can be combined with simultaneous positive initiatives that seem presently to be negotiable and also consonant with some of the key objectives of the South. In particular, the fears over the international debt situation, in the midst of a profoundly disturbing world slump, have opened up a genuine area of mutual concern that draws into its ambit a number of influential countries of the North and the South.[4] The resulting recent exploratory thoughts by Mr. Regan, and in response by several Europeans, suggesting that an international monetary conference might be organized outside the IMF framework, and evidently with wider participation, represent an opportunity for the South to enter the scene actively. The South's spokesmen ought to move in on the ground floor of this idea, ensure that they participate constructively in its agenda, and thereby promote both their interests and their desire for more effective participation in the design of the resulting changes in the international monetary regime. Such an initiative would require both political action (e.g., active mobilization of the political leadership of the South, to get the US administration to support the conference proposal) and economic preparation (which would mean that the South provides the expertise to itself and assurance to the North that its participation at the conference would be mutually rewarding).[5]

I must emphasize the need for a thorough and careful preparation for entering and performing at such a conference. It is important that the Southern interests be realistically defined, and interests that do not concern us directly be dealt with at arm's length. In my view, the South ought to urge steps by the North for a quick recovery of the world economy. However, it should leave the matter of macroeconomic coordination and management, including the disharmony on exchange rate stability, as a debate between the Europeans and the United States. Nor should the South get involved in OPEC concerns (which were yesterday's Northern concerns) about stabilizing oil prices. The Southern interests lie, of course, in world recovery but the methods ultimately settled upon to institute it are for the most part not ones where we have special expertise or immediate interests.

I stress this last point particularly since the South, especially India and Colombia, attracted unnecessary irritation from the United States at the November 1982 GATT ministerial meeting in Geneva by opposing the proposal to extend the GATT to services. This matter was of special concern to the United States, which sees its comparative advantage shifting to services, and since the threat was greater to the Europeans and Japanese, who were nevertheless willing to go along with the studies of this proposal, the appropriate response of the developing countries should have been simply to say: "If you wish to open up this can of worms, fine; but we assert our right to protect our infant service sectors and therefore any extension of GATT to services will have to exempt the developing-country members through suitable clarification of Part IV et al."[6] I might also add that the South missed a fine opportunity at the GATT ministerial meeting in Geneva of putting UNCTAD into the services picture by reminding the developed countries that UNCTAD already had been studying the services for many years and that the proposed studies could be organized jointly under UNCTAD and GATT auspices.

Furthermore, the South should not attempt to resurrect the grandiose notions that have no bearing on the present crisis: a world central bank or the SDR-link are proposals that, no matter how attractive in certain circles and meritorious perhaps in the classroom, have simply no place in the South's current repertoire if it is planning to play a constructive, self-helping role at such a conference.

In my view, the South ought to concentrate instead on two interrelated items. First, the question of appropriate institutional structure and governing principles for debt management for the lucky few "middle-income" developing countries who borrowed heavily during the 1970s and who now have the Northern banks in their embrace: and second, the question of how to assist the unlucky low-income developing countries, many in Africa, but also including Bangladesh, which need official assistance, official debt relief and the like, especially in view of the collapse of their primary earnings.[7]

While the monetary conference, if it transpires, can provide an instructive departure from the specialized agencies in favor of a wider participation, it would also bring into play a possible role model for a compromise between the South's and the North's positions on the specialized agencies versus the UN as forums for negotiating on North-South issues. The monetary conference would discuss the substance of what ought to be done, trying to reach a consensus. But it does not rule out, in its present conception, the possibility that the ultimate negotiations would be conducted at the IMF itself (unless of course new institutions outside of the IMF were to emerge from these deliberations, as seems unlikely). A way of breaking the impasse at the Global Negotiations would be precisely to explore this possibility: that the UN Global Negotiations become, in effect, a discussion forum where the different issues are addressed within a comprehensive view of the problems facing the world economy and the North-South relations therein; whereas the actual negotiations are conducted at the specialized agencies. A possible enlargement of the UN role could then also be to bring the negotiated agreements at the specialized agencies back to the UN for a wider ratification. Attention would then have to be paid also to strengthening the specialized agencies in the direction of a greater Southern voice and Southern interests, a phenomenon that has certainly occurred, albeit slowly, in the preceding two decades. But this overall shift in focus and conception of what Global Negotiations ought to aim at and accomplish is something that we need to discuss seriously at this conference.

Notes

1. These diverse schools of thought were delineated and discussed at some length in my introductory essay in a book that I edited, *The New International Economic Order* (Cambridge, Mass.: MIT Press, 1977).

2. For an illuminating discussion of several of these changes, see John Ruggie, "Political Structure and Change in the International Economic Order: The North-South Dimension," paper presented to the conference "Rethinking Global Negotiations," International Economics Research Center, Columbia University, and Indian Council for Research in International Economic Relations, New Delhi, 6–8 January 1983.

3. The increasing influence of Secretary of State Shultz, however, may blunt the cutting edge of this reversal of the US role.

4. In this context, it is relevant to note that where genuine mutual interests obtain, North-South cooperation seems to emerge without our urging. The problem with the Brandt Commission's eloquent plea for more aid for the South, among other things, was simply that it appealed to mutuality of economic interests that simply were implausible except to those who wished to assist the South anyway. In this, the Commission was of course playing the same game, and with even less success, as the early aid advocates who proposed enlightened self-interest as an argument in favor of aid, but who invoked it in a political form (i.e., that aid would make the world safer for democracy).

5. The serious handicap under which the South operates in international negotiations owing to inadequate technical preparation has been documented by several observers. A particularly frank appraisal is to be found in *The North-South Dialogue: Making It Work* (London: Commonwealth Secretariat, 1982).

6. I should add that the United States also erred in trying to open up GATT to services while simultaneously trying to raise the graduation issue, thus arousing the fears of the SOUTHNICs that they would be under pressure to sign a service protocol without necessary exemptions eventually.

7. There is enough mutuality of interests in the case of the middle-income countries, between Northern banks and Southern borrowers, for such a dialogue to be rewarding. The question of the low-income countries has, rather, to be put on the moral plane, much like famine relief.

3

Another Round, Another Requiem? Prospects for the Global Negotiations

John Gerard Ruggie

The international community is in the twentieth year of what has come to be known as the North-South dialogue. The record of this dialogue is not only mixed but also confusing to those who seek to assess it: "Some of those who think there has been progress do not dispute the lack of movement in areas that others see as a sign of deadlock or stalemate. Those who think there has been stalemate do not dispute that change has taken place in areas that the former perceive as examples of 'enormous progress.' "[1] It is clear that the discrepancy is accounted for by whether it is believed that negotiations between North and South can or should achieve fundamental, structural change in the international economic order. The "structuralists" have been disappointed, blame lack of political will in the North for lack of success, and look for new strategies and tactics that might engage the North in serious reform efforts. At the same time, they may acknowledge that closer bilateral relations have been established between some Northern and Southern countries and that improvements have been made in some functionally specific multilateral arrangements.

The Global Negotiations are the most ambitious expression yet of the structuralist objective, and they reflect the most recent strategy on the part of the South to convince the North to be forthcoming. The first strategy, characteristic of the 1960s and early 1970s, attempted to extend the international normative consensus in favor of independence to international support for development. Declaratory commitments to the goal of development, and more programmatic commitments to official development assistance targets, preferential trade arrangements, and the like, were sought repeatedly. Structural change was defined in essence as "closing the gap." The early UNCTAD concerns illustrate this first strategy. The second strategy was more explicitly redistributive and combined the threat of negative sanctions with the promise of mutual gains. This phase is exemplified by the New International Economic Order (NIEO) program of the mid-1970s, which was to have been realized largely by the sort of commodity power that OPEC demonstrated together with the advantages to producers and consumers alike of agreeing to stabilize commodity prices. The third and most recent strategy focuses on the efficient and equitable functioning of the world economy as a whole. It maintains that greater efficiency requires greater equity, in the sense that noninflationary and sustainable recovery in the world economy can best be achieved by resource transfers to the South. Growth in the South would be stimulated thereby, in turn increasing Southern demand for Northern exports and pulling the North out of its recession without rekindling inflation. The report of the Brandt Commission advances both intellectual and political justifications for the pursuit of this strategy, and the Global Negotiations are its institutional manifestation.[2]

To date, none of these strategies has succeeded in engaging the North in serious reform efforts. There is every indication that the Global Negotiations are destined to be the least successful round yet. It is my purpose here to show that, of the many political factors that explain this outcome, the perennial charge of lack of political will contributes very little insight. More basic and profound factors are at work.[3]

Regime Design

International economic regimes are governing arrangements constructed by states to coordinate their expectations and organize aspects of their behavior in such issue areas as trade and monetary relations.[4] The Global Negotiations reflect an effort by developing countries to achieve more equitable international economic outcomes by redesigning existing international economic regimes, creating new regimes in certain areas of interest to them where none now exist, and enhancing their influence in forums in which decisions are made concerning the structure and functioning of these regimes. How plausible a set of objectives is this in view of what we know about the determinants of international economic regimes?

Among political scientists the configuration of state power in the world political economy generally is taken to be the most basic factor explaining the characteristics of international economic regimes.[5] This is so because the world political economy is a self-help system, lacking a central authority. As a self-help system, it exhibits certain collective action problems, including generating and enforcing the rules required to maintain a stable international economic order. The severity of these problems is thought to be a direct reflection of the number of great powers. If economic capabilities are so concentrated that a hegemon exists, as in the case of Great Britain in the mid- to late nineteenth century and the United States after World War II, an "open" or "liberal" international economic order is hypothesized. Specific regimes that serve such an order (in the areas of trade and monetary relations, for example) are expected to exhibit at least such basic features of multilateralism as nondiscriminatory trade arrangements and convertible currencies. If and as the concentration of economic capabilities erodes, the liberal order is expected to weaken and its regimes to unravel, ultimately being replaced by mercantilist arrangements. The interwar period is usually cited as evidence of the disintegrative effects of the absence of a hegemon.

Although useful and necessary, the "hegemonic stability thesis" cannot by itself fully account for patterns of the rise and demise of regimes in the economic field. One reason is that it conjoins the formal features of an integrated economic order with the substantive features of economic liberalism.[6] The existence of a Liberal International Economic Order (LIEO), however, has more to do with the international projection of a particular configuration of domestic state-society relations than it does with the projection simply of state power. In a liberal order, pride of place is given to market rationality and political authority is designed to give maximum scope to market forces rather than to constrain them. An LIEO will exist, then, when this form of state-society relations enjoys a hegemonic status among the major economic powers. For example, under the classical gold standard levels of domestic prices and economic activity were strongly conditioned, if not directly determined, by the balance of payments. The adjustment process ultimately was geared toward securing external stability—that is, the gold parity of one's currency. Although cheating took place, this objective nevertheless was widely adhered to by the major economic powers in the last third of the nineteenth century.[7] In the interwar period states sought to establish the primacy of domestic stability over external financial discipline. Governments everywhere developed increasingly active forms of intervention in the domestic economy in order to affect the level of prices and employment and to protect them from external sources of dislocation. Configurations of state-society relations, however, were so divergent that no common ground existed on which to construct viable international regimes. As a result the domestic policies pursued by states triggered mutually destructive external consequences that deepened and lengthened the Great Depression from which governments were seeking relief.[8] The task of post–World War II institutional reconstruction was to maneuver between internal and external stability by striking a compromise rather than by sacrificing one to the other.[9] Under the formula arrived at, which I have elsewhere termed the compromise of embedded liberalism, the postwar regimes for money and trade were designed to provide vehicles for liberalization as well as means for stabilization.[10] Also, they were designed to stabilize the domestic consequences of external developments that impinged on the pursuit by governments of their new economic and social objectives, as well as the external consequences of the domestic measures that governments undertook in the pursuit of these objectives.

Thus, a sufficient degree of congruence is necessary in the balance of state-society relations characteristic of the regime-making states in order for viable economic regimes to be constructed. Once they are constructed, the collective purposes these regimes serve must still be operationalized and justified as policies. Here a third set of factors becomes important: the prevailing bodies of economic theory and ideology to which the regime-making states hold. For example, under the gold standard state abstinence was prescribed so as not to undermine what were assumed to be equilibrating linkages between the balance of payments and changes in gold reserves and in domestic credit supply, income, and demand. These notions were understood within the framework of classical economics and justified by the ideology of laissez faire. In the interwar period there was no reigning theory or ideology. The United States experimented with the New Deal, the Soviet Union with its Five Year Plans, Sweden with unorthodox budgetary policies, Italy with *corporativismo*, Germany with *Wirkschaftslenkung*, and so on. All the while the Financial Committee of the League of Nations and its various endeavors to establish international economic regimes continued to adhere to doctrines of financial orthodoxy.[11] In the post–World War II era, among the capitalist countries social-democratic doctrines and methods have coexisted with more traditional economic forms, but there has been a substantial area of theoretical and ideological overlap in the Keynesian middle.[12]

In summary, the distribution of state power may be said to determine whether an integrated international economic order can exist. Beyond that, the degree of congruence in the balance of state-society relations characteristic of the regime-making states determines the collective purposes that regimes will pursue. Finally, the extent to which the prevailing economic theories and ideologies held by the major economic powers are compatible determines the ease with which collective purposes are operationalized as policies and legitimated as doctrine within regimes.

Applying these notions to the post–World War II international economic order, we can say that its basic design reflected the interstate hegemony of the United States, coupled with the characteristic form of state-society relations that emerged in the advanced capitalist world from the Great Depression. Within the parameters set by these two structural features, the postwar negotiations, as at Bretton Woods, worked out the more detailed provisions of this design. The neoclassical-Keynesian synthesis came to provide the means both to legitimate the prevailing social objectives of the major economic powers as well as to operationalize those objectives into specific policies that the economic regimes were programmed to coordinate.

Thus, the Bretton Woods monetary regime provided for free and stable exchanges and also for a "double screen" to cushion the domestic economy against balance-of-payments constraints.[13] The double screen consisted of short-term assistance, made available conditionally by the IMF, to finance payments deficits on current account, and the ability to change exchange rates so as to correct fundamental disequilibria. The conditionality provisions of the IMF were predicated on a specific interpretation of the nature of payments deficits, as reflecting idle productive capacity or stocks of unsold goods and services, which temporary deflationary measures would quickly cure.[14] The GATT-related trade regime made obligatory the most-favored-nation rule and prohibited quantitative restrictions on imports (which, however, were deemed suitable measures for safeguarding the balance of payments, explicitly including payments difficulties that resulted from domestic full-employment policies). A substantial reduction in tariffs was also called for but was coupled with several escape mechanisms to buffer the extent of domestic dislocation produced by imports.[15] The pattern of multilateral tariff reductions through GATT encouraged the growth of intrasectoral trade, which, compared to intersectoral trade, is "less valuable from the viewpoint of increasing economic welfare" but also socially and politically less disruptive.[16] And where trade in industrial products is based on a more classical notion of comparative advantage, as it is with imports from the NICs, the trade regime has encountered difficulty and is cluttered with various forms of "voluntary" export restraint arrangements. Despite the best efforts of some of the developing countries present at the initial postwar negotiations, no development regime came into existence alongside the trade and monetary regimes, and the industrialized countries rejected the notion that these two regimes should specifically acknowledge the special needs of developing countries.[17] By about 1960 one can speak of a quasi-regime for development assistance, consisting of the lending program of the IBRD, development assistance targets by the members of the OECD Development Assistance Committee, and the technical assistance programs of the United Nations.[18]

It follows from this line of reasoning that the prospects for the developing countries' succeeding in fundamentally renegotiating the status quo are not great, irrespective of such situational factors as who holds power in Washington, Tokyo, Bonn, or London. And yet these regimes have adapted in recent years and in some cases appear to be more responsive to the developing countries than they were in the past.

Regime Change

Since the early 1960s the monetary and trade regimes have generated a number of arrangements specifically aimed at the developing countries. In the monetary regime, a Compensatory Financing Facility (CFF) was established by the IMF in 1963 and a Buffer Stock Facility in 1979. During the 1970s the low-conditionality Oil Facility was added, as was a Supplementary Financing Facility. And a Trust Fund was established by the IMF for developing countries, financed by the sale of IMF gold holdings. Perhaps most important, in the early 1980s the conditions under which IMF drawings were allowed began to change to include, as in the case of an SDR 5 billion drawing by India, the objective of "structural adjustment . . . with a view to achieving balance of payments viability in the medium term."[19] Moreover, the length of time permitted for repayment was extended. As a result, new commitments by the IMF in 1981 totaled SDR 15.2 billion, all to developing countries.[20]

In the trade regime, the GATT adopted a new text for article XVIII of the General Agreement in 1957, making it easier for developing countries with development-related payment difficulties to invoke this escape provision; in the period from 1974 to 1981 the non-oil-exporting developing countries accounted for some 37 percent of all invocations by GATT members of its major escape clauses.[21] In 1964 GATT added a new chapter to the General Agreement concerning Trade and Development, which released members from the obligation of reciprocity in trade negotiations with developing countries. In the 1970s the General System of Preferences (GSP) came into being, which multilateralized preferential treatment to some extent. Beyond this traditional concern with tariffs and tariff policy, a number of commodity agreements were reached during the 1970s, and the Common Commodity Fund was established.

However, these and related changes are limited in scope. Increased access to IMF resources is dwarfed by Third World debt problems. The changed conditionality provisions of the IMF are coupled with a much more rigorous application of performance criteria. The GSP has benefited relatively few developing countries, which at the same time have also been the primary object of export restraints imposed by the industrialized countries. The Common Fund is deliberately underfunded so that it can have little impact on commodity flows and prices.

Moreover, in most instances the rationale for these changes itself exhibits little discontinuity from past practice. In the case of the IMF, the developing countries had come to represent a source of vulnerability in the international adjustment process and in the international financial system. Both were due to the fact that these countries enjoyed greater access to private capital markets during the 1970s, which meant that the more developed among them could bypass the IMF altogether. Additional IMF resources, their allocation to developing countries, and changed conditionality provisions for certain developing-country borrowers that were not under immediate duress was the price of reasserting IMF influence.[22] As for the GSP, the United States came to take the view that a global system constituted a less onerous form of preferences than those the European Economic Community (EEC) had evolved for particular subsets of developing countries, which included reverse preferences, and which the Latin American countries were also requesting from the United States.[23] Besides, this deviation from the MFN rule is balanced by "graduation" beyond the preference categories, and it has not been made a permanent feature of the international trade regime.

In short, the adaptation of the trade and monetary regimes to accommodate the developing countries is limited in scope and does not reflect any fundamental deviation from the existing rules of the game. This is not to say, however, that the North-South dialogue has had no impact at all. Three types of impact can be discerned.

The first is that the dialogue has put issues on the international agenda that would not be there otherwise. In no case has the preferred outcome of the developing countries been realized, but in several instances arrangements now exist or are coming into existence that owe their origins to the dialogue. The GSP is one example, as is the Common Fund and the codes of conduct that are evolving in the areas of restrictive business practices and technology transfer. Some developing countries derive at least some benefits from each of these. Moreover, the programmatic activities of UN agencies in virtually every instance have changed dramatically over the course of the past twenty years to reflect the particular concerns of developing countries.

The second impact is normative. No order of relations can long endure unless it enjoys some legitimacy or, at minimum, acquiescence. Both sides in the dialogue know this. The ritual of negotiations provides a useful instrument in the global legitimation struggle because it is carried on in universalistic terms and in the language of common interests. The dominant party will seek adherence to, or the rule-governed extension of, what we might call the hegemonic consensus.[24] This, however, may require that it yield certain concessions and offer some side payments, though not such as would endanger the underlying structure of power. Various export-earnings-stabilization schemes, including the Common Fund, illustrate this point; they do not supplant market forces but provide marginal compensatory mechanisms to help buffer the impact of fluctuations. As for the subordinate party, it will look to the same negotiations as a means to undermine the legitimacy of the existing order and to advance counterhegemonic ideas and principles. The short-term significance of these efforts is likely to be minimal and overshadowed by attempts to maximize whatever concessions and side payments may be available. They may, however, have long-term effects of some significance. For example, the recent changes in IMF conditionality provisions are undoubtedly due in considerable measure to fears about global financial instability. But the particular kinds of modifications that were adopted are also due to the gradual acceptance of the idea, repeatedly stressed by the South in the dialogue, that there is such a thing as a structural development deficit that differs from the more transient deficits of fully industrialized countries and that the two should be treated differently. The process of eroding and creating norms does not end at this point, however. To continue with the same illustration, tacit acceptance of the idea of differential treatment of developing country deficits is bound to reinforce pressure from the industrialized countries for more precise differential categorization among the set of developing countries, and eventually the routinized graduation beyond it altogether. The legitimation struggle proceeds in zigs and zags. It is never far removed from the structure of power, nor is it entirely reducible to it.

The third area of impact of the dialogue has been at the institutional level, both within governments and in the international system. Development policy constituencies are now embedded in the bureaucracies of all the industrialized countries, in large measure because of the need to prepare for and respond to the never-ending rounds of the dialogue. The power of these constituencies varies widely across countries, but nowhere is the game of bureaucratic politics quite the same as it would be in their absence. Moreover, in international organizations the need to service negotiations has become an effective means to justify all manner of activities, some of which may be not even remotely connected with the substance of any particular negotiations but are interesting or useful nonetheless and would lack financial support otherwise.[25]

In the long run, perhaps the most important of these consequences of the dialogue is the extensive institutionalization that it has triggered among the developing countries, particularly in and through the Group of 77 (G-77).[26] The G-77 has become pervasive throughout the UN system. Its annual meetings in New York alone increased nearly tenfold in number during the 1970s, and some form of permanent machinery to support and coordinate its activities is imminent. Although the initial impetus for these developments came from the dialogue, one of their unanticipated by-products has been to create an institutional infrastructure that could be used for South-South economic negotiations, the advent of which may be hastened by the very existence of this infrastructure together with its lack of substantive success on the North-South front.

The North-South dialogue has had little to do with transforming international economic regimes, but it has not been entirely irrelevant to this process. The limited impact it has had is felt less on the first-order level of substantive outcomes, though there has been some, as on the second-order level, in the realm of legitimation and institutionalization, circumscribed by the structure of power but not fully determined by it.

The Next Round

I have suggested some of the political factors that account for the design of existing international economic regimes and for the manner in which they have responded to demands for change by the developing countries. Proponents of the Global Negotiations may or may not agree with my analysis. Nevertheless, they would uniformly claim that the current context is so radically different from past contexts that previous patterns offer little if any guidance for the future.

Two sorts of discontinuities in particular are often mentioned. The first is that those factors that I have called the basic political determinants of the current crop of international economic regimes themselves have become unhinged. The interstate hegemony of the United States is eroding. There are signs of increasing divergence in state-society relations among the major economic powers, some tugging toward the Left and others to the Right. And everywhere the death of Keynes is proclaimed. The second is that the developing countries are far more important to the industrialized countries than ever before. Throughout the 1970s the South constituted the most dynamic market for Northern exports; by the end of the decade nearly 40 percent of U.S. exports were purchased by Southern countries. Moreover, developing countries now owe some $600 billion in foreign debt, the repayment of which depends on their ability to generate foreign exchange. In the words of the Brandt Commission: "The South cannot grow adequately without the North. The North cannot prosper or improve its situation unless there is greater progress in the South."[27] Neither of these arguments is wrong, but neither warrants the belief that Global Negotiations will succeed where previous rounds have failed.

If the political structure on which international economic regimes are based is unraveling, large-scale institutional innovations in the international economic order will become more, not less, difficult to achieve. This is so because the diversity of economic interests, objectives, and policies will increase while the ability of anyone to control the centrifugal organizational forces that affect all will decline. Historically, this type of configuration has generated economic blocs rather than an integrated economic order.[28] The implications for the developing countries, then, would be to abandon Global Negotiations forthwith and to scramble for the best possible regional and bilateral deals with specific industrialized countries.

But what of the new interdependence? Is it not sufficient to break through this "tyranny of small decisions"? The idea that North-South interdependence can be constitutive of a new order of North-South relations is flawed in four important respects.

First, closer economic ties between Northern and Southern countries have had negative as well as positive effects in the North. For example, although increased trade between the two has created jobs in the North, in specific sectors it has also led to a loss of jobs. The sectors so affected increasingly include those basic industries that no industrialized country will willingly phase out in the foreseeable future and that are also the most seriously affected by the current recession.[29] Thus, while long-term adaptation to changes in international comparative advantage may be inevitable, Northern countries are likely to weigh any prospects of "mutual gains" so derived against the adjustment costs that closer economic ties entail in the interval.[30]

Second, as the OPEC case amply demonstrated, great care must be taken not to overgeneralize from specific interdependent relations. There is relatively little economic interdependence between North and South *per se.* A small handful of developing countries, primarily oil exporters and newly industrializing countries, account for virtually all of the increase in trade and financial transactions between North and South. The relative share of the rest of the developing countries in fact has declined.[31] This small group of countries by and large is also the weakest link in the Southern chain, least supportive of the NIEO program, and most anxious to maintain favorable bilateral relations with Northern countries.

Third, as was also shown by the OPEC experience, it is extremely difficult to leverage specific forms of interdependence into generalized influence. For example, the fact that the external debt of developing countries exceeds $600 billion already has produced some changes in the policies of the IMF and in bilateral financial and trade relations between the major borrower and lender countries. It may even increase pressure for a lowering of interest rates and thereby lower the value of the dollar, both of which would ease the present debt strain. However, there are neither historical nor theoretical grounds for extrapolating from the debt problem or from any other sector-specific source of Southern influence to some generalized global restructuring.

Fourth and finally, international economic interdependence in any case is not directly constitutive of international political order. In the North-South dialogue, the Marshall Plan is often cited as a precedent that demonstrates the mutual economic benefits that resource transfers can produce. The example, however, confuses consequences with causes. The Marshall Plan was a unilateral response to an economic situation that had immediate implications for the global strategic balance and therefore involved the direct security interests of the United States. That was its cause. That it also produced mutually beneficial economic expansion was a consequence. If the U.S. Congress had been asked to adopt the Marshall Plan as a countercyclical measure, it would have met with the same fate as Keynes's Clearing Union. International resource allocation to benefit the South so that the North in turn can benefit would require the prior existence of a tightly knit political community such as exists in domestic societies. Thus, like so many previous North-South proposals, the idea of a North-South Marshall Plan, as proposed by the Brandt Commission, advances solutions that cannot be achieved through the means that the international political system makes available.

The foregoing discussion points to an inescapable conclusion: If new approaches are going to be devised and more favorable outcomes achieved, pride of place will have to be given to indigenous efforts within and among developing countries. These efforts can take a variety of forms.[32] For some developing countries, though probably not for many, it may be possible in the foreseeable future to achieve the domestic transformations required of successful export-led strategies. For others, it may mean at least a temporary delinking from or highly selective association with the international economy. Greater South-South ties would be supportive of either stance. In any case, change in self-help systems requires self-help measures. Serious negotiations take place only among parties whose relationship is already characterized by a reasonable balance of effective demand; negotiations are unlikely in themselves to produce such an outcome. Thus, in the long run the desultory status of the Global Negotiations may yet turn out to mark both an end and a beginning: the end of the North-South dialogue as the central axis of international development diplomacy and, as a result, the beginning of a new order of North-South relations.

Notes

1. Michael W. Doyle, "Stalemate in the North-South Debate: Strategies and the New International Economic Order," *World Politics* 35 (April 1983): 428.

2. Independent Commission on International Development Issues, *North-South: A Program for Survival* (Cambridge, Mass.: MIT Press, 1980). A second report

has since been issued by the commission, but all references here are to this, the first, report.

3. I draw on several previously published essays: "International Regimes, Transactions, and Change: Embedded Liberalism in the Postwar Economic Order," *International Organization* 36 (Spring 1982); "A Political Commentary on Cancún," *Third World Quarterly* 4 (July 1982); and "Political Structure and Change in the International Economic Order: The North-South Dimension," in Ruggie (ed.), *The Antinomies of Interdependence: National Welfare and the International Division of Labor* (New York: Columbia University Press, 1983).

4. The most comprehensive analysis to date of the character, determinants, and consequences of international regimes may be found in Stephen D. Krasner (ed.), *International Regimes* (Ithaca, N.Y.: Cornell University Press, 1983), first published as a special issue of *International Organization* 36 (Spring 1982).

5. For a review of the relevant literature and a test of its major hypotheses, see Robert O. Keohane, "The Theory of Hegemonic Stability and Changes in International Economic Regimes, 1967–1977," in Ole Holsti et al. (eds.), *Change in the International System* (Boulder, Colo.: Westview Press, 1980).

6. Ruggie, "International Regimes, Transactions, and Change."

7. "The view, so widely recognized and accepted in recent decades, of central banking policy as a means of facilitating the achievement and maintenance of reasonable stability in the level of economic activity and prices was scarcely thought about before 1914, and certainly not accepted, as a formal objective of policy." Arthur I. Bloomfield, *Monetary Policy under the International Gold Standard* (New York: Federal Reserve Bank of New York, 1959). Bloomfield shows that central banks did, however, attempt partially to "sterilize" the effects of gold flows.

8. Charles P. Kindleberger, *The World in Depression, 1929–1939* (Berkeley: University of California Press, 1973).

9. "There was a growing tendency during the inter-war period to make international monetary policy conform to domestic social and economic policy and not the other way round. Yet the world was still economically interdependent; and an international currency mechanism for the multilateral exchange of goods and services, instead of primitive bilateral barter, was still a fundamental necessity for the great majority of countries. The problem was to find a system of international currency relations compatible with the requirements of domestic stability. Had the period been more than a truce between two world wars, the solution that would have evolved would no doubt have been in the nature of a compromise." League of Nations (Ragnar Nurkse), *International Currency Experience: Lessons of the Inter-War Period* (Geneva: League of Nations, Economic, Financial and Transit Department, 1944). p. 230.

10. Ruggie, "International Regimes, Transactions, and Change."

11. Dean E. Traynor, *International Monetary and Financial Conferences in the Interwar Period* (Washington, D.C.: Catholic Universities Press of America,

1949); Karl Polanyi, *The Great Transformation* (Boston: Beacon Press, 1944); and Benjamin Rowland (ed.), *Balance of Power or Hegemony: The Interwar Monetary System* (New York: New York University Press, 1976).

12. For a discussion of the role of social knowledge in international economic regimes, see Ernst B. Haas, "Why Collaborate?" *World Politics* 32 (April 1980); for the role of ideology, Robert W. Cox, "The Crisis of World Order and the Problem of International Organization in the 1980s," *International Journal* 35 (Spring 1980).

13. Richard N. Cooper, "Prolegomena to the Choice of an International Monetary System," *International Organization* 29 (Winter 1975).

14. The lack of congruence between these expectations and the actual situation of developing countries is discussed by Ismail-Sabri Abdalla, "The Inadequacy and Loss of Legitimacy of the International Monetary Fund," *Development Dialogue* 2 (1980).

15. Gerard Curzon and Victoria Curzon, "The Management of Trade Relations in the GATT," in Andrew Shonfield (ed.), *International Economic Relations of the Western World* (London: Oxford University Press for the Royal Institute of International Affairs, 1976), vol. 1.

16. Richard N. Cooper, *The Economics of Interdependence* (New York: Columbia University Press, 1980), p. 76.

17. Richard N. Gardner, *Sterling-Dollar Diplomacy in Current Perspective* (New York: Columbia Unviersity Press, 1980); and Joseph Gold, " '. . . To Contribute Thereby to . . . Development': Aspects of the Relations of the International Monetary Fund with Its Developing Members," *Columbia Journal of Transnational Law* 10 (Fall 1971).

18. Andrew Shonfield, "Introduction: Past Trends and New Factors," in Shonfield, *International Economic Relations*. I call it a quasi-regime because (1) the donor countries fully understood that certain norms, particularly those concerning the quantity of Official Development Assistance, represented aspirations rather than commitments; (2) the various component parts of the would-be regime were almost totally unrelated; and (3) compliance mechanisms were few and weak.

19. *IMF Survey*, November 23, 1981, p. 365.

20. Ibid., January 25, 1982, p. 28.

21. Ruggie, "Political Structure and Change in the International Economic Order," table 9.3.

22. "A Conversation with Mr. de Larosière," *Finance and Development* 19 (June 1982): 5.

23. The formulation of the U.S. policy is traced effectively by Ronald J. Meltzer, "The Politics of Policy Reversal," *International Organization* 30 (Autumn 1976).

24. Robert W. Cox, "Labor and Hegemony," *International Organization* 31 (Summer 1977).

25. For an extended discussion of the relationship between UNCTAD and the North-South dialogue, see Robert Rothstein, *Global Bargaining: UNCTAD and the Quest for a New International Economic Order* (Princeton, N.J.: Princeton University Press, 1979); cf., more generally, Ruggie, "On the Problem of 'The Global Problematique': What Roles for International Organizations?" *Alternatives* 5 (January 1980).

26. Carol Geldart and Peter Lyon, "The Group of 77: A Perspective View," *International Affairs* 57 (Winter 1980–1981), and Stephen Taylor, "The Group of 77 and International Organization," (paper prepared for delivery at the 1980 Annual Meeting of the American Political Science Association, Washington, D.C.).

27. In addition to the Brandt Commission Report, *North-South*, this view is also expressed by Roger D. Hansen, *Beyond the North-South Stalemate* (New York: McGraw-Hill for the 1980s Project of The Council of Foreign Relations, 1979), and by several of the contributors to Khadija Haq (ed.), *Dialogue for a New Order* (New York: Pergamon Press, 1980).

28. On this point, consult the literature cited by Keohane, "Theory."

29. Statistics on North-South trade and employment effects may be found in Bela Balassa, "The Changing International Division of Labor in Manufactured Goods," *Banca Nazionale del Lavoro Quarterly Review*, no. 130 (September 1979), Stephen Marris, "The Case of the Newly Industrializing Countries NICs)," *OECD Observer*, no. 96 (January 1979), and "OECD and the NICs: The Current Trade Pattern," *OECD Observer*, no. 113 (November 1981).

30. In the basic industries, response is likely to take the form of retooling and automating rather than phasing out. As Felix Rohatyn has put it with respect to the United States: "That this nation can continue to function while writing off such industries to foreign competition strikes me as nonsense." Rohatyn, "Reconstructing America," *New York Review of Books*, March 5, 1981, p. 16. Bhagwati has reminded me that Rohatyn's view about the importance of basic industries would be rejected emphatically by many economists. Possible responses to foreign competition, including nonadjustment have been analyzed by several distinguished economists in Jagdish Bhagwati (ed.), *Import Competition and Response* (Chicago: Chicago University Press, 1982).

31. For example, the share of world exports in 1980 accounted for by all nonoil developing countries, including the NICs, was less than half their share in 1950. Calculated from UNCTAD, *Trade and Development Report, 1981* (New York: United Nations, 1981), p. 116.

32. For a review of the available options and an examination of the conditions under which they may be feasible, see the contributions to Ruggie, *Antinomies*.

4 The Time for Painful Rethinking

Albert Bressand

Global Negotiations can be discussed within two different perspectives. The normative way is by far the easier. Anyone confident of the fundamental importance of North-South issues, anyone committed to speaking in favor of international justice, simply needs to reaffirm support for the long-term objectives embodied in the New International Economic Order (NIEO). Calling for the launching of Global Negotiations is, then, an almost self-evident first step on a long list of best wishes.

Unfortunately, this comfortable normative approach is increasingly at odds with the policy-oriented one. In policy terms, one of the major questions that must be accounted for, in addition to why Global Negotiations are desirable, is why three years of negotiating on negotiations have produced only disagreements, bitterness, and resentment. Why has the dialogue so obviously lost touch, in spite of an unprecedented summit of the heads of state, with "high politics"? It is only too clear in this perspective that if these negotiations could ever be launched, their actual policy relevance and their chances of success would still be extremely limited.

I have chosen to address the issue from this second, more uncomfortable, perspective. I am well aware that this midpoint between normative dream and cold-hearted disinterest is bound to be unpopular both with the "true believers" (for whom a ten-year story of repeated failure is of marginal importance when assessed in the light of the true faith) and with those who see little point to any North-South exercise outside of a few specialized topics. Yet in my mind there would be no point adding to the voluminous literature already available from these two schools of thought.

Universal Values and Ephemeral Contexts

One could argue rightly that the proposal to launch Global Negotiations, and for that matter the Brandt proposal to hold what became the Cancun summit, represent attempts to recreate the policy context that briefly prevailed at the time of the sixth and seventh special sessions of the UN General Assembly. Indeed, North-South issues had come to occupy for a couple of years a central place on the world political agenda. Not that North-South issues had not been raised earlier; most of them had been identified many years before through the work of pioneers such as Raul Prebisch in the framework of the Economic Commission for Latin America (ECLA) and later of UNCTAD. But the Charter of Economic Rights and Duties of States, as well as the program of action for a New International Economic Order, symbolized a new awareness. Addressing North-South issues came briefly to be seen as a central element of any international strategy to deal with the new economic dilemmas confronting all nations in the 1970s. It is therefore important to analyze, more carefully than has been done so far, why this identification between the high politics of international relations and the specific set of issues encapsulated in the NIEO agenda was able to take place.

Two elements combined in a way that was unusually beneficial for the NIEO approach. However, this useful and welcome coincidence is quite unlikely to reappear, at least before the end of the 1980s. The first element was the intellectual heritage of the 1960s. During those prosperous years of almost universal rapid growth, a new set of values, objectives, and concerns had gradually come to the forefront. At a time when basic issues of production and growth were considered solved forever (remember "fine tuning"), attention could shift gradually to issues of redistribution and social organization. Much of that thinking took place within each society (witness the student turmoil of the late 1960s), but some of it also worked its way into the international realm. Today, when production issues have come back to the forefront and when the fabric of the "welfare state" is everywhere under irresistible pressure, the visionary appeal of Barbara Ward in the early 1970s to move from national welfare states to a world welfare state appears even more optimistic as far as our political capacities are concerned.[1]

The second element instrumental in propelling NIEO to the top of the international agenda was of course the first oil shock and the radical redistribution of power that it seemed to illustrate. The belief in the possibility for far-reaching changes in the power structure was all the more potent as the dramatic example administered by OPEC could be seen against the value system of the late 1960s and early 1970s. Its coincidence with the new ethics of scarcity preached by the Club of Rome was one of those amplifying factors. In this context, the first oil shock could be greeted as the first visible sign of a historical process of change, with NIEO as its logical result. Hence the unwillingness of most LDCs and the even greater unwillingness of Third World thinkers to recognize the full impact on non-oil-exporting Third World countries of what they liked to see as only the first stage of world power sharing.

This intellectual and policy context is gone. Not to acknowledge this simple fact appears to me the most effective recipe for failure and disillusionment. Leaving its analysis to conservative thinkers is also the best service anyone concerned with North-South issues could render to status quo diplomacy.

The first change is that the spirit of the 1960s, which managed to survive more or less through the 1970s, is now gone for good. A process of economic slowdown, which had been perceived for almost a decade in terms of temporary difficulties, is now increasingly perceived as a long-term shift toward reduced growth, at least in Europe. In this respect there is far more difference between 1982 and 1977 than there was between 1977 and 1972 or 1965 if we remember that 1977 was the year when the MacCracken report could attribute world economic problems to "exogenous shocks" and "policy mistakes." Since then, policies have made two U-turns. One turn was toward quasi-universal monetarism in the wake of the second oil shock. The other, in the wake of elections of the early 1980s, was toward "miracle policies" of painless reflation ("supply side" in the first Reagan period, "consumer-led recovery" in the first Mitterand year). However, faith in the capacity of the world economy to regenerate itself rapidly has almost vanished in Europe and is open to erosion in the United States and even Japan.

Whether one does or does not believe in the Kondratieff fifty-year cycle, the basic policy assumption is increasingly becoming one of a prolonged period of exacerbated difficulties. The capacity of various societies to foster or even welcome international change is reduced in proportion. Of course there is still awareness in some intellectual quarters that only fundamental changes can put an end to the present stalemate, but this awareness is not shared by public opinion. Attempts to change the political climate and to spread this awareness, as the Brandt commissioners and a few Cancun summiters bravely undertook to do, simply did not succeed.

The second major change is that the economic power structure now appears much less prone to radical changes than was briefly assumed in 1974–75. The 1970s had seen several groups of "newcomers" make rapid headway in the various fields of international relations: OPEC in oil and finance, the NICs in trade and basic industries, Germany and Japan in monetary affairs. But in a clear reversal of this trend toward a "multipolar" system, the early 1980s have seen most of these "challengers" experience major difficulties.

OPEC is no longer the main exporter of oil and has great difficulty preserving its influence and coherence despite a cut of almost half in its production level. The Latin American NICs have reached the limits (if they have not gone beyond it already) of their externally financed strategy of fast growth. "Structuralist" economics and industrial machismo have to be buried while the support of a little-loved IMF is sought. Even the East Asian NICs are feeling increasingly unsafe as shrinking markets and growing trade barriers undermine the central elements of their outward-looking strategies.

Europe and Japan may well be in the process of discovering that much of their previous success had more to do with a thirty-year process of "catching up" than with an inescapable "American decline." As they now have more or less caught up, a whole new game opens in which American energy and technology resources, the supremacy of the dollar, and the depth and dynamism of the American financial markets will make for a much more disputed and bitter competition.

What I have called elsewhere "the hardening of hierarchies" is translating into an ever more hostile environment for countries at the periphery of the economic power system. The middle-income countries are quite unlikely to repeat during the 1980s the success stories of Korea, Brazil, and other NICs during the 1960s and even the 1970s. Bankers are unlikely to be very forthcoming as they struggle with the quasi-compulsory refinancing of mammoth commitments to the first-generation NICS. Thailand and the Philippines will not become the Koreas of the 1980s as Korea became the Japan of the 1970s. Spain will not become the France of the 1980s, and France has a hard time trying to catch up with the Japanese-American technology condominium.

The plight of the least developed countries was already worsening in per capita terms during the 1970s. For them the 1980s are bound to be times of extreme hardship. Prospects for commodity prices, foreign investment, and concessional aid are similarly worrisome.

The policy relevance of the North-South dialogue is thus challenged from two sides at once. The erosion of faith in growth and progress makes change less desirable; the rigidification of power distribution makes it appear less necessary.

The Narrowness of Globality

One would like to object that the present dangers facing the international economic system have never made the dialogue more urgent. This is true in general terms, but it is not true of the North-South dialogue as we have come to define it. Here, very clearly, a high price is being paid for the quite remarkable institutional and even intellectual rigidity that has characterized the negotiating stance of the South as well as of the North.

The NIEO was the result of lumping together the specific interests of various LDC groups. As such, it was particularly prone to internal contradictions and to rigidity. Frankly, a certain tendency on the part of Southern diplomats to look at the 1974 NIEO program in religious rather than economic terms, although it is understandable in a narrow tactical perspective, has not served their interests well over the long term.

Whatever the reason, this rigidity has allowed major issues to appear or change without being reflected more than rhetorically in the agenda of the "dialogue." Of course, as the United States and others tried to reduce a program for power sharing into a limited set of nonconflictual "global issues" (food, environment, population), some form of intellectual resistance was in order. But more fundamental factors were at work to keep the NIEO agenda insulated from real-world challenges. For example, some of the major issues facing the most advanced of the LDCs lent themselves very little to the global, multilateral approach with which the United Nations community has come to identify the dialogue. Exploding debt and imploding markets were therefore quietly dealt with outside this majestic framework. The global approach has turned into a narrow one.

The North-South Dialogue: The Sleeping Beauty

Thus, the North-South dialogue, for a short while the symbol of the great changes and hopes of our time, has lapsed into a state of lethargy.

It seems increasingly unlikely that it can be revived without a major change in the present framework.

The last veil of contrite good will that concealed the growing emptiness of North-South negotiations is now being torn away by the new American economic nationalism. And because multilateral cooperation has already lost much of its substance and has been incapable of engendering a new foundation of political consensus, it is an easy target for the new economic dogmatism of an American administration that has decided to be guided only by its most immediate national interests. Rather than seek multilateral rules of the game that would be acceptable to all, the Reagan administration is turning to bilateralism as offering a more propitious frame for flexing its military and financial muscle.

As a result, whereas the basic demographic, economic, and strategic trends should have made the dialogue a central factor, it has become a marginal aspect of international affairs. The main issues of the 1980s—energy, recycling, the vulnerability of the banking system, and the need to bring development (food, in particular) back onto a regional basis—do not fit into the conceptual framework that seems to have crystallized in the mid-1970s. Meetings and resolutions are increasingly taking on the form of ritual rather than of political acts: incantation by the poor countries and purification by the rich countries, old and new.

This immobility is the more lasting in that it is fed by dogmas that, although in apparent conflict, have reached a cozy accommodation through long contact with each other. At the root of the first of these dogmas is the absence of a strategic vision by the West of its long-term interests. Instead its attitude has been determined by the balance of power existing at each point in time and its own immediate economic interests. Western nations sought a debate with oil-producing countries when prices flared, but then they were unable to make suggestions for a joint approach to energy security when the market situation made such an offer more credible. Similarly, the Reagan administration, in the name of a naive conservative view of the world, cast its weight against the very multilateral organizations that were created three decades ago to guarantee the economic *Pax Americana*.

The Southern countries have also committed strategic blunders. Drawn up in the euphoria of still recent independence and the early victories of OPEC, NIEO was more a program for securing economic power than a charter for development and cooperation. The admittedly legitimate objectives of accelerating industrialization, securing market shares, nationalizing resources, and capturing more power in the international financial institutions, which are the backbone of the plan of action, overlooked the importance of the development of agricultural production, education and training, and the patient quest for the conditions needed for independent development.

Only in specific circumstances, such as the first economic summit of the Organization for African Unity at Lagos in 1980, did Third World countries fully take into account, for example, the dangers that food and energy dependence represent for most of them. Similarly, the renegotiation of the Multifiber Agreement (MFA) would have deserved to receive from the Southern countries some of the political priority that they concentrate on the United Nations forum. It is quite remarkable indeed to see how little of the "G-77 spirit" has actually been mobilized (in form other than ritualized reference to protectionism) during the MFA renegotiation. Although it may be the most important trade issue in the field of manufactures from the point of view of the South, this type of businesslike discussion is at the margin of, if not outside, the field of vision of the UN community.

What with the frigidity of Anglo-Saxon diplomacy, bereft of historical vision, and Third World rhetoric that is rapidly becoming cluttered with the clichés of official speeches, the issues and language of a genuine dialogue for the 1980s still remain to be invented.

The New Agenda of "Economic Security"

My intention is not to draw in detail the outline of an alternative plan that might serve as a bridge between remote visions of the future and the current paralyzing constraints. Nevertheless, in examining field after field and region after region, it would seem that the concept of world economic security might provide the impetus for a renewed and revitalized dialogue. This concept, described in greater detail in the second RAMSES report on the state of the world economy, is an attempt to put the immediate problems of today (which decision makers have to address in any case) in the perspective of a long-term reconstruction of the international framework.[2] A modicum of international "security" (stability, predictability, reduction of disturbances) has come to be seen as essential even by politicians whose agenda has long been purely domestic. International economic security could therefore be described as the minimum element of an international strategy, the absence of which would jeopardize any national policy to ride out of the recession and to maintain a lasting growth.

Such a program is most understandable today in the field of finance, whereas memories of the 1930s underline the importance of the trade elements. However, the point can be least be made that energy and monetary relations also have to be an essential part of any concerted strategy.

Energy

Whereas the oil markets are currently working (albeit at a price level that would have looked extremely high a few years ago) in favor of the consumers, the "energy crisis" cannot be regarded as over. In Robert Mabro's words, it has simply taken the form of an economic constraint. As underlined by the IEA, about half of the "energy savings" can be accounted for by the direct and indirect impact of the world recession. Yet the short-term market signals currently are jeopardizing both the long-term transition effort toward another energy mix and the short-term effort at oil exploration.

Launching a realistic dialogue between oil-producing and oil-consuming countries therefore remains one central element of the international agenda. "Realistic" here implies that security is based on a balance of interests and of power, not merely on presumed purity of intentions. The fact that OPEC is in disarray and that pressure on oil prices is clearly downward, far from being the reason for complacency that myopic decision makers like to think, provides the type of opportunity that we shall lament once it passes away.

In suggesting (as my colleagues and I do in our RAMSES report) price-stabilization measures and a concerted international stockpiling policy, we will no doubt disappoint both the producers, who condemn any effort by consumers to reduce their vulnerability, and those who currently rejoice in the present OPEC setbacks without measuring the dangers that fluctuating prices represent for energy transition and their own long-term security. Yet each of these groups has paid dearly for its policy of relying on the short-term balance of power.

The security of the non-oil-exporting developing countries warrants stepped-up action on the part of the multilateral organizations (the ill-fated World Bank's energy affiliate deserves to be revived) for the development of energy resources, even though such resources might be of purely local interest. In the present context the Third World can be expected to be even more neglected by international companies than previously. Yet in 1980 only $4 billion worth of oil exploration was conducted in the South, as against $20 billion in the United States alone. Clearly, considerations of "political risks" are pushing us far from the economic and geological optimum.

If no agreement can be reached within the World Bank, then the San Jose de Costa Rica Agreement signed in August 1980 by Mexico, Venezuela, and the Caribbean countries appears to trace a path worth exploring more fully. The regional level indeed offers opportunities for joint schemes of funding or guarantee. In my view, such a scheme should be included in the next Lome convention between Europe and the Africa, Carribean and Pacific (ACP) countries.

Trade: GATT Is Too Narrow a Forum.

In the field of trade, plans for new multilateral negotiations (such as the one that the United States recently tried to push at the GATT ministerial meeting and, more successfully, at the Williamsburg Summit) appear unlikely in themselves to offset the protectionist trend. More than ever the monetary dimension of the shifting competitive balance must be taken into account. Combating protectionist practices will also require a concerted stance by the major industrial democracies to put trade issues in the broader context of industrial relations, where they belong. Relations with Japan in this respect call for a special, broader approach.[3]

Third World exports cannot be considered a major cause of economic difficulties in the North, outside of a few sectors and regions, and Third World imports have a major role to play, if not as an "engine for growth" (the analogy of the Marshall Plan is not very appropriate) then at least as a buffer against a deeper recession.

Yet Southern countries should take a second look at the emphasis they have put on "nonreciprocal" arrangements. Whereas the poorest of them clearly deserve protection for their very fragile structures, the medium-and higher-income LDCs have deprived themselves of bargaining power. By refusing to play the game, LDCs have received "nonreciprocal" concessions that, they now discover, often have very limited value. Furthermore, since they have cast themselves as permanent exceptions to the rules, their complaints against Northern neglect of the rules cannot be, and are not, taken as seriously as they should. The situation is the more worrisome because protection is now clearly hurting many of the more advanced "infant" industries. India's mechanical and engineering industries, for instance, clearly suffer from the exorbitant tariffs granted to the specialty steel makers.

Yet it must also be realized in the West that greater openness in the South is simply impossible if "adjustment" policies attempt to deal with financial difficulties by extreme reductions in growth and imports. It is time indeed that the "invisible hands" of finance and trade stop undoing each other's work.

Finance: Country risk and System Risk

As the Mexican and Brazilian debt problems clearly illustrate, financial security is the most clearly threatened part of our global economic security. It is well known that financial security is overshadowed by "country risks," but in addition it is threatened by what can be referred to as "system risks." An example of the latter concerns the distortions in the implementation of national monetary policies caused by the particular development of international liquidities. These distortions might one day lead the United States, whose role is far more decisive than that of the OPEC surplus countries, to restrict the supply of dollars to the Eurosystem. The consequences for the LDCs of a contraction of the Euromarkets or of a recentering of the world financial system on the U.S. domestic system could be enormous.

Ideally, the required control mechanism would be a "variable geometry," allowing the system to retain its flexibility in periods of financial pressure while at the same time moderating speculative fever in times of monetary instability. We must overcome the awe that the mere mention of these unregulated markets evokes in many European quarters as well as the limitless fascination aroused in others by their remarkable resilience and capacity for adaptation.

Country risks are due less to the absolute level of Third World debt than to short maturity and its concentration in a small number of countries. Development, a very long-term process, is now financed on a short- or medium-term basis. In reality, this does not guarantee the security of the lenders (who are obliged to roll over their loans and even increase their exposure to avoid compromising their repayment) while, at the same time, rendering the borrowers vulnerable to short-term fluctuations exacerbated by U.S. interest rates. Clearly, the effectiveness of mechanisms such as the Club de Paris and the assistance of consultant banks have made it possible to confront many situations that would be termed bankruptcies were it not for a linguistic convention.

But one may wonder whether the time has not come to move from constant "debt rescheduling" to a more thorough restructuring that would restore long-term financial instruments to their rightful place.

The most disquieting trend, however, is the risk of fragmentation of a financial market to which many countries have no access. This exclusion is especially hard on the African nations, and it will intensify as OPEC countries, now encountering difficulties, withdraw their funds and increase their borrowing. On purely economic criteria, certain "threshold countries" deserve greater access to the market, but they are penalized by the growing timidity of banks that have their fingers burned in Brazil or Mexico—hence the interest of various proposals for a partial guarantee of loans to such threshold countries.

For the poorest countries, aid will remain the best means of promoting the development of human resources and basic infrastructures. The greater awareness of risks, which has led to the decision to increase IMF quotas by 47.5 percent and to the extension of the General Agreements to Borrow, should be extended to World Bank and IDA; only long-term capital can offer a solution for long-term problems. SDR allocations also need to receive special attention at a time when the danger of illiquidity is far greater than their marginal impact on inflation. The risk of marginally increasing inflation is much less frightening, especially at a time of lower oil prices, than that of deflation and protectionism. In that respect the situation of the least developed countries, and notably of Africa, calls for special efforts.

Africa, the Last "ODA Continent"

The 1970s witnessed a substantial decrease in relative terms of the role of international organizations and aid agencies in two of the three continents of the Third World. The exception is Africa. The issue now is whether official development assistance of all sorts will remain available at present levels and, even if it does so, whether those external sources of support will be proportionate to the difficulties now confronting the continent.

Whereas the more advanced countries of Latin America and Asia were able to gradually substitute access to international capital markets and to foreign export markets for reliance on Official Development Assistance (ODA), only a handful of African countries were able to do so during what appears in retrospect to have been a much more favorable period for rapid development. Twenty of the thirty so-called least-developed countries are situated in Africa, and official development assistance is bound to remain an essential link with the world economy.

The problem in the 1980s is likely to be compounded by the acute economic and financial problems now facing the few middle-income countries that had managed, like the Ivory Coast, to achieve high growth rates. Plummeting commodity prices and rising debt-service ratios are already compelling them to make dramatic downward adjustments, more often than not under some form of international supervision. Even the recent oil-based wealth of the few African members of OPEC (Nigeria, Gabon, Algeria, and to a lesser extent Libya) is beginning to appear as much more fragile than anticipated as the world recession makes its impact felt on the oil market also. Only those countries that have been able to combine a strong agricultural base with sufficient energy resources and some form of economic and political prudence appear in a relatively favorable situation. Cameroon is one of the very few examples.

The sheer scale of the social and economic problems points to the likelihood of breakdown. On the economic front any real chance of improvement is not likely, and for many the situation is catastrophic. Edem Kodjo, secretary general of the Organization of African Unity, was led to declare at the first African economic summit in Lagos in April 1980: "The future seems to be without future. And we are blithely told that if things go on in the same way, only five to nine of the fifty or so African countries will be able to survive for any length of time. This is indeed an apocalyptic prospect but it reflects better than any speech what lies in store for us. . . . The very survival of Africa is at stake."[4]

In this increasingly gloomy context, the role of foreign governments and international organizations is bound to be more critical than ever. This is true not only in terms of supplying much-needed financial resources but also in terms of the "conditionality" that increasingly accompanies, at either the macroeconomic or the project level, official assistance.

Yet the remedies proposed by the international organizations all too often suffer from a tunnel vision in which all reality is reduced to the economic dimension. In its simplistic zeal, the Reagan administration has put forward its own instant panacea: that the recipes for economic success that have shown their worth in the United States, Korea, and Taiwan can be transposed *en bloc* to Africa. The outward-looking policies frequently advocated often run the risk of excluding whole segments of the population from the development process while the elites continue on the domestic front to turn a blind eye to these contradictions and present a picture of uniform and common poverty to the outside world.

Commodities: No Easy Answer

In a large number of least-developed countries, the only alternative to increased ODA is increased commodity export earning. On this subject, too, the debate has been sterile and uselessly ideological.

It is clear that no grandiose "stabilization" scheme is feasible. Many commodities lend themselves poorly to price stabilization as envisioned by UNCTAD, and LDCs with specific positions to protect (Morocco in the case of phosphates is only one example) have been opposed to commodity agreements.

However, to look at the issue in economics-textbook terms, as the United States, the United Kingdom, and West Germany are doing, is also self-defeating. It is clear that countries risk collapse. No commodity producer in Kansas, Yorkshire, or Bavaria would ever be treated one-tenth as brutally as the most deprived producers of the world are treated in the name of "optimality."

The solution has to be pragmatic, which means that it cannot be organized only around the "Common Fund" as currently set up. Some commodities are clearly meeting a falling world demand. The assistance should then be aimed at opting out of reliance on these commodities. Others, notably minerals, undergo extreme fluctuations. Then a combination of supply-side policies and expanded earnings-stabilization schemes should help countries maintain coherent development programs in spite of these vagaries. A few commodities can be managed through full-scale commodity agreements. When this is the case, and if consumers and producers find an interest, no ideological opposition should remain.

In the European context, the immediate problem is the financial difficulties of Stabex, a stabilizing scheme that has itself become destabilized. Indeed the launching of Sysmin in the framework of the second Lome convention and the growing interest aroused by Stabex in the face of the very limited success of the efforts at commodity price stabilization (Common Fund, commodity agreements) should not blind European governments to the limits of their contribution to raw-material development in Africa and to the commodity issue more generally. As illustrated by the financial difficulties that have recently plagued Stabex, these mechanisms are not sufficient to deal with a generalized commodity slump. They work well when a few commodities are affected by cyclical and moderate price downturns or when a few producers experience very adverse local conditions, but it would clearly be overambitious for the EEC to hope to provide a global "safety net" for all African producers against the impact of a world-wide depression.

The Challenge of International Economic Management

North-South issues appear, therefore, as one important dimension of a more global problem. Our failure to account for the specifically international dimension of the present crisis is the major factor of insecurity. The occasional respites in the monetary field and in the field of oil have often merely produced complacency. Every opportunity should now be seized to propose ways of controlling the international risks.

The launching of Global Negotiations at the United Nations might afford one such opportunity, if the participants have the courage to set the agenda not according to the symbolic weight attached to the issues but in the light of their relative relevance for world security. Western economic summits have a key role to play if they pursue the path traced at Tokyo toward genuine collective commitment. These summits might be followed up with meetings modeled after Cancun extended to Third World countries, whose influence is increasing in world affairs. In the longer term the door should also be left open for including the Eastern countries, on the basis of the balance of power, in the multiform process of cooperation for security.

However, this procedure will be valid only if it helps lend shape and effectiveness to a collective desire to strengthen the international foundations on which to build prosperity and development. Let us not give way to fear or helpless awe in the face of the profound complexity of interdependence. We should refuse to succumb to the belief expressed by the romantic poet Novalis that "this adaptation, transformation, dissolution of the divine and the human into uncontrollable forces is the spirit of the awful, devouring power that is nature."[5]

Notes

1. See, for example, Barbara Ward's foreword to Mahbub ul Haq, *The Poverty Curtain: Choices for the Third World* (New York: Columbia University Press, 1976).

2. *RAMSES, 1982: The State of the World Economy*, Annual Report by the Institut Français des Relations Internationales (Paris: Economica et Documentation Française, 1981; Cambridge, Mass.: Ballinger, 1982; London: Macmillan, 1982).

3. For an elaboration of these issues, see Albert Bressand, "Mastering the "Worldeconomy," *Foreign Affairs* (Spring 1983).

4. Edem Kodjo, Opening Speech, First Economic Summit of the Organization of African Unity, Lagos, April 1980.

5. Novalis (Friedrich Freiherr von Hardenberg). *The Novices of Sais*, trans. Ralph Manheim (New York: Curt Valentin, 1949).

5   A Third-World Perspective

Muchkund Dubey

Background and Present Position

It will be instructive, though frustrating, to trace the course of Global Negotiations. This can throw interesting light on the motivations behind the proposal for these negotiations, their purpose, the reason it has not been possible to launch them, and the ways out of the present impasse.

The negotiations that were launched in principle in 1980 are still struggling to cross the procedural hurdles in order to be launched in practice. The global approach to negotiating North-South issues can be defined as one covering all major North-South issues, designed to bring about a restructuring of international economic relations based on the principle of equality and mutual benefit, involving the participation of all the member states of the United Nations, and conducted in the global forum of the UN General Assembly in a simultaneous manner in order to ensure a coherent and integrated approach to the issues under negotiation. Since the early 1970s two attempts have been made to embark on such Global Negotiations, and it is of some significance that each arose out of dramatic and substantial increases in oil prices and that the initiative for both came from the OPEC countries. It is also significant that each turned out to be a long, drawn-out process and that a year or two after their launch—the first in reality and the second in principle only—the interest of the participants, including that of the initiators, started waning.

Paris 1975–1977

An attempt to negotiate, simultaneously and in an integrated coherent way, all major North-South issues was made for the first time in the

Conference on International Economic Cooperation (CIEC) held in Paris from 1975 to 1977. These negotiations, which were the first to acquire the now popular and almost ubiquitously applied designation of North-South dialogue and were conducted among 27 countries, ended without producing any significant results. As happens with most international conferences, the failure of the Paris conference was rationalized with the notions that it had promoted a better understanding of each country's difficulties and fostered general awareness of interdependence. Soon after the Paris negotiations were convened, the Northern countries were able to absorb the shock of the first oil-price increase through an increase in the prices of manufactured goods exported by them and through recycling to them of most of the OPEC surplus revenues. Many of the oil-importing developing countries learned to live with this phenomenon by increasing their own exports to OPEC and other destinations and by adjusting their planned economic activities downward. These developments seemed to have deprived the negotiations of their principal justification. After that they turned into a charade, which continued until all the parties, out of a sense of sheer futility, decided to call them off.

Manila, May 1979

The second large increase in the oil prices, in 1979, cast a long shadow on the Fifth United Nations Conference on Trade and Development, held in Manila in 1979. The item on the world economic situation, of which the oil-price increase was an important aspect, received a great deal of attention, and some of the other major substantive issues were relegated to the sidelines. Some non-oil-producing developing countries, mainly in Latin America, felt obliged to cast aside the veil of decency that had come to be expected in talking about the oil-price issue in North-South forums and made a strong case for energy's forming a crucial part of the North-South dialogue. It was in this context and at this stage that Algeria mooted the idea of a new global round of negotiations in which energy would be discussed along with other North-South issues. All this happened in informal group meetings. No formal written proposals were made, nor did the documents of the Conference reflect this aspect of the debate.

Colombo, June 1979

The Manila controversy was carried forward to the ministerial meeting
of the coordinating bureau of the nonaligned countries. Most of the
substantive discussion in the economic committee of the meeting centered on energy. This was the first time that the energy issue was openly
and substantively debated in a forum of developing countries. A number
of oil-importing developing countries presented a grim picture of their
economic plight and prospect, attributed this mainly to the second large
increase in oil prices, and made an appeal, in the name of the unity
of the Group of 77 and the nonaligned movement and addressed mainly
to OPEC countries, for urgent measures to alleviate their condition.
Regarding the suggestion for global negotiations, their position was
that their grave and urgent problems could be tackled most effectively
within the framework of economic cooperation among nonaligned and
other developing countries and that, in the context of their sad economic
situation, hopes held out by Global Negotiations were like the brave
music of a distant drum. A series of other objections to the idea of
Global Negotiations were also raised. After protracted discussions and
consultations, a compromise was reached according to which the meeting decided to set up a consultative group of government experts to
elaborate proposals for reinforcing mutual assistance and solidarity
among nonaligned and developing countries. At the same time it was
agreed to consider the proposal for Global Negotiations at Havana in
September. It was clearly understood that the main purpose of the
consultative group would be to devise and agree on measures for assisting the nonaligned and other developing countries severely hit by
the second large oil-price increase, that the position of the nonaligned
countries on the idea of global negotiations was wide open, and that
satisfactory progress on the former would be an important factor influencing the position of the oil-importing nonaligned and other developing countries on the latter.

Georgetown, August 1979

A meeting of considerable importance but one generally forgotten in
the discussion of Global Negotiations was that of the consultative group
convened by Guyana in pursuance of the decision taken at the Colombo
meeting. Government experts from nine OPEC and oil-importing nonaligned countries participated in this meeting. In spite of its title of a

more general nature (consultative group of government experts to elaborate proposals for reinforcing mutual assistance and solidarity among nonaligned and developing countries), it was the first meeting of nonaligned countries devoted exclusively to the discussion of the oil problem. Its report contained ideas and recommendations on the question of compensating for the oil-price increase and assuring supply to oil-importing developing countries. Moreover, in deference to the position of the OPEC countries that the oil-price increase did not by itself impose any special responsibility or liability on them, the terms "essential commodities in short supply" and "developing countries in a position to supply such commodities or disposing of surplus resources" were used in place of "oil" and "oil-producing countries." However, the background of the discussions in both Colombo and Georgetown made it abundantly clear that oil had been at the center of the discussions and that the recommendations were addressed to the OPEC countries. Another significant aspect of the recommendations was that the difficult economic circumstances facing many nonaligned countries, as well as the need to adopt mutual cooperation measures in the areas that could alleviate these circumstances, were recognized. These circumstances, however, were attributed not to oil-price increases but to "the failure to effect fundamental structural changes in the existing international economic relations."

The meeting made detailed, specific recommendations on oil supply to oil-importing developing countries. Nonaligned and other developing countries supplying essential raw materials would seek to meet the requirements of the importing developing countries on a preferential and priority basis. They would take measures to ensure that the latter would secure an equitable share of the world's consumption of such raw materials. Specific measures for achieving these objectives were spelled out, including earmarking a minimum proportion of total supply and exporting this minimum proportion on the basis of government-to-government contract. Recommendations were also made for redirecting the investment of the OPEC surplus resources toward developing countries, augmenting the resources of the existing funds of the developing countries (the reference here was obviously to the OPEC Fund), keeping in view the needs of these countries, and cooperation among developing countries for promoting the development of both conventional and new and renewable sources of energy. The meeting could not reach agreement on and therefore only took note of the proposals outlining some features of a possible rebate scheme on commodity purchases in favor of developing countries.

Havana, September 1979

At the Havana summit conference of the nonaligned countries there was no surge of enthusiasm for the proposal for global negotiations. Until the last couple of days before the end of the conference, there was no serious negotiation on the proposal. Similarly, all moves on the report of the Georgetown meeting were kept suspended until the last moment. The only significant development consisted of a few informal meetings of selected ministers of oil-importing developing countries and OPEC countries to discuss the plight of the former countries. It was through these meetings that the resolution on Policy Guidelines on the Reinforcement of Collective Reliance Between Developing Countries emerged. This resolution represented a breakthrough for the entire Havana summit. It cleared the decks for negotiating the resolution on Global Negotiations and for reaching agreement on the parts of the text of the economic declaration dealing with energy. The entire package was negotiated and wrapped up in one continuous effort lasting 36 hours.

The guidelines are a summary version of the Georgetown recommendations. Predictably, the idea of a rebate on oil purchases was quietly dropped, but most other elements of the Georgetown recommendations were retained with such qualifications as "without prejudice to their [OPEC countries'] national interests or to their existing commitment." As in the case of the Georgetown recommendations, though "oil" and "oil-producing countries" were not mentioned there was a clear understanding that the terms used in the text were mere euphemisms.

However, the most significant development was that these recommendations even in a somewhat diluted form, were adopted by all of the members of the nonaligned movement, and at the summit level.

The policy guidelines turned out to be an important stage in the process of economic cooperation among developing countries. They triggered a whole chain of decisions and activities in this area. Soon after the Havana summit the OPEC countries took their own decision for guaranteeing supply of oil to oil-importing developing countries, thus imparting operational content to the exhortative Havana resolution.

The summit resolution on global negotiations had a very important provision. In its operative paragraph 7, it called for convening preparatory ministerial meetings of the Group of 77 to define the strategy of the developing countries for these negotiations and to ensure that the implications of this strategy would be conducive to the strengthening of their collective self-reliance. By this it was understood that a continuing and vigorous process of South-South dialogue at the ministerial level could be carried out simultaneously with the Global Negotiations so that the former, by virtue of strengthening the bargaining position of the developing countries, could reinforce the latter. This part of the resolution contributed in no small measure to the convening of the Caracas meeting of the group of 77 at the ministerial level and all that has followed since then in the field of economic cooperation among developing countries (ECDC).

Thirty-fourth Session of UN General Assembly, 1979

The most important step toward launching Global Negotiations was the adoption of General Assembly resolution 34/138, which was an immediate follow-up of the decision taken at the Havana summit. By this resolution the General Assembly decided to launch the negotiations at its Eleventh Special Session and outlined the distinguishing features, broad purpose, and major objectives and themes of the negotiations. It also designated the Committee of the Whole of the General Assembly as the Preparatory Committee for the Conference.

Ministerial Meeting of the Group of 77, March 1980

The Group of 77 set about preparing for the negotiations in a serious and businesslike manner. An expert group worked out the draft agenda, time frame and the procedures for the negotiations. These were finalized in a meeting of the senior officials of the group and approved by the ministers in their March 1980 meeting.

Committee of the Whole, March–July 1980

The Group of 77 formally submitted its proposals on the agenda, procedures, and time frame for the negotiations to the first substantive session of the Committee of the Whole held in March 1980. The principal emphasis in the agenda was in the direction of changing the structures of the international financial, monetary, and trade institutions and systems to make them just and equitable and to serve the purpose of the development of the developing countries.

Under the "energy" item there was reference to "measures to meet the growing requirements of the developing countries" and to assistance for exploration and development of energy resources in these countries. The proposal for creating an "energy affiliate" was not mentioned, nor was there any mention of measures for alleviating the financial burdens of the oil-importing developing countries arising out of the increases in oil prices. The Iraqi proposal for compensation for developing countries for effects of imported inflation was included in the agenda. There was no suggestion regarding negotiation on the pricing of oil. Two specific matters of direct interest to OPEC countries included in the agenda, were the improvement and protection of the purchasing power of the unit value of developing countries' energy exports and guaranteeing the real value of the financial assets of developing countries.

The U.S. position on the negotiations was revealed formally for the first time in a statement made by the U.S. representative in the first substantive session of the Committee of the Whole. The United States suggested a preliminary phase of the negotiations to take up urgent issues related to food, energy, protectionism, and recycling. Mention also was made of "demographic issues" and developing countries' own efforts for development. The United States was in favor of a highly selective agenda and found the agenda suggested by both the G-77 and the EEC as too long. Apparently the United States was trying to divert the negotiations from issues involving structural changes in the world economy and world economic relations. The second major thrust of the U.S. statement was to restrict the role of the central forum and to safeguard the role, mandate, and structure of the specialized agencies (particularly the IMF, the World Bank, and GATT). The role of the central forum, according to the United States, should be to "stimulate action" and provide "political impetus" to work already underway and to "summarize" results received from specialized forums.

At the time of the final meeting of the Committee of the Whole, there was no agreement on how to launch the negotiations. The total stalemate situation reached in the committee was recognized, and the entire matter was refered to the Eleventh Special Session of the General Assembly.

Eleventh Special Session of UN General Assembly, September 1980

A revised proposal on the procedures and time frame for the Global Negotiations was submitted after intensive negotiations. This, however, could not command the support of the United States and the few other developed countries that stood by its side.

The developing countries made a number of concessions in agreeing to the revised proposals. The most far-reaching concession made by them was to agree to "reach agreement by consensus on all important matters." In the first UNCTAD the developing countries had refused to agree to the application of such a procedure in the decision-making process through the UNCTAD machinery. The maximum that they conceded was to agree on a conciliation procedure in the event of a difference on a substantive issue. The principle that decisions must be taken in the ultimate analysis by majority voting was kept intact. The G-77 also accepted the U.S. suggestion of taking up the negotiations in two phases and commencing, for the time being, with only the initial phase.

The Eleventh Special Session of the General Assembly, having failed to reach an agreement, decided to transmit to the Thirty-fifth Session all the documents relevant to the global negotiations.

Thirty-fifth Session of UN General Assembly, 1980

During this session intensive informal negotiations on all aspects relating to the launching of the Global Negotiations, including the agenda, took place. The results of these negotiations were incorporated in informal texts issued by the president of the General Assembly on December 14, 1980.

The developing countries made further concessions in these negotiations. They agreed that the resolution on the subject would state specifically that the conference on global negotiations would not prejudice the competence, functions, and powers of the specialized forums within the UN system. In the agenda for the negotiations, they further agreed to rephrase the items in such a manner as to delete direct reference to restructuring. Most of the agenda items were couched in neutral terms, and the focus of the negotiations was going to be the problems of all countries, not only those of the developing countries.

Once again the text did not command the support of all countries. The OPEC countries did not agree to a mention of "criteria for pricing."

The developing countries insisted on retaining the general idea of re-structuring. The United States dissociated itself from the draft in spite of concessions made by the developing countries. However, the fact remains that, up to that time, the maximum degree of consensus was reached in these negotiations; 90 percent of the agenda was agreed on. The only issues that remained to be settled concerned a few aspects of the agenda on money, finance, and energy and the question of the role of the specialized agencies.

Developments in 1981

The year 1981 turned out to be a barren one for the progress of the concept of Global Negotiations. No worthwhile negotiations on the subject were undertaken during this period, mainly because of the position taken by the United States. After the inauguration of the Reagan administration, the United States was not prepared to discuss the matter until the concluding stages of the Thirty-sixth Session of the General Assembly. The United States backtracked on even the agreements reached with it on procedural matters in the previous negotiations. When the Thirty-sixth Session opened, the United States said that the Ottawa Summit of the industrialized countries had made no difference to its position, which would be reviewed only after the Cancun summit; however, after this summit, the United States informed the president of the General Assembly that it was not prepared to discuss the subject until the Thirty-seventh Session of the General Assembly in 1982.

There was an understanding from the beginning of the Cancun summit that there was no direct formal link between the summit and the Global Negotiations. However, a principal objective of the summit was surely to facilitate agreement on these negotiations. In fact, the idea of launching Global Negotiations received highly tentative and qualified support in the chairman's summing up at Cancun. Subsequent developments showed, however, that discussions on the subject at Cancun had made no dent in the position of the United States.

Developments in 1982

In March 1982 the Group of 77 took a major step by drafting and adopting a revised resolution on the subject in which they made a number of further concessions in the hope that it would broadly meet the requirements of the United States and thus would be acceptable to the developed countries. Among the concessions, they agreed that the central forum would function throughout on the basis of consensus, and in this context they dropped the words "in all important matters'; they dropped the concept of "package agreement"; and they gave up the concept of "integrating" the end result.

The outcome of the discussions on Global negotiations at the Versailles summit (June 1982) was much more impressive, at least on paper, than that of the Cancun summit. All participants in the summit accepted the launching of Global negotiations as a major political objective. The March 1982 resolution of the G-77 made a good impression on the leaders of the summit, but instead of accepting the draft as it was they agreed to accept it only as a basis of consultation with the G-77.

Some amendments arising out of the Versailles discussion were suggested to the draft by Canada on behalf of the summit contries. The G-77 accepted a few of these amendments but suggested counteramendments to two of them.

The entire difference on launching the Global Negotiations has now boiled down to two procedural points. First, the industrialized countries are not prepared to accept any reference to resolution 34/138, which has the intent of making it binding for them. This is mainly because of the U.S. objection to references in this resolution to NIEO and a restructuring of international economic relations. (The Carter administration had accepted this resolution.) Second, the industrialized countries want to make it clear that *ad hoc* groups should be created "without duplication of the existing appropriate fora." The developing countries are not prepared to accept the resolution because it drastically restricts the role of the central forum and because of the fear of the OPEC countries that the net result of this provision could as well be the creation of only one *ad hoc* group on energy.

The industrialized countries have stuck to the draft reformulated in the light of the Versailles discussions. There has been no progress in the recently concluded session of the General Assembly in bridging the gulf separating the positions of the two groups. The Global Negotiations continue to lie in limbo.

Principal Features of the Idea of Global Negotiations

The feature of the Global Negotiations that stands out clearly is their emphasis on the pressing need to establish a new system of international economic relations based on the principle of equality and mutual benefit.

This calls for structural changes in the present international industrial, trade, monetary, and financial institutions and systems. In short, this is an attempt to establish a new international economic order virtually in one fell swoop.

The concept of interdependence, both between nations and between negotiating issues, is another distinguishing feature of the approach. The new system that is expected to be brought into being by these negotiations must promote the common interest of all. The proposal has been advanced because of the realizations that the present system not only is unjust and inequitable but also has proved inefficient and incapable of serving even the interests of those after whose image it has been created, and that if it is permitted to be left in its present state of uncertainty and chaos it will inevitably destroy the economic prosperity of the developed countries while dragging the developing countries further down the ladder. There is now a wide acceptance that the concept of interdependence has matured to a point where it can be the force for striking new comprehensive and strategic bargains for saving nations from economic disaster. Whereas for a long period after World War II the developed countries viewed international economic relations in terms of asymmetrical positions of industrialized and developing countries, they recognize today that these relations are more complex and diversified. Even one of the U.S. representatives stated in a debate on this subject that, whereas until recently interdependence was only a perception, today it is a fact.

Including all major issues within the scope of the negotiations not only enables them to be seen in their mutual interrelationship but also offers a wider canvas for mutual bargains. In this connection, the inclusion of the item on energy at the initiative of the developing countries themselves is of considerable importance.

Other special features claimed for Global Negotiations are not unique to them. Universal participation, for example, is claimed to be a special feature. But organizations like UNCTAD have the same membership as that of the United Nations as a whole. Therefore, any general negotiation within these forums would have universal participation. Moreover, even under the aegis of the General Assembly there can be and have been other negotiations like those on international development strategies in which the participation has been universal.

Universal participation has both merits and demerits. If not properly structured and orchestrated, it can become unwieldy. Moreover, the strength of the number of the developing countries in such negotiations can make the developed countries less enthusiastic, if not outright indifferent and even hostile, to such negotiations. On the plus side, negotiations based on universal participation are truly democratic. Solutions emerging from such negotiations will have the widest measure of support. There is also considerable political significance attached to bringing the socialist countries of Eastern Europe and China within the ambit of such negotiations. This is, of course, justified on economic grounds also. Moreover, if solutions to major North-South issues emerging from these negotiations ultimately have to be universally endorsed, then why not begin the negotiations on the basis of universal participation? Finally, the strength of their number, which puts off the developed countries, is the main bargaining strength that the developing countries have. They can hardly afford to deny themselves the use of this strength. Therefore, on balance, any negotiation with a very large sweep and broad scope should be based on universal participation.

Inclusion of all major issues is again not unique to global negotiations. The negotiations on the two international development strategies adopted by the United Nations involved practically all North-South issues. If energy was not included in the negotiations for the second international development strategy, it was not because the conceptual framework of the strategy did not admit of this issue but because the major interests involved decided not to allow it to be discussed within the framework.

Motives behind Sponsorship of and Support for Global Negotiations

Different countries or groups of countries have endorsed and pursued the idea of Global Negotiations for different reasons. Even the United States has never opposed the idea openly; it has concentrated its energy on raising obstacles to ensure that the negotiations never got off the ground.

The OPEC countries sponsoring the proposal for Global Negotiations seem to have had the following purposes in mind:

1. They wanted to demonstrate that the world economy was afflicted by a malaise of a long-term structural nature, and that it was therefore wrong to allege that oil-price increases were responsible for the current global economic crises.

2. They recognized that their main economic objectives—safeguarding the real value of their surplus financial assets and ensuring their se-

curity—could not be achieved except in a global context and through global arrangements, possible only by presenting a solid front with other developing countries.

3. They were interested in devising new institutions and exercising increased influence over those and existing institutions for facilitating the flow of their surplus resources to both developed and developing countries on satisfactory terms and conditions and on a secure basis.

4. They wanted to use the negotiations as a ploy to head off oil-price pressures mounted against them by oil-importing countries, both developed and developing.

5. After the 1979 oil-price increase, there were hints of a separate dialogue between the Persian Gulf states and some of the West European countries. The OPEC countries, in taking the initiative for launching global negotiations, wanted to forestall such a move.

The oil-importing developing countries supported the move for two reasons. First, they thought that if OPEC was able and willing to agree to an arrangement for ensuring reasonable security of supply and predictable prices this would not only benefit the former countries directly but could also be used as a weapon to obtain concessions from the North on other major North-South issues. This would provide them with a good opportunity to restructure international economic relations. Second, they wanted the OPEC countries, within the framework of the Global Negotiations, to focus attention on the need to alleviate the financial burdens imposed on them by the increase in oil prices.

The EEC countries saw the value of a new comprehensive North-South dialogue mainly in terms of its providing an opportunity to establish a new dynamic balance in the supply and demand of energy and to avoid the imminent collapse of the Third World market. They also realized that the world economic situation had deteriorated to such an extent that political tensions had been engendered that might pose a threat to world peace. They recognized that it was in their interest to explore the possibility of maintaining and reactivating economic growth by stepping up North-South economic relations. The EEC's interest in finding a solution to the problem of supply and prices of energy and its stake in the economic viability of the developing countries evidently derived from the facts that the EEC is the world's largest importer of energy and raw materials, accounting for over 30 percent of the world imports of these products, and that the markets of the non-oil-producing developing countries alone absorb over 20 percent of the EEC's exports.

The agenda proposed by the EEC naturally reflected its objectives and concerns, and it was almost as wide in scope as the one suggested by the Group of 77. The three broad headings for the agenda suggested by the EEC—energy and development, food supply and development, and external balance and development—covered practically everything. However, it did not include any explicit suggestion for changes in the institutional structures or in the rules of the game. Under the item on energy, the EEC made an explicit provision for discussing pricing of oil with a view to ensuring that oil prices would follow a steady and predictable pattern and any future increases would be progressive rather than sudden. The agenda the EEC proposed also showed an interest in assisting developing countries in the development of their energy resources, making joint arrangements for financing their balance-of-payments deficits, ensuring steady growth in their exports, and assisting the poorest countries through food security, increased ODA flows, and development of their mineral resources.

The United States has been the only country that has remained opposed to the Global Negotiations. This stance reflects the shift that has taken place under the Reagan administration, in its entire thinking on developmental issues, on U.S. foreign-policy objectives and the means to be deployed for achieving these objectives, and on its attitude toward multilateral development cooperation.

This policy has a number of elements. There is a belief in the magic of the marketplace, and in this light all proposals for joint international action are regarded as interventionist. Security and political interests are given precedence over other interests. This has relegated U.S. interest in the progress of the developing countries to a secondary position. In pursuing national security interest, the United States prefers dealing with developing countries on a bilateral basis rather than within a multilateral framework. And it believes that self-reliance is more important than international assistance for developing countries. In pursuing self-reliance, these countries should apply the recipes that constitute the essential components of the Reagan Administration's domestic economic policy: demand management, a nonwelfare state, nonintervention, and encouragement of private capital enterprise and initiative. The administration expects international organizations and institutions also to follow these precepts. The negative and sometimes even obstructionist attitude of the United States toward various activities and proposals for international cooperation, including the initiative for Global Negotiations, derives mainly from these policy assumptions.

Reasons for the Delay in Launching the Global Negotiations

Except for the initial agreement in principle to launch the Global Negotiations, until now there has been no worthwhile progress toward
actually launching them, despite the fact that the G-77 made its most
serious and painstaking preparations for such a conference. All ideas
and concrete proposals relating to the procedures, time frame, and
agenda for the negotiations came from the G-77. All preparations were
agreed on at the ministerial level. Heads of government of important
members of the G-77 took initiatives to establish contact and made
direct appeals to the heads of government of important developed
countries in an attempt to develop enthusiasm for these negotiations.
The G-77 also made all concessions, short of sacrificing the very notion
of Global Negotiations, that they thought would facilitate agreement
for launching the negotiations.

Seldom in the history of the United Nations have procedural problems
proved so stubborn and held up the process of negotiations for such
a long period. Such procedural hurdles have been encountered in the
past, but until now it had always been possible to overcome them. For
example, the problem of how detailed the agenda should be was faced
at the time of the formulation of both international development strategies, and each time a solution was found by not being too prescriptive
from the beginning or by being prescriptive on some items while ex-
pressing other items in neutral terms. There is, in any case, very little
prudence in joining at the procedural stage the battles that will have
to be fought when the substantive negotiations commence.

Similarly, seen in the light of experience, the fears expressed by the
industrialized countries regarding the role of the specialized agencies
are highly exaggerated and their position on this issue is wholly un-
tenable. All their fears have been taken care of by the concession made
by the G-77 to their position that all decisions will be made by consensus.
Even if a consensus is imposed on the developed countries in the central
forum against their will, this will have only recommendatory value,
as all other UN decisions have, and the commitments that they would
undertake under such decisions will be only of a moral character. The
question of the developing countries' effectively altering the power
structure and control over specialized bodies like the IMF, World Bank,
and GATT through decisions in the central forum does not arise, because
these alterations simply cannot just be legislated. They have to be
translated into specific amendments to the statutes or the articles of

agreements setting up these bodies and then approved and ratified by sovereign member governments through their respective legislative and executive procedures.

Finally, the role of the UN General Assembly in suggesting alterations or improvements in the decisions taken by specialized agencies have always been accepted. No objections have been made to such a role, precisely because it is only recommendatory. It is left to the specialized bodies to take whatever decisions they want on such recommendations. Moreover, it is always open to sovereign governments to reach agreements, in the General Assembly or in any other forum, of a more binding and far-reaching nature than has been possible in a particular specialized forum. For example, quite a few such agreements were reached in the General Assembly at the time of the negotiations on the First International Development Strategy.

All this shows that the procedural objections are only a smokescreen to hide objections of a more serious and substantive nature. The Global Negotiations have not been launched for essentially the same reasons that have made all other North-South dialogues exercises in futility. The developed countries, particularly the United States, do not want their authority over the present international economic order to be eroded in any manner. The existing order has admirably served their purpose. Even though it has started failing them, they still do not see any need for change and want to preserve it at all costs. On the other hand, the main objective of the developing countries in taking the initiative for Global Negotiations is to restructure the present international economic order. The agenda proposed by the developing countries called for changes of an entirely different magnitude. The subitems of the agenda struck at the very root of the economic power of the industrialized countries. This is why the conflict has been created.

It was hoped that including energy on the agenda would make the exercise worthwhile for the developed countries. Most of the European countries certainly viewed it in that light and therefore supported the proposal. However, because of its unique position, the United States saw the problem differently. The United States does not depend nearly as much on foreign energy sources as do most of the European countries. The United States has felt confident it can manage the energy situation. It views the energy problem as a short-lived one that would be alleviated without making any drastic concessions to OPEC. Moreover, the United States was confident of being able to deal with leading OPEC countries bilaterally.

The ambiguous position taken by the OPEC countries on the inclusion in the agenda of an item on oil pricing did not help matters. The OPEC countries rejected the wording for the item on energy suggested by the EEC ("trends and predictability of energy supply, demand and prices and their consequences for economic growth and development"). They also did not accept the item "recycling" proposed by the United States. Part of the reason for the U.S. indifference is, perhaps, the foreknowledge that OPEC was not going to allow energy to be discussed in any meaningful way in the Global Negotiations.

There are also indications that at least some major OPEC countries have not thrown their full weight behind the Global Negotiations—in any case, not behind the measures that must be taken for strengthening the position of the developing countries in these negotiations. These countries remain lukewarm toward the proposals to create an energy affiliate. They have been indifferent to the initiatives for promoting and expanding ECDC activities. They have not even attended some of the major conferences and meetings on ECDC.

Prospects for Global Negotiations

Those who are optimistic about the prospects of Global Negotiations pin much of their hope on the general consensus that still prevails in favor of launching them. This consensus was reiterated in unambiguous terms at the Versailles summit. Moreover, on the procedural issues, there are now differences on only a few points, and they are not of a nature that should continue to defy solution indefinitely.

The argument that the current deepening world economic crises cannot but adversely affect prospects for the negotiations, or that the future of the negotiations will ultimately be determined by developments in the world economy, cuts both ways. On the one hand, the current economic problems of the developed countries seem to preclude the possibility of their making concessions essential for the success of the negotiations. On the other hand, Global Negotiations should be launched precisely because they can show the way out of the present difficulties. After all, the worldwide recession was already with us when the idea of launching the Global Negotiations was first discussed. It is true that since then the situation has deteriorated further and the recession is now threatening to develop into a worldwide depression. But, then, this common adversity should heighten the sense of common destiny and alter the perception of those who want to maintain the status quo at all costs. There are already indications of such a shift of perception, such as that reflected in the reported statement of the U.S. treasury secretary that the international monetary system may need to be reexamined. The changed energy situation has, of course, weakened the developing countries' potential bargaining power. However, in spite of this, the overriding factor of interdependence remains as strong as, if not stronger than, before. Thus, there remains a strong intellectual justification for launching the global round.

The problem is basically one of will. It is far from clear that the developed countries really have the intention of negotiating any drastic changes of a structural nature or accepting the drastic remedies that the present situation calls for. In spite of the brave words used, what these countries seem to have in mind may very well turn out to be one more exercise in tinkering with the existing international economic order. All that the industrialized countries are likely to do, as an increasing number of developing countries approach default in the payment of their debts, is to bail out those few developing countries whose bankruptcies threaten the former's banking system and to keep afloat, by ad hoc concessional financial flows and marginal trade concessions, the economies of the vast number of the poor developing countries facing bankruptcies. In the process, the industrialized countries' stranglehold on the economic and political life of both these groups of developing countries will be increased, mainly by making their economies hostage to international commercial banks, the IMF, and the World Bank. The disappearance of the OPEC surpluses, the fragility of the economies of many oil-importing developing countries, the growing economic and political tension within OPEC, and the political disarray and vulnerability in which many developing countries find themselves today due to the weakening of détente and the intensification of big-power rivalry have further complicated the situation and have made the prospects of Global Negotiations very uncertain.

Thus, the prospects for global negotiations are fairly bleak. Yet it will not be possible to give them up, because no initiative in the UN of such a momentous nature is ever buried.

Consequences of Global Negotiations

Has the debate on Global Negotiations held so far done any good for the cause of international development cooperation? Two positive results claimed for the debate are that it has influenced in the right direction the negotiating approach of specialized forums and that it has been of considerable educational value. There is no evidence to substantiate the first claim. Since the beginning of 1980, when the Global Negotiations were launched in principle, there has been no worthwhile progress in the negotiations in any of the specialized forums. On the other hand, some of these agencies have been subjected to pressures of a negative kind and have witnessed retrogressive attempts and measures such as graduation, privatization, and sanctification of departures from the standstill principle. It is said that the discussions on the Global Negotiations served the educational purpose of enabling the participants to be better aware of each other's position and difficulties. This, however, can be said about any negotiation. In the case of Global Negotiations, even this limited purpose was not served, because the discussions so far have remained confined to procedural issues. Moreover, the process of better knowing each other's position has some value only if there is a desire to use this knowledge for taking the dialogue to a successful conclusion. Unfortunately, in the case of Global Negotiations this desire has been conspicuously lacking.

On the other hand, as stated in the chairman's summing up after the New Delhi consultations in February 1982, "the protracted and, so far, inconclusive preparations for the launching of Global Negotiations has held up progress in other forums dealing with North-South issues." This is so regardless of the provision in the Havana summit resolution and the General Assembly resolution (34/138) that the Global Negotiations should not interrupt the process of negotiations in other forums but should reinforce and draw upon them. Progress in other forums can be slowed down by Global Negotiations simply because, even if the Group of 77 displays a firm unity of purpose, the developed countries can always use the pretext of Global Negotiations to withhold progress in other forums. Also, a venture like Global Negotiations cannot but be protracted and time-consuming. The time period of about nine months suggested by the G-77 in its initial proposals was highly unrealistic. Even the more limited and unsuccessful Paris dialogue lasted for about three years. If the limited diplomatic, bureaucratic, and financial resources of the developing countries are to be devoted to the inevitably long Global Negotiations, these countries will not be able to address other negotiations effectively. The worst casualty in this respect could be the South-South dialogue, itself a very demanding exercise.

There is evidence that excessive preoccupation with Global Negotiations has been responsible for withholding progress in other negotiations. In mid-1979, some OPEC members seriously suggested that the negotiations on the second international development strategy should be postponed until the Eleventh Special Session of the General Assembly, when Global Negotiations were expected to be launched. This was mainly responsible for the very lean period for the negotiations on the strategy in the second half of the year.

Future Strategy

Developing countries now generally agree that they cannot put all their eggs in the one basket of Global Negotiations. There is also wide recognition that in the ultimate analysis what is important to persist with is not the exact format of Global Negotiations but the spirit and the general objectives. This was clearly reflected in the remark made by Prime Minister Gandhi of India at Cancun: "We are not wedded to certain ideas. We are more interested in the results and the substance. While preparing for [Global Negotiations], other pressing problems brook no delay." In the New Delhi consultations also it was agreed that "efforts should be made concurrently to achieve progress in areas of critical importance to developing countries . . . in the forthcoming conferences and meetings of specialised agencies." This feeling was reflected by the heads of government or state of the industrialized countries participating in the Versailles summit: "At the same time we are prepared to continue and develop practical cooperation with the developing countries" in different specialized areas and issues.

Undoubtedly, serious efforts will be made in all appropriate forums for finding solutions to the short-term and long-term development problems of the developing countries and generally for achieving the broad purposes of the Global Negotiations. At the same time, efforts will continue to reach an agreement on launching Global negotiations; however, it will not be an exclusive concern.

It is tactically important for the developing countries to change gear without changing direction. They should now seriously explore the possibility of making progress in negotiations with developed countries in the following areas:

1. Issues of mutual interest: Stabilization of commodity prices; balance-of-payments support, including the additional allocation of SDRs; debt reorganization; resources flow; energy and natural resources.

2. Issues that do not call for immediate and apparent changes in structure, such as food security.

3. A program of emergency assistance.

4. Issues that can lead to changes within the framework of well-recognized and widely accepted policies by developed countries; import liberalization; combating protectionism; assistance in developing indigenous capacities and infrastructure in developing countries.

5. Issues that a group of developed countries want to raise with other developed countries and at the same time are the concern of developing countries, among them the fight against protectionism and dispute settlement in GATT.

Changing the issues and the form should not imply, however, the discarding of the basic rationale and objectives of the Global Negotiations. As a matter of fact, the negotiations on the above-mentioned issues in specialized forums will have very little meaning if they are insulated from the basic objectives of the Global Negotiations. Therefore, the spirit of Global Negotiations must prevail in these negotiations also. These negotiations, without being called global, must be inspired by a global perspective. This is of critical importance for the unity of the G-77 and a necessity for the North also. The North must realize that the present trends in the world economy, particularly increasing interdependence, require coordinated international action and call for far-reaching changes in the structure of the world economy and international economic relations if major tensions and strains are to be avoided in the coming years.

A change in the negotiating strategy is being suggested here simply because, for the time being, the best prospect for success lies in modifying the existing system rather than changing it radically and comprehensively at one go. However, a mere change in the strategy of negotiations is not going to make them much easier. Even in the negotiations on the issues indicated above, many substantive problems are likely to arise, just as in the negotiations under the proposed global round. For example, when we negotiate on issues like energy, food security, and balance-of-payments adjustments, we come face to face with the same problems of restructuring, making additional resources available to developing countries, and providing increased access to them in the markets of the developed countries.

The so-called mutual-interest issues are never unequivocally so. There are conflicts of interest inherent in all mutual-interest issues. Moreover, mutual interests in an issue evolve over time. Even proposals for a "link" between SDR and development finance and for an international taxation system are arguably in the interest of North in the medium and the long term.

The approach of global negotiations was advocated in 1979 because multilateral development cooperation between developed and developing countries was stalemated at that time on a number of key issues and a series of international conferences had not succeeded in providing the necessary breakthrough for progressing toward the achievement of the goals of an NIEO. Given this background, it may be argued that there is no point now in changing the strategy and reverting to the earlier sterile phase. The answer to this argument is that the dialogue must be continued in all circumstances. The dialogue keeps the ideas alive. It influences the various parties' positions and makes them aware of inperfections and inadequacies in those positions.

In order to be effective, the dialogue must be sustained, and at the substantive level. Unfortunately it has not been so with global negotiations that have assumed the character of unproductive sparring rather than really facing the issues. Therefore, other approaches must be tried.

The developing countries, while conducting negotiations with developed countries in specialized forums and on issues in which developed countries may perceive their immediate interest, will have to be extra vigilant. It will be of supreme importance for them to maintain their unity and make progress in implementing programs of mutual cooperation in order to strengthen their bargaining position. Moreover, they will have to be very careful about not making any concessions that will undermine the prospects of their independent and autonomous growth. For example, vigilance will be required in considering various aspects of IMF and World Bank conditionality, facilitating flows of private capital, and the application of GATT rules to sensitive sectors of their economies.

6

Global Negotiations: Path to the Future or Dead-End Street?

John W. Sewell and
I. William Zartman

North-South negotiations are now nearly three decades old. It was at the Bandung Afro-Asian conference in Indonesia in 1955 that the developing countries began to call for redefinition of the relationship between what came to be known later as the "North" and the "South." The new countries of the developing world—many of which gained national independence in the late 1950s and the early 1960s—not only wanted equal participation in the international political system but also started asking for far-reaching changes that would lead to a "more equitable" international economic system.

Although the idea of reforming the international economic system evolved over a long period of time, it was the success of OPEC in raising oil prices in the early 1970s that led the developing countries to aggressively demand fundamental reforms in the international economic system. OPEC's success in increasing oil prices and the attempt by some of its members to use oil as a political weapon had a significant impact on both the developed and developing countries. It suggested to both sides that the South will be able to wield formidable economic power if and when it is united.

In the early 1970s the developing nations introduced the idea of a New International Economic Order (NIEO). The Third World countries questioned the fundamental premises of the present international order and hoped that their proposals would correct inequalities, redress existing injustices, and permit them the opportunity to participate in reforming the existing system and in shaping their destinies. As a result, since the early 1970s there have been multiple negotiations between the developed and the developing countries on a wide range of issues and in many different forums.

The year 1983 marked the end of a decade of intensive negotiations between the developing countries of the South and the developed countries of the North. It was the tenth anniversary of the meeting of the nonaligned countries in Algiers that issued the Charter of Economic Rights and Duties of States calling for a New International Economic Order, which in turn gave rise to an intensive and unprecedented set of North-South negotiations. It is now time to take stock and to see what can be learned from these negotiations.

North-South negotiations have been extensively analyzed in other chapters in this book and elsewhere. The focus of almost all of these studies, however, has been either on the politics or economies of the issues or on specific problems such as commodities, trade, and debts.[1]

In contrast, this chapter assesses the reasons for the seeming stalemate in North-South negotiations and examines analytically not only the "center ring" negotiations, such as the Conference on International Economic Cooperation (CIEC) or the UN's Committee of the Whole (COW), but also other equally important negotiations, such as the Multifiber Agreement and the International Wheat Agreement.

Our analysis is based on several assumptions. The first is that North-South negotiations of various kinds will continue in the 1980s and the 1990s. These negotiations will be unavoidable because the developing countries are of increasing economic and political importance to the North; because they are much more numerous and dominate international forums, from whence they will continue to exert pressure for more negotiations; and because they have a well-founded sense of grievance and are pressing for a greater share of benefits and power within the international system.

The second assumption is that lessons can be learned from negotiation theory and the experiences of actual negotiations that can explain the negotiating behavior of the parties and provide useful procedural guidance for future negotiations.

The third assumption is that North-South negotiations do not have to be a zero-sum game. Both sides will benefit from a restructuring of the current international economic system. The needs of the developing countries are obvious, but the North, particularly given the world's current economic problems, needs a new international economic order just as much as the South does.

First Questions

Before we can examine the contributions of negotiating theory, several issues must be discussed. These include whether the terms "North" and "South" reflect reality, whether the issues are truly negotiable, and whether some degree of power has shifted from the industrial countries to the developing world.

In the last decade North-South negotiations have been very diverse. They have ranged from global issues that affect almost all countries (like COW) to quite specific discussions (such as the Multifiber Agreement); from universal participation (the Law of the Seas Conference) to representational (CIEC); from successes (the Lome Convention) to dismal failures (CIEC).

Some observers in the developed countries maintain that a North-South division is not real and that North-South negotiations therefore do not reflect reality. They base their conclusions on the wide and growing diversity among developing countries. It is true that at times it almost seems as though North-South negotiations were carefully structured not to come to any agreement. But North-South negotiations will continue, if only because both sides take them seriously enough to be obliged to continue. Although there are differences on the issues to be discussed and the locus for discussions, there is no doubt that negotiations between the North and the South in one form or another are here to stay.

But although the dialogue will continue in one form or another, there is no escaping the fact that the positions and expectations of the developed and the developing countries are fundamentally different. The North, by and large, is satisfied with the status quo and feels that the international system is working well and does not need major restructuring. The predominant view is that changes must be gradual and marginal. Most developing countries, on the other hand, feel precisely the opposite. They maintain that the present economic order systematically discriminates against them and denies them equality of opportunity. The South argues that the international economic system— with all its mechanisms and decision-making institutions—was created to serve the needs of the industrialized countries and lacks the capacity to respond to the needs and interests of the poor countries. Since most of the Southern countries were not present at the creation of the present order, they feel that the system does not allow them to receive an adequate share of the benefits and power. Moreover, there has been a strong subtheme in their presentation that the North "owes" the South a debt due to past exploitation—hence the far-reaching proposals to change the international economic system radically.

The choice of a forum for negotiations has also been a source of differences. The South wishes to negotiate in the universal forums where decisions are made on the basis of one vote per country, for the simple reason that Southern countries command the majority of the votes. It prefers, therefore, to locate discussion in the UN, particularly the General Assembly. It also wants multipurpose and comprehensive negotiations that deal with a wide variety of issues simultaneously. The North, on the other hand, wishes to negotiate issues in the forums where voting power reflects economic reality and where it has substantial influence and control. It therefore emphasizes the World Bank and the International Monetary Fund as forums for negotiations on financial and monetary issues. The North also prefers negotiations that deal with specific issues, and it has been reluctant to enter into negotiations whose agendas include a range of international economic issues. Both sets of differences—over the objectives and over the forums of negotiations—have contributed greatly to the current stalemate in North-South negotiations.

There are, of course, differences of opinion on the above issues among the Northern and Southern countries themselves. The Nordic countries and the Netherlands, for example, have been more interested in accommodating to the proposals of the developing countries than, say, the United States or West Germany. There have also been differences of attitude and approach among the developing countries. While the radical countries among them have been pressing for more fundamental and far-reaching changes in the international economic system, the moderate states have been willing to accept more limited and gradual changes. In fact, differences among developing countries have often been a major factor in negotiations. For instance, the developing countries that had been most successful in tapping commercial credit markets in the industrial world refused to allow discussion of debt moratoriums for fear it would affect their credit ratings.

In spite of the difference of opinion about the objectives and locus of the negotiations and the repeated failures and frustrations, both sides have continued to carry on the discussion, to discuss the issues, and in some instances to negotiate seriously. Contrary to the views of many people who thought that North-South negotiations were dead after the failure of CIEC between 1975 and 1977 and later on after the impasses at the COW between 1977 and 1980, negotiations on various aspects of the NIEO issues have continued in various forums. For example, trade negotiations have taken place in the Multilateral Trade Negotiations (MTN) in Geneva in 1979 and at the GATT meeting in 1982. Debt issues have been discussed at UNCTAD and other forums, and monetary issues have been negotiated within the international financial institutions. These activities as well as the emerging political and economic circumstances in the world indicate that negotiations between the developed and the developing countries will remain an important aspect of international relations in the decade ahead.

The Issue of Negotiability

Given these differences, some observers have raised the question of whether the NIEO issues essentially are negotiable. They argue that, since the developing countries are working for a redistribution of wealth, income, and power and since they do not have the ability to impose costs or to offer immediate benefits, the industrialized countries should not and need not negotiate. The proponents of this view maintain that the present economic system works quite well and should not be tampered with. They view the demands of the developing countries as an empty rhetoric and North-South negotiations as impossible, undesirable, and unnecessary.

There is a growing sense in the North, however, stimulated by the current global recession, that both sides can benefit from the outcomes of North-South negotiations. Although the present international economic system, which was created after World War II, has served the world rather well, they contend that it is time to improve and change some aspects of it. They argue that it is now time to reform the system so that it reflects the new economic and political importance of the developing countries. In addition to the matters of justice and fairness, a reform of the system, they maintain, is necessary if the world is to avoid serious economic and political dislocations. With growing interdependence between the North and the South, they argue that both parties will benefit if they solve their common problems by negotiation rather than confrontation.

Of course, no party negotiates unless it wants to—that is, unless the costs of not negotiating are higher than those of negotiating. But negotiating does not necessarily mean that all parties want to reach an agreement either. Indeed, some parties participate simply to be able to stall any agreement. Issues are negotiable only if one rejects the idea of the total conversion of one party to the views of the other. The issue therefore becomes how much change has to be made in the positions of both sides in order to get the parties to negotiate. The need is to formulate the possibilities of a favorable outcome and to change the perception of non-negotiability. It is here that the analysis of the negotiating process is important, and it is such an analysis that is the purpose of this chapter.

Negotiations, it is said, are essentially reflections or ratifications of shifts in power between two parties. The important question is whether power has shifted to some degree from North to South in the last few decades. Many in the industrialized countries believe that there has been no significant shift of power and that the North can ignore Southern demands without incurring substantial costs. Others argue that the question of the shift of power should not be raised at all. They point out that the South has become an important part of the international economic system, and they believe that the North cannot ignore the South's interests and demands for long without incurring substantial costs.

The South clearly now has more weight in the global economy than it did three decades ago, and in some areas—most notably energy— it has considerable importance. The South also is an important market for the exports of goods and capital of the North and an essential supplier of a wide range of raw materials, including strategic commodities. The Southern countries have also become important participants in international finance, particularly as major borrowers from commercial banks in the industrial world. Indeed, the importance of the South for the North has increased so much in the last two decades that growth or lack of it in the South directly influences the rate of growth in the North.[2]

In short, although the difficulties in defining power and in quantifying it make it hard to say how much power has shifted from North to South, there is no doubt that the South is more important and more powerful now than it was a generation ago. The fact that the two sides have come to negotiate on various issues is evidence of some shift in power in favor of the South. The North recognizes this, and the recognition is implicit in its continuing feeling that it has to respond by participating in the negotiations. In any event, the South collectively certainly has the power to block agreements the North considers important, as it did in the case of the International Wheat Agreement. For purposes of negotiating, however, the issue should not be so much one of power transfer as one of power sharing. In sharing power the gains of one party are not necessarily translated as a loss to the other.

The gains can be important to both the stronger and the weaker parties even if they do not result in a fundamental restructuring of the relationship.

The Negotiating Process: What Can Be Learned from Theory?

North-South encounters are full of exhortation. Much of the literature is occupied by one side's telling the other, in beguiling or condemning tones, how it should behave for the greater good of humanity, while the other side spends a somewhat smaller portion of the debate telling how this is not so. The thesis of this chapter is that something might be learned from the process by which North and South seek to resolve the problems of economic order. A better understanding of the negotiation process can permit an understanding of how better to conduct North-South negotiations.

The focus on process is admittedly unusual—indeed perplexingly so. War is studied and taught as a process, as are love, cooking, tennis, and expository writing. Why then is it so hard to focus on the process of negotiation and learn from past performance rather than getting stuck on substantive positioning and debates? The question may be only intellectually (rather than practically) interesting, but it may also bring some insights with its answer. Negotiation is not usually studied because it is caught among three more common deterministic explanations—the economic, the political, and the moral. Much of the discussion on North-South matters is carried on (primarily by the North) in terms of established economic mechanisms with determinate outcomes—comparative advantage, supply and demand, pricing, and so forth. The rest of the discussion in the North is in terms of simple power determinacies, in which the stronger parties decide and the weaker lack even the choice of rejection. In the South discussion is usually in equally determinate terms of morality, according to which what must happen is what should happen.

Determinacy does not kill debate, as any economist, political scientist, or philosopher knows, but it does deflect attention from process. Outcomes are the subject of debate rather than the business of getting to them. Yet, as every baseball player knows, how one plays the game has much to do with whether one wins or loses. Process dominates—even if it does not determine—outcome. For instance, the "parliamentary negotiations" that marked the Law of the Sea negotiations helped to determine the agreements finally reached as a result of that long process.

And since the economic, political, and moral determinants of outcomes are less sure than their advocates would have us believe and are in any case mutually contradictory, it is worthwhile to focus on the process of negotiation, in which economic, political, and moral factors all have a rightful place.

Characterizing the Process

Like many other procedures, negotiation has serious implications for substance. To say that a problem is to be negotiated or solved by negotiation is not to say that two points of view can simply be glued together to form an outcome, or that one point of view is to be adopted over the other, or that both sides will lay aside conflict and practice cooperation. Negotiation is a mere continuation of policy by other means. The means chosen have costs and implications, however, which impinge on the unaltered continuation of policy. A party's policy preferences are essentially unilateral creations, designed to further aims and handle problems, and are frequently in conflict with other parties' unilateral policies. Negotiation is joint decision making in which unilateral positions in conflict are turned into multilateral decisions that are deemed preferable by the parties on the combined basis of cost, goals, and effectiveness. In order to examine some of the implications of this process, it is appropriate to highlight its most important, and frequently paradoxical, characteristics.

The most important characteristic of negotiation is that it is a creative process aimed at providing the parties with a preferred outcome. No party will agree to a negotiated or multilateral outcome, or even agree to negotiate for one, if such an outcome is not seen as preferable to the outcomes attainable by going it alone. Unilateral action may simply not be able to solve the problem, and hence be ineffective, or it may be able to attain its goals only at high cost, and hence be inefficient, but these elements will be weighed against the cost of not overcoming the problem and the viability of the present situations and also against the benefits to be gained by a unilateral outcome. Preferability calculations must take into account the relations among these four points; for example, a marginally preferable multilateral outcome may not be attractive enough to outweigh a current nonsolution viewed as viable. But negotiating parties also have an opportunity in such calculations, since they can seize on the elements to improve and sell their proposals. Negotiations can therefore be seen as a combination of competitive efforts by parties to offer outcomes to each other that are sufficiently preferable over unilateral outcomes to gain their support.

The competing characteristic of negotiation is that it is an alternative means to a policy end. Parties first judge preferability of outcomes by constant objectives and criteria. Negotiating opponents may push back these objectives onto prior levels and into previous referents, but they are unlikely to change their nature; thus, negotiators can help other parties see alternative means of achieving their ends. Yet parties can be expected to resist. Diplomats receive their basic credits for effectively defending their country's policies, and this results in a foreign-policy debate that is essentially one of attack and defense. In these kinds of interaction, diplomats are conducting barrage diplomacy on fixed targets—shooting at the other's positions and fortifying their own. An improvement in prospects for negotiations is effected when diplomats turn from position warfare to mobile warfare, attempting to get the other party to move from its fixed position to one more favorable to the first party. When both parties begin to seek movement rather than defense, meeting at a common position becomes possible (even if not predictable).

Negotiation takes place when there are not agreed terms of trade (that is, when there is no agreement on how much of what one party wants is required to pay for how much of what the other wants) and the main purpose is to establish such terms of trade. Even in the most positive and cooperative encounters, when a new good is created by the sole act of multilateral agreement, the conflictual task remains that of distributing the benefits of agreement—that is, deciding how much of what one party gets is worth how much of what the other party gets—and this is a terms-of-trade exercise. Terms of trade are established when items are exchanged; items valued highly by one party and less costly to the other are exchanged for items valued highly by the other and less costly to the first. The more the items fall into two separate and equivalent piles, the greater the chances of agreement. When items are divided, the terms of trade become more difficult to arrange and depend on agreed principles of justice. In the latter case, process may become even more important, since concessions from initially posited systems of justice may determine an outcome quite distinct from any notions of justice that established the starting points. Furthermore, concession behavior frequently has its own norms and signals and may break down for procedural as well as substantive reasons.

Negotiation also is a reflection of power and a register of power changes. To some observers negotiation is nothing more than a ratification of power positions, although to more discerning analysts there is a margin of tactical power than can be exercised in consonance with particular power positions to produce secondary changes in them. No analysis has shown that negotiation can be used to effect major changes in power positions, although it can give structure to changes that have already taken place or are in the process of doing so. In a more dynamic sense, negotiation can provide structures and institutions to handle ongoing changes in power relations and allow for transitions that might otherwise prove unmanageable and disruptive. Thus, in power terms, negotiation has a past and a future dimension in regard to power position and a present dimension in regard to tactics of power. Parties in negotiation often trade off present against future positions: Negotiation frequently takes place when a dominant power is slipping and a weaker party is rising in power, and the former negotiates to maintain some of its privileges before it loses everything while the latter negotiates to consolidate its gains rather than holding out over the long run for additional but costly advantages. Power is the fundamental consideration in negotiations, underlying other basic values such as well-being, interests, and even existence, and it is not traded loosely. Exhortations are part of the process of changing perceptions of power shifts, but they are rarely sufficient; conflict, tests of strength, and suffering are almost always required to bring home the message, with all the problems of countermeasures and embittered feelings that such encounters imply.

Negotiation is persuasion. It involves changing the views of suspicious, resistant individuals and transmitting such changes through institutional groups and networks structured to resist change. Three characteristics of negotiation that set it aside from other decision-making processes underlie its peculiar nature as a problem in persuasion: variable values, side payments, and partial information. Negotiators come to negotiations with different and uncertain evaluations of various items, events, ingredients, and outcomes under discussion, rather than with fixed positions. Even the scope of discussions is fluid, enabling negotiators to set aside items too intractable to be the subject of agreement and to bring in items strictly extraneous to the problem but useful as side payments for other concessions. Negotiators deal with uncertainty; not only are values flexible, but information about them can be manipulated tactically and even misleadingly, or, in other instances, can be sought expanded cooperatively and creatively to expand the terrain of possible agreement. Furthermore, as in any other exercise of persuasion, positions can be altered by bringing out their future implications, by attaching contingent deprivations and gratifications. Such contingencies can depend on the action of the persuading party, through his use of threats and promises, or they can be nonvolitional and inherent in the position itself, indicated through the use of warnings and predictions. In either set of cases, the deprivation and gratifications are not self-evident but must be convincingly conveyed to the other party if they are to be effective in bringing about a change in his position.

Finally, in terms of the immediate encounter and also of the broader evolutionary context in which it fits, negotiation is a problem of timing. If it did not matter when the parties agreed, it would not matter whether they agreed at all. Time has its costs, and so parties negotiate their cost-resistances against each other. Negotiations come to a successful conclusion when the parties are convinced they have arrived at the best deal possible from the other party and when that deal is better than no agreement. This means that it is in each party's interest to make an offer the other cannot refuse just before the negotiation is about to end for a procedural reason—just before an external deadline is lowered, or just before the other party is about to break off and go home. This, in turn, implies a fine sense of timing. Unless there is a sense of a clear rise in time costs—an external or internal deadline—negotiations can go on forever. But time costs rest on three analytically discernable elements that are hard to separate in reality: the procedural rhythm of the negotiations (the concession rates), the substantive discount rates of the items under discussion (the rotting rate), and the long-range evolution of the relative power and fortunes of the parties (the historical rate of change). It is an unusual encounter that benefits from a coincidence of all three.

Thus, negotiation can be analyzed as six different problems—a creation problem, a defense problem, a bargaining problem, a power problem, a persuasion problem, and a timing problem—each to be solved according to its own theoretical components. All can be applied to the analysis of a common negotiating process that runs through three phases: diagnosis, formulation, and elaboration. On the basis of this understanding of the negotiation process and its various natures, we can turn to some operational lessons for North-South negotiators.

Improving the Process

This section addresses the question of how the North and the South can improve the process of negotiations. It is drawn mainly from an analysis of negotiations in general but more particularly from seven case studies of North-South negotiations over the last decade that were analyzed in a series of seminars at the Overseas Development Council (ODC).

Schematically, suggestions for better negotiation merely indicate that each of its basic three phases should be developed to the utmost—that the diagnostic phase be devoted to a fuller preparation of information, that the formulation phase be used for the satisfactory development of a common definition of the problem and of an acceptable solution, and that the elaboration phase be used for the balanced implementation of the formula in detail in the jointly best terms possible.

Developing a Better Information Base

North-South negotiations have usually had a highly inadequate information base. There often has been a chronic lack of basic information on the issues under negotiation, and at times this has prevented the parties from reaching an agreement. This is true of both the North and the South, but it is particularly serious for the South. Even if they are technically qualified, Southern negotiators are often too busy to undertake the time-consuming work of assembling the necessary statistical and technical information. The negotiators of the South are invariably outnumbered by their counterparts from the North and overwhelmed by routine work. They are burdened by the paperwork produced in the course of the negotiations alone. They frequently lack the time and energy to cope with new developments and to adjust their negotiating positions. In the International Wheat Agreement negotiations, for example, the Southern negotiators lacked sufficient technical expertise and information, and because neither FAO nor UNCTAD was involved in the negotiations the South could not rely on their resources. The same is true of the negotiations on the Integrated Program for Commodities (IPC) negotiations, where the lack of information on complex and uncertain issues was very great. Similarly, in the Lome II negotiations the ACP countries had to depend on the EEC for statistical information and other issue-specific expertise.

The negotiating process could be improved if all parties could develop the best possible informational base beforehand, especially where subject matters are filled with unknowns and controversy. Better information will not eliminate all conflicts (it may well heighten some while reducing others), but it will put debate on a more factual level. In the realm of persuasion, to the extent that future implications can be agreed to and predictions or warnings shared, the need for threats and promises, with the attendant implications of interference and coercion, is reduced, and parties can turn to a common attack on the problem rather than on each other's positions. This common problem-solving aspect of North-South negotiations can be enhanced if information sources are shared, if background studies are jointly sponsored or prepared by independent agencies, and, as negotiations proceed, if joint technical briefing sessions are offered by independent agencies.

There are two aspects to the preparation needed for North-South negotiations. One concerns the technical information needed to master the subject; the other concerns preparation of each party for a better understanding of its own position and of the basis of the position of the other parties. Both are often wanting. Developed and developing countries alike enter economic negotiations with insufficient preparation, even on their own positions. They also devote little effort to understanding the ingredients in the other parties' positions. Yet the two are crucial to the creation of positive formulas that bring the parties' positions together.

Examples of this need come in numbers from the Law of the Sea Conference, where the very length of the negotiations was in part explained by the necessity for new information. Briefings offered by nongovernmental groups helped fill this need. A model developed by Nyhart at MIT was used by diverse delegations to test their proposals, and when implications became clearer proposals were modified accordingly. In the Lome II negotiations, the consulting firm of Tate & Lyle advised both Great Britain and the Caribbean countries, with positive results.

In order to facilitate the flow of information between the parties and among them, there is a need for more unofficial forums where experts from both sides can discuss the issues and exchange ideas that will lead to better understanding and appreciation of the various viewpoints and negotiating positions. Informal study groups and problem-solving exercises between both sides can help a great deal. Expert groups from the developed and developing countries will have to be encouraged to meet frequently to promote the dialogue, explore acceptable negotiating proposals, and develop ideas and strategies that can accommodate the diverse interests of the parties. Groups such as the Society for International Development's North-South Roundtable need to be supported and expanded to fulfill this function. In addition, expert groups could meet before major negotiations to help establish a common information base.

The Third World has particular needs in this regard. Although misinformation and uncertainty are very great on both sides, the South clearly is at a disadvantage in trying to sort out facts from fiction. As a Commonwealth Group of experts has put it, "In the conduct of negotiations, Southern spokesmen often operate under a handicap and are put on the defensive or easily deflected from their negotiating positions, as they find themselves unable to respond convincingly to queries relating to the analytical foundations, cost-benefits implications or the time frame of their proposals."[3]

A common theme running throughout the analysis of the ODC's case studies was the need to make greater analytical capability available to Southern negotiators so that they could better understand issues and judge trade-offs and therefore be more prepared to handle compromise in specific negotiations.

Many observers have proposed that the South should establish its own secretariat to undertake the necessary technical, statistical, and analytical work and provide advice on strategy and tactics.[4] Such an institution would not only provide technical support but would also be in a position to coordinate the diverse interests of the developing countries in the various North-South negotiations. It should not only provide analytical support but should strive to identify priorities and to develop and propose strategies and tactics for the negotiations.

Although we realize the political, institutional, and economic problems associated with the setting up of such a secretariat, we believe that the South needs an organization that will provide technical and analytical support for its negotiators. Some have suggested that UNCTAD should fulfill this role, if only because it is perceived in the North as a "Southern" institution. However, UNCTAD is a part of the UN system and is governed by both developed and developing countries. The South needs its own institution, analogous to the Organization for Economic Cooperation and Development (OECD). In view of the fact that negotiations between North and South are here to stay, the argument for such an organization becomes even more compelling. A relatively small organization with a highly competent and qualified staff could provide the critical support system that the South now clearly lacks. In order to avoid duplicating the work done by other institutions, a Southern secretariat can and should work closely with the various UN bodies and other international institutions.

The Need to Develop a Formula

The inability to develop a formula that reflects the real interests of each party may have been the greatest failing in North-South negotiations over the past decade. The failing is particularly marked in the formulation of the issues by developing countries. In many cases the South tends to rely on moral arguments, although there are strong economic and political arguments to be made for reform of the international economic system. The debt negotiations are a good example. The South based its arguments essentially on moral grounds when there was a real and strong case to be made for Northern self-interest in global financial stability and trade expansion. The trouble is that moral arguments carry very little weight when real economic and political interests are at stake and are not therefore an effective bargaining chip.

If future North-South negotiations are to prove fruitful, the issues must be posed in such a way that the agreements can be sought on the basis of mutual gains. The South has to make it clear that it is asking not for charity but for a reform of the international economic system in order to make it more efficient, more equitable, and more open for both developed and developing countries. It has to show that a gain for the South does not necessarily mean a loss to the North and that benefits can accrue to both sides. It has to demonstrate that, in this period of intensifying interdependence, growth and development in the South is in the economic and political interest of the North.

Many of the North-South encounters to date have failed to reach agreement because they represent a clash between basic notions of redistributive justice ("to those that have not it shall be given") and equitable justice ("to those that have it shall be given"), with each side holding out for its victory. The negotiations in the COW foundered on this conflict; the Lome Convention succeeded because it found a formula for agreement, whose compromise nature is testified to by the attendant debate over its real degree of success.

Negotiation should be a positive-sum process, not a matter of victory and defeat. Each party must receive something within the framework for agreement. The agreement must be fair to both sides, and, although each side naturally seeks a formula that is closest to its own positions, it must make an effort to broaden that position to include something for the other party. An invitation to find a common solution to a common problem is the beginning of a search for a jointly satisfactory formula. It can begin with an examination of the other party's position for weakness, not in an effort to discredit it but rather in an attempt to complement it with positions that will remedy its deficiencies.

The specifics of this general approach will vary with the different matters under discussion. The International Wheat Negotiations of 1974–1979 and the Law of the Sea negotiations are contrasting examples of formulas that did not and that did work, respectively. The drafters of the International Wheat Agreement sought a limited agreement that took excess price fluctuations out of the market rather than a broader and more radical resource transfer; it failed to win agreement from all parties. In the United Nations Conference on the Law of the Sea (UNCLOS), the imaginative parallel banking system for deep-sea mining is a striking example of a formula that bridges the redistributive demands for an enterprise monopoly and the equity demands for free-enterprise mining. The course of North-South negotiations, however, is marked more by the absence of the search for such a formula than its presence, one of the causes of the current stalemate.

Coalitions and Alliances

If North-South negotiations are to produce the desired results in the future, coalitions and alliances that cut across North-South lines must be established. While we do not question the validity of the North-South framework, we believe that the negotiating process will be greatly improved if the parties can transcend the strict division into "North" and "South." Admittedly, this is a delicate matter that has to be handled carefully. The impression must not be given that the North is trying to divide the South and to co-opt some groups of the developing countries.

The developing countries have seen their strength lying in their unity. This perception has been essentially correct, and it has paid dividends in that it has created a group solidarity and has brought the developed countries to the bargaining table despite the fact that developing countries wield little real power in a traditional sense. This means that developing countries put a high premium on obtaining an agreed-upon group position and go to considerable lengths to achieve one.

Yet this very unity often has blocked real compromise, as shifting positions during negotiations often has been cumbersome. It also has prevented natural alliances from emerging across North-South lines. Perhaps the most obvious example is the field of trade. There now appears to be emerging the potential for creating alliances between countries interested in a more open trading system and those favoring more protection of national markets. In practice the United States and the newly industrializing countries have a considerable interest in trade liberalization; the European Community and Japan do not. Yet, as the negotiations over the Multifiber Agreement (MFA) and the Wheat Agreement indicate, group lines are hard to transcend. In both cases negotiations among the industrial countries were long and arduous and resulted in the case of the MFA in a more restrictive agreement and in the case of the wheat negotiations in no agreement at all. There are other similar examples. Only during the Law of the Sea negotiations were cross-cutting alliances achieved, and then only on some issues.

If cross-cutting coalitions cannot be achieved, the prospects of continuing stalemate are high, especially as differences within the Third World grow. Negotiations will continue to be cumbersome and confrontational. Natural alliances cannot be made. The challenge is how to get the parties to see themselves as bargain makers rather than antagonistic groups.

The Creation of Trade-Offs

The need for trade-offs is closely related to the challenge of creating formulas that bring gains to all sides. There are two aspects to this issue of trade-offs. While global negotiations, given their diversity and complexity, are so broad that the balance sheet is hard to keep track of, excessively narrow topics provide little chance for trade-offs. The definition of specific agendas, therefore, is terribly important for the success of negotiations.

Since negotiation is generally less a process of deciding a matter than one of providing counterbalancing payoffs that make a new outcome possible, an array of items is necessary to provide the basis for agreement. Trade-offs require disarticulating issues, in itself a useful way of overcoming intransigence over large problems. Fractionating and packaging are necessary to provide the ingredients of an agreement and the material for the procedure of exchanges and compensations. Admittedly, like any other human interaction, trade-offs are a matter of perception; Nicolson's famous confrontation between the Warrior, who negotiates only to win, and the Shopkeeper, who negotiates to strike a mutually satisfactory deal, remains a standoff as long as the Warrior sees it as a contest of principle rather than a search for a trade-off of price and quantity. But perception is theoretically vulnerable to effective persuasion and to the skillful use of side payments, both items that return the discussion to the level of trade-offs.

In the last ten years of negotiations, trade-offs were very evident in UNCLOS but not to any great extent in the other North-South negotiations. For instance, the African, Caribbean, and Pacific (ACP) countries refused to trade off in an acknowledgment of human rights or the EC's need for investment guaranty provisions in the Lome II negotiations. On the other hand, in debt negotiations agreement was reached because the Third World countries were willing (albeit reluctantly, as they had little choice) to trade off their insistence on overall rescheduling of their debts in turn for Northern agreement to adjust the debts of the poorer countries from past foreign aid from loans to grants.

Only UNCLOS provides some important examples. Coastal control over resources, in the form of the 200-mile exclusive economic zone (EEZ) and the modified archipelago concept for the South, was exchanged for transit rights through straits and archipelagic waters and a 12-mile territorial sea limit for the North as one of the basic compromise formulas of the negotiations. In all the other cases (even those with some mutual satisfaction in the outcome, such as Lome II), trade-offs were scarce. Often there was a missed potential, as in the MFA, where the United States could have offered liberalization in textiles against continual restrictions on apparel. More frequently, as in the COW, the International Wheat Agreement (IWA), and the Integrated Program for Commodities (IPC), the South promoted the idea that it had nothing to trade off against Northern concessions and the North agreed, believing either that the South had nothing to offer or that it would offer nothing it had.

One fundamental problem in the provision of trade-offs is that the negotiations of the issues to be traded are carried out in different forums. There is an obvious interrelationship between trade liberalization and debt financing, but trade and debt issues are negotiated at different times and in different places by different negotiators. It is therefore critically important to develop a mechanism that can promote coordination in the negotiations of related issues in different forums and that can encourage and facilitate trade-offs. So far there has been little coordination between the different forums and institutions, such as GATT and UNCTAD, that deal with trade issues and the World Bank and the International Monetary Fund, which handle debt issues. Unless urgent steps are taken to rationalize the system or to provide some overview mechanism, the proliferation and compartmentalization of the negotiations process will continue to hinder progress and create misunderstanding.

A related problem is the unwillingness and inability of the South to look at issues in disaggregated form and to think of ways to offer some tangible concessions to the North other than to promise long-term self-interest. Unfortunately, long-term self-interest is not a sufficient incentive where the costs are seen by the North as short-term and real. Politicians in the North—like their counterparts in the South—are preoccupied with short-term problems and likely to resist concessions unless they are offered some short-term advantages. As the Commonwealth study has observed, "it is time to recognize that the Southern attempt to achieve its goals by frontal assault has become counterproductive in present circumstances; that its persistence results in negotiating strategies which hamper rather than facilitate progress; and that an approach which takes seriously both the claims of the South and the interests of the North should be adopted."[5]

Negotiators Need to Ensure Domestic Support

In general, North-South negotiations over the past decade have been divorced from domestic concerns. This phenomenon has had two important effects. The North has had trouble generating domestic political support when agreements needed ratifying. In spite of the fact that a great deal of time is spent in domestic negotiations to come up with negotiating positions, support for the results of negotiations is usually wanting. In the United States, where congressional approval is necessary, the problems are compounded. For instance, it is likely that the Law of the Sea agreement would have been in trouble in Congress even if the administration had decided to sign it. Similarly a more liberal U.S. position on the MFA was changed to a more restrictive provision in a direct trade for legislative support on an entirely unrelated issue of foreign aid.

The South has had the problem of the dichotomy between discussions taking place in formal North-South negotiations and those taking place in national capitals between representatives of functional bureaus from Northern and Southern governments. Frequently there are considerable differences between the way LDC negotiators in Geneva and New York approach the negotiations and the way officials in their home ministries look at them. While the negotiators push hard for concessions, officials in ministries usually have little knowledge of and little interest in the negotiations. Northern officials therefore often get the impression that the negotiations are not an issue in their bilateral relations. This lack of coordination between the representatives of the LDC governments at the negotiations and their counterparts back home not only has generated confusion but also tends to undermine the credibility of Southern negotiators in the eyes of their Northern counterparts. It is therefore important for the developing countries to develop a mechanism at the national level to coordinate their negotiating positions at the various forums.

International negotiation is only the interface between complex political systems. In their efforts to come together on an agreement, the negotiators should not leave their home teams behind, eventually to reject the negotiated results. American trade negotiators have estimated that two-thirds to four-fifths of their time is spent putting together their position in domestic negotiations before the rest of the time is expended in international negotiations; American arms negotiators estimated that 60 percent of their time was spent in domestic negotiations, 35 percent in negotiations with allies, and the rest in negotiation with the Soviets. Domestic negotiations are necessary to provide a coordinated, thought-out national position, and then more time is necessary to provide some flexibility and understanding of the adversary.

Problems often come down to administrative details that require more planning than effort to overcome. Ministers often launch the sessions with principled statements and then leave or else arrive only at the last minute to restore rigidity to a process that was gaining flexibility. Exchanges among contending parties at the appropriately high level are often absent and left to lower-level technicians and implementers. In the case of democratic politics, where negotiation is essentially ad referendum to the legislature, it may slow down the process to retain several legislators—even opposition legislators—as advisers to the negotiators, but that is probably preferable to a legislative disavowal at the end because of a lack of communications during the preparation of the agreement. American negotiators particularly may be able to negotiate a harder bargain by casting their legislators in a "tough cop–good cop" routine, but they can negotiate a better deal if they are able to convince the other parties that they can carry the home folks with them in support of their agreement.

The fact that many North-South negotiations have been marked by very mixed levels of representation has also been a source of problems. Partly because of the frequency of North-South negotiations, partly because of lack of resources, and partly because of the lack of decisive interest in all issues, the developing countries usually have been represented by relatively lower-level officials. Consequently the developed countries have tended to send delegates of comparable rank, thereby reducing the effectiveness of the negotiators. For instance, the United States started out at the first session of the COW represented at a high level but quickly moved back down when it was obvious that the LDCs were not sending delegates of similar rank. The question was not of protocol but of negotiating effectiveness. This phenomenon not only contributes to the slowness of the negotiations (because the negotiators lack the authority to make quick decisions) but also affects the quality of leadership, particularly on the part of the South.

Negotiations Need a Deadline

Unlike negotiations to end or prevent wars, economic negotiations usually do not have an inherent deadline. The most frequent tactic is to announce a deadline or cite the need to report to the coming UN session; neither is very effective. Pro forma deadlines can be cast aside with impunity since they do not contain the basic ingredient of a real deadline, an automatic application of sanctions. In this regard, internally imposed deadlines tend to be pro forma, whereas externally imposed deadlines have a greater chance of being real since the sanction—if it exists—cannot be removed by the parties to whom it applies. Unfortunately, the nature of economic problems makes sanctions a long-term rather than an immediate matter.

Examples of external deadlines in North-South negotiations are notably absent. Although much of the Law of the Sea Conference was a healthy exercise in learning, the negotiations suffered badly from the lack of a deadline; they could go on seemingly forever with impunity.

The COW, like the UNCLOS, passed deadlines provided by UN General Assembly sessions without a murmur. A further problem is that the procedural and substantive aspects of deadlines must jibe; if even an effective deadline is too early, parties will meet in only symbolic negotiations, without any effect on the substance of their conflict, or will start preparing negatively for it by shifting their behavior from a search for agreement to an attempt to pin the blame for breakdown on the other. Thus, the CIEC met its deadlines by a meaningless token agreement. Yet a deadline remains a crucial element in reaching an agreement. The very nature of negotiation is such that parties will continue to try to improve terms if they are under no constraint to wrap up an agreement.

There are three elements that can be put to greater use in building deadlines into North-South negotiations, each with its strengths and weaknesses. One is the unilateral deadline. Although the threat of one side to impose some sort of sanctions if agreement is not reached is a form of ultimatum, it is not as harmful to the negotiating atmosphere as ultimatums that aim at a specific (substantive) agreement. Nevertheless, the threatening party is in an awkward and thereby somewhat ineffective position: It must enforce its deadline impartially, but it must also (for other reasons) try to take advantage of it to make the best deal. Generally a threat to withdraw or a threat to go it alone is the preferred form of a unilateral deadline. Each must be credible, but the threatening party must also credibly commit itself to negotiate fairly if the procedural deadline is respected. The example of the United States at the Law of the Sea Conference is fascinating. The threat not to sign could have led to revised terms more closely to the liking of the United States. But a year elapsed before the United States put forth a new position, and by that time the other parties had agreed to push ahead without the United States.

The second element is the use of scheduled political change in a negotiating country as a deadline. In this case the deadline is externally or impartially imposed; it works directly on one party, but there needs to be an even greater awareness among other parties of its effects. Countries with regular democratic elections risk changes of government that could affect negotiations. The CIEC negotiations, for example, were adjourned in late 1976 to await the inauguration of the Carter administration. The results, however, were not any more favorable to the developing countries.

If a favorable government is in power, future elections serve above all as a deadline for the other parties who wish to get an agreement. In calculating the deadline, it is important to count the time required for ratification lest one administration's agreement be turned down by a new legislature. Although individual circumstances may vary, it is generally wrong to hope for better results after the election and more appropriate to aim for a conclusion of the agreement under the administration that entered into the negotiations.

Third, other North-South encounters can be used as deadlines and played against each other. This aspect has been somewhat of an ingredient in past encounters. North-South negotiations have often failed because (or at least at the same time as) parts of their agenda have been picked up by concurrent encounters and enacted. The result has been a patchwork of partial measures, but nevertheless there has been uneven progress to complement a more wholly negative record of the negotiations. The North-South negotiations then become a deadline even for other forums. The Lome II convention is a case in point. The Europeans saw their own self-interest in agreements with the ACP countries, but they also wanted to reduce pressure for more demands from the South at other forums.[6]

Refining the Process: The Virtues of Incrementalism

Thus far, one of the assumptions has been that a general agreement is necessary for success. This assumption needs examination. North-South negotiations are exercises in incremental change. They are not puzzle-solving applications of a permanent paradigm (even to those who want no basic change in the current economic order), nor can they be seismic alterations from one order to another (as much as that might be the wish of some who feel that the current order has already failed). The question then becomes how incrementalism is best negotiated.

The previous section dealt with lessons to be learned for North-South negotiations in the future from the experience of the past decade; this section suggests specific alternatives that could be chosen to advance North-South agreement. They stem from the belief that, at least in the next few years, there is no prospect for any grand "global compact" such as was envisioned by some observers of North-South relations in the 1970s. The NIEO is not going to be created in the near future; therefore, the North can stop worrying and the South can stop hoping for immediate results. But both sides need changes in existing international economic structures and policies for their own and everybody else's benefit. Those interested in achieving those benefits, therefore, need to be ingenious in seeking incremental steps that will lead to a more efficient and beneficial global economic order.

Functional Incrementalism

The first and current answer is that of functional incrementalism. Since global negotiations are too complex and of a magnitude too great to set up a new economic order, partial improvements and transitional tinkering are needed. Those who feel that costly repairs on the older order (as on an old car) are an expensive and nostalgic impediment to buying a new one reject functional incrementalism. Many examples—the Multifiber Agreement, the International Wheat Agreement, and the Lome Convention, from various points of view—give grist to their argument. Yet the futility of seeking grand global compacts is most evident in the area of commodities. Ten years' effort has been expended negotiating the IPC, with relatively few results. Both the North and the South might have gotten greater direct results through negotiating various expanded schemes of compensatory financing.

It is also worth remembering that there have been some incremental changes already in the system. This is particularly marked in the policies of the multilateral development banks and the International Monetary Fund. The establishment of new facilities and the enlargement of quotas at the IMF to meet the needs of the developing countries is a clear example. Progress has also been made in the Tokyo Round trade negotiations, where the industrialized countries agreed to cut tariffs and in the area of development assistance, particularly where special attention has been given to the least-developed countries. One example for future functional incrementalism would be full participation of the LDCs in the GATT, which could become their best defense against Northern protectionism. In general, a strong case can be made for progress in global negotiations by seeking agreement on those issues where common benefits and mutual trade-offs are possible, even if they do not immediately bring fundamental changes.

Participant Incrementalism

A different answer is that of participants' incrementalism. Instead of looking merely for agreement on those topics where it is possible, negotiators may also seek agreement among those parties among whom agreement is possible, leaving the rest outside. Obviously, not any number of parties will do; they must be large enough in number or important enough in economic weight to matter and to form a pole of attraction for those who remain outside. But if the purpose of the negotiations becomes an agreement among most instead of all the parties, tactics and implications change considerably. An example is the negotiations that led to the adoption of the Charter of Economic Rights and Duties of States in 1974. Originally the parties intended to reach agreement by consensus, but, when this proved difficult to attain, the Third World pressed for a vote in the UN General Assembly, which adopted the charter by a roll-call vote of 120 in favor, 6 opposed (including the United States), and 10 abstentions. Similarly, the countries that agree on the current Law of the Sea treaty have decided to go ahead without the United States (a decision that will decrease the bargaining power of the United States when it does decide to sign). The purpose of such negotiations becomes not only agreement among those who can agree but also isolation of the recalcitrants, to be brought in at a later date. Since recalcitrants no longer block agreement, the price they can extract for adhesion drops. At the same time, the agreement in operation may allay some of their fears and make their later accession easier.

In seeking such partial agreement, it is important to resist the temptation to turn the outcome against the recalcitrant or to use it to reinforce existing camps and divisions. This obvious temptation and difficulty would worsen rather than improve the chances of later change and broader agreement. To the contrary, the partial agreement should seek to build on cross-cutting cleavages, bringing in additional items and interest if necessary to break up broad existing coalitions. To be sure, such tactics will lead to struggles over marginal members between the signatory majority and the isolated recalcitrants, but North-South negotiations are already and naturally the scene of such struggles. Partial agreement should be not an initial goal of negotiations but one that can be adopted during their course when unanimity appears unlikely; in that event, it may serve as a threat position that can actually help the last chances of unanimity.

The distribution of positions on many North-South issues gives rise to further ramifications for negotiations once partial agreement becomes an acceptable goal. Preference distribution is frequently not bimodal, with two strong, equal, and opposing camps, just as it is usually not "normal," with a common peak and minority fringes. More commonly it is a skewed distribution with a strong peak and a tail, with many different states (not necessarily all Southern) belonging to the peak and lots of other differences of opinion tailing off, not all in total opposition to all aspects of the majority. Such a distribution provides the basis for a broad, if partial, agreement. What then are the implications for further negotiations between the agreeable peak and the recalcitrant tail?

The tail has a number of different strategies to chose within two general options: to accommodate or to bargain. The accommodation options include acceding and abiding. The recalcitrant can join the agreement at a later moment according to its original terms, or it can abide by it without formal accession, much as the United States abides by the Universal Declaration of Human Rights. In both cases the outsider joins the provisions of the negotiated settlement without change. The advantage of this procedure is that the terms of the agreement have been set by the majority, to which the minority accommodates later on. The bargaining options are more numerous. In bargaining a new relationship, the minority can try to buy in, buy out, or buy off the majority. In the buy-in strategy, it can seek to join the agreement while bargaining its accession against new concessions that preserve the nature of the agreement and giving the new members a special place in it. Buy in is what Britain did in joining the European Communities, at the price of some special provisions. In buy-out strategy, the minority can bargain with the majority by negotiating a new agreement between the two groups of parties, offering a new universal agreement if the majority will dissolve its own former agreement. Universality is bargained against changes in the nature of the agreement, an outcome sometimes possible only when both sides have crystallized their positions. Buying out was characteristic of the relations between the Casablanca and Brazzaville groups as they came together in the Addis Ababa Charter in 1963. The buy-off strategy is the most hostile type of relation, consisting of minority attempts to woo away some members of the majority from their agreement and into a counteragreement with the minority. Carried to an extreme, buying off could lead to two competing agreements and a disorderly economic arrangement. More likely, however, the competitive order would lead to new attempts to bargain a universal agreement from the newly elaborated positions of strength (buy off lending to buy out). Early relations between the EEC and the European Free Trade Area (EFTA) might stand as an example. Cases of the bargaining options are less frequent in North-South relations because of the current emphasis on universality. It may be, as this review of the options seeks to suggest, that partiality is a better road to universality. Partial agreements can provide stepping-stones to universal agreements by creating new negotiating conditions.

Within North-South negotiations, examples of these strategies occur more frequently as a means to full agreement than after partial agreement. Buying in was the Ratiner tactic at the last UNCLOS session. It failed for related reasons: lack of domestic support and lack of a perceived commitment to success. Buying off perpetuated the stalemate before the CIEC meeting. The strategies are also used in the reverse of the commonly held notions of majority and minority: In the Yaounde and Lome negotiations, in the International Wheat Agreement, and in the Multifiber Agreement, it was the North that established the terms and left the South with the option of accommodating or bargaining. Various strategies were picked within the two options. Further analysis is needed of the use and implications of these tactics within negotiating sessions before they are applied to negotiations to complete partial agreements.

Structural Incrementalism

The third way to use incrementalism is through gradually changing relationships. Structural incrementalism, in which evolving relations are brought about by steps reflecting incremental shifts in power, is often typical of political decolonization and has been analyzed in this connection. Such studies have brought out conclusions that could be taken to heart in North-South economic relations; for example, structural imbalance was the occasion for active but tacit (informal) bargaining, whereas structural balance with interlocking interests was the occasion for direct bargaining. In other words, in decolonization, the two sides negotiated informally from positions of inequality until they finally reached a power balance, then they held a formal session to negotiate the terms on which power would shift from one side to the other, and then they continued to negotiate informally within the new power relation.

Carried over to economic negotiations, this implies that a long program of preparation is needed before formal restructuring sessions can be envisaged—involving occasions, both governmental and private, to exchange views and understand each other's interests. Problem-solving exercises (study, not negotiation sessions) can be particularly useful in turning government delegations' attention from refuting each other's positions to joining in a common, diversified attack on a problem.

The one basic lesson of studies of structural incrementalism is that bargaining occurs after structural changes (changes in power relations) have taken place, and not as a means of making them take place. But negotiations need not aim at all or nothing or await the moment when a total reversal of roles is possible. Smaller changes can be ratified by negotiation, giving parties the opportunity to work together—including working for new changes—in the new relation. Since power is participation, structural changes merely concern the ability to take part in substantive decisions. Just as structural change need not be total, all parties cannot be expected to accede to full participation at once. New participants from the South—NICs, OPEC members, group interest representatives—can work for institutionalized roles at moments when their fortunes are most favorable. In contrast with political decolonization, the goal of economic negotiations is not power transfer but power sharing (broader participation). If this sounds like a Northern strategy of co-optation, it should also be remembered that refusing access offered to a few because others are excluded merely prolongs problems instead of moving them by steps toward a solution.

Parties

Mediators
Mediators could play an important role in North-South negotiations. When parties do not feel equally the imperative to negotiate, when power or aims are out of balance, or when trust is elusive, a mediator is especially useful. Mediators make communication possible when it breaks down, think up new formulas for agreement when the parties run out of ideas, can add side payments when it becomes otherwise hard to come up with a positive sum, become the vehicle of trust when the parties do not trust each other, and can provide some pressure to move the parties to agreement. In a large multilateral negotiation, it is difficult to find an appropriate external mediator, but international organizations can serve as an internal mediator. In that case some of its powers are limited. International organizations composed of state members—or even more so private organizations—have few resources for side payments and little other than moral leverage over states, but they can provide communication, formulas, and trust. The case of the

IPC negotiations is one example where the UNCTAD secretariat could have played the role of a mediator. It did not do so, however, because it was a party to the negotiations. It was identified with the proposal being negotiated and therefore had a great bureaucratic stake in seeing its realization.

There are two types of mediators: partial and impartial. Impartial mediators are hard to find, although in international economic negotiations the secretariats of international organizations are particularly well placed to play the role, and the need for technical information and expertise as the basis for trust indicates the direction in which to develop the role. Partial mediation is equally possible (contrary to common misperceptions) and may be easier to find in the North-South context, but the mediators have a special role. Partial mediators are expected to "deliver" the party to whom they are partial, as they bring together the two sides to make up an agreement. The role thus requires leverage as well as expertise. One of the great weaknesses of the South's position is that it could not deliver OPEC either at the CIEC or at the COW. When the North saw that OPEC would not use the oil weapon or would not bankroll commodity arrangements, the leverage of the developing countries was attenuated.

The EC Commission and the Commonwealth Secretariat are bodies that have worked as mediators; in the case of the COW, of UNCLOS, and of the International Wheat Agreement, mediators might have been able to salvage the negotiations. In the future more creative use could be made of mediators in a variety of North-South forums. The caveat, however, is that partial mediators need to be able to deliver their side.

Coalitions

The creation of coalitions based on mutual or common interests is probably crucial to any further progress on North-South negotiations, but the current bloc system militates against the forming of coalitions. The South sees its interests furthered by solidarity, but this very solidarity stymies compromise (which is the heart of any negotiation) and is further weakened when individual members make side deals or let the opposite party know that their position differs from that of the group. This leads back to the point that perhaps the most important single innovation needed in North-South relations is ways and means to develop coalitions between Northern and Southern countries on various specific issues without undermining the unity of the Third World.

The problems related to the diversity of issues and the range of interests of the developing countries are succinctly summarized in the Report by a Commonwealth Group of Experts:

> Its size and diversity have made the determination of priorities especially difficult for the Group of 77 and have led to agendas that are neither well focused nor adequately selective. They have also led to consultations which are complex and laborious. Those at UNCTAD are further complicated by the fact that (unlike in New York) the Group's three regional groups caucus separately to prepare their initial positions, whose reconciliation at Group level introduces its own inflexibilities. This system tends to introduce such delicate balance that failure to reach agreement on any one issue delays or even prevents consideration of others. Divergent national interests also encourage the tendency to maintain the bargaining at the broad level of principle and to prevent each regional group from moving at anything more than the pace of the slowest. The balance struck in establishing the Group's position is therefore inherently fragile and introduces a significant measure of rigidity into the negotiations. Reluctance to endanger internal compromises pre-empts effective bargaining and militates against optimal and creative solutions.[7]

Coalition formation is possible only when the monolithic sides break down into smaller groups, with the parties or small groups of parties free to seek out common or complementary interests in other camps. Common interests permit consensus; complementary interests allow trade-offs. To be sure, coalition building may lead to the creation of new sides, but it is more likely to yield a series of cross-cutting and interlocking ties and agreements that make a final outcome more likely and a final collapse more costly to already partially agreeing parties. Coalition building among interest groups was used with great success in the UNCLOS, to the point where observers have concluded that it was scarcely a typical North-South negotiation. The success of cross-cutting coalescing would be to reduce the confrontational elements of international economic bargaining.

Representation

This issue is closely related to that of coalition building. Although representation has proved a mixed blessing in past North-South negotiations, we think that it will be effective and efficient to form representative groups that can negotiate on behalf of the Group of 77. The benefits of negotiations by representative groups are obvious. In a world of 122 developing-country governments, small groups make discussion easier, coalitions with cross-country interests are simpler to form, and representational bargaining is less time-consuming and less costly.

Depending on the issue to be negotiated, representative countries can be selected from among the various subgroups within the G-77: oil-importing countries, OPEC, newly industrialized nations, least developed countries, or from different regions such as Asia, sub-Saharan Africa, the Middle East, Latin America, or the Caribbean. Similar representational formulas for the North also can be designed.

However, in past North-South negotiations the idea of representation has proved more efficacious in theory than in practice. Both the CIEC and the North-South summit at Cancun were representational discussions, but there were considerable tensions and problems, particularly in the South but also in the North in choosing the representative countries. Tensions between representatives and their constituencies during negotiations have been high. Often there has been a constant need to refer back to the constituencies for clarification on negotiating positions, which meant that Southern negotiators had to carry out two sets of negotiations at the same time. Only the Law of the Sea negotiations involved some representational activities that proved crucial in overcoming serious obstacles.

For representative negotiations to be successful, certain conditions have to be fulfilled. First, the representatives should have sufficient expertise and knowledge about the issues under negotiations. Such negotiators can be innovative and flexible. They will not also spend time in acquainting themselves with the issues and in asking for clarifications from their constituencies. Second, the negotiators have to be high-level officials if they are to be taken seriously. They should have the respect of their peers and the necessary political clout. Finally, it is important that the representatives come from countries most centrally involved in the issues being negotiated. If they come from these countries, they are likely to speak with more authority and to have experience in negotiating the issue at hand. One reason for the lack of success in the debt negotiations, for example, was the fact that the Southern negotiators came not from the major debtors but from the poorer developing countries.

Representation assumes fixed interest groups, to the point where enough trust and commonality is developed for one member to be able to act as the spokesman for the group. In some circumstances representation can go hand in hand with coalition building, since representatives can talk with each other to build interlocking ties. To the extent that the represented groups are large and inflexible, however, representation is an alternative to coalition, since the chances for formation of new groups and interrelations and of belonging to several interest groups are reduced.

Timing

The discussion thus far has borne for the most part on conditions in the North-South negotiation process that can be changed to make that process more productive. There is another category of variables that cannot be changed but nevertheless have a powerful impact on chances of success.

The Ripe Moment

Foremost among these are conjunctural elements. It is possible that the ripe moment in economic bargaining cannot be identified in the same terms as in political conflict resolution, since the political characteristics of a ripe moment (such as deadlock and deadline, alternative tracks, and power relations) are more gradual, long-term phenomena.[8] The ripe moment needs to be understood in other ways; indeed more conceptualization needs to be developed for a more thorough and detailed presentation. Furthermore, the lessons of this type of inquiry are often unwelcome, since statesmen in a term of office do not want to hear that now is not the moment to tackle a problem that may eventually put them out of office. However, identification of conjunctural elements can be used to highlight characteristics that make some tactics more appropriate than others or at least raise awareness of difficulties and lower expectations of success.

Timing has clearly been important in North-South negotiations and has facilitated or hindered agreements. The years 1973 through 1975, for example, were a ripe moment for North-South negotiations, because of the emergence of OPEC as an economic power and the fear in the North that other primary commodity producers might also create cartels. A few years later, however, the willingness of the North to negotiate dissipated when OPEC failed to exercise enough leverage and when commodity power was seen to be a chimera. On the other hand, it is ironic that debt negotiations ended in stalemate just before the question of Third World debt was to become a major issue. Debt was not seen as a problem in 1977 and in 1978, but in 1982 it was seen as a major crisis. Similarly, the COW negotiations were helped by the failure of

CIEC because neither side wanted a vacuum. And in commodity negotiations timing is very crucial. The problem is that producers want agreements when prices are dropping and customers want them when they are rising. One of the reasons for the failure of the wheat negotiations was that none of the parties found the time propitious in 1976 for an accord.

The Solidarity Function

Parties often need an initial period of consciousness raising and solidarity making before they can turn to problem solving. Aspects such as identity, awareness of interests, and ability to speak with confidence are all effects of the solidarity-making phase of activity and are best built through confrontation. What is not clear is whether such confrontation can be successful in creating these effects if it is kept only on the symbolic level, or whether separate development and self-reliance must be pursued for a founded sense of equality to occur. In any case, such identity building is a compensatory function, necessary to the South and not to the North, and is an important precondition for subsequent coalition formation. If coalitions form before solidarity is established they are treasonous to the common cause, whereas if solidarity is established beyond question members can build cross-cutting ties without undercutting their own new independence and Southern identity. With the absence of perspective that comes from being in the midst of history, it appears that the confrontational phase of the mid-1970s is passing and that conditions are more propitious for problem solving; some countries such as Algeria have moderated, and group membership (as within the G-77) is an established fact. On the other hand, the temporary collapse of a number of Third World forums (NAM, OAU, LAS) and the rise of Third World disputes may mean that symbolic solidarity becomes paramount because real solidarity is so thin.

The Crisis Function

Another conjunctural element is the crisis function. The downturn of economic conditions that began in late 1979 brought home to all countries the need to take serious measures and makes less tenable the argument that all is well with the old order. Since the basic calculation in any negotiation concerns the viability of the present course as a baseline comparison for any negotiating alternative, the fact that things are getting bad is all to the good. Crisis at least means that new answers must be sought. It does not decide between deep reform and palliatives, but it at least makes that debate necessary. It is now less likely that crisis will permit a purely defensive reaction, since the interdependence of the world economy and its political ramifications make continued recalcitrance by the North not even a palliative.

One fundamental question in the analysis of negotiations is whether parties make greater concessions when they are weak and therefore vulnerable, whether they make greater concessions when they are strong and therefore have a cushion, or whether both effects obtain under the differentiating impact of some yet-unknown intervening variable. Politically the effect seems to be the third; beleaguered parties do not concede if the implications are immediately costly, if the concession is touted as a defeat, if zero-sum perceptions are high. But beleaguered parties do concede if concession raises the siege, if concession can be recast as victory, if positive-sum perceptions can be made dominant. Obviously, much depends on the way the argument is presented. This reinforces the notion of negotiation as persuasion, which seems to have eluded many Northern and Southern negotiators.

Now the key question is whether the perceived global economic crisis makes this a "good" time for serious North-South negotiations. Is the crisis deep enough? Or is the crisis too deep and are the constraints to action too great?

Conclusions

What does this analysis imply for global negotiations? The answer to this question has to begin with a recapitulation of the points made at the beginning of the chapter.

First, North-South negotiations in a generic sense are likely to be as much a feature of the decade ahead as of the decade past. Second, they do not have to be a zero-sum game. Indeed, the benefits to both the North and the South of changes in the existing international economic order are likely to be considerable. If both those points are true, improving the process of negotiating between developed and developing countries will be a critical element in addressing urgent global problems. It is, of course, not true that improving the negotiating process alone will bring about agreement between North and South. Differences of viewpoints are still too deep and fundamental to be resolved simply by changing the process. Nevertheless, it is probably equally true that the very process of negotiations, as it has been manifested in the past decade, is likely to prove a barrier to serious address of these global problems.

However, an analytical examination of the last decade's negotiations and their meager results leads one to be cautious about the prospects for future negotiations in the absence of serious address of the negotiating process itself. Our discussion here suggests some of the issues that need to be addressed if any real agreement between North and South is to be achieved in the future.

Perhaps the paramount need is to break down the division of the parties into "North" and "South." Differentiation within both North and South is increasing, and interests are diversifying, forcing either group to assume a common position. It is almost a prerequisite to stalemate. Until the North-South divide can be bridged so that countries can form coalitions and associations of only alliances of their real interests, progress in North-South negotiations is not likely to be great.

There is a need to transcend or perhaps isolate those who do not want to reach any agreement. It now seems that partiality is a better (and in any event the only) road to universality. There is no other plausible alternative. The challenge is to pick countries that for one reason or another can reach agreement. It is necessary to assemble groups of countries that the Commonwealth report calls "like-minded" to develop cross-cutting links. Unfortunately the process now tends to be driven by the lowest common denominator; the most recalcitrant countries (the United States for the North and the radicals for the South) tend to set the agenda.

Second, the North must take North-South negotiations more seriously and participate in them more actively. As much as the South's rhetoric and confrontationist stance have contributed to the lack of progress in the negotiations, the North's rejectionist strategy and indifference have also led to deadlock. If North-South negotiations are to move beyond stalemate, therefore, the North, instead of being defensive, has to take an active part in the negotiations. It has to accept that North-South negotiations are an effective part of the management of the evolving international economic system. Negotiations have to be seen as an alternative to chaos and confrontation. What is more, instead of dismissing Southern proposals as rhetorical and impractical, it has to come up with counterproposals that will take some of the grievances of the South into consideration and will attract the developing countries that are interested in reaching agreement. Without a strong commitment by the North to continue the dialogue and negotiations, and without the North's active participation, North-South negotiations are likely to remain adversarial, tense, stalemated, and unproductive.

The third urgent need is a reformulation of North-South issues in order to ensure that concrete benefits will accrue to both sides. No agreements or bargains will be reached when the concessions and costs will largely have to be borne by one set of parties and the benefits (real or potential) accrued by the other. North-South issues in the past decade, unfortunately, have been posed in precisely this manner (with a large dollop of guilt thrown in). Yet a growing number of analyses demonstrate quite clearly that there are a variety of mutual gains to be received by both North and South from restructuring the international economic system established after World War II.

Fourth, there must be some agreement on forms of representation in the negotiating process. It is impossible to conduct any serious negotiations in universal forums where over a 150 governments are represented to one degree or another. There needs, however, to be active exploration of different modes of representation. Various formulas suggest themselves, but the common element should be that the states with the most interests in negotiations should be the prime representatives. Here again a division between North and South needs to be transcended. There may be more commonality between commodity producers in both North and South and commodity consumers than between North and South. Similar examples were discussed earlier in the field of trade.

Fifth, there needs to be agreement on ways of negotiating in functional forums while maintaining some sort of overview of the process. Insisting on negotiating monetary or trade affairs in the General Assembly of the United Nations is a guarantee of continuing stalemate. It would be much preferable for the developing countries to participate to a much greater degree in the discussions of the GATT or to search for ways of linking the functions of GATT and UNCTAD. Similarly, the developing countries need to coordinate their activities in the deliberations of the World Bank and the International Monetary Fund on monetary and financial issues.

Negotiations in functional forums are likely to be successful if the structure of representation is modified to ensure effective South participation. In monetary and financial negotiations, for instance, it would be helpful if the Development Committee and the Interim Committee of the World Bank and the International Monetary Fund were modified by accommodating more equitable South representation (perhaps by including the Group of Twenty-four as a whole) rather than limiting the South to quota structure in the Bank and the IMF. Decisions in such forums could be reached on the basis of consensus. There will, however, also be a need for some mechanism where results can be judged and new bargains across issues broached. In this regard, serious consideration should be given to periodic North-South summits, following on the meeting at Cancun, Mexico, in 1981. Such summits are not a panacea, but they do give world leaders a chance to exchange views and (with good management) a chance to break deadlocked negotiations and to arrive at bargains across different forums. Those who feel that North-South summits are counterproductive should be challenged to provide some alternative to fulfill the same function.

Finally, there clearly needs to be much more analysis of North-South issues available to governments, both in the North and in the South. There is a considerable need for some sort of Third World secretariat available to negotiators from the developing countries. However, the North too has neglected analysis of North-South issues and particularly the creative exploration of solutions that, while not yet politically viable, will inform the discussions of the future.

In this regard, too, the need for unofficial forums where representatives of developed and developing countries can discuss common positions and better understand those of the other party is important. They can be organized on a global level (such as the North-South Roundtable) or on regional levels (such as the continuing discussions among North American and Latin American leaders that have taken place under various auspices over the last ten years). No matter what the formula, the need is the same: Policymakers from both North and South need to have opportunities to better understand each other's position in order to arrive at creative compromise and bargains.

Implementing these suggestions will change the fundamental nature of the process, at least as it currently is described, but the economic and political stakes for both rich and poor countries leave no choice. If these issues can be addressed, global negotiations may well be the path to the future. If not, they are likely to be a dead-end street.

Acknowledgments

This chapter is based on and draws from a project of the Overseas Development Council. It included seven case studies of specific North-South negotiations conducted during the last decade. The project, directed by Zartman, was generously supported by the Rockefeller Foundation. A book containing the case studies will be published in 1984. Amha Selassie of the Overseas Development Council made a major contribution to the drafting of this chapter.

Notes

1. The major exception is *The North-South Dialogue: Making it Work*, Report by a Commonwealth Group of Experts, Commonwealth Secretariat (London, 1982). The study reviews the negotiating process between North and South, examines the principal obstacles in the negotiations, and suggests improvement to overcome or reduce the obstacles.

2. See John W. Sewell, "Can the North Prosper without Growth and Progress in the South?" in *The United States and World Development: Agenda 1979* (Washington, D.C.: Overseas Development Council, 1979), pp. 45–76. John P. Lewis, "Can We Escape the Path of Mutual Injury?" in *U.S. Foreign Policy and the Third World: Agenda 1983* (Washington, D.C.: Overseas Development Council, 1983), pp. 7–48.

3. *North-South Dialogue*, p. 74.

4. See Mahbub ul Haq, *The Poverty Curtain: Choices for the Third World* (New York: Columbia University Press, 1976), pp. 182–183. Shridath S. Ramphal, "Not by Unity Alone: The Case for Third World Organization," *Third World Quarterly* 1 (July 1979): 43–52; *North-South Dialogue*, p. 17.

5. *North-South Dialogue*, p. 11.

6. The effect needs further investigation to see whether it can be used in reverse; since deadline is essentially a juxtaposition of alternative courses and their consequences, the possibility of scheduling competitive alternatives to be examined.

7. *North-South Dialogue*, p. 72.

8. See I. William Zartman, *Ripe for Resolution: Conflict and Intervention in Africa* (New Haven: Yale University Press, 1984).

Strengthening the Framework of the Global Economic Organizations

Catherine Gwin

This chapter is about one of the main issues in the North-South "dialogue": the South's demand for a greater voice in the management of international economic relations. Since the mid-1970s, when this demand was made a part of the call for establishment of a New International Economic Order, the South has sought to win acceptance for three kinds of reforms: a redistribution of votes in those international economic institutions that operate under a system of weighted voting, the establishment of new institutions based on a different structure of voting (specifically, institutions that would give developing countries as a bloc an equal share of decision-making power) and a shift in the focus of economic negotiations and broad international economic policy making into the central United Nations organization, which operates on the principle of one vote per nation and in which developing countries make up the majority.

In all, the aim of the developing countries has been to gain a more equal share of control in the collective management of the international economic system—control, that is, over the definition of norms, the setting of rules, and the operation of procedures that states agree to in order to regulate areas of economic interaction.

Third World spokesmen have often been asked by First Worlders why they care more about form than substance, more about decision-making than decisions. For example, a common criticism in the United States of the Brandt Commission's report was that its recommendations put too much emphasis on the need for new institutions with new decision-making structures at the expense of focusing attention on how to strengthen existing institutions in ways that would be mutually acceptable to North and South. Similarly, observers in the North have questioned the wisdom of the South's position on "Global Negotiations"—a position that holds that satisfaction on the procedural issues of where negotiations occur and how decisions are reached are as important as the beginning of substantive talks on major issues. In reply, Third World spokesmen have explained that they are concerned about substance and that this is why they care about the forum.

The emphasis on decision making reflects, in other words, a deep dissatisfaction with existing norms, policies, and practices which, in the view of Third World countries, were designed by and for the First World and will not be significantly changed unless the Third World gains greater decision-making power. One can go farther and say that the emphasis that has come to be placed on the issue of who exercises control is a reflection of a wide divergence of views between developed and developing countries about the principles that ought to underlie the rules of the game in international economic relations and about the reconcilability of interests.[1] While the South argues for restructuring of institutions to provide for greater "equity," the North stresses achievement of greater "efficiency" through the reinforcement of existing institutions. Although the two goals can be mutually reinforcing, neither side in the North-South dialogue has advanced a program of reform that seeks to make them so. This divergence of substantive views makes it difficult to address the issue of control separately from the broader issue of institutional reform.

Concern with substance is, however, but one reason why the Third World has pressed the issue of control. Another reason is the Third World's strategy of "solidarity." As various analysts have observed, the desire to strengthen their joint negotiating capacity was the reason for the LDCs' establishment of the Group of 77 in 1964 and for their continued emphasis on a group approach to international economic negotiations through the 1970s. Sauvant writes:

At UNCTAD I, the first major North-South conference on development questions, the divergence of the economic interests of the developing from those of the developed countries emerged sharply and crystalized along geopolitical-group lines. The Joint Declaration of the Seventy-Seven, adopted on 15 June 1964 at the end of UNCTAD I, was the result. In it, the developing countries justly celebrated their own unity . . . as the outstanding feature of this conference and they expressed their strong conviction that there is a vital need to maintain, and further strengthen, this unity in the years ahead. Since then, the Group of 77—which, by December 1981, counted 125 members—has become the Third World's principal organ for the articulation and aggregation of its collective economic interest and its representation in the negotiations with the developed countries within the United Nations system. Thus, the Group has represented the Third World in all major international economic events since 1964: the UNCTAD Sessions, the

UNIDO General Conferences, the special sessions of the United Nations General Assembly on Development, the Paris Conference on International Economic Cooperation, and the discussions in the IMF and the World Bank.[2]

Analysis of the dynamic of this group strategy has indicated that "what usually emerges from the deliberations of the Group of 77 (after prior caucuses among its various sub-groups) is an exceedingly complex package proposal, "with the operating principle of the group strategy being "equal benefit for all the participating Third World countries in each package of cooperation."[3] This has led to the developing countries' insistence on a comprehensive or "integrated" approach to economic negotiations, and it has reinforced their preference for wide-ranging negotiations under the aegis of the General Assembly—a forum in which they have the controlling votes—instead of negotiations within the functionally specialized agencies that would offer LDCs little opportunity for linking and making trade-offs among issues.

The importance that this dynamic of Third World solidarity has had for the issue of the appropriate negotiating forum is clearly evident in the sequence of events that run from the Paris Conference on International Economic Cooperation (CIEC) through the debate on the launching of a round of Global Negotiations.

The CIEC, a meeting of 27 country representatives (19 from developing countries and 8 from developed countries), was convened in 1975 after the United States indicated its willingness at the Seventh Special Session of the United Nations to turn away from confrontation. First proposed by the president of France as a context in which to discuss energy matters among a representative group of oil-exporting, industrial, and oil-importing developing countries, the CIEC ranged over a full array of North-South issues for some 18 months. It concluded "undecisively" in June 1977, marking the end of the first and only effort of a representative group of countries to negotiate across a broad range of issues. In explaining the reasons for the failure of the CIEC, one observer has noted that there was a lack of political will on the part of the North and a lack of political realism on the part of the South.[4] Also, there was evidence of "constant tension" between the Group of 77 and the Group of 19 developing countries that "represented" the G-77 at the CIEC, owing to the concern of most G-77 members that the G-19, which heavily overrepresented the "upper-tier" developing countries (and included seven OPEC states), would not appropriately represent the interests of the larger group.[5] After the

CIEC, therefore, a core principle of the G-77 was that the system of universal participation should be the framework within which North-South negotiations would take place. This principle, which grew out of the perceived failure of the CIEC, led first to the G-77's demand for the establishment within the UN of the Committee of the Whole (COW) and then, when the COW also failed to provide the LDCs with the momentum on North-South issues that they sought, led to the call for a round of Global Negotiations that would be under the aegis of the UN General Assembly and would, like the COW, involve the direct participation of all member countries of the United Nations.

It hardly needs to be said that this series of North-South negotiations (or attempted negotiations) has brought little improvement in the collective management of contemporary international economic problems. Two recent reports by prominent independent groups of both "Northerners" and "Southerners"—one a Commonwealth Experts Group, the other the Brandt Commission—have emphasized that the negotiating process, as well as the issues under discussion, has become a serious obstacle to international economic cooperation and that in this regard too rigid a reliance on group negotiating methods has proved particularly detrimental. As the Commonwealth Report observes,

The time available for effective negotiations between groups is often shortened by the laborious and time-consuming task of reconciling internal differences in order to establish group positions. This applies particularly to the functioning of the Group of 77. . . . Its size and diversity have made the determination of priorities especially difficult for the Group of 77 and have led to agendas that are neither well focussed nor adequately selective. . . . Divergent national interests also encourage the tendency to maintain the bargaining at the broad level of principle and to prevent each regional group [within the G-77] from moving at anything more than the pace of the slowest. The balance struck in establishing the Group's position is therefore inherently fragile and introduces a significant measure of rigidity into the negotiations. Reluctance to endanger internal compromises pre-empts effective bargaining and militates against optimal and creative solutions.[6]

While the South has made clear its sense of grievance against the existing system, neither North nor South has, separately or together, advanced ideas for change that would produce a better balanced, widely acceptable system more responsive to diverse needs and changing conditions. In the belief that such proposals are needed now more than ever, this chapter will argue the following points.

The developing countries have been right to press for reform of the international economic institutions. There has been much change in the international system since the central international economic institutions were established at the end of World War II. As a result, there is a need for more international economic cooperation at the global level than exists today and a need to revise various norms, rules, and procedures currently governing economic relations among states. Developing countries, even more than developed countries, stand to gain from such a development, for a strengthening of global institutions is essential to providing smaller and weaker states a legitimate voice in the management of international economic relations. However, a continued proliferation of new institutions—which in recent years has resulted more from a lack of basic consensus on institutional reform than from a broadly shared conception of a more appropriate institutional framework—does not seem the right response. Rather, there is need now to agree on certain principles of collective management and to revise, streamline, and strengthen the central framework of global economic organizations accordingly.

Developing countries have also been right to call attention to a wide range of aid, trade, money, investment, commodity, and other issues, and they have been right to emphasize the need to look at the whole array of international economic institutions. As Miriam Camps has written, "one of the keys to agreement on reform is to focus on the overall picture and be concerned with balance in the system as a whole." But, as Camps goes on to argue, this does not mean that "all pieces on the board must be moved if one piece is to be moved."[7] Nor does this mean that the best way to deal with the interconnectedness of issues and interests is by means of universal participation in continual omnibus negotiations whose most successful outcomes tend to be agreements at the lowest common denominator satisfactory to no one. Instead there needs to be a strengthening of key functional organizations along lines that will achieve a balance of interests in the system as a whole, particularly regarding the structure of rights, obligations, and responsibilities in the institutional arrangements for trade, money, and resource transfers, and there needs to be better coordination among those functional agencies.

Developing countries have been right to insist that there be more participation in the making of rules and the carrying out of procedures by all countries with interests at stake in the management of the system. As a general proposition, dependence on the system as well as ability to affect the system ought to be reflected in the distribution of decision-making power in global organizations. However, if governments are going to agree to more global-level collective management, there must also be acceptance of the fact that in any organization that is more than a forum for airing views the one-nation, one-vote rule is inadequate. Some form of participation that matches "voice" with needs, responsibility, and weight is inescapable if the purposes that the key institutions are designed to serve are to be met.

Finally, developing countries have been right to argue that failure to reach agreement on reforms has often been due to a lack of political will or what might better be termed unenlightened self-interest. Despite growing recognition of the fact of increased interdependence, there continues to be a propensity, on the part of governments and citizens alike, to cling to unrealistic notions of national autonomy and thus to assume that purely national actions can ensure reasonable economic conditions. Yet the very reforms that are most needed stem from the facts that no country can singlehandedly deal effectively with the kinds of shocks that have occurred in recent times and that national actions (especially those of the most powerful states) need increasingly to be taken with the interests of others in mind. The realities of interdependence do not mean, however, that one group of countries can issue a set of demands to which other countries should be expected to accede. Better management of economic relations will result only from the realization of the potential for shared or mutual gains. That realization is not likely to arise out of the agenda of international secretariats that see themselves as the brain trust for one group of countries or another, or from negotiations among national representatives that become isolated from policy makers in their national capitals. Instead, reform of the international economic order requires the buildup of mechanisms of structured collaboration that involve in a continuous way those in capitals with national policy-making responsibility, as well as the further strengthening of the staffs of the key global organizations.

Stated briefly, the thesis of this chapter is, in other words, that an adequate response to the LDCs' legitimate demand for greater voice requires more effective collective management of a broad range of international economic issues, that better collective management requires a reformed and strengthened framework of institutions at the global level, and that a strengthening of the key institutions—to make them more acceptable, more responsive, and more efficient—requires fuller agreement than now exists on appropriate forms of "representational diplomacy." This argument differs significantly from earlier calls for world order through the establishment of supranational organizations to which nation-states were expected to cede considerable authority. It also differs from proposals that would further the trend toward indiscriminate universalism and those that would settle for incremental tinkering. In developing this argument, I will discuss the need for institutional reform (including reform of decision-making structures), offer an approach to and some specific ideas for reforming the key global economic organizations, and suggest ways of giving LDCs greater voice in these organizations that would be consistent with a general strengthening of the global economic framework.

The Need for Institutional Reform

It is no coincidence that LDCs' demands for institutional reform have intensified over a period in which major changes have also occurred in the structure of the world economy. Both the political demands and the shifts in patterns of production and trade reflect real changes in the distribution of economic power, which in turn have created new problems as well as new opportunities for the management of international economic relations. In addition, after some 30 years of dynamic multilateral institution building, governments today are faced with an unwieldy array of organizations and agencies whose operations are increasingly overlapping but inadequately coordinated. These three developments—proliferation of multilateral organizations, shifts in the structure of the world economy, and demands for greater equity—make it necessary to give serious consideration to reform not only of economic policies but also of economic institutions. Only if all three of these developments are considered together will it be possible to devise appropriate reforms. Unfortunately, too many recent proposals have chosen to pay attention to only one or another of these trends. This is as true of some of the NIEO demands for new institutions based on equal voting rights among all states or blocs of states as it is of some Northern proposals for bolstering existing specialized agencies without revising their patterns of governance.

The growth of the international institutional framework since the end of World War II has been the result of at least three factors. First, there has been recognition on a worldwide basis of new tasks that require new efforts at international collaboration. Broad recognition of development as an international problem and an international responsibility has quite clearly given rise to the greatest amount of new institution building, but other issues, such as the peaceful uses of atomic energy, environmental control, and international monetary and financial affairs, have spawned important institutions. Second, in the development field in particular, there was a time when it was believed that more spigots would mean more aid, and therefore functionally specific agencies (such as the United Nations Fund for Population Assistance), regionally specified agencies (such as the Caribbean Development Bank), and member-specific agencies (such as the OPEC Special Fund) sprang up in considerable number. Third, it is also the case that the proliferation of institutions, particularly in the development field, has sometimes reflected a lack of consensus on policies and priorities (e.g., not all aid donors are participants in the UNFPA) and has recently been motivated primarily by the demand for new power-sharing arrangements (as in the case of the International Fund for Agricultural Development).

At different times in this period of postwar institution building, and for different reasons, both developed and developing countries have alternately argued for more centralization or more decentralization. The situation has given rise over the years to various official and nonofficial restructuring reports and recommendations. A principal problem with most of these efforts is their failure to find an acceptable accommodation between the Northern governments' concerns about efficiency and the South's demands for a "fair" distribution of decision-making control.

What eludes the reform and restructuring debates is any consensus on the patterns and principles that ought to guide a much-needed streamlining as well as strengthening of the multilateral institutional framework. In recent debates on institutional reform, developing countries have sought to give greater operational responsibility to such bodies as ECOSOC and UNCTAD and decision-making authority to the General Assembly (particularly in the form of the Committee of the Whole), or to create new operational agencies with decision rules that in the past have been applied only to non-task-oriented bodies. Neither of these approaches will lead to a more effective system, nor will needed institutional reform result if complacent Northern governments continue to argue that existing institutions are working well and that all that is needed is minor, incremental change. Instead, major reforms are needed that will lead to greater efficiency as well as greater equity. The reforms need to rest on a clearer distinction than is now frequently made between organizations that should have operational or executive functions and those that should not, and the decision-making structures of each of those kinds of organizations should reflect that difference. Specifically, the central UN organization, whose deliberative bodies correctly operate on the basis of the one-nation, one-vote majority rule, should not be given new operational responsibility. Rather, the major weight of needed global economic management ought to be borne by a reformed and strengthened set of functional organizations in which there is a correspondence between voting strength and economic power (i.e., ability to affect the system), responsibility, and interest.

A viable process of institutional reform also needs to be based on a recognition of the world as it is and is becoming, not the world as any one country or group of countries might wish it were. This means that no country—strong and rich or weak and poor—can ignore the policy implications of increased international economic interdependence except at a cost (which may or may not be politically acceptable) of slower technological development and, over the long run, slower economic growth. On the positive side, changes in the structure of the world economy have meant expansion of world trade, development of international capital markets, and an enormous increase in financial flows worldwide, as well as growth and diversification of many developing countries' economies. On the negative side, benefits have not been shared equally among or within nations, and there is a heightened sense of vulnerability, exacerbated in today's environment of worldwide recession. Yet despite the complexities of increased interdependence there continues to be reluctance among publics and policy makers to recognize the limits of national autonomy and the need for all countries to accept the obligations as well as the rights that come with more collaborative action. There also continues to be a strong belief, at least within some of the major economies of the world, that free markets, or what have come to be known as free markets, provide a kind of automatic regulator for the economic system that relieves governments of the need to make their policies compatible with the policies of others. Thus, despite the clear evidence of the inability of the "free markets" to absorb the shocks that have occurred in the past decade, few steps have been taken at the international level to smooth the functionings of international markets (e.g., for capital or for commodities). As Roger Hansen, among others, has repeatedly argued, the situation calls for a "new statecraft" to cope with changing relationships.[8] In whatever field of activity one looks at—trade, money, finance—one sees that, as a result of shifts in economic power and increased economic interconnectedness, there is not only a need to revise old rules and procedures but also a growing need for more and better cooperation among governments in the management of economic interactions and for more of that collaboration to occur at the global level.

This does not mean, however, that international economic institutions should be viewed as vehicles for restructuring the world economic order. Such organizations are "reflections of the economic order determined by—not determining—economic realities," and "any international economic organization that does not reflect actual economic forces, in its operations as well as its decision-making processes, has little promise as an active, effective agency.[9]

The United States, which dominated the world economic scene at the start of the postwar period, is no longer in quite so commanding an economic position today as during the 1950s and 1960s. It still remains undeniably the leading actor in the world economy, but it cannot dictate rules of the game or control by universal actions most economic outcomes. How the United States manages its economy has a major bearing on conditions in the world economy; for example, economic revitalization in the United States today is a necessary condition for a healthier world economy. But increasingly the United States cannot successfully manage its domestic economy except by acting in collaboration with others, it cannot achieve its national economic goals independent of conditions prevailing in the world economy, and it cannot, acting alone, ensure desirable conditions. Nor can any other country or small group of countries play the role once played by imperial Britain or imperial America. The diffusion of economic and political power makes it impossible any longer for a single country to combine and coordinate the functions that shape the world economic order and makes necessary a closer collaboration among states if there is to be adequate provision of international liquidity and management of exchange rates, maintenance of rules governing trade in goods and services, movement of capital, technology, and labor, the transfer of resources to speed economic growth and alleviate poverty, or other processes essential to the functioning of a dynamic world economy.

For some purposes, such as the management of exchange rates, only a small number of countries may need to cooperate closely and agree to regulate their actions in common. Willingness by other countries to view this collaboration as legitimate must be matched, however, by acceptance by those in the "inner group" of the obligations that their weight carries to supply certain kinds of public goods to the system as a whole. Accordingly, "their policies must be designed not simply with their own national needs in mind but should be informed as well by systemic concerns," and "there must exist an effective set of institutions in which the interests of other affected countries are fully represented and fully taken into account."[10]

There will always be need, moreover, to find ways of accommodating the interests of groups of countries that choose to cooperate closely together (through regional integration schemes or other arrangements) with norms, rules, and procedures agreed to at the global level. And for some activities over some continuing period of time, "North" and "South" will remain politically relevant groupings of states. However, in thinking about the principles that should guide global economic institutional reforms, it will be increasingly important to think in terms of a continuum of states and to recognize that on different issues both the interests of states and their abilities to affect the system will vary enormously. Accordingly, it would seem to make greatest sense for countries to play a greater or lesser role in particular institutional arrangements depending on their importance to the issue in question and its importance to them. This does not mean that small or weak countries cannot or should not be given a larger voice in the key economic institutions—they should, as part of an effort to make the operations of those institutions both more responsive and also more acceptable. This will require some redistribution of weighted votes in the Bretton Woods institutions. However, the structure of voting should not be all that receives attention. Of perhaps even greater real importance would be a change in the staffing patterns of the international organizations and developments in consultative mechanisms within the framework of the organizations involving, on a regular basis, officials from member countries' capitals.

Clearly, not all international problems are global problems that need to be dealt with at the global level. Indeed, some of the most impressive examples of interstate cooperation may occur in the coming years below the global level; for example, there may well be increased cooperation among states bordering the Mediterranean to control pollution or greater cooperation among Amazonal states to solve water-management problems. Certain regional or subregional groupings may decide that there are increased benefits to be gained from closer economic or security cooperation. And in some areas of activity there may be groups of countries that, because of political or cultural affinities or because of similar levels of economic development, may choose to cooperate more closely. But none of these subglobal arrangements will eliminate the need for institutional reform at the global level. It is the increased interconnectedness of the prospects for achieving societal goals that is the principal reason for the need for more and better global-level collective management. In addition, as conditions in all parts of the world become known (or knowable) in all other parts of the world, there is a kind of indivisible humanitarian imperative that demands cooperative action on behalf of the world's truly needy.

Revamping the Institutional Framework

Despite the fact that the North-South dialogue is, at its core, a debate about reform of international economic institutional arrangements, surprisingly few attempts have been made to map out the essential changes that would be required to provide for a more efficient, more responsive, and more acceptable institutional framework. Various proposals have been put forward that call for some new institution or another, but until recently few proposals have tried to look at the system as a whole and to give a sense of what a new, more balanced array of institutions might look like. Moreover, both North and South have expressed considerable ambivalence about the kinds of institutional changes they would like to see.

Although the developing countries have sought in recent years to strengthen the UN's role in international economic negotiations, policy making, and policy implementation, they have neither devoted the kind of high-level participation to UN economic sessions that successful negotiations would require nor shown a willingness to grasp the nettle of UN institutional reform, which is much needed if the central organization is going to function effectively. While attacking the World Bank and IMF in formal declarations, they argue strongly in substantive debates for increasing the resources and expanding the mandates of these key specialized agencies. Moreover, while the South calls for a more efficient international response to the problems of development, the South's solution to almost any issue is to propose the creation of yet another international institution rather than to find mutually acceptable ways of reforming and streamlining the existing structures. Finally, although developing countries probably stand to gain the most from any agreement to bring more international economic management under the aegis of global institutions, their concern that collective management limits their freedom of maneuver and their reluctance to adhere to obligations of multilateralism seem as great as that of developed countries.

For their part, the developed countries have championed the specialized agencies in which they maintain a dominant position. Yet from time to time they have also been critical of inefficiencies in the present array of institutions, and they have frequently argued that there is need for more centralization and coordination to provide for greater coherence. While insisting on protecting the "integrity" of the specialized agencies, the developed countries (in particular the United States) have shown a reluctance to increase the resource base of the key international financial institutions to levels that would enable the agencies to fulfill adequately their intended roles, preferring instead the political advantages that derive from bilateralism. They have also been reluctant to treat within the context of international institutions policy issues that have important international ramifications but have traditionally been viewed as purely domestic matters (such as the range of governmental measures that constitute a country's industrial policy and many of its macroeconomic policy responses to inflation and recession). Finally, while insisting that international economic cooperation must give rise to mutual benefit, developed countries have been unwilling to adjust decision-making procedures in ways that will ensure developing countries that their own interests are more adequately represented.

Some who have been either witnesses to or participants in the nearly decade-long dialogue on system reform now believe that the only way both to break through the substantive and procedural stalemate that has developed and to overcome bureaucratic rigidity in the existing institutions is to begin a series of meetings at the highest level: a period of North-South summitry somewhat analogous to the series of seven-nation economic summits that have been held among the heads of government of the leading industrial economies since 1975. What supporters of summitry hope will have been only the first of a number of such meetings was held in Cancun, Mexico, in October 1981. Although the Cancun meeting did not achieve any significant breakthroughs on existing issues or set the North-South dialogue off on a constructive new course, it has been praised as a beginning of useful exchanges at the highest level, and calls have been issued for subsequent summits with follow-up procedures built in.[11]

In light of the current depressed and unstable state of the world economy and the accumulated mistrust and ill-formed opinion on each side of the North-South divide about feasible policy options on the other, Cancun-type meetings may perform some useful interim function by introducing a new sense of realism as well as purposefulness into regular economic negotiations and dealings. But North-South summits are no more (indeed, they are probably rather less) of an adequate response to the need for continuous policy dialogues and specific regularized cooperative actions among groups of developed and developing countries than are the seven-nation summits an adequate means of ensuring that the steering and leadership that the system requires and that only few countries can really provide will be supplied continuously and in a way that takes account of the legitimate interests of others.

Nor is any serious attempt to restructure the international economic system likely to be composed of ingredients that can be brought together in one overall negotiation of the sort that the UN Global Negotiations were intended to be. It is in the nature of universal negotiations that the interests of all participants are somehow supposed to be served equally. Therefore, progress on any single issue tends to become hostage to progress on all others, irrespective of the fact that diverse issues rarely are all ripe for resolution at one time. Moreover, those issues on which some agreement might be possible tend to get distorted or bogged down by attempts of parties with unrelated and unresolved interests to piggy-back or link other actions to particular potential agreements. (For example, negotiations on the establishment of a common fund for commodity stabilization were distorted by demands of African states to add a resource transfer function to any fund agreed on.) Obviously the principal motivation for the kind of issue linkage that tends to occur in broad-ranging, universal negotiations is the desire of countries or groups of countries to enhance their bargaining power—either as a means of advancing or blocking action on a particular issue. In proposing the CIEC the French government seems to have thought that it could get oil-importing developing countries to ally with oil-importing developed countries in pressing OPEC for some kind of international oil agreement in exchange for progress on other issues, and in pressing for a round of global negotiations the non-oil-exporting LDCs have sought to enlist the support of the oil exporters in eliciting concessions from the North in areas of money, finance, and trade in exchange for putting "energy on the table." OPEC, for its part, seems to have been willing to participate in such enterprises mainly as a means of keeping energy from being addressed in isolation and of letting the failure to reach agreement on other issues mitigate the blame that might be placed on the oil exporters for the deterioration in world economic conditions. In neither of the first two examples has the bargaining tactic proved successful. Rather, what nearly a decade of experience suggests is that there may be a far greater likelihood of success in issue-specific negotiations than in global rounds that try to address broad agendas of disparate issues.

Moreover, though clear interconnections exist between certain issues (for example, the avoidance of greater trade protectionism and the ability of deficit countries to service their debts), there would seem to be far less likelihood that those interconnections could be adequately dealt with through bargains struck in omnibus negotiations than that the interconnections could be handled by regularized improved co-ordination among a reformed and much strengthened set of specialized international agencies that have operational responsibilities in specific functional areas.

What might a reformed and much strengthened set of key institutions look like? Some proposals by the Group of 77 seem to suggest that the answer to this question lies in strengthening the UN General Assembly's control over the operations of the specialized agencies. Among these who would concentrate instead on strengthening the role of specialized agencies themselves, there are some who doubt that existing institutions can be sufficiently revised and therefore prescribe the establishment of wholly new institutions based from the start on "more democratic" principles of participation than exist today. The position this chapter takes differs from both of the above, though it too looks forward to substantial renovation.

Rather than give major responsibility to the UN General Assembly (or to that body acting in Special Committee) or wipe today's institutional slate clean, the restructuring endorsed here would, as a matter of priority, provide for a much-altered IMF and World Bank and an essentially new trade organization in the form of a much-enhanced GATT at the center of the system. (Oddly, after more than a decade of North-South debate, no sustained effort has yet been made to explore in depth the possibility of reforms in the Bretton Woods institutions that might be both intrinsically desirable and acceptable by North and South.)[12] In addition, contrary to the prevailing view in the North (at least in the United States) that the central organization should play little or no role in the international economic policy sphere, the UN organization performs an important function as the world's central forum, and from time to time there will be cause for high-level negotiations on specific problems that for various reasons will need to take place in the universal forum. Therefore, a strengthening of the UN organization is a desirable complement to a strengthening of the trade and financial organizations—not so that the General Assembly can exert greater control over the operations of those institutions that must carry the major weight for the collective management of international economic relations, but so that the UN's legitimate role can be improved.

Though it is not possible in the space of this brief chapter to discuss in much detail this approach to restructuring, some ideas about desirable directions of change are outlined in the following pages.

Trade Organization

Miriam Camps has argued that the greatest need for institutional innovation seems to be in the trade field, which is principally governed today by "an uneasy combination" of GATT and UNCTAD. Camps suggests that the time has come to consider a new production-and-trade organization to replace both GATT and UNCTAD, taking over some functions from each but having some new tasks as well.[13] One can envisage this change as bringing into being an updated version of the proposed postwar international trade organization or an essentially enhanced GATT. Camps offers several strong reasons for proposing this change, including the failure of today's arrangements to deal adequately with two major, interrelated issues of the present decade: the need to find ways to incorporate the LDCs more fully into a global trading system that they accept as both being responsive to their needs and requiring certain obligations on their part and the need to cope efficiently with the process of structural change and shifting patterns of international trade and production.

GATT's effectiveness in handling trade issues has clearly declined since the end of the 1960s, as evidenced by a decline in strict adherence to the rules of GATT and widespread resort to nontariff measures of various kinds. This trend has reflected, at bottom, a widespread feeling that the rules do not adequately respond to the situations that were posing the most acute problems for governments—neither those governments that had written the rules nor the new members of GATT who had not shared in the rule making. Moreover, it is increasingly apparent that there are other important inadequacies and omissions in the present trade regime: an almost total lack of rules or procedural arrangements to deal with restrictions on services or controls on foreign direct investment, continued high protectionism in agriculture, problems of trade between market and command economies, and the organizational problem of the lack of any widely supported global body where discussions of trade policy take place on a continuing basis.

Many of today's trade-related problems involve questions that extend beyond the policy areas now covered by the GATT, raising issues not likely to be handled adequately within the context of today's GATT, with its primary reliance on market forces, its strong emphasis on rule making, and its quasi-legal approach. Nor does it seem likely that UNCTAD could develop, as LDCS have always wanted it to, into a new international trade organization, a full-fledged specialized agency with the range of functions originally proposed in the Havana Charter. Camps writes that "given the history of the organization and the continued unwillingness of the developed countries to see it become, in effect a new [international trade organization], there is no easy way out of the problems that stem from the organization's over-identification with one group of countries." Although it is possible to envision an evolving partnership between GATT and UNCTAD, the record of the past, writes Camps, "offers few reasons to believe that a fruitful relationship between the two organizations could be developed."[14] It therefore seems desirable to think in terms of major organizational renovation in the trade field that would, in effect, create a new organization.

Among those improvements that ought to come out of such renovation are the following:

ways of reconciling the need to have as many states as possible accept some rights and duties with, on the one hand, special arrangements for developing countries and, on the other, freedom for sets of states to go further than the membership as a whole would be prepared to go in accepting obligations vis-à-vis one another,

a new pattern that would combine more use of limited groups with arrangements that effectively protect the rights of those not represented, and

new processes whereby various functional problems that need to be looked at more closely together with trade issues and arrangements can be addressed in that way. (Centering the responsibility for trade activities within one institution and then establishing clearer lines of authority and closer working relationships between it and the World

Bank and the IMF would open the way to a less cumbersome and a more fruitful coordination within the UN system generally.)

As Camps notes,

If handled in the right way, agreement to establish what would, in fact, be a "new ITO" would go a very long way toward meeting the argument of the LDCs that the modern world needs a new international economic order. Rather than the existing practice of meeting bit by bit and frequently in a grudging way the most legitimate arguments put forward by the Group of 77 (and not infrequently making dubious concessions on some of their less legitimate claims for the sake of harmony), the international community would be taking a bold new step, one which did entail a new distribution of costs and benefits and sought to reconcile in a new way the competing demands of efficiency, equity, order, and autonomy. In this context, it would be reasonable to anticipate LDC agreement to the progressive assumption of responsibilities and commitments to a freer and more orderly trading system.[15]

Some have argued that the creation of a new trade organization is not feasible and therefore not worth discussing, and that it is more useful to consider instead ways of improving GATT. There may, however, be less substantive difference between asking what an improved GATT or a new trade organization should look like than this objection suggests. Camps argues that for various reasons it might be easier to think in terms of a new organization. But a GATT sufficiently enhanced to cope with today's and tomorrow's trade problems would be in effect a new institution. It therefore seems instructive to consider how an effective organization might best be structured.

The new organization that has been proposed would be a specialized agency paralleling the IMF and the World Bank and with similar formal relations to the United Nations. It would deal with trade and industrial policy, broadly defined, and specifically including problems of structural change and shifts in the global distribution of production. Its mandate would also extend to certain service industries, to issues of foreign direct investment and business practices, to commodity arrangements affecting conditions of trade, and to trade-related aspects of agriculture.

Finally, in terms of organizational structure—outlined not as a blueprint but as suggestive of desirable directions of change—the proposed new trade and production organization would be different from any existing specialized agency in that membership would be open to any state prepared to accept certain few basic principles. However, the weight of the institution would rest in an array of formally subordinated groups or committees whose membership would vary according to task and would operate with considerable autonomy. For instance, among the principal subordinate bodies there might be a tariff and trade code (which would be the main, but not only, successor body to the GATT), an LDC trade committee, an advisory council on the structure of the global economy, and a council on foreign direct investment. Most important there would be a trade policy review board that would be roughly analogous to the executive boards of the bank and the IMF (in that there would be weighted, constituency representation of all members of the full organization on it) and would be the main global trade policy body as well as the body to review and settle many types of complaints.

Even if that much institutional remodeling is not feasible within a period of time that is reasonable to plan for, it would seem desirable to take steps, through the better functioning of and improved cooperation between GATT and UNCTAD, that would move in directions consistent with the reforms that would be entailed in the establishment of a new international trade organization.

The IMF

Turning from the field of trade to money and finance, one confronts no less serious a set of problems. Indeed, with fears growing that the world is on the verge of financial collapse, wide-ranging consensus seems to be emerging on the need for new and renewed efforts of international financial cooperation. In the money and finance fields the kinds of actions that are needed to respond to both current and long-range problems seem to be ones that can best be handled through the further evolution of the existing institutions, especially the IMF and World Bank, rather than by the replacement of those institutions with new ones. The reasons for this difference are as follows. Both the IMF and the World Bank have changed over the years in response to international economic conditions and expanded memberships. They now need to be further reformed and strengthened in various ways. However, unlike the existing trade organizations, they have in most respects the right basic structures, and it ought to be possible to continue to revise each institution to meet today's concerns and those of the future. Some of the ways of thinking about what might be built into an enhanced GATT or a new trade organization would seem useful in thinking about how to reform the IMF and the World Bank. For example, it would seem desirable to see both financial institutions evolve more into umbrella organizations with a number of different bodies for different tasks (this is in some sense how the World Bank Group is now organized, but further moves in this direction seem appropriate), and it would be desirable to have more broad-ranging global monetary and financial policy reviews take place on a continuing basis under the aegis of each of the two institutions. To the contrary, it does not seem desirable to create a wholly new World Development Authority out of a merger of the IMF and the World Bank, as some have suggested.

This is obviously a controversial point. Those who argue for a new global monetary and financial institution correctly point to a number of real weaknesses in the existing system:

the failure of governments to agree, after the abandonment of the Bretton Woods par value system, to any meaningful rules or guidelines for managing exchange rates or to act effectively to moderate wide fluctuations and alter serious currency misalignments that have had negative systemic effects,

the limited ability of the international financial institutions to respond to the new (structural) adjustment problems that have plagued most economies since the mid-1970s and the continued inability of the IMF in particular to promote or influence, as might be needed from a systemic perspective, adjustment efforts of strong economies,

the absence of anything more than ad hoc mechanisms to deal with serious debt-management crises that disrupt the debtors' economies and have the potential for creating system-wide instability,

the failure, in certain specific ways, of the lending policies of the international financial institutions to adequately meet legitimate financing needs of countries, particularly those without access to the private capital markets, and

the persistence of decision-making procedures that deny the less powerful countries adequate voice on issues that have major impact on their well-being.

At least three main reasons are frequently given in support of the notion that further evolution of the existing institutions will not provide the means for overcoming these inadequacies. First, it is argued that the functions that the IMF and the World Bank now perform or should perform are so overlapping as to make their continued separate operations inefficient, if not counterproductive. Second, it is argued that the international financial institutions (IFIs) need to take on new tasks but that simply adding new tasks to the existing institutions would "overload their circuits." Third, it is argued that the existing institutions are too set in their ways and too heavily dominated by a few developed countries to be able to be reformed.

The problem of overlap has become increasingly real in the last few years as both the IMF and the World Bank have sought to respond to problems of structural adjustment and as developing countries have become major borrowers of IMF as well as World Bank resources. The fact that structural adjustment problems fall within the mandates of both institutions does not seem reason enough to propose a merger of the two, however; indeed, such a merger would seem likely to undermine rather than to clarify and enhance the two different sets of functions these institutions are intended to perform.

The IMF stands at the center of the world monetary system as "guardian of the rules of the game" in international money relations. In playing this central role it performs three main functions: It serves as a forum for discussion of the management of the international monetary order; maintains surveillance over the exchange-rate policies of member countries, and affects the supply of international liquidity in the system [in particular by providing short-term finance to members to allow them to ride out temporary balance-of-payments difficulties or more smoothly adjust to permanent (fundamental) changes, and, since 1970, by periodic issues of SDRs]. The role of the IMF in all three of these activities needs to be significantly strengthened, espcially if the IMF is to evolve, as it should, into something more closely resembling a world central bank. In contrast, the World Bank is a development investment institution whose long-term loans are directed to the promotion of economic growth and development worldwide and will likely be needed for this purpose for a long time if the full human and economic capacities of the world's people are to be more fully and efficiently realized. It too can and should be improved in particular ways. The challenge that current and continuing problems of structural adjustment pose for each of the institutions clearly suggests the need for closer coordination between them (as well as closer coordination of each with the GATT and UNCTAD or a new international trade organization). But the differences in the operations of an institution resembling a world central bank and those of an institution resembling more an international finance corporation are sufficiently great to warrant separate, autonomous bodies.

Moreover, the second problem, of overburdening the institutional framework, would be made worse not better by a merger of the World Bank and IMF into a single world development authority. While more coordination and more consistent policy guidance is needed, each of the two Bretton Woods institutions needs to take on certain new tasks. At least in the case of the World Bank, that change, which must involve more nonproject financing, should be accompanied by closer cooperation with the regional development banks that should be providing, over time, more of the traditional (project) development finance. This move, in itself, would affect somewhat the issue of participation within the multilateral development banks. Though other steps ought to be taken as well to give developing countries greater voice in the international financial institutions, the right principle for the key economic institutions is a system of weighted voting, and any new institution that both more and less developed countries could agree on would surely have to be built on this principle. The approach this chapter supports is thus to revise and strengthen the IMF and the World Bank.

There are at least three important areas for IMF reform: a strengthening of the surveillance process, a rationalization of lending policies and procedures that would better meet the liquidity needs of member countries (both those countries that normally have access to the international capital markets and those that do not), and the establishment of a debt-management mechanism involving, not only the IMF but also the World Bank and the major private international banks.[16]

From the outset, surveillance has been a major feature of the IMF— a way to guard against abuse of exchange-rate intervention and to promote order in exchange markets. With the shift from fixed to floating rates, surveillance has become an even more important key to adjustment. Under the Second Amendment of its Articles of Agreement, the IMF is required to exercise "firm surveillance over the exchange rate policies of members" and must adopt "specific principles for the guidance of all members with respect to those policies" (Article IV, Section 3b). To carry out this obligation, the IMF conducts regular consultations with its member governments, in most instances annually. In addition, the Executive Board conducts an annual review of the world economic outlook, based on a report prepared by the staff using current information on the policies of the major countries. In accord with the adoption of the Second Amendment in 1977, the IMF's board also agreed to guidelines for countries with floating exchange rates, and the Managing

Director was authorized to initiate discussions with a member government if its policies appear to violate these guidelines.

Although IMF surveillance still focuses on exchange-rate policies, its consultations with member governments now range widely over current policies, including monetary and fiscal policies. This is wholly appropriate, because exchange rates are heavily influenced by macroeconomic developments and policies and exchange rates are especially sensitive to monetary policies. The process of surveillance is therefore the one way by which the IMF can influence the economic policies of its members, including those of the major industrial countries that have not been drawing on IMF resources. Through its surveillance function, the IMF can (and indeed has begun to) give more attention to the consistency of policies across countries and emphasize the need for coordination of macroeconomic policy among key countries.

Nevertheless, the IMF's ability to influence those policies is quite limited, because it cannot readily impose penalties on countries that do not need its help. A deficit country coming to the IMF to make a drawing must agree to conditions set forth by the IMF. It may be compelled to make major changes in its economic policies. A country that does not need IMF resources cannot be subjected to this sort of influence. A surplus country cannot be compelled to modify its policies.

If the IMF is to play a larger role in the overall management of the international economic system, more needs to be done to strengthen the surveillance function, combine it with more coordination of the macroeconomic policies (not just exchange-rate policies) of key countries, and bring this coordination within the context of the fund.

In this regard there should be more frequent consultations on the economic policies of the industrial countries since these policies have such an enormous effect on the world economy. Ways should be found to publicize the process. For instance, the report on the world economic outlook should be published more promptly, and the text of that report should devote more attention to the polices of individual countries.

Most important, however, the IMF should encourage groups of members, particularly the key currency countries, to hold multilateral consultations under its auspices and with the participation of its staff. What this means is that those responsible for national economic policy making should become more closely and continuously involved in deliberation within the IMF, and IMF staff should become more actively involved in ensuring that macroeconomic policies of the key countries do not conflict but reinforce one another and contribute to an international economic system that is open, orderly, and conducive to noninflationary growth.

A step in this direction was taken after the June 1982 seven-nation economic summit at Versailles. In a Statement of International Monetary Undertakings annexed to the summit communiqué, the authorities representing the currencies of North America, Japan, and the European Community announced:

1. We accept a joint responsibility to work for greater stability of the world monetary system. . . . We are determined to discharge this obligation in close collaboration with all interested countries and monetary institutions. 2. We attach major importance to the role of the IMF as a monetary authority and we will give it our full support in its efforts to foster stability. 3. We are ready to strengthen our cooperation with the IMF in its work of surveillance; and to develop this on a multilateral basis taking into account particularly the currencies constituting the SDR. . . .

This statement was followed by a meeting of the Group of Five in Toronto at the time of the 1982 annual meetings of the IMF and the World Bank. The managing director of the IMF was invited to a portion of this meeting for discussion of better coordination of macroeconomic policies. What is needed now is to regularize this process and bring it more formally under the aegis of the IMF, perhaps by the creation of a "committee of the Interim Committee or, better, the Council that was foreseen in the Second Amendment as the successor to the Interim Committee," which would include "representatives of all those countries whose rates (and the policies underlying those rates) have to be considered together" and "in the deliberations of which the Fund's Managing Director would play an active role."[17]

The second major issue for the IMF involves its role as lender. According to Article I of the Articles of Agreement, one of the main purposes of the IMF is to "give confidence to members by making the general resources of the Fund temporarily available to them under adequate safeguards, thus providing them with opportunity to correct maladjustments in their balance of payments without resorting to measures destructive of national or international prosperity." On this basis, the IMF has over the years provided relatively short-term balance-of-payments assistance to countries whose economies were in disequilibrium. Just how the IMF has carried out this role has been a controversial issue for many years, particularly as regards the relative availability of high-conditionality and low-conditionality finance, the content of the conditionality applied by the IMF to its lending at higher credit tranches (or levels high relative to countries quotas within the IMF), and the overall levels of financial assistance that the IMF can provide.

Recent events have made it increasingly clear that there are at least four distinct sets of problems that would seem to necessitate some alterations in the IMF's lending practices (as well as substantial increases in its resources).

First, there is the particular problem of the liquidity needs of low-income countries that do not have regular access to the international capital markets. For these countries, the IMF needs to play something other than a lender-of-last-resort role, both by increasing the availability of its low-conditionality finance and by doing more to help promote adjustment when necessary through its more highly conditional higher credit tranche lending.

As argued by various analysts, the availability of low-conditionality finance from the IMF has not been maintained over the past decade at levels relative to growth in world trade or to increases in IMF conditional finance.[18] This is because IMF quota increases (and thus drawings from its low-end credit tranches linked to quotas) have not kept up with the expansion of world trade. The result has been particularly hard on low-income countries that have not benefited from liquidity expansion from other sources—notably, in the 1970s, commercial-bank lending to advanced developing countries and increases in the price of gold which raised the level of reserves of those countries, primarily industrial ones, that held gold in sizable amounts.[19] For the poorer member countries of the IMF with limited access to balance-of-payments financing, the unconditional and low-conditionality facilities of the IMF remain of critical importance. These countries "have an interest in the retention and extension of the low-conditionality facilities so as to provide them with access to low-conditional credit whenever a payment deterioration is due to circumstances beyond their control."[20] Some extension of low-conditionality finance to the commercially noncreditworthy countries faced with exogenous shocks could be accomplished in various ways without detracting from the continued provision of high-conditionality finance to encourage effective adjustment when a country encounters what is judged to be a permanent adverse-payments shock and/or to help restore the creditworthiness of countries with regular access to commercial credit.

The second challenge is to improve the role of the IMF in promoting orderly adjustments to structural imbalances. As has been evident since the mid-1970s, the structural nature of adjustment problems faced by many countries calls now for larger amounts of longer-term finance than was previously the practice of the IMF. In this regard it has recently been suggested that the terms of reference for extended (or medium-term) IMF financing be reformulated to make more explicit the role that the IMF, in keeping with its traditional mandate as an adjustment institution, has in helping countries to adjust to structural deficits. The current terms of reference authorize extended financing for a country "characterized by slow growth and an inherently weak balance of payments position which prevents pursuit of an active development policy." The proposed reformulation would specify the role of the IMF's extended facility as that of "aiding a country to adjust to a structural deficit.[21] In addition there is the related issue of need for improved coordination between the IMF and the World Bank as each institution seeks to cope with structural adjustment problems from its distinct institutional mandate and perspective.

Third, there is a need to improve the role of the IMF in response to financing emergencies. Here the issue is "in the short run, to ensure that financial flows to countries with serious debt or liquidity problems continue at an appropriate rate so as to avoid a liquidity crisis that could force these countries to suspend debt payments and to allow them to undertake an orderly adjustment process that does not place unbearable strains on their political and social fabric."[22]

To deal with the debt-management problems and the structural imbalances that countries have come to face, it might make sense to think of an institutional innovation that would link the IMF, the World Bank, and perhaps the private financial institutions in order to better help meet both the emergency, quick-disbursing financing needs and the longer-term adjustment financing requirements that have become features of the international financial system.

While there is clear evidence that the "recycling" handled by private institutions was for a time beneficial to countries of the world, it is now equally clear that the virtual abdication of responsibility by official institutions for the management of international capital flows has not worked well and that some better balance between the roles of public and private institutions needs to be reestablished if there is to be stability over time in the international financial system and if there is to be a continuing flow of international credit that will be conducive to non-inflationary worldwide growth. While private banks and not governments or intergovernmental institutions will continue to provide the bulk of international credit, the roles of official institutions need to be strengthened in various ways. Many proposals for how to do that have been made recently, most of which focus on the single, immediate issue of keeping credit flowing to countries experiencing what everyone hopes will be only short-term liquidity problems that can be overcome by a combination of policy adjustments in the debtor country, public and private debt rescheduling, and worldwide economic recovery. These proposals tend, therefore, to deal largely with finding better (less ad hoc) means of handling debt-rescheduling crises, with the IMF assuming a more central role in facilitating both the needed adjustment and the rescheduling of debt. But there is good reason to doubt that adjustment and rescheduling is enough of a response. That response assumes that countries will be in a position to come back to economic health if they are given a brief (two to three years) breathing space, and it assumes that new net private funds will be there to help finance adjustment and recovery; neither is a safe assumption. Recent arrangements (e.g., with Mexico) will help a debtor country meet its interest payments, but the net effect is more indebtedness and larger future debt-servicing outflows. Moreover, the country involved is being asked to slash imports and reduce its domestic standard of living so that more of its export earnings will be available for interest payments and less net borrowing will be needed. The external accounts will then look better, but the internal economy will be greatly weakened.

If there were a certain prospect of a vigorous worldwide economic recovery in the next year or two, it might make sense to provide even the very heavily indebted countries with substantial new credit to tide them over. There would at least be some likelihood that the debtor country could export its way out of trouble in a short time. But there is widespread concern among economic analysts (within and outside the leading international organizations) that the impact of economic recovery on LDCs will be slow, that protectionist pressures will remain strong because of prolonged high unemployment, that demands for LDC exports will remain depressed, and that therefore the "debt problem" will not be a short-term one. Moreover, there is a need for substantial net increases in new medium-term to long-term financing to provide countries with the capital to make necessary structural adjustments. And there is a need for public institutions, both national and international, to improve on a more permanent basis the management of international financial flows. What this means, in part, is that a more comprehensive response to debt management is needed than has yet been put together—one that sees as the solution to the

immediate problems not simply crisis management but an actual reduction of debt in real terms and that over the longer term encourages
a more efficient allocation of credit, including measures to discourage
overborrowing and overlending as well as insufficient access. Perhaps
one useful step in regard to the immediate problems would be to establish a new international institutional mechanism, requiring little
initial financing, that would swap its own debt (backed by guarantees
of creditor nations) for some of that of the private banks at a discount.
Whereas the existing private debt is mostly short-term to medium-term
and carries high rates of interest, the new officially issued loans would
be somewhat longer-term and at somewhat lower interest rates. While
this does not seem an appropriate task for the IMF, it is one that the
World Bank could and should be empowered to perform. But it might
also make sense for the longer term to establish a formal link between
the Bank and the IMF to ensure better coordination of their respective
roles in adjustment and debt management.

Currently, debt problems are handled in three poorly integrated
phases: quick-dispersing bridging finance needed to get countries
through that period of time that it takes to put together an adjustment-
rescheduling package, short- to medium-term adjustment assistance
intended to help countries reestablish creditworthiness, and longer-
term finance for needed structural adjustment. The first is handled by
ad hoc intergovernmental arrangements, usually involving creditor
countries (through their central banks) and the Bank for International
Settlements, the second by the IMF, and the third partially by the IMF
and partially by the World Bank.

Since the middle of 1982 the IMF has sought to play a more activist,
integrating role, but its institutional capacity in this regard is limited.
To encourage a more coordinated and more comprehensive set of arrangements over the long run, it might be useful to establish a joint
standing committee of the World Bank and the IMF. Such a joint committee would create the functional link between the World Bank and
the IMF that is now lacking and would promote better coordination
on "adjustment" problems that in the past have tended to fall between
the two institutions or to be handled in part by each but not always
in complementary or mutually reinforcing ways. In addition, the joint
committee might serve as both the decision-making body for a new
emergency fund that would provide bridge financing and an advisory
body for a World Bank debt-restructuring mechanism. While debt
"crises" brought to this facility would be looked at on a case-by-case

basis, the buildup of "case law" ought, over time, to make the development of certain guidelines and criteria possible.

Fourth, it would seem desirable to have the IMF "take greater account of the world cyclical situation in framing its lending policies."[23] One ambitious way the fund could do this would be to considerably enlarge its Compensatory Financing Facility. An expanded CFF, designed to serve as "a sturdy international firstline of defense against depressions," might focus on expected real export earnings rather than on nominal shortfalls; cover all exports whether of manufactures, services, or primary commodities; and automatically and fully cover shortfalls from expectations that would be repaid quickly when real export earnings surpass expectations.[24] A more modest step would be to have the IMF vary its conditionality over time in response to cyclical variations.[25] Either way, for the IMF to play more of a countercyclical role it will need a larger amount of resources than will be available to it for lending even after the 1983 eighth quota increase.

Underlying these proposals for change in the IMF's lending practices is a recognition that structural changes in the world economy, growing diversity among developing countries, and changed patterns of international capital flows are all contributing to a diversification of financial needs worldwide. These same trends bear centrally on the future role of international resource transfer institutions, notably the World Bank and the regional development banks.

The World Bank

To respond adequately to the increasingly diverse financing problems, it will be necessary in the decade ahead not only to increase the volume of international resource transfers between richer and poorer states but also to make substantial innovations in the multilateral resource-transfer process.

While some improvements are still needed in the process of project financing, the major reforms needed in the years ahead are ones that broaden the range of international financial assistance beyond the traditional focus on project financing to include more nonproject lending of various kinds. The key to many of these needed improvements would seem to lie in expanding the range of activities of the World Bank Group and strengthening the bank's ties with other international economic institutions.

Through the 1980s the core activity of the World Bank and the regional development banks should remain much the same to provide financing for a wide range of development projects. But as the lending capacity of the regional banks is increased, much of today's project financing ought to be provided by them, and the World Bank should, increasingly, be carrying out a number of different functions.

The World Bank is today the major international development institution and the leading coordinator, having increased the level and the breadth of its lending program greatly during the years of the McNamara presidency. Consequently, it is the most diversified of the multilateral development banks, providing loans for capital projects and heavy infrastructure, social and human resources development, and balance-of-payments support (in the form of new structural adjustment loans, old program loans, and loans for specific sectoral purposes). Each of these types of loans requires a different expertise and approach to be successful. Structural adjustment, program lending, and sector lending require substantial macroeconomic analysis and the fixing of goals and priorities of a broad policy nature. Capital-intensive and infrastructure projects depend heavily on engineering and construction expertise and are the simplest type of lending. Social projects are generally labor-intensive in both the project development and execution stages. Although they do not require as high a level of analytic ability as some others, they do require close involvement in execution and monitoring.

The World Bank is big enough to retain a diversified staff with the requisite skills to engage in these three kinds of lending operations. The regional banks are not. Moreover, they depend heavily on the World Bank for the macroeconomic analysis on which their country programs and project developments are based. Hence, the Asian Development Bank has focused on infrastructure projects while doing some balance-of-payments lending, the Inter-American Development Bank has also focused on infrastructure but has increasingly been lending for social projects that directly benefit poor people, and the African Development Bank has so far concentrated principally on brick-and-mortar projects.

In the future, some greater overlap of activities among the institutions is inevitable and probably constructive. However, for each of them to engage heavily in all categories of lending would be inefficient. Each institution should concentrate its activities on those areas of its greatest advantage. This suggests that the regional banks should focus on capital-intensive and heavy-infrastructure projects. Reduced pressure by the United States and other donors on the regional banks to engage in "basic needs" projects would probably result in a natural increase in capital projects infrastructure lending and would, over a period of time, increase the relative importance of the regional banks at the expense of the World Bank. Such an outcome would seem an acceptable way of achieving both economies of scale and a better distribution of responsibilities in the development field.

For its part, the World Bank should place increased emphasis on the most complex aspects of lending—structural adjustment, program, and complex sector lending—and should take the lead on most of the "new style" and social projects. Especially for the more advanced World Bank borrowers, structural adjustment lending should become more dominant, with increased coordination between the bank and the IMF. In addition, the role of the World Bank in relation to the more advanced developing countries should shift from direct project lending (except for essential large-scale investment projects that ought typically to be co-financed) toward the somewhat more "aloof" activity of providing financial guarantees.

The World Bank should also do more to help the least developed countries with their own development programming, enhance coordination among concessional agencies, and (as part of that effort) provide an increasing amount of its concessional "credits" in the form of program loans and become more of a gap filler and residual lender.

The World Bank might also do more to encourage an increase in foreign direct investment in developing countries. Even if the availability of commercial bank credit to LDCs proves greater over the course of the 1980s than now seems likely, it is not obvious that a continued buildup of external debt would be highly desirable. The present system has led to an inefficient allocation of risk, whereby exogenous changes in economic policy (such as OPEC surpluses and U.S. interest rates) have heavy effects on the capacity of LDCs to service debt. Increased reliance on direct investment may be a way to spread these risks more widely and to help stabilize the entire system. Tapping this source of investment financing in a substantial way will require changed attitudes on the part of both developing countries and firms. LDCs will have to adopt more open policies toward foreign private enterprise and the repatriation of their profits, and foreign companies will have to maintain investments for long periods of time. At a minimum there will have to be improved fiscal and contracting arrangements that are fair to all parties, and it would seem appropriate for the World Bank to play an increased role in this regard, perhaps through the establishment of a multilateral investment insurance scheme (now under discussion within the bank's executive board) to which countries could chose to affiliate on a wholly voluntary basis.

In all of this the World Bank should be concerned increasingly with the financing needs not only of individual countries but also of the "global economy." Entry into energy and minerals development and into structural adjustment lending moves the bank in this direction, but the bank needs to develop a greater advisory capacity in the trade-policy field and work more closely with the existing GATT-UNCTAD framework or, preferably, a new international trade organization.

Finally, if the World Bank is to play the principal long-term financing role in the years ahead, there should be established under its auspices a new development assistance review committee as a locus for the kind of continuing high-level discussion of resource transfer needs, policies, and practices that the management of change in a global economy requires.

Today there is no place where the full array of needs is adequately reviewed and discussed on a regular basis, although there are a number of different forums in which parts of the problem are discussed. The annual meetings of the boards of governors of the IMF and World Bank Group are occasions for broad-ranging discussions but not for in-depth review and long-term planning. The executive board of the World Bank discusses broad policy issues, but it is responsible for the running of the bank and addresses issues primarily in terms of bank activities, not issues that go beyond that. Outside the World Bank framework, the Development Assistance Committee (DAC) of the OECD holds regular reviews and appraisals of the OECD donor countries' policies and procedures. But these are discussions by a "club" of donors. Recipients do not participate. Nor do OPEC and other aid-giving countries take part, which means that DAC reviews now cover a smaller percentage of total aid transfers than they once did.

Recently UNCTAD has done some good studies of international financial issues. However, it was not set up to deal with development-financing problems, and the attempt by its secretariat to carve out an expanding role for the agency in this field adds to the bureaucratic and political confusion that already hampers the development-assistance effort. Within the central United Nations, the Committee on Development Planning, established in 1961 to follow the progress of the

First United Nations Development Decade, continues to function as a review and advisory body. But the committee is an expert group, and its deliberations are not a substitute for the kind of high-level, continuing discussion that ought to go on between donor and recipient governments concerning criteria, objectives, gaps, and ways of improving the flow and use of resources. The joint IMF–World Bank Development Committee, established in 1974, is an experiment along these lines, but it was designed mainly to deflect pressures for other, more radical changes in the IMF and the bank, and it is composed of finance ministers rather than heads of development-assistance agencies and planning ninisters. Partly for this reason, it has too limited a view of its role to carry on the broad, regular, multilateral review of resource-transfer policies and practices that is needed.

The proposed development assistance review committee would have a limited membership composed of high-level government officials. All members of the review committee would represent groups or constituencies of countries. Because of the nature of its activity, it might be desirable for the review committee to be somewhat larger than the executive board of the World Bank, and it might also be desirable for the constituencies of the review committee to be composed in a somewhat different way. That is, rather than having committee members who mainly represent groups of countries within geographical regions or subregions, it might be useful to try to give representation to categories of countries defined according to their economic capabilities and needs. For example, constituencies might be composed of groups such as low-income resource-poor countries, less-developed resource-rich countries, middle-income LDCs, LDC donors, and advanced donor countries. The membership of the committee should not be static but should be reviewed often.

The review committee, which might meet several times a year, would have research support from the World Bank's staff, not a large separate secretariat, but it should also make use of expertise in other parts of the UN system, particularly the IMF and the proposed trade organization.

In essence this committee would be a policy review group. It would discuss a broad range of issues relating to the transfer of real resources, including the development-assistance policies and procedures of donor countries, the assistance and lending criteria of both bilateral and multilateral programs, appropriate performance criteria, and the goals and priorities that should guide the distribution of official long-term resource transfers and official policies affecting long-term private transfers. If the committee did not become simply another forum for rhetorical exchanges, there would cease to be a need for OECD's DAC because the review committee would be a multilateralized DAC. Over time one can envisage the new committee moving beyond today's familiar discussion of resource transfers for development to a broader discussion of the adequacy of resource allocations and the distribution of investment on a global basis.

These changes in the World Bank and those proposed in regard to money and trade would make the international economic institutions significantly more responsive to the interests of developing countries as well as those of developed countries. But still to be addressed are the issues of the role of the central organization and the structure of governance in the specialized agencies.

The Central UN Organization

The economic role of the United Nations has been evolving continually. Initially the UN was concerned with narrowly described technical assistance efforts. For a time, some economic-assistance measures associated with decolonization were added. Then the organization became increasingly centered on problems of development broadly construed. With this changing role (which reflects the interests of an expanding membership) came the proliferation of UN agencies and the attempts to strengthen the General Assembly [and, under it, the Economic and Social Council (ECOSOC)] in order to give greater direction and cohesion to the activities of the UN system. The outcome of these two institutional trends, each of which has been supported at different times by developed and developing countries, has not, however, produced a well-functioning organization. To the contrary, criticisms have been heard from all sides. For example, in two fairly recent "Northern" assessments one finds the following comments:

The UN system—particularly the General Assembly, Security Council, and certain of the specialized agencies—has been increasingly dominated by the Third World's drive for greater economic, social and technological equality. In the same historic period the great powers have downgraded the United Nations as an instrument for negotiating important disputes, choosing more and more to act unilaterally, often in disregard of UN Charter obligations. Compounding the negative picture is the spread of the Middle East conflict across the UN system, poisoning the atmosphere for constructive action in the major political organs and politicizing several professionally oriented specialized agencies, seriously hampering their important work.[26]

It was thought in the early years of the UN that clearly defined programs for the general welfare could be insulated from the members' "high politics" and that agreements could be reached on monetary policy, investment, trade, agriculture, labor, health, education, science, culture, communications, nuclear energy, civil aviation, merchant shipping, and other important issues. It was hoped, too, that habits of cooperation in these specialized areas would spill over into such politically sensitive areas as security.

In fact, the opposite has too often happened: The politics of the General Assembly and the Security Council have been replicated in various specialized agencies and functional conferences. . . . Unhappily, the efforts of some of the agencies—UNESCO, ILO, World Health Organization and others—have been threatened by the injection of extraneous political issues ("politicization") that provokes friction and confrontation and hinders cooperation. Two closely related patterns are involved in this regrettable development: taking action on matters outside the specific functional domain of a given specialized agency or conference, and reaching decisions on matters within their functions competence on the basis of political considerations irrelevant to the technical or scientific problems at issue. . . .

In the Secretariats of the UN and its specialized agencies, hiring and promotion have been influenced increasingly by political pressure rather than by merit. This has brought many poorly qualified officials to important positions and, as a consequence, eroded confidence in the integrity of international officials in general.[27]

Numerous "Southern" spokesmen have also voiced a variety of other criticisms: According to some, the major problem is bigness and bureaucratic sprawl. ("A lot of agencies are really a waste of money. Often we have no choice but to send a man just to keep up appearances.") According to others, the greater problem is that the UN is not adequately used by its members.[28] The Secretary General has spoken out on the "underlying deficiencies" of the present system that make the UN "unable to play as effective and decisive a role as the charter certainly envisaged for it."[29] But as these comments themselves suggest, while there is agreement on the need to address shortcomings of the organization, there is little agreement on the nature of the problem or how the organization should be strengthened.

According to the UN charter, the organization "shall make recommendations for the coordination of the policies and activities of the specialized agencies" (article 58). In particular the Economic and Social Council is empowered to "make or initiate studies and reports with respect to international economic, social, cultural, educational, health and related matters and may make recommendations with respect to any such matters to the General Assembly, to the Members of the United Nations, and to the specialized agencies concerned" (article 62); and it "may coordinate the activities of the specialized agencies through consultation with and recommendations to such agencies and through recommendations to the General Assembly and to the Members" (Article 63). Though these authorized functions of coordination and recommendation on policy establish for the UN a more limited role than current G-77 positions acknowledge, they also anticipate a more active role for the organization in economic affairs than most developed countries now seem willing to allow or than the UN is able to perform effectively. Beyond the concerns of the developing countries, the needs of the system would seem to call for better fulfillment by the organization of its full, authorized role.

The UN is the one place in the system where all problems can be looked at, where the views of all countries can be voiced, and where (at times) consensus can be reached on what new tasks are urgent and what policies need reassessing. At a high level of generality, the UN, specifically the General Assembly, performs a global goal-setting role and sets the general international policy framework in the sense that it reflects and helps mold global views. However, it would be undesirable, except in one respect, to make the central UN organization more operational or to create new bodies with executive tasks as part of the main UN structure.[30] But this is not to say that the role of the central UN organization is not vitally important and that weaknesses in current UN operations are not in need of serious attention.

If the UN's "forum function" could be made to work well, the level of understanding on key issues among all groups of countries could be raised. Moreover, a well-functioning central forum might help to provide early warnings on emerging global problems. It might also reverse the trend of costly bureaucratic expansion within the UN system. (For example, the establishment of UNCTAD, which was in part a response to the inadequate functioning of ECOSOC, has led in subsequent years to the growth of a separate secretariat that duplicates in many ways work that is done or should be done by the central secretariat.)

Some of what ought to be done to improve the UN's role was spelled out in 1975 in the Report of the Group of Experts on the Structure of the United Nations.[31] Though few of the ideas in the report were adopted (largely because of lack of interest on the part of key countries and the press of economic events at the time), many of its recommendations remain valid and should be reexamined as part of any serious consideration of international reform. In that report particular emphasis is placed on revitalizing ECOSOC, increasing the level of expertise in and the consensus-building role of the UN Secretariat, and consolidating and streamlining UNO development-related funds.

After the submission of the experts' report, an ad hoc committee of the General Assembly (open to all members) was established to deliberate the issue of UN restructuring. Those deliberations continued between 1975 and 1977. In the end the committee (and the resolution put by it to the full General Assembly) endorsed many of the experts' recommendations but departed from the report in certain significant ways.[32] Most important, the committee, in contrast to the experts' group, gave particular emphasis to strengthening the General Assembly to allow it to function as the principal forum for policy making in international economic and social matters, establishing overall strategies, policies, and priorities for the entire UN system, and reviewing and evaluating developments in other UN forums. As recently observed,

This recommendation had the full backing of the South, but the North had reservations. The United States considered the Assembly's role was "neither to negotiate precise agreements nor to place restraints on the negotiations in other fora," which should maintain their own integrity.

The two positions are exemplified in the protracted, and so far unsuccessful, attempts by the Assembly to agree on procedures to launch a Round of Global Negotiations on international economic cooperation for development.[33]

The committee also approved the establishment within the Secretariat of a post of Director-General for International Economic Cooperation and Development, called for in the experts' report as one means of bolstering the Secretariat's role and competence in giving guidance and direction to the UN system's work on development issues. Furthermore, the committee endorsed the experts' call for a revitalization of ECOSOC, as does this chapter. Although the role the experts envisioned for ECOSOC (as the central organ in the system for "global policy formulation and implementation and the setting of priorities for the system as a whole") seems neither a feasible role in today's political climate nor a practical way of handling highly complex and rapidly evolving economic problems, the focus on improving the workings of ECOSOC as one key to a better-functioning UN does seem right. What ECOSOC ought to do principally, but does not now do well at all, is provide for a continuous stocktaking of world economic conditions. It ought to serve "as a kind of 'global watch' group, scanning the international horizon for new problems and providing a forum for a wide ranging exchange of views on issues that are important but in danger of being overlooked, or issues that although critical are still too controversial for settlement but do need airing."[34] ECOSOC cannot in any operationally meaningful way coordinate the work of the separate, specialized agencies; such coordination can be accomplished only by the talking and working together of those people who are actually responsible for the operations of those agencies and should occur as part of a strengthening of the key specialized agencies. But ECOSOC can, through continuous stocktaking, promote greater coherence and draw attention to un-attended-to problems or interconnections among issues that are being ignored. It can also serve as a useful place to follow up decisions reached in global conferences for which no specialized agency or other body has responsibility. To perform this role well, there would have to be a higher level of representation at ECOSOC meetings and better substantive backstopping by the UN Secretariat. In addition it would be useful to have ECOSOC hold shorter, more frequent, subject-oriented sessions. Although these changes have long been addressed, no move in this direction has yet occurred.

Both the experts' group and the General Assembly committee correctly emphasized the value of issue-specific discussions within a revitalized ECOSOC, and both endorsed the idea of varying patterns of participation according to countries' interests in and their importance to the handling of the specific issue at hand. The discussions that would take place in the issue-oriented ECOSOC sessions could not dictate changes in policies, procedures, or programs of other organizations with their own governing structure and membership. Nonetheless, there is something to be said for the G-77's point that UN recommendations should carry some weight. Therefore, it would be reasonable to think about follow-up procedures to ECOSOC resolutions (for example, in the form of reports from governments or agencies on actions taken or not taken). But the legitimacy of follow-up actions in ECOSOC will be accepted by governments only if decisions are reached or recommendations made on the basis of consensus in the first place.

In sum, there seem to be a number of concrete steps that could be taken to strengthen the role of the UN and that would meet with broad international agreement. But there are also at least three conditions essential to an enhanced role for the UN in economic affairs: higher levels of representation in more frequent, issue-oriented ECOSOC sessions; more expert secretarial support for both ECOSOC and the UNGA; and willingness on the part of governments to take decisions in the UN forums on a consensus basis.

Presumably, if ECOSOC, the UN Secretariat, and the functional agencies were working better—along the lines proposed—there would be less frequent calls for high-level, wide-ranging economic negotiations under the auspices of the General Assembly. The need for special conferences will continue, and, as demonstrated by the 1974 World Food Conference, these can serve a useful purpose when they are focused, well prepared for, and deal with a problem ripe for concerted action. But no amount of squabbling over procedures for omnibus negotiations can make that sort of effort a success, and the time of government representatives would be far better spent on putting the overall institutional framework in order and dealing with specific, high-priority problems in a focused way. This approach to institutional reform will be seen to be valid, however, only if it provides for the interests of all countries to be fairly represented and fully taken into account.

Representation and Voice

For anyone who holds to the view that international organizations can and should be vehicles for redistributing economic power or restructuring the world economic order, the approach of this chapter will surely seem inadequate. From all that has been said above, however, it should be clear that the view of the chapter is that international organizations are reflections of economic and political realities and that only those organizations that accurately reflect (in their operations as well as their decision-making processes) those realities have any chance of functioning actively and effectively. Moreover, it is my view that the test of decision-making rules has to be whether they are conducive to the achievement of the purposes an organization is intended to perform. This means that for operational organizations the decision-making rules should enable members "to make decisions, without undue delay, that are accepted and followed by the majority of members whose acceptance is crucial to accomplishing the agency's goals."[35] This in turn requires that there be a correspondence between interest in the issue at hand, ability to affect the system, obligations and responsibilities, and voting strength. Accordingly, there should be a pattern of representation (voting structure) combined with safeguards (veto power) that reflects a balance between the interests of those most affected by and those able to affect the rules, policies, and procedures.

Voting procedures in international organizations in the period between the Congress of Vienna in 1815 and the Bretton Woods Conference in 1944 underwent a move away from "egalitarianism" (equal voting among states on the basis of unanimity consistent with the doctrine of sovereign equality) to majority rule and weighted voting. This shift paralleled the emergence of international institutions engaged in technical activities with little or no political character or mandate.[36]

Even in some of these early technical organizations, however, the issue of weighted voting was the subject of intense debate both in the negotiation of constitutional treaties and in the operation of the organizations created by them. While the disputes were provoked both by the attachment of countries (especially the weaker ones) to the doctrine of sovereign equality and by the difficulty of finding rational formulas for weighting votes, the advocates of weighted voting "regarded themselves as contributing to the progressive development of international relations, because this arrangement would be more realistic and therefore give greater assurance of effectiveness."[37]

In the negotiations on the Bretton Woods institutions, both Keynes and White apparently supported the principle of weighted voting, and there is said to be no record of any objection by others. There was some dispute, however, between how much to weight votes and what use to make of special majorities—distinct though related issues that bear importantly on the current power-sharing debate.[38]

In recent years pressure has mounted to reverse the post–World War II tendency to create organizations based on weighted voting and restore relative equality in decision procedures or to adopt procedures that group nations into voting blocs with balanced voting strength. Yet neither the proliferation of universal one-country, one-vote institutions nor institutions where voting shares are allocated among economic blocs will provide an adequate foundation for stronger, more effective global institutions able to bear the weight of more and better multilateral economic management.

The choice of universalism wastes the scarcest resource the world commands: skilled manpower. It bears hardest on poor and small countries, which are nevertheless its strongest advocates since they see their interests as otherwise underrepresented. Moreover, it reinforces tendencies of the rich and powerful countries to resort to arrangements among themselves rather than encouraging them to cooperate more under the aegis of global institutions in which account can be taken of the concerns of all affected parties.

Although developing countries have been the ones to espouse the one-country, one-vote principle, equal voting is in fact resisted by the more powerful developing countries, and therefore the LDCs have placed greater emphasis on equality among groups of nations—or bloc voting—as instituted in the International Fund for Agricultural Development (IFAD). This trend aims to institutionalize bloc voting along political rather than functional lines. Blocs formed along functional lines exist in, for example, international commodity agreements that assign an equal number of votes to exporting and importing countries.[39] The more recent emphasis on political blocs is designed to ensure certain voting proportions to like-minded countries.

As an alternative to universalism, this political bloc representation may offer some greater measure of efficiency, at least in the short run.[40] But over the long run such an agreement seems certain to give rise to serious rigidities in management efforts at the global level. Within each bloc there will inevitably be diversities of interest and capabilities that must first be resolved before accommodation among blocs is attempted. In more than a decade of North-South negotiations, this has proved to leave little room for maneuver and compromise. By insisting on this approach, "developing countries may succeed in adjusting the decision-making machinery, only to find the machinery grinding to a halt."[41]

Yet, in light of changes in the structure of the world economy and shifts in relative economic power, the institutional patterns and principles endorsed here require that ways be found to increase LDCs' influence in the key international economic institutions. In considering how this ought to be done, three kinds of measures deserve attention: measures having to do with formal voting arrangements, including both the reweighting of votes on the executive boards of the IMF and the World Bank and the use of special majorities in the taking of votes, changes in other (nonvoting) procedures that bear on how policy decisions are made and how organizations are operated, and steps that would make for a greater divorce between the distribution of decision-making power and both the provision of and access to funds.

As regards the first issue of formal voting arrangements, it follows from what has been said above that, although operational institutions should function on the basis of weighted voting, some reweighting can and should take place in the key organizations. In the IMF votes are allocated among countries according to a formula that gives major but not exclusive weights to quotas, which themselves are largely a measure of the position of members in the world of trade and payments. Reweighting in this case might entail changing the way quotas are determined and/or readjusting the relative significance given to quotas and to basic votes in the allocation of total votes among member countries. In addition, the use of special majorities for deciding major issues might be reconsidered. Each of these possible reforms requires some elaboration.

According to the IMF's Articles of Agreement each member country has 250 votes plus one additional vote for each part of its quota that is equivalent to 100,000 SDRs. At intervals of not more than five years IMF members conduct a general review to determine whether an adjustment of quotas is needed, and at any time consideration may be given to the adjustment of any single member's quota at its request. If ratified, the 1983 eighth quota increase will result in a minor increase in the percentage share of votes for all OECD countries taken as a group (from 59.59 to 60.52 percent) and an equivalent minor decline for all LDC and other member countries. The 1983 quota increase will also result in some modest shifting of relative weights among OECD and among LDC countries. For example, the shares of the United States and United Kingdom will decline slightly, and those of West Germany, France, and Japan will increase a bit.

In commenting on this most recent quota review, the Group of 24 (the LDC coalition within the IMF) argued that it is past time to reexamine formulas used in determining quotas—specifically the economic criteria and the weights attached to them in the quota formulas.[42] The Group of 24 also urged that the basic votes, which have remained unaltered since the inception of the IMF, should be raised so that the share of basic votes in total votes will return to something approaching the original proportion. In other words, formal provision ought to be made to protect the proportion of basic votes to total votes even as the quotas increase and shift among countries over time. Both points would seem to have considerable validity. There are reasonable, fairly technical, arguments for adjusting the measurement of variables that enter the quota formulas and for altering other procedures that bear on the determination of each member's quota. Furthermore, as a result of successive quota increases since the late 1950s, the share of basic votes in total votes has steadily declined from 15.6 percent (1958) to 9.3 percent (1971) and 8.2 percent (1980) and will decline further if the

1983 quota increase is implemented. If the proposals of the Group of 24 were adopted, the quota share of developing countries could increase from its present level of 32 percent to something in the order of 45 percent.

The second issue concerning the voting arrangement in the IMF that deserves attention—the use of special majorities—is less frequently discussed but no less important. Indeed, a fact that most LDC spokesmen have failed to recognize is that, as part of the agreement on the second amendment to the Articles of Agreement of the IMF (authorizing a shift from fixed to flexible exchange rates), the number of issues on which special high majorities are required was increased, and this means that the power to veto a decision on an increased number of important issues is now held not only by the United States but also by LDCs as well as by the countries of the European Community when either group of countries votes as a bloc. This step is an important one in better satisfying groups of countries that their legitimate interests are being safeguarded. As the IMF's leading legal authority, Joseph Gold, has noted,

The effect of the requirement of special majorities combined with the efforts of established groups of members to adopt common positions on important issues is to moderate the influence of weighted voting power and to approximate the effect of a rule of unanimity in the resolution of these issues. This phenomenon gives formal recognition to the informal policy of taking decisions by consensus or by broad consent. It is the result in part of the wider distribution of economic and financial strength among the members of the Fund or groups of them than in the earlier years of the organization, the increased number of developing members, and the coordinated approach of developing members in international negotiations.[43]

If, however, the IMF is to play the role it should play at the center of the monetary system, it would seem a desirable innovation—and one that would both strengthen the position of the Managing Director and limit the blocking power of high-quota countries—if certain kinds of decisions required lower, not higher, majorities when proposed or endorsed by the Managing Director. This would seem particularly appropriate for decisions that bear on all the member countries' economies as well as the general health of the global economy—for example, decisions concerning the allocation or cancellation of SDRs that bear on the adequacy of global liquidity and the overall composition of reserves. The effect would be to reduce the use of the veto power, but that power would remain widely shared for issues left to be decided by large majorities.

The allocation of votes among member countries of the World Bank resembles in general the procedure used in the IMF. Member countries receive 250 basic votes plus one additional vote for each share of stock held. Clearly, this has meant that donors have the controlling share of votes. Indeed, as with IMF quota increases, successive capital increases to the World Bank have decreased the proportion of basic votes in the total votes of member countries. It would seem to be as appropriate in the World Bank as in the IMF to correct this decline. Moreover, since the World Bank, unlike the IMF, is a development institution, and since therefore developing countries are the ones predominantly affected by its operations, it would seem appropriate to ensure LDCs an even more equal share of votes in this second Bretton Woods institution.

As of mid-1982, the United States controlled 20.6 percent of the votes in the World Bank and 18.9 percent in the IDA. The advanced industrial countries, taken as a group, controlled over 60 percent of the votes in each institution. In the late 1970s there was much discussion of giving a greater voice to the surplus-oil-exporting countries commensurate with their growing contributions to development financing. But giving more voice to new donors does not address today's issue, which is whether and how to increase the voice of recipient countries. Rather, that calls for changing the way votes are weighted so that somewhat less emphasis is placed on a country's contribution to the institution and somewhat more emphasis placed on a country's dependence on the institution. There are various ways this could be done. The simplest and most straightforward way, suggested nearly a decade ago, would be to increase each member country's number of base votes, say, by one per million people in its population.[44] Although this would not be a wholly accurate way of achieving a better balance between developed and developing or between donor and recipient countries, it seems that some variant of this proposal (involving perhaps a somewhat more complex formula that would put a reasonable limit on the advantages that this arrangement would afford very populous countries such as India and, particularly, China) would be a reasonably good way of moving into better balance.

This change, coupled with larger capital contributions by some oil-exporting developing states, could reduce the developed countries' shares to close to 50 percent. Since the United States, which now has over 20 percent of the votes and therefore the power to veto, would likely see its share fall below that percentage, it might prove necessary to increase the number of issues requiring special, high majority votes in the World Bank, as was done in the IMF. This would allow the United States to retain a veto power on some issues, but, as in the IMF, it could also give the European Community and the developing countries a veto on the same set of issues. There might, however, be some risk that a redistribution in the relative voting power of developed countries would lead traditional donors to reduce their contributions to the World Bank or that the bank's bonds would become less attractive to the market and as a result the bank would have less money to lend. There are more gradual changes that would result in a less dramatic redistribution of voting power; for example, votes might be weighted differently for different kinds of decisions, perhaps giving borrowers considerably more voice than they have now in decisions regarding World Bank lending policies and practices but retaining control for creditor countries in decisions concerning the capitalization of the bank and regulations governing its borrowing. In principle, however, the simpler and more radical change seems the more desirable one for a universal, multilateral organization.

Although much of the discussion to date on representation and voice has focused on this issue of voting arrangements in the World Bank and the IMF, there are other (nonvoting) procedures by which inter-national economic decision making is now controlled by the developed countries that might also be changed. One step (which has been em-phasized throughout this chapter) would be to bring more issues, or more of the consultation on issues that now occurs in other limited-group settings (such as the OECD, summits, and G-5 meetings), under the aegis of the key global agencies. Although this change alone would not be directly responsive to the LDCs' demand for greater voice, to-gether with other changes in decision-making procedures it would be a key step in giving greater meaning to the process of collective man-agement, especially if, as part of this change, the executive heads of the global organizations were encouraged to play more of a role in consultations and decision making as the neutral arbiters or represen-tatives of the global interest. Thus, it would be desirable for consultations among key currency countries to take place within the IMF with the participation of the Managing Director, for a multilateral development assistance review committee to be established and associated with the World Bank, and for discussions of industrial policy and structural change to be a more regular feature of a global trade organization.

In bringing more issues into the global institutions, there would also have to be a greater involvement of officials from capitals on a regular basis—since for the most part the kinds of issues one is talking about are not those that can be the responsibility of the country representatives on executive boards concerned necessarily with the day-to-day operations of the institutions they govern but rather involve broader issues that are the business of national policy makers and for which the global institutions, with expert staff, can provide important forums.

Still another step that should be taken is to alter staffing patterns in the key institutions. Although there has been an increase of personnel from developing countries, the developing world is still underrepresented at the upper echelons of management. It would make no sense to destroy the World Bank or the IMF by imposing on it the kind of member-country personnel quota system that now cripples the United Nations. Nonetheless there ought to be more LDC nationals in senior positions. The desirability of these changes has been recognized for some time. They have become more important with the passage of time, and they are necessary if the World Bank and the IMF are to play the roles envisaged for them.

One related way of introducing more flexibility into the economic institutions would be to have more fixed-term appointments. At present only the Managing Director and the Deputy Managing Director of the IMF and the president of the World Bank have limited (five-year renewable) terms. Perhaps the same arrangement should apply to a few other key staff members. A system providing for some rotation between the institutions' staffs and national governments would seem to offer the advantage of injecting a more systemic view into thinking at the level of national governments and more political sensitivity into the international organizations. This might also be one way of bringing in high-quality people from LDCs without permanently draining talent away from national posts. (Though this change seems particularly important for the staffing patterns of the World Bank, the IMF, and the GATT, it probably ought also to be applied to the UN Secretariat.)

Finally, it seems worth asking whether steps can and should be taken that would produce some delinking between decision-making power and both provision of and (at least in the case of the IMF) access to resources. Again, there are some overlapping aspects of this issue as regards the IMF and the World Bank, but there are significant differences to warrant separate discussion of the issue as it relates to each institution.

One of the reasons that discussion of change in the voting structures is so difficult in the IMF is that the quota shares that largely determine voting shares also serve several other purposes: to set members' contributions to the fund, their access to the fund's resources, and their shares of SDR allocations. Increasingly it would seem desirable to delink quotas from this multiplicity of purposes and thereby break the automatic connection that now exists among votes, contributions, and drawing rights. Already some of the links with quotas have been stretched and modified. For example, for certain drawings from the Witteveen (Supplementary Financing) Facility there was no mandatory connection with quotas, and as a result of a decision in 1981 for countries' "facing serious payments imbalances that are large in relation to their quotas" total purchases can exceed 450 percent of quota in any three successive years. But these remain quite delimited changes; more radical rethinking is needed in the way IMF resources are used.

In the area of development finance, the question that now receives much attention is whether new, "automatic" sources of funding could be devised—such as certain forms of international taxation—that would allow for some delinking of a country's ability to provide international finance and its degree of control over the transfer of funds and the operations of resource transfer institutions.

Today's system of development finance is characterized largely by donor discretion in each of three regards: who determines the magnitude of resource transfers from rich to poor countries, where (as between a resource-transfer agency and a recipient country) responsibility lies for determining how aid resources should be used, and how decisions are made in the international agencies. The effort to set an internationally agreed-upon target of 0.7 percent of GNP has not done much to make aid appropriations less discretionary, especially since the target has never been accepted by the world's largest economic power. It is also the case today that donor countries exercise considerable leverage over how aid is used within recipient countries. According to donors, they have a legitimate interest in maximizing the effectiveness of their aid and they must have assurances that assistance will be used effectively if they are to satisfy their publics that appropriated resources are being used well. A decade ago the reaction of aid-receiving countries to the too-interventionist character of aid was to urge that more assistance be channeled through multilateral agencies. However, as recipients have argued with increasing force, the multilateral agencies that handle the bulk of international assistance are themselves too controlled by a few donor countries. This set of circumstances has now led to calls for new ways of mobilizing resources for development that would not be dependent on periodic decisions by national governments and whose distribution would therefore not be subject to their control.

In a highly integrated world with broad consensus on both the goals of economic cooperation and the distribution of rights and obligations among states, this would be an attractive idea. But an international resource-transfer system that would operate wholly automatically—in the sense of raising funds by nonappropriated means and distributing them on some formula basis—is beyond the bounds of political feasibility today or in any future period of time worth planning for. Indeed, this idea would seem to assume a set of international agencies with more supranational authority than either developing countries or developed countries are prepared to accept today. Perhaps a modest move in this direction might be taken in support of a program to meet very basic needs and as a way to strengthen today's incipient sense of global community. Other than that, what would seem more worthy of the attention of government officials would be other sorts of reforms that would transform today's highly discretionary resource-transfer system into one that would give recipients a greater voice in the international resource-transfer institutions and that put the resource-transfer process more firmly on a basis of agreed-upon criteria and standards—a transformation toward which the reforms already proposed in World Bank procedures and governance are aimed.

Conclusion

The ideas for institutional reform presented here are, for the most part, not ideas that will help to deal with today's most pressing problems, but they could improve the way countries deal cooperatively with problems over time. They are meant to be both responsive to the key issues in the North-South dialogue and suggestive of more useful ways of thinking about organizing international economic cooperation.

This chapter argues for giving much more attention in North-South discussions to streamlining and strengthening global-level economic institutions; vesting principal weight for the organization of global economic cooperation in a few key specialized agencies that operate on the basis of weighted, representational voting; making changes within those institutions in the weighting of votes and in other decision-making procedures to give recognition to the idea that dependence on the system as well as the ability to affect the system ought to be a factor in decision making and management and, thus to give developing countries a greater voice; and involving national policy makers more closely in consultations within these institutions while at the same time strengthening the role of the international staffs so that full account is taken of the interests of all affected parties and of the requirements of the world economic system as a whole. The central UN organization ought not to be empowered to exercise "control" over the operations of the specialized agencies, but it should play a more effective role as the universal forum, as a global monitoring organ, and as an embodiment of what Stanley Hoffman once referred to as the "flickerings of 'universal consciousness.'"

Acknowledgment

This chapter draws heavily on the book *Collective Management: The Reform of Global Economic Organizations* (New York: McGraw-Hill, 1981), which was designed and largely written by Miriam Camps with contributions by me, particularly on certain chapters. I accept full responsibility, however, for the way in which ideas, themes, and specific recommendations from that volume are presented herein.

Notes

1. This same point is made in a recent report by Commonwealth Group of Experts, "The North-South Dialogue: Making it Work" (London: Commonwealth Secretariat, 1982), p. 28: "Basically a struggle has been taking place between two different concepts of international negotiations. The South favours a universal, multilateral system of public negotiation which gives due recognition to the weight of numbers. It wants comprehensive negotiations dealing with packages of issues and giving full weight to the linkages between them. It believes that needs, equality and redistributive justice, rather than power, should be the criteria adopted. The North, on the other hand, favours traditional bilateral forms of negotiations or those involving limited participation, and views multilateral diplomacy in the North-South context sceptically, both on technical and political grounds. It prefers negotiations which are specific and issue-oriented. It believes that economic power and responsibility for the implementation of decisions must be fully reflected in the negotiations, and it has been stressing technical soundness in considering proposals. In this situation, neither side is able to prevail entirely and the outcome is a compromise which attempts to fit together bits of each approach in a way which reflects political realities more than rational consistency. The North-South dialogue is largely about what the precise nature of this compromise should be."

2. Karl P. Sauvant, "Organizational Infrastructure for Self-Reliance: The Non-Aligned Countries and the Group of 77" (paper presented at the conference

on International Institutions and Evolving Development Strategies, Rio de Janiero, August 1982), p. 19. On the Group of 77, see also Robert A. Mortimer, *The Third World Coalition in World Politics* (New York: Praeger, 1980), and Robert L. Rothstein, *Global Bargaining* (Princeton: Princeton University Press, 1979).

3. Robert L. Rothstein, "Commodity Bargaining: The Political Economy of Regime Creation" (unpublished manuscript, June 1982), p. 21. This point is confirmed by Jahangir Amuzegar in an article describing the failure of CIEC. As Amuzegar writes, "The strategy of the Group of 19 was to hammer out a whole 'package' of agreements, and not to accept the other side's separate or incremental offers. Since the interests of the Group varied, and the possibility of a split in ranks was always present, they decided that unless they stood firm in getting something for everyone, they might end up getting nothing for anyone. A dominant thread running through the Group's thinking was the importance of solidarity at all costs. They were thus willing to trade off some partial short-run gains for a more comprehensive and lasting success." "Requiem for the North-South Conference," *Foreign Affairs* (October 1977):152.

4. Amuzegar, "Requiem."

5. Roger Hansen, *Beyond the North-South Stalemate* (New York: McGraw-Hill, 1979), p. 99.

6. Commonwealth Group of Experts, "North-South Dialogue," pp. 53–54.

7. Miriam Camps with the collaboration of Catherine Gwin, *Collective Management: The Reform of Global Economic Organizations* (New York: McGraw-Hill, 1981), pp. 56, 58.

8. Hansen, *Beyond the North-South Stalemate.*

9. Stephen Zamora, "Voting in International Economic Organizations," *American Journal of International Law* 74 (1980): 608.

10. Camps, *Collective Management*, p. 60.

11. See, for example, Brandt Commission 1983, *Common Crisis North-South: Cooperation for World Recovery* (London: Pan Books, 1983).

12. Although the original Brandt Commission report would have been far more impressive if it had tried to do just this, it took the far easier approach of proposing that consideration be given to the establishment of a new World Development Fund. Within the last year, however, both the Commonwealth Secretariat and the North-South Roundtable have begun efforts to review the Bretton Woods system.

13. See Camps, *Collective Management*, chap. 5.

14. Ibid., p. 146.

15. Ibid., p. 149.

16. See ibid., chap. 6.

17. Ibid., pp. 233–235: "Although the Second Amendment envisages the new surveillance functions as coming within the purview of the Council, it is difficult to see how the kind of intimate multilateral consultation on all the closely interrelated aspects of policy that affect the exchange rate could really occur in any body except one composed only of the representatives of those countries whose rates must be examined together. The language of the Second Amendment would seem to permit the Council to establish committees, and there would seem to be no insuperable impediment to its vesting this multilateral surveillance function in a Special Surveillance Committee, even though it is somewhat at variance with the rest of the structure of the Fund. . . . The role of the Managing Director of the Fund in this new surveillance and consultation process would be crucial: not only . . . should the Managing Director be specifically mandated to see that the discussions in the Special Surveillance Committee never lose sight of the larger needs of the system as a whole, but there must also be more acceptance of his right—and duty—to push the big countries to modify their policies than has been traditional, or deemed expedient, thus far in the Fund's history."

18. See, for example, Sidney Dell, "Stabilization: The Political Economy of Overkill," in *IMF Conditionality*, ed. John Williamson (Washington, D.C.: Institute for International Economics, 1983).

19. This point is made in Gerald K. Helleiner, "The IMF and Africa in the 1980s" (paper prepared for the African Studies Association Meeting, Washington, D.C., November 1982), pp. 14–15.

20. John Williamson, "The Lending Policies of the International Monetary Fund" (Washington, D.C., Institute for International Economics, August 1982), p. 19.

21. Ibid., p. 58.

22. Ariel Buira Seira, "Prospects for Private Financing and the Role of the Fund in the 1980s" (manuscript, November 30, 1982), p. 12.

23. This idea is put forward in Williamson, "Lending Policies," pp. 43–52.

24. Carlos Díaz-Alejandro, "International Financial and Goods Markets in 1982–83 and Beyond" (manuscript, March 1983).

25. Richard Cooper, cited by Williamson, "Lending Policies," p. 44.

26. Atlantic Council Working Group of the United Nations, *The Future of the UN: A Strategy for Like-Minded Nations* (Boulder, Colo.: Westview Press, 1977), p. xix.

27. Report by Ad Hoc Group on United States Policy toward the United Nations, "The United States and the United Nations: A Policy for Today" (October 1981), pp. 15, 17.

28. Quoted in "The UN: Keeping Alive a Withering Dream," *South*, no. 11 (October 1981): 7–11.

29. United Nations, "Report of the Secretary-General on the Work of the Organization" (New York: United Nations, 1982).

30. The one exception would be a UN basic support program that would be in concept an expanded and better funded "UNICEF plus UNDRO (United Nations Disaster Relief Organization)" and would take over the functions and formally supersede UNICEF, UNDRO, and the World Food Program. The specific functions of this proposed program would be to offer help in emergencies, to provide grants to poor countries in support of programs designed to provide basic goods and services to people in extreme need and to organize and oversee the carrying out of certain "global welfare tasks," such as an attack on starvation and acute malnutrition, which would be accepted as "obligations," by the world community and therefore funded at least in part by some form of international tax. The principal reason for making this program an operation of the central UN organization has to do with the nature of the obligation that ought to be felt to exist for underwriting the essential needs of all people. That obligation is a humanitarian one, one that runs not between states but between people. A program built on the recognition of that obligation would be appropriate to the UN and would perhaps contribute to a greater sense of global community than exists today. For a further description of this proposed program, see Camps, *Collective Management*. chap. 4.

31. United Nations, "A New United Nations Structure for Global Economic Cooperation," Report of the Group of Experts on the Structure of the United Nations System, E/AC 62/9 (May 1975).

32. United Nations, "Report of the Ad Hoc Committee on the Restructuring of the United Nations System," Official Records, Thirty-second Session, UNGA, Supplement No. 34 (A/32/34) (1978).

33. Commonwealth Group of Experts, "North-South Dialogue," pp. 44–45.

34. Camps, *Collective Management*, p. 338.

35. Zamora, "Voting," pp. 603–604.

36. Ibid., pp. 571–576.

37. Joseph Gold, "The Origins of Weighted Voting Power in the Fund," *Finance and Development* 18 (1981), no. 1: 26.

38. Ibid.

39. For a description of this trend, see Zamora, "Voting," pp. 600–601.

40. The term *universalism* is being used here to mean something different from universal membership. While the latter is to be encouraged, the former—i.e., equal participation of all member countries in the decision-making procedures of an organization, as distinct from constituency representation with weighted voting—cannot be applied to operational agencies intended to work effectively.

41. Zamora, "Voting," p. 601.

42. Group of Twenty-Four, communique, February 9, 1983 (mimeo), p. 3.

43. Joseph Gold, "Voting Majorities in the Fund: Effects of Second Amendment of the Article," IMF Pamphlet Series No. 20 (Washington, D.C., 1977).

44. See Escott Reid, *Strenghtening the World Bank* (Chicago: Adlai Stevenson Institute, 1973).

II   Debts, Finance, and Trade

8 Some Economic Lessons of the Early 1980s

Carlos F. Díaz-Alejandro

Preliminary data indicate that the magnitude of the external shock to LDCs during the early 1980s is comparable to that which those countries received during the early 1930s. Depending on the circumstances of each nation and the policies pursued, the external shock has had different effects on the growth and development of various LDCs, as during the 1930s. This chapter focuses on selected characteristics of the international monetary and financial systems and their vulnerability to events such as those experienced during the last few years. The basic viewpoint is that a major lesson of the early 1980s is simply a variation on that of the 1930s: Deep and prolonged slumps, especially if accompanied by protectionist pressures in industrialized countries, are incompatible with international financial markets of tolerable efficacy and threaten international monetary cooperation and stability. This viewpoint does not deny that there are important microeconomic imperfections in international financial markets, even during favorable stages in the business cycle; it simply suggests that those imperfections are quantitatively less important and also less tractable to international reform, under foreseeable circumstances, than the system's vulnerability to macroeconomic disturbances.

Liquidity, the LDCs, and Gold

At least under some plausible definitions, aggregate international reserves increased dramatically during the 1970s. Reserve composition was also drastically altered. Neither event was foreseen, much less planned, during the 1960s. The increase in the price of gold was the major cause for both events. By the late 1970s gold had become de facto the major international reserve asset, although its price fluctuations limited its classical reserve function.

During the 1960s the LDCs were encouraged, if not presssured, to hold reserve increases in the form of interest-earning, key-currency-denominated assets. The dollar was said to be not just as good as gold; because it could earn interest, it was said to be better. Choosing gold was regarded as an unfriendly act, and LDCs were lectured on the irrationality of gold holding. Three-fourths of the world reserve gold remained in the hands of the United States, the Federal Republic of Germany, France, Italy, Switzerland, the Netherlands, and Belgium, countries that registered massive (paper) profits as a result of gold-price increases. Brodsky and Sampson (1981) estimate those profits at more than $300 billion. Gains to LDCs from the gold-price increase, including those from the liquidation of IMF gold, are tiny next to that figure. The disadvantages of peripheral members of the international monetary system may be put another way: The inflation tax levied on LDC reserves by the unexpected dollar inflation of the late 1960s and the early 1970s was followed in the late 1970s and the early 1980s by a new surprise tax. Many LDCs, partly encouraged by the low ex post real dollar interest rates of the early 1970s, piled up debts that by the late 1970s exceeded their reserve dollar assets, making them vulnerable to the unexpectedly high real interest rates registered since 1979.

The instrument intended as the principal reserve asset of the international monetary system, the SDR, accounted for around 2 percent in the growth of international reserves during the 1970s, and the figure is unlikely to be much higher during the 1980s. Even without the "link," the LDCs would be better off today had the increase in international liquidity registered since the late 1960s taken the form of expanded SDR allocations. Ironically, the countries that benefited from the increase in gold prices during the 1970s now argue that further SDR allocations are not needed and would be inflationary. By the early 1980s nongold international reserves had fallen sharply relative to trade. IMF quotas have slipped way behind world trade and payments imbalances, reducing access to its low-conditionality facilities.

Tables 8.1 and 8.2 present the postwar evolution of international reserves of nonoil LDCs. Several points may be highlighted. During 1965–1967, before the increases in gold prices, the share of gold in nonoil LDC reserves fell. Table 8.1 also shows a rapid increase in reserves between 1965–1967 and 1972–1973, followed by remarkable fluctuations. Unless gold is valued at market prices, no persistent upward trend in real reserves can be detected after 1972–1973; the 1978–1979 peak is followed by steep declines. Table 8.2 shows that, even if gold

Table 8.1
International reserves of nonoil developing countries (billion U.S. dollars at 1975 prices; end-of-year figures and averages)

	A Total reserves minus gold	Total reserves		A as percentage of B	A as percentage of C
		B Gold valued at 35 SDRs per ounce	C Gold valued at market prices		
1952–1954	14.5	21.2	21.2	68.5	68.5
1955–1959	12.9	19.6	19.6	65.7	65.7
1960–1964	12.6	19.6	19.6	64.3	64.3
1965–1967	18.0	24.9	24.9	72.2	72.2
1968–1971	27.1	36.1	37.0	75.2	73.4
1972–1973	50.9	58.7	65.8	86.6	77.3
1974	39.2	44.4	58.5	88.3	67.0
1975	33.5	37.8	51.2	88.5	65.4
1976	45.5	49.7	58.4	91.6	78.0
1977	56.0	60.5	71.6	92.6	78.3
1978	64.8	69.3	83.8	93.5	77.3
1979	61.7	65.6	87.6	94.1	70.5
1980	51.0	54.2	94.6	94.1	53.9
1981	47.9	50.7	79.5	94.5	60.2
1982	46.9	49.6	72.9	94.6	64.4

Note: Basic data were obtained from IMF 1983. Nominal magnitudes were deflated by import unit values for non-oil-exporting developing countries for 1954–1981; export unit values of industrial countries were used for 1952 and 1953. Gold market prices refer to the London price, given in line 76 kr of IMF 1983. The exchange rate between the U.S. dollar and SDRs was obtained from the U.S. pages in IMF 1983.

Table 8.2
Nonoil developing countries: reserves as percentages of imports

	Reserves minus gold	Reserves with gold at 35 SDRs per ounce	Reserves with gold at market prices
1952–1954	26.2	38.2	38.2
1955–1959	20.0	30.4	30.4
1960–1964	15.9	24.8	24.8
1965–1967	19.1	26.4	24.4
1968–1971	21.6	28.9	29.7
1972–1973	33.1	38.3	42.8
1974	22.2	25.2	33.2
1975	19.6	22.2	30.0
1976	25.6	27.9	32.8
1977	29.3	31.6	37.4
1978	31.4	33.6	40.6
1979	28.1	29.9	39.9
1980	21.7	23.0	40.2
1981	19.4	20.6	32.3
1982	20.5	21.7	31.9

Note: End-of-the-year reserves have been compared with merchandise imports during that year. Basic data as in table 8.1.

is valued at market prices, reserves expressed as a percentage of imports never recovered their 1972–1973 peak; by the early 1980s nonoil LDC reserves expressed as percentages of their imports were, depending on gold valuation, either near or below postwar lows. If to these figures one adds that rescheduling discussions during 1982–1983 have brought to light the illiquid nature of some assets included in the reserves of some non-oil-exporting LDCs, it would appear that additional SDR allocations to these countries are likely to be devoted to an important extent to the rebuilding of depleted international reserves.

International Monetary Fund and Other Lenders of Last Resort

Those who launched the IMF in 1944 expected a world with adjustable but mostly fixed rates, a low degree of international private capital mobility, and exchange controls. An influential report of those days, reviewing the experiences of the 1920s and 1930s, put it this way: "The only effective answer to any serious capital flight proved to be the imposition of exchange control. . . . after the experience of the 1930s, it is most unlikely that any government will ever again allow complete freedom to private individuals to menace the economic stability of their [and other] countries and to sabotage their economic policies by sending their money abroad" (Arndt 1944, p. 286). The IMF's articles of agreement specifically prohibited use of the fund's resources to finance capital flight and imposed no obligation to liberalize capital transactions. The IMF was to be a club of members wishing to insure each other against unexpected shocks that could not be handled by commercial borrowing or exchange controls.

Is the IMF really necessary in a world of floating rates, in which private finance seems plentiful to creditworthy countries and exchange controls are viewed with horror by predominant economic opinion? Before 1944, after all, there were some periods of tranquil international prosperity without an IMF.

Many small countries (not all LDCs) prefer to maintain parities pegged to key currencies or baskets of them for good optimum-currency area reasons. Even authorities in charge of key currencies have not foresworn intervening in exchange markets. In other words, exchange rates will not bear the full burden of adjusting to shocks to the balance of payments in the foreseeable future. In spite of other adjustment policies, there will remain deficits and surpluses generating financial transactions. Microeconomic and macroeconomic considerations suggest that purely private financial markets may not be optimal for handling deficits and surpluses; informational and organizational flaws may lead to circumstances where the required finance will not be forthcoming at a reasonable cost when it is most needed. Countries could be pushed into emergency adjustment measures that have substantial externalities and are less than optimal from both national and international viewpoints. This is why, leaving aside advocates of a return to the gold standard, immediate world revolution, or free banking, there is widespread agreement that a desirable international monetary and financial system should have at its center something like an IMF to act as a lender of last resort to national central banks, in a manner partly similar to and partly different from the manner in which those central banks act with respect to their commercial banking and financial systems. This systemic consideration also explains why LDCs, which are harsh critics of the IMF, also advocate a large increase in its quotas. Much of the 1944 case for some kind of IMF remains, and the circumstances of 1981–1983 have underlined the importance of truly multilateral financial institutions.

Neither at the national nor at the international level is there a robust theory of a lender of last resort; we have instead history and ad hoc judgments (see Solow 1982). First, note the differences between the IMF and central banks. In most countries the latter have a good deal of power over their national financial institutions, even when located abroad, while the IMF must generally wait until central banks come to it before it can influence their policies. National central banks, however, have tighter limits on their ability to print internationally acceptable money than the IMF has. It appears plausible to argue that whoever acts as international lender of last resort should have enough of those funds that are likely to be demanded during a crisis to make its reassurances credible. It should also be on speaking terms with potential customers for funds and with those providing its financial muscle. It must be able to move very quickly during emergencies. Since at least the first oil shock, there have been doubts, on all counts, whether the IMF is really up to the role of an international lender of last resort (ILLR). Its lending potential has not kept up with possible balance-of-payments deficits, and its authority has been eroded by proposals for ad hoc "safety nets." Its long estrangement from many LDCs, including key ones such as Brazil, has not been fully overcome. Its rules call for time-consuming negotiations and procedures.

During 1979–1980 the IMF seemed on the way toward enlarging its lending capacity and adopting more flexible lending conditions, culminating in a large loan to India. This trend was suddenly stopped during 1981, under pressure from the new U.S. administration. Events during 1982 have persuaded at least some skeptics of the wisdom of the 1979–1980 initiatives, although it remains to be seen how forcefully those initiatives will be pursued. The crucial issues remain both a major increase in the IMF financial resources and a substantial improvement in its lending practices.

John Williamson (1982) has provided a helpful survey of crucial points in this area. His discussion can be criticized as minimizing past IMF inflexibility in dealing with LDCs, especially in the Western Hemisphere, and as exaggerating the theoretical (in contrast with the practical) grounds for advocating the use of credit ceilings in stabilization plans. However, his estimates indicating the need to raise IMF resources to at least SDR 100 billion (from SDR 61 billion) and most of his suggestions on how to liberalize IMF lending practices are persuasive. Williamson's characterization of the IMF theoretical position as eclectic and his conclusion that criticisms of the IMF are largely misplaced will be tested by how that institution reacts to his proposals over the next few years. The standbys negotiated during the second half of 1982 and early 1983 do not appear to have taken Williamson's recommendations to heart; indeed, the targets set in some of those agreements (such as that with Brazil) do not seem credible to many observers unless sharp recessions are induced.

Few would deny that the IMF, or any ILLR, should attach some form of economic conditionality on its loans. (See Dell 1981 for a masterful review of the evolution of conditionality.) The lack of consensus on macroeconomics, not just among academics but also among IMF patrons (contrast macroeconomic policy in France and the United States), strengthens the case for IMF conditionality focused narrowly on balance-of-payments targets. It is true that observed performance in the balance of payments is the result of both domestic policies and factors beyond the country's control. Yet a number of indicators, such as staple prices and market shares, could be used to evaluate performance and failure to meet agreed targets. The compensatory facilities of the IMF have accumulated experience in this area.

It is the business of the IMF to insist on balance-of-payments targets consistent with the repayment of its short-term loans, to monitor closely performance in this area, and to suspend its credit (either subsidized or cheap relative to alternatives) to countries that do not repay promptly without a good reason, such as unexpected exogenous shocks. It is not the business of the IMF to make loans conditional on policies whose connection to the balance of payments in the short or even the medium run is tenuous, such as food subsidies, utility rates, controls over foreign corporations, or whether the banking system is public or private. It was a brilliant administrative stroke for the IMF staff to develop the "monetary approach to the balance of payments" during the 1950s, allowing the translation of balance-of-payments targets into those involving domestic credit, but for many LDCs the assumptions needed to validate such translation, such as a stable demand for money, have become less and less convincing.

Focusing on balance-of-payments targets would keep the IMF away from the more political aspects of short-run macroeconomic policy making. Countries could, of course, actively solicit IMF advice on those aspects, and under those circumstances the IMF staff could give full expression to its views on inflation control, optimal trade regulations, food subsidies, and so forth. A clear balance-of-payments focus would eliminate incongruities such as an IMF conditionality that benignly overlooks serious distortions in the South African labor market while sternly insisting on higher food and gasoline prices elsewhere.

Balance-of-payments flow targets will be naturally intertwined with estimates of the stock of a country's foreign debt. A country asking the IMF for a loan will have to discuss its other outstanding loans, if for no other reason than to clarify priorities in debt servicing. IMF conditionality thus inevitably involves this institution in discussions about debt limits and servicing, including rescheduling exercises. In principle all of this could be handled so as to reduce uncertainty and informational flaws so that both private lenders and borrowing countries, as well as innocent bystanders, could on balance gain relative to a laissez-faire counterfactual. As noted, a lack of resources and overly intrusive notions of conditionality have kept the IMF from fully playing that constructive role. Until there are clear indications that a "new" IMF has come into being, some countries may continue to handle their debt, and possible debt reschedulings, on their own. To make even a new IMF a kind of central committee of an international credit cartel would under normal circumstances be a remedy worse than the disease, at least from the viewpoint of many borrowing countries.

Difficulties servicing the Mexican and Brazilian external debts during 1982 showed that not even the Reagan administration expects financial crises and potential bank failures to be handled by the magic of the marketplace. As noted by the Managing Director of the IMF, in a commendable brief period the central banks, the Bank for International Settlements (BIS), the U.S. Federal Reserve Bank and Treasury, the commercial banks, and the IMF acted in full cooperation. Similarly, the government of the Federal Republic of Germany appears to have had an influence in containing the impact on German banks of Polish difficulties with punctual debt servicing.

A practical lesson of the second half of 1982 may turn out to be that, under present political and economic conditions, the real ILLR is the U.S. government, whose treasury and Federal Reserve can mobilize vast sums of dollars with more secrecy and speed than the IMF or even the BIS. The mechanisms available to the U.S. executive for these purposes are plentiful and free from ex ante congressional checks. Big and politically centralized LDCs, such as Brazil and Mexico, may even prefer in a crisis to deal directly with the U.S. government. IMF blessings to bilateral deals may or may not come ex post. One may conjecture that big borrowers will trade off foreign-policy autonomy (for example, by lessening their opposition to U.S. policies in Central America and in GATT) for more resources and somewhat more lenient economic conditions.

Strengthening Built-in Defenses against International Slumps

Commendable as the learning curve of the Reagan administration appears since August-September 1982, there is a need to look beyond crisis management and be aware of dangerous side effects of the emergency medication dispensed since then. Economists and practitioners, even when sharing similar ideologies, historically have differed in their views on desirable mechanisms for carrying out and underpinning long-term international lending. For most likely scenarios covering the next couple of decades, an international financial system having both strong and truly multilateral governmental institutions, such as reformed IFM and the World Bank, as well as a competitive private sector with a variety of financial intermediaries, seems both possible and desirable. The public institutions should remedy the most salient imperfections in international financial markets, including the "rationing out" of most LDCs (especially the poorest and riskiest), from private lending. A vigorous and competitive private sector would save the many good features of the international financial system of the 1970s.

Crises encourage cartelization, and there have been ominous signs pointing in this direction during 1982–1983. We have a brand new International Banking Institute. Special committees made up of major lenders are "advising" countries on how to reschedule their debts, in some cases even writing draft telexes for ministers of finance. The Managing Director of the IMF is telling banks how much each should expand its net credits to which country and when. The Federal Reserve Board has been twisting the arms of U.S. regional banks. Much of this seems necessary to handle the emergency, and it is even imaginative and innovative. But it is also threatening to destroy the flexibility and competitiveness displayed by international lending during the 1970s. The politicization of international lending, not surprisingly, has also been encouraged by the crisis. It is not only within the U.S. Congress that questions are asked as to why, at a time of general distress, emergency attention is channeled toward selected countries and institutions. In the Third World, countries such as Colombia wonder whether what they perceive as their virtuous adjustment policies and modest growth targets are not keeping them from access to subsidized external funds. There is also a visible tendency toward spheres of influence—the United States is supposed to look after Mexico, Japan after South Korea, and Western Europe after Poland and Zaire. Umbrellas decorated with national flags will naturally be held only over special borrowing and lending friends, and at a political price. More than one developing country having difficulties servicing its debt is being advised from abroad that perhaps it should reconsider its regulations over transnational enterprises, international banks, and inflowing direct investment. Discriminatory trading arrangements could result from financial spheres of influence.

Cartelization and politicization, reminiscent of the 1930s, may be partly arrested by repairing and expanding international defenses against slumps and by encouraging a swift recovery from the present one. Beyond the already agreed-upon modest expansion of IMF quotas, it seems desirable to revive old ideas for turning the IMF's Compensatory Financing Facility (CFF) into a sturdy international first line of defense against depressions and, in some ways, into the international equivalent to those domestic programs in the North that are designed to stabilize the income of farmers and provide safety nets to other debtors. The basic notion behind the CFF—stabilizing the purchasing power of LDC export earnings without commodity price fixing—has received widespread support for many years. A reinvigorated CFF facility could be focused on expected real export earnings, rather than on nominal magnitudes as at present. The facility should cover all exports—manufactures, services, and primary commodities. Expected medium-term real export trends would be worked out jointly by the CFF staff and the authorities of each country, refining present practice while relying on accumulated expertise. Shortfalls from expectations could be fully, automatically, and speedily covered by SDR credits, which would also be quickly repaid when real export earnings surpassed expectations. Credits to cover shortfalls could charge standard SDR interest rates or embody an interest-subsidy element for the poorest LDCs. In obtaining estimates of the capacity to import, the import-price deflator could be broadened to include not just the prices of merchandise imports and of nonfinancial services but also the price of servicing loans (interest rates and fees charged to LDCs).

If "full and automatic" coverage of shortfalls is found too permissive and vulnerable to moral-hazard imperfections, less than 100 percent insurance could be provided and some low conditionality could be required; however, credits should go substantially beyond the present quota-limited ceilings. The expanded CFF should be expected to break even over the business cycle, inclusive of whatever concessional funds it receives to subsidize interest rates to the poorest nations. Eventually an expanded CFF could be merged with the Stabex scheme, strengthening the multilateral character of both institutions. The expanded CFF could remain within the IMF or be transformed into an autonomous body. The latter option has the advantage that the autonomous CFF, with its clear guidelines and reasonably objective criteria, could move more quickly and forcefully into medium-term countercyclical finance without impinging on the more traditional short-term, revolving-fund preoccupations of other IMF lending, which would be expected to maintain stricter conditionality than the CFF. Indeed, the advantage of expanding the CFF over less-specific proposals to increase the IMF's lending capacity and to give conditionality countercyclical flexibility lies in the clearer and more automatic rules of an expanded CFF. An important task for the CFF staff will remain the analytical separation of those export shortfalls that are due to unexpected external and internal shocks and those that are a consequence of misguided domestic policies. CFF funds would be expected to handle only the former type of shortfalls. Another tricky task, hardly unknown to present CFF staff, is the sorting out of cycles and trends in the international economy—for example, how much are the troubles of the early 1980s due to cycle and how much to the beginnings of a less vigorous growth trend?

The purpose of an expanded CFF would not be to stabilize the international price level or to bring to IMF closer to becoming a world central bank. Those possible longer-term goals should be kept distinct from the automatic-stabilizer character of an expanded CFF. The proposed scheme, however, would be facilitated by the simplification of IMF procedures proposed by Polak (1979), which would consolidate its general account and its SDR account. Under that scheme the IMF's lending capacity would be limited only by the willingness of member countries to accept SDRs in payment for their goods and services. As Cooper (1983) has noted, that limit is unlikely to be binding during world recessions.

An expanded CFF could yield better-functioning private international markets for both commodities and finance, reducing extreme risks arising from depressed circumstances such as those of 1929–1932 and 1979–1982 as well as from inflationary booms. It would rely on fairly objective criteria and would cover all the LDC membership of the IMF rather than just the super-borrowers. It would reduce the need for emergency rescues, thus offsetting trends toward the politicization and cartelization of international financial markets. If the recovery from the recent major recession turns out to be very sluggish, an expanded CFF could be started by an emergency SDR issue to cover ex post the export shortfalls of 1981–1982—a formula that would benefit both Brazil and Colombia and may be worked out with a minimum of political haggling.

In making projections of LDCs' real export earnings, an expanded CFF will have to take into account not only expected growth rates in the major industrialized economies but also their commercial policies affecting their imports from LDCs. Ongoing, quantitative, and publicized studies of how protectionist policies in the North harm Southern export earnings should be carried out regularly by joint committees made up of the staffs of the CFF-IMF, GATT, and UNCTAD. Authoritative international estimates of the impact of old and fresh Northern protectionist measures on the South's capacity to service its external debt could have a sobering and restraining influence on legislators and could be helpful information in debt-rescheduling exercises. These studies need not wait for an expanded CFF and could be rapidly started with the research already available in the three institutions. The joint committees could also be extended to explore ways in which gradual Southern import liberalization could be financially supported by the international community. The joint committees could become, if not the core of, at least important predecessors to a global (not just OECD) body coordinating trade, financial, industrial, and macroeconomic national policies.

The 1981–1982 international depression has exposed, one more time, the clumsiness of existing debt-restructuring mechanisms. For many LDCs debt rescheduling is a necessary first step in recovering from a recession, and the question may be raised whether those mechanisms could be improved and whether an expanded CFF would eliminate the need for such an improvement. First of all, historically moratoriums and reschedulings have been mechanisms to deal ex post with unexpected shocks in the international economy; although clumsy, they involve a more sensible attitude toward risk sharing between lenders and borrowers than that found in the letter of most loan and bond contracts. Within national economies having bankruptcy laws, it is not always in the interest of lenders to foreclose on a debtor; one frequently sees creditors voluntarily rescheduling and even expanding loans to promising firms having temporary liquidity troubles. Similarly, in international lending many reschedulings could be Pareto optimal after unexpected innovations have occurred and are clearly perceived by all agents. Sanctimonious remarks pointing out that LDCs could maintain punctual debt servicing if only they would tighten their belts and show proper respect for the sanctity of contracts are quite beside the point, and such rhetoric seems peculiar on economists' lips. Most LDCs could meet 1983 debt-service commitments, as written down some years back, at a cost. The interesting question is whether this behavior would be rational in the light of widely available new information as well as well-known alternative arrangements. A rational lender concerned with his long-term stake in the Brazilian economy would be unlikely to insist on the strict observation of past debt-service commitments if in the process Brazilian growth prospects were to be seriously damaged. How the gains from recontracting are shared between borrowers and lenders will depend on the specific characteristics of the renegotiations. Also, lenders seek in reschedulings reassurances not only from troubled borrowers but also from other lenders, who they fear may be paid more promptly or who may squeeze better conditions from hapless borrowers, thus jeopardizing other lenders' chances of repayments. In other words, reschedulings do (badly) at the international level what federal bankruptcy courts do more efficiently in the United States. Poor rescheduling mechanisms at the international level increase the probability that debtors will attempt unilateral rescheduling programs.

Even as U.S. farm-support programs have not eliminated rural bankruptcies, an expanded CFF cannot be expected to eliminate all debt reschedulings; indeed, that is unlikely to be a desirable policy goal. With an expanded CFF in place, one would be tempted to adopt a laissez-faire position toward rescheduling conditions and terms, perhaps only suggesting some improvements in the awkward existing arrangements for debt restructuring (hardly a novel idea; see Pearson et al. 1969, p. 157). In 1983 that position is harder to justify, as there are alarming reports about some of the "first round" rescheduling negotiations of late 1982 and early 1983. The alarm is due partly to reported fees and spreads, which are justified on grounds of greater risk but could also be the fruit of cartelization. Creditor governments, banks, and the IMF are also said to be moving back to a "short leash" approach where only amortizations coming due within a year or so are rescheduled (see Garten 1982, pp. 285–286). Perhaps most disturbing are the reported attempts to force some borrowing countries to ex post guarantee external debts of purely private borrowers when both lenders and borrowers were told at the time when the transactions were made that they were on their own. Banks are reported to have threatened to curtail short-term commercial credits if such bailouts are not carried out. The IMF, while taking a more activist stance in the rescheduling process, apparently has ignored such pressure tactics, and has not visibly intervened in the determination of spreads and rescheduling fees. Higher spreads and fees in reschedulings, which also involve new IMF stabilization plans, are hard to reconcile with the notion that past lending was made riskier by the absence of the IMF. Why is the combination of Delfim Netto and IMF monitoring perceived as riskier than Delfim Netto alone? What new information about the Brazilian economy could justify such an abrupt change in lending conditions? Evidence so far suggests that possible Pareto gains from 1982–1983 reschedulings have been unequally shared between banks and their debtors; the banks, in spite of their complaints about mental anguish, continue to register remarkable crisis-resistant earnings.

The World Bank and Other Multilateral Financial Intermediaries

As with the IMF, one may question whether the 1944 justifications for creating a World Bank remain valid for the 1980s. In what follows the role of the World Bank and of other multilateral lending agencies (such as the Inter-American and Asian development banks) as financial intermediaries will be separated from their role as dispensers of concessional finance or aid (as with IDA and other "soft" windows).

Why should the World Bank borrow in more or less open financial markets to lend to Colombia, which has had direct access to those markets on its own? Why would Colombia want to use the World Bank as an intermediary anyway? The answer must be sought again in the informational imperfections of capital markets, which can be reduced by multilateral banks, whose solvency is backed by financially powerful countries and who can exploit economies of scale in monitoring borrowers. Faced with rationing or steeply rising marginal borrowing costs, Colombia could welcome indirect borrowing channels, which might expand credit availability and reduce costs. Colombia's public-sector borrowing from the World Bank, in turn, will increase its creditworthiness among private lenders, both internationally and domestically. These considerations apply with greater force to LDCs whose direct access to international private credit markets is less fluid than that of Colombia. Although international capital markets revived since the

1960s beyond 1944 expectations, the World Bank still has the role assigned to it in Bretton Woods: to substitute partly for private international markets for long-term bonds, which collapsed in the 1930s. The 1982–1983 international financial crisis has done nothing to weaken this role. Even in industrialized countries with fairly well-developed credit markets, there are public institutions acting as financial intermediaries or guarantors to channel resources toward borrowers overlooked or neglected by purely private markets; examples include the Small Business Administration and student loans in the United States.

With an IMF devoted to short-term balance-of-payments financing and an expanded CFF stabilizing the capacity of LDCs to import, the World Bank and other multilateral financial intermediaries could focus on financing investment opportunities with high social rates of return which are not being banked by private sources. This type of lending need not involve much more than a minimalist banking "conditionality," assuring itself of the soundness of specific projects and of the broadly defined "collateral" offered by the borrowing country to demonstrate its willingness to repay loans.

An international financial system made up of private lenders plus multilateral agencies following the policies sketched above would still lack what may be called Alliance for Progress–type lending. Such lending covers general balance-of-payments support; that is, it is not linked to specific projects, it is of a medium- or long-term nature, and it is accompanied by a special type of conditionality (a pledge of policy reforms by the borrowing LDC going beyond the short-term commitments made to the IMF and those made when obtaining loans for specific projects). Depending on the fashions of the day, policy reforms may range from land redistribution to import liberalization to population control. The terms of AFP-type lending may be softened relative to purely commercial rates to "buy off" those hostile to the reforms within the borrowing LDCs. In circumstances when the international economy has been subjected to unexpected shocks, such as the oil-price increases of the 1970s, the line between policy reform and structural adjustment may become blurred, and general balance-of-payments support may underwrite a blend of both.

The experience with AFP-type lending has been mixed, whether in the context of the original AFP or in the paler versions of the 1970s. A cautious case can be made, however, that the World Bank and regional multilateral banks should continue to devote a modest part of their activities to that lending, especially for the poorest LDCs. In particular, those institutions should remain receptive to initiatives from borrowers presenting reform packages involving sustained efforts for several years, going beyond what the IMF or an expanded CFF should finance yet not involving specific steel-and-cement projects. A fund to encourage reform and experimentation, prudently managed, could support innovative LDC officials at critical junctures. Even with an expanded CFF in operation, some LDCs may face severe stabilization problems whose efficient correction could involve horizons going beyond those of IMF lending. In those circumstances a blending of IMF and World Bank balance-of-payments support (a very old proposal) could prove useful. The temptation to use AFP-type lending to push from above the pet ideas of whoever happens to be World Bank president should, however, be resisted.

Especially with an expanded CFF and a reformed IMF in place, countercyclical lending need not be a major objective of multilateral banks. But care should be exercised so as to keep their lending from being procyclical, as appears to have been the case during the early 1980s. These years have also witnessed renewed debates about "graduating" the more advanced LDCs from multilateral borrowing and experimentation with new lending modalities. Though Colombia may want to borrow from international markets both directly and via multilateral banks, the option to do either reduces the leverage the latter institutions have over that type of borrowing country. At the same time, abrupt "graduations" of NICs from multilateral banks during the circumstances of the early 1980s appear unwise. Multilateral banks during the 1980s could pioneer in experimenting with financial instruments and loans with repayment schedules contingent on borrowers' export earnings and various forms of indexing. Cofinancing of loans with private lenders, as practiced by the International Fnance Corporation, could play a useful but modest role in expanding the volume of finance so long as this practice would not distort priorities in the rest of the World Bank system.

LDCs without direct access to international credit markets will have to rely on the intermediating role of multilateral banks and on multilateral and bilateral aid if they want to invest beyond what they save, either temporarily or for a longer term. Among LDCs, the dependence of the sub-Saharan African countries on multilateral institutions and on aid remains singularly acute and worthy of special emergency attention (Helleiner 1983). Willy-nilly, LDCs of this type will continue to participate in a "dialogue" with multilateral lenders and donors about their investment plans and other development policies. The apparently correct conventional wisdom argues that such a dialogue is best handled multilaterally rather than bilaterally; it is therefore strange that the Reagan administration appears to favor both tighter "development conditionality" and a weakening of multilateral institutions.

Some Final Observations

Throughout history international monetary and financial arrangements have been an aspect of the world economy obviously connected to political power. The Pax Romana, the Pax Britannica, and the Pax Americana had counterparts in coinage and credit. Between Pax and Pax, chances for panics and depressions grew (Kindleberger 1973). It may be argued that, although in the early 1980s the hegemonic power of the United States has been seriously eroded, a gret deal of consensus remains among capitalist industrial powers about desirable international economic arrangements, so that a repetition of past inter-Pax catastrophes may be avoided (Ruggie 1982). Yet the diffusion of commercial, financial, and political power of the early 1980s remains historically unprecedented, generating large actual and potential frictions among major international actors, including those arising from attempts by the United States to reassert hegemony and discipline among its allies. This dangerous situation, however, can also be interpreted as a necessary precondition to the building of a more equitable and participatory international economic system.

Most LDCs having economic development as their highest priority are peripheral spectators in this turmoil. They are often lectured to adjust to the realities of the 1980s. If the adjustment is compatible with the maintenance of a minimum rate of development, they are likely to go along. Most, however, are unlikely to put up with a pseudo-adjustment involving long periods of stagnation. Rather, they will face possible new international realities by reorienting their development strategies. Quite sensibly, they will not for very long "adjust" by having high rates of unemployment and excess capacity and wasting opportunities for capital formation. Some LDCs are in a better position to carry out such reorientation than others, because they have larger domestic markets and a greater availability of and willingness to use policy instruments. A reorientation of LDC development policies would involve (as during the 1930s) a greater emphasis on import substitution, this time perhaps involving more South-South cooperation. The new strategy could also involve import postponement and investments intensively using nontraded goods (such as housing); these elements are consistent with greater attention to the welfare needs of the population at the bottom of the income scale. If stagnation and protectionism in the North were to become chronic and hamper the reverse real transfer involved in debt servicing, financial arrangements would have to be reexamined and renegotiated. The IMF, the World Bank, and other multilateral lending agencies would have to exercise some imagination to serve as more than debt-collecting agencies.

How much pressure can LDCs exercise in international financial bargaining? Can Southern debts be aggregated into one powerful bargaining chip? One is skeptical. Mexico is unlikely to want its debt lumped with that of Bolivia or even Brazil for bargaining purposes. During the December 1933 Pan American conference at Montevideo, the Mexican delegation proposed a general moratorium on external debts—an initiative promptly shot down by the Argentine foreign minister (Hull 1948, pp. 335–336). Yet demonstration effects among debtors could occur during a severe international crisis, leading them to sequentially suspend normal debt service, as during the early 1930s. This may be enough to give at least some semi-industrialized LDCs a bit of influence to press for a reexamination of international monetary and financial arrangements, perhaps in the context of a "new Bretton Woods." Ideas put forth at the UNCTAD Manila conference and elsewhere on rescheduling and on how to ameliorate the real consequences of the cycles and financial scares that are inevitable in private financial markets are worth a fresh look.

In spite of troubles in formal South-South integration schemes, intra-LDC trade grew vigorously during the 1970s. Scattered data for 1981 and 1982 indicate an alarming contraction in that trade, greater than the shrinkage in overall international transactions. Before bold new proposals are launched, this disappointing experience should be analyzed carefully; political and military tensions along a number of South-South borders should also be discussed frankly in this context. These gloomy considerations notwithstanding, one may conjecture that the 1970s trend in South-South trade can be resumed during the rest of the 1980s once the international crisis is overcome. That trend could be accelerated by the adoption of modest steps, such as by greater cooperation among LDC central banks. More generous reciprocal credit lines could be particularly important for encouraging trade in machinery and other capital goods. This type of financial cooperation, say among the central banks of Brazil and Mexico, may be quite useful in the environment of the 1980s and may indeed pave the way to joint bargaining with third parties.

Acknowledgements

This chapter owes much to comments made on earlier drafts by Jagdish Bhagwati, Jonathan Eaton, Gerald K. Helleiner, and John Williamson. Discussion and comments made by many participants at the conference on Rethinking Global Negotiations held in New Delhi, India, January 6–8, 1983, were also very useful. Virginia Casey kindly and ably typed the manuscript.

References

Arndt, H. W. 1944. *The Economic Lessons of the Nineteen-Thirties*. London: Cass.

Brodsky, David A., and Sampson, Gary P., 1981. "Implications of the Effective Revaluation of Reserve Asset Gold: The Case for a Gold Account for Development." *World Development* 9, no. 7.

Cooper, Richard N. 1983. "The Evolution of the International Monetary Fund toward a World Central Bank." Harvard University, April.

Dell, Sidney 1981. *On Being Grandmotherly: The Evolution of IMF Conditionality*, Princeton Essays in International Finance, No. 144. Princeton, N.J.: Princeton University, International Finance Section, October.

Garten, Jeffrey. 1982. "Rescheduling sovereign debt: Is there a better approach?" *World Economy* (November), pp. 279–289.

Helleiner, Gerald K. 1983. *The IMF and Africa in the 1980s*. Princeton Essays in International Finance, No. 152, Princeton, N.J.: Princeton University, International Finance Section.

Hull, Cordell 1948. *The Memoirs of Cordell Hull*. New York: Macmillan.

International Monetary Fund. 1983. *International Financial Statistics*. Washington, D.C.

Kindleberger, Charles P. 1973. *The World in Depression, 1929–1939*. Berkeley: University of California Press.

Pearson, Lester B. et al. 1969. *Partners in Development; Report of the Commission on International Development*. New York: Praeger.

Polak, J. J. 1979. *Thoughts on an International Monetary Fund Based Fully on the SDR*. Pamphlet No. 28. Washington: International Monetary Fund.

Ruggie, John G. 1982. "International Regimes, Transactions, and Change: Embedded Liberalism in the Postwar Economic Order." *International Organization* 36 (Spring): 379–415.

Solow, Robert M. 1982. "On the Lender of Last Resort." In Charles P. Kindleberger and Jean-Pierre Laffargue, eds., *Financial Crises: Theory, History and Policy*, pp. 237–248. Cambridge: Cambridge University Press.

Williamson, John. 1982. *The Lending Policies of the International Monetary Fund*. Policy Analyses in International Economics, No. 1. Washington, D.C.: Institute for International Economics, August.

9

Two-Edged Sword: Demands of Developing Countries and the Trading System

Martin Wolf

The separate economic blocs and all the friction and loss of friendship they bring with them are expedients to which one may be driven in a hostile world, where trade has ceased over wide areas to be cooperative and peaceful and where are forgotten the healthy rules of mutual advantage and equal treatment. But it is surely crazy to prefer that.— Lord Keynes, House of Lords, British Parliament, December 18, 1945.

With these words, delivered shortly before his death, Lord Keynes defended the Financial Agreement with the United States, the Lend-Lease settlement, Bretton Woods, and the commercial policy proposals that led ultimately to the General Agreement on Tariffs and Trade.[1] As a result of his efforts and those of many others, an open world economy was recreated after World War II. That achievement is now under threat. Yet if it was "crazy" then to remain wedded to controls over trade and payments, when liberalization was a painful experience still to be undergone, how much more crazy would it now be to throw the achievement away?

The liberal economic order was established after World War II by the industrial market economies. These countries continue to bear the principal responsibility for both its maintenance and its further strengthening. Not only does it reflect their economic philosophy, but commercial and financial transactions involving their citizens still account for by far the greater part of international exchange.[2] It is undoubtedly the failure of the industrial countries to live by the rules to which they themselves had earlier agreed that presents the greatest present danger.[3]

This failure, grievous though it is, is not the subject of this chapter, which is instead the role of developing countries—past, present, and prospective—in the trading system. More precisely, the chapter deals with the consequences of demands which Robert Hudec of the University of Minnesota, a leading authority on the GATT, has described as follows:

The developing country bloc has sought two kinds of change in general. It has urged the developed countries towards a greater "legalism"—more effective enforcement of developed country obligations, and adoption of new developed country obligations for the particular benefit of developing countries. On the other hand, the bloc has worked just as hard to remove inconvenient GATT obligations controlling its own conduct.[4]

The desire of developing countries to create a world in which one group of countries has most of the obligations and another most of the rights is long-standing. It goes back to the discussions that led to the Havana Charter of 1947. As Kenneth Dam has remarked,

It was the U.S. position that the less-developed countries could best develop by participating fully in a multilateral nondiscriminatory system with the lowest possible levels of tariffs and no quantitative restrictions. This position proved totally unacceptable to the less-developed world, which sought both affirmative commitments by all member countries to further the process of economic development, and, more important, specific exceptions to many of the prohibitions of the Charter in order to permit the less-developed countries to follow an independent commercial policy. The reigning view in less-developed countries was that economic development . . . required the creation of import substitution industries. It was asserted that such industries could flourish only behind high tariff walls supplemented . . . by quantitative restrictions.[5]

In effect, developing countries have engaged in a sustained assault on the liberal international trading system, including the principle of nondiscrimination, embodied in article I of the GATT. They have argued that "equal treatment of unequals is unjust" and have urged, instead, that there be discrimination in favor of developing countries. Thus, they began pressing for the following:

to be excused in multilateral trade negotiations from making reciprocal tariff reductions, which they formally secured in part IV of the GATT, added in 1964,

to be accorded tariff preferences in the markets of developed countries for their exports of manufactures and semimanufactures, which they formally achieved in the "waiver" of the most-favored-nation (MFN) clause, granted in 1971, sanctioning the Generalized System of Preferences (GSP), and

to be afforded "special and more favorable treatment . . . in areas of the negotiation where this is feasible and appropriate," which they formally obtained in the Tokyo Declaration setting out the terms of reference for the multilateral trade negotiations of 1973–1979.

These and other developments over the past quarter of a century have resulted in a very considerable divergence in the formal application of GATT principles and rules to the trade of developing countries, on the one hand, and to that of developed countries, on the other. As the Brandt Commission report has correctly stated; "The Tokyo Round agreement has recognized that preferential treatment of developing countries should be accepted as a permanent feature of the world trading system rather than as a temporary exception."[6]

It is the principal purpose of this chapter to argue that the United States was correct in its original view and that the demands of developing countries, however understandable in origin, were mistaken and were indeed damaging to the sustainability of the liberal trading system where they were not directly damaging to developing countries themselves. In effect it argues that the demand for special treatment has proved a two-edged sword.

Certain caveats are in order. The discussion is concerned largely with the international trading system and focuses on the diplomacy of international rule making. Thus, two closely related issues are treated only in passing—world trade itself and optimal policy for a single country—although the relation between both of these and the rules of the trading system is considered when necessary. Second, the question of commodity-price stabilization is not discussed. The focus is on market access, namely the terms and conditions on which citizens or organizations of one country may enter into transactions with those of another. Furthermore, with few exceptions the discussion deals with the traditional GATT concern: trade in goods. Third, although the topic of "graduation" (as it has come to be called) is related to that of this chapter, the discussion below concerns more than graduation. The idea of graduation presumes a world of two distinct status groups, the problem then being how to manage the transition of countries between the two. The discussion below questions whether a world of two distinct groups is desirable in the first place. Fourth, the heterogeneity of the group referred to as "developing countries" must be recognized. There can be no serious prospect that all developing countries will make the recommended commitment to the liberal international order. In practice, the countries that might make such a commitment are the more advanced market economies. There are therefore difficult questions concerning negotiating tactics, which can only be touched upon below. Finally, although the emphasis here is on what developing countries have done to damage the liberal trading system and might do to restore it, this does not imply that the developing countries bear the main responsibility for either that damage or that restoration. The principal responsibility rests with the industrial market economies.

Reason for Action

The trading system is already under serious threat, with numerous "dead spots" in the GATT code and the proliferation of restraints outside its purview.[7] The protectionist pressures revealed by the almost calamitous GATT ministerial meeting of November 1982 are very strong.[8] In consequence, it may well be that even a strong commitment by the most successful developing countries to the principles of the liberal trading system will not reverse the trend. Nevertheless, there is no reasonable alternative for them. The collapse of the liberal international order, with attendant consequences for financial flows to developing countries, is most threatening to those rapidly growing countries that require a smooth accommodation by the rest of the world to their growth. Thus, it is the importance of the task, rather than the probability of success alone, that should determine their actions.

The Underlying Concept of GATT and the Interests of Developing Countries

Rules of the international economic order exist to bind governments and restrict their actions, in order to allow agents, wherever located, to make long-term plans in a stable policy environment and so participate fully in an integrated world economy. In this way extensive economic specialization across national frontiers is made possible. These international rules therefore help to ensure the survival of an international economic system based on market principles.

The Essence of the Trading System

In order to achieve their desired goal in international trade, those who framed the GATT decided that the commercial policies of participating states should have four fundamental attributes: nondiscrimination, liberalism, stability, and transparency.[9] The tariff was selected as the sole instrument of commercial policy because it is intrinsically transparent, easy to negotiate, and fully compatible with the market. Tariff bindings were agreed in order to give economic agents the security to invest on the assumption of long-term market access. Restrictions on the circumstances and ways in which protection could be increased (including articles and codes on nontariff measures) were also intended to ensure stability and transparency. Finally, it was agreed that trade policies would not retain the desired attributes without acceptance of the principle of nondiscrimination. In this view the authors of the GATT were influenced by the experiences of the 1930s. The same principle, nondiscrimination, ensured that global benefits were derived from liberalization by a relatively small number of countries.

None of the four basic elements was newly invented in the GATT. On the contrary, they were also the central elements of the trading system that grew out of the Cobden-Chevalier Treaty of 1860 and led to the great expansion of world trade of the second half of the nineteenth century. The similarity between that period and the period after World War II was, therefore, no accident.

The rules of the international trading system were not designed to achieve free trade. It was accepted that individual countries were bound to differ on this issue and that many would wish to reserve the right to protect. At the same time, it is politically difficult to sustain greater liberalism in one democratic country than in another when they are in apparently similar circumstances. Moreover, since mercantilist prejudices are strong, it is virtually impossible to liberalize unilaterally. Reciprocal bargaining over trade barriers therefore became in practice the principal instrument of general trade liberalization. Even though it is an effective technique of liberalization, the emphasis on reciprocity is also a source of fragility, tending (as is now clear) to generate conflicts and resentments where no economic justification exists.

From the point of view of the world order as a whole, adherence to the rules by major market economies is much more important than adherence by smaller countries. If Sri Lanka were to pursue free trade one year and autarky the next, the upheaval would be a legitimate concern for its own citizens but would be of little importance to the rest of the world. The same is not true for the European Community or the United States. They face consequences and therefore constraints—entirely beneficial ones from the point of view of their own long-term interests—that do not affect others to the same degree.

The most important role of large market economies in world trade is as the major open markets on which all can rely and in which global supply and demand can be balanced relatively smoothly. If a major market is suddenly cut off from the rest of the world, especially by quantitative controls, the impact of global supply and demand fluctuations will be felt more sharply in the remaining open markets. Partly for this reason, such protection tends to spread rapidly. If, however, all major markets are controlled, no exporter can enjoy predictable market access. All trade becomes subject to permanent negotiation and is in consequence determined by political rather than economic considerations. Exporters will then come to depend on ex gratia favors by governments of importing countries, and potentially efficient investments will inevitably be curtailed and development prospects impaired. Thus, adherence to the rules by the governments of the major economies makes possible a global public good: a reasonably stable, yet dynamic, world economy.

It is possible, therefore, to consider the trade policies of any country (or group of countries) from two perspectives. For a country, looked at in isolation, the question is whether the government's policies allow for efficient international specialization. This is the classic problem in international trade theory, and the current view is that—except where the aim is to exploit monopoly power (a dangerous game)—the best trade policy is simply free trade.[10] From the point of view of outsiders, however, the question is whether the country's policies contribute to a harmoniously functioning international economy. What are required for this, especially in the case of large economies, are simply the stable, transparent, and liberal policies that the GATT attempted to ensure.

The Interest of Developing Countries in the Adherence of Other Countries to GATT Principles

Developing countries are individually fairly weak and are latecomers to economic growth. The value for the weak of the binding of the strong by international rules has been brought out clearly in the following remarks, in which Sidney Golt, formerly deputy secretary in the Department of Trade and Industry in the United Kingdom government, explains how the GATT originated in a reaction against the abuses of power in commercial relations that characterized the 1930s:

... a significant element [of the justification for the GATT system] was the view of the body of international rules, customs and practices as not only governing the relationships of the strong countries towards each other, but also as safeguards for the weaker powers in the international system. ... There was to be no repetition of what was seen as a particular evil of the 1930s—the operation of bilateral bargaining through which a strong country, by the sheer use of its commercial power and, even more objectionably, its political power, imposed its own desired patterns of trade upon a weaker trading partner.[11]

Equally, it has been the historical experience that in periods of liberalism—the second half of the nineteenth century and after World War II—dynamic latecomers have performed better than established economic powers. A liberal world economy does not, of course, guarantee the success of any economy, but it does at least ensure the accommodation of others to it. In an open, nondiscriminatory market, the more competitive suppliers will automatically shoulder aside the less competitive suppliers. This automatic accommodation is particularly important for small countries, for which trade is certain to be a central element for growth, but even a large country like Japan could hardly have achieved its extraordinarily rapid growth after World War II in a more restrictive environment.

For each individual developing country it is also desirable that other developing countries follow the rules. It is true that industrial countries are the world's largest market, accounting for 64 percent of world imports in 1981, but developing countries themselves accounted for 25 percent.[12] Secure and predictable access to these markets would undoubtedly be a boon for the development of each country.

Optimal Trade Policy, the GATT, and Reciprocity

If it is accepted that any given country would want other countries to adhere to basic GATT principles, what of its own policies? In general, there is no conflict between optimal, unilateral trade policy and GATT rules. Indeed, a country following an optimal policy would avoid taking advantage of virtually all the loopholes in the GATT, especially such devices of "administered" or "contingent" protection as the escape clause.[13] There are three areas in which conflict can arise. Two of these—export subsidization and infant-industry protection—pose trivial problems, but the last—reciprocity and GATT mercantilism—creates much greater difficulty.

Developing countries claim the need to be free to subsidize exports. The principal justification is that of offsetting the effects of their own protection. This justification could, of course, be made unnecessary by a compensated devaluation and lowering of import barriers. Furthermore, in practical terms the Code on Subsidies and Countervailing Duties, negotiated during the Tokyo Round of Multilateral Negotiations, allows developing countries to subsidize exports if the subsidies are not used "in a manner which causes serious prejudice to the trade or production of another signatory."[14] At the same time, the code grants substantial freedom to employ domestic subsidies.[15] Similarly, there is plenty of room in the GATT (probably too much room) for infant-industry protection (under article XVIII).

A more substantial problem is that of reciprocity, the principal technique of trade liberalization under the GATT. Four issues arise:

An optimal trade policy would approximate free trade, but a country following a policy of complete free trade has, as Hong Kong and Singapore know well, no bargaining power whatsoever.

Small countries have, in any case, limited bargaining power, and they tend therefore to obtain modest reductions in trade barriers on products of direct export interest to them, especially when tariff negotiations are carried out under the "principal supplier" rule.[16]

To the extent that the GATT performs the role of a weak constitutional constraint on trade policy, the failure of reciprocity for small countries works both ways. Just as small countries know they can get rather little in return for tariff "concessions," they know also that retaliation against withdrawal of "concessions" by them is unlikely. *De minimis non curat GATT*. Thus, the fear of retaliation is of modest help to the government of a small country wishing to pursue liberal policies and to resist domestic pressures for protection.

The GATT, like other constitutional arrangements, has an educational function. Unfortunately, its mercantilist language concerning tariff "concessions," combined with the language of its escape clauses, all of which emphasize the cost of increased imports, teaches the wrong lesson: that, as Gustave Flaubert once put it, "imports are the canker at the heart of trade." For this reason, membership in the GATT is of little help in explaining the value of an efficient trade policy.

It may be concluded that small countries will have at best limited influence on the trade policies of others via GATT mechanisms; that the more efficient their policies, the smaller their direct leverage; that GATT mechanisms will provide only modest assistance to them in achieving an efficient trade policy; and that such a policy will involve a liberalism that goes well beyond that of the GATT.

Nevertheless, the notion of reciprocity is not useless for developing countries. Collectively, developing countries (even the group of more advanced developing countries) have substantial weight in world trade.

If they can coordinate their offers and the withdrawal of offers, they can hope to influence the trade policies of others. Moreover, most developing countries now have trade policies that are much more illiberal even than those consistent with GATT principles. For them there is no contradiction between offering "concessions" on trade barriers and simultaneously moving toward more efficient policies.

Developing Countries' Demands and the Erosion of the GATT System

Although the central principles of the GATT are strong and sensible, it had to be constructed with a multitude of loopholes. The GATT permits the renegotiation of bound tariffs (article XXVIII), imposition of (nondiscriminatory) emergency protection against competitive imports (article XIX), protection for balance-of-payments reasons (article XII), countervailing action against dumped or subsidized goods (article VI and the code on subsidies and countervailing duties), formation of customs unions and free-trade areas (article XXIV), and the imposition of quantitative restrictions against agricultural imports (article XI).

Unfortunately, the industrial countries have found it increasingly difficult to live by even this enfeebled system. Their great achievement was the progressive liberalization and binding of tariffs in a series of seven multilateral negotiations. When the Tokyo Round tariff cuts are completed, the weighted average MFN tariff of industrial countries on all industrial products will be only 4.7 percent.[17] Meanwhile, however, there have been the following major derogations and failures.[18]

The principle of nondiscrimination has been seriously eroded. Preferential trade arrangements, including the European Community's agreements with associates and arrangements among developing countries that fall far short of satisfying the conditions of article XXIV, have proliferated. In addition there has been a renewed trend toward bilateralism with the growth of "voluntary" export-restraint agreements, negotiated mainly with Japan and the advanced developing countries. As the principal authors of the GATT had anticipated, this mushrooming of discrimination has proved increasingly incompatible with the maintenance of stable, transparent, and liberal trade policies.

The growth in discrimination has been associated with the failure of the provision in the GATT (article XIX) that permits the imposition of emergency protection against import surges, but only on a nondiscriminatory basis. Governments have found "voluntary" discriminatory arrangements a more attractive alternative.

Whole industries have been excepted from liberalization. Since the early 1950s, trade in temperate-zone agricultural products has been effectively removed from GATT governance. From 1961, a plurilaterally agreed-upon system of discriminatory restraints against developing countries' exports of textiles and clothing has been in force, and these restraints have become increasingly restrictive over time. Since 1977, there has been a rapid movement toward a not dissimilar system of restraints on trade in steel. Trade in automobiles appears now to be on the verge of similar global cartelization.

The reciprocity technique of trade liberalization has meant disproportionately small liberalization of trade in products of immediate interest to developing countries.[19]

A complex system of "administered" or "contingent" protection has been built up in industrial countries, as a substitute for tariffs, through exploitation of the loopholes present in the GATT and corresponding domestic laws.[20]

Finally, the process of multilateral consultation and collective judgment has fallen into disuse. The formal process of dispute settlement has proved an ineffective replacement, especially where complaints of small powers against the great are concerned.[21]

Many of these exceptions, especially those involving resort to discriminatory protection outside the purview of the GATT, were the result of an accommodation to protectionist pressure that might otherwise have threatened the achievement of tariff liberalization. Such trimming of the sails has not been unsuccessful; certainly the liberal framework of trade policy has endured in a way not experienced in the 1930s. Nevertheless, the damage being done by the cumulation of individual exceptions, each justifiable on its merits to practical men—damage in terms of increased uncertainty, misallocation of resources, and failure to adjust—threatens to overwhelm the open trading system. Moreover, since adjustment at the margin is resisted most, developing countries are likely to be the most damaged by the growth of the discriminatory protection that is the principal symptom of decay.

The Demands of Developing Countries and the Responses of Industrial Countries

As a result of the above trends, developing countries have found it easy to agree—quite rightly—that constraints on industrial countries in the GATT are feeble and that their practice has fallen short of even these far-from-exalted standards. They have attempted, therefore, to impose a sterner discipline. For example, spokesmen for developing countries have demanded tighter and more specific definition of the concepts of injury and market disruption, which are central to various GATT clauses and codes, to the textile arrangement, and to domestic law.[22] Similarly, they have demanded in the hitherto abortive discussion of the code on safeguard protection that procedures be made more open, that duration of safeguard protection be limited, and in other ways that the right to safeguard protection be circumscribed.

Developing countries have gone still further. They have demanded of industrial countries discrimination in their own favor, the principal result being the GSP. Moreover, they have consistently argued that the fetters to be placed on industrial countries are inappropriate for themselves since they need greater sovereign discretion.

So automatic has become acceptance of this double standard that it is even to be found in an excellent pamphlet by Carlos F. Díaz-Alejandro and Gerald K. Helleiner, who state: "These lessons [of economic history] maintain their relevance in 1982. They should strongly discourage departures from the broad principle of *non-discrimination* in commodity trade, except for transitional preferences for LDCs . . . and customs unions formed by those countries."[23]

While developing countries have won a number of formal concessions in the GATT, it has also become increasingly the practice of industrial countries to discriminate against the more successful among them. In effect, industrial countries have been prepared to grant the appearance of compliance with developing countries' demands while denying the reality. They fear the consequences of dynamic growth of new competitors, but they are willing to offer the carefully controlled favors of what Harry Johnson once described as neo-neo-colonialism, thus dividing developing countries into disruptive goats, against whom discriminatory protection is appropriate, and less successful sheep, for whom favors can be done. It is because of the supposedly more favorable treatment accorded to all, in principle, but the less favorable treatment accorded to the more successful, in practice, that the problem of graduation has become so vexed. A country has little incentive to graduate into hostile and discriminatory, rather than equal, treatment.

An interesting historical example of industrial countries' divide-and-rule tactics was the Brasseur plan for selective preferences in favor of developing countries, advanced by the Belgian representative at the

1963 GATT ministerial meeting.[24] It was in part a response to years of sustained pressure for a general liberalization of barriers facing developing countries, just as was the vague rhetoric of part IV of the GATT.[25] Preferences—a side issue at best—then became a principal concern of the United Nations Conference on Trade and Development of 1964.[26] Unfortunately, developing countries were willing to take the bait. They had doubted the appropriateness of liberal trading policies for themselves from the beginning. Equally widespread was their belief that special favors and concessions were needed if their exports were to grow.[27]

In consequence, developing and industrial countries' attitudes present a mirror image. Both fear the general application of universal and liberal rules vis-à-vis one another, and both are prepared to accept derogations from such universality, hoping thereby either to obtain special favors, as in the case of developing countries, or to avoid liberalism toward the more dynamic developing countries, as in the case of industrial countries. In the process, a Gresham's Law of negotiations has come into effect: Bad (or marginal) issues have driven out good.

Consequences of Developing Countries' Demands

What is the value of the concessions that developing countries have obtained? This question can be treated under four heads: the economic effects of industrial countries' preferences, the effect on industrial countries' attitudes, the effect on the body of trade rules, and the effect on developing countries' policies.

The literature on the economic consequences of preferences is vast and cannot be reviewed here in any detail.[28] Three conclusions can legitimately be drawn from it, however: that the dramatic growth of developing-country-manufactured exports after 1960 (at a volume growth rate of close to 13 percent a year) was not due to preferences, that trade creation has probably been a larger source of the benefit from preferences than trade diversion, and that the greater part of the benefits go to relatively advanced developing countries such as South Korea and Brazil.

Industrial countries regard this as an ex gratia favor to an arbitrarily defined group of countries. For this reason the preferences are neither generous enough nor secure enough to have the impact on infant industries that had been hoped for.[29] It is also to be noted that the difference between the effects of preferences and equivalent general liberalization consists of trade diversion. Not only is diversion a small part of the benefit to developing countries, however; it is also the part that is threatened by further general trade liberalization. Moreover, because the preferential element (as opposed to the liberalization per se) works by promoting exports in which other suppliers have a comparative advantage, this element of the GSP is unlikely to stimulate development in line with the global comparative advantage of the developing country itself. It is therefore just insofar as the benefit derives from the preferential element that it is most dubious. In effect, preferences are a combination of general liberalization, desirable to both parties, and an inefficient form of aid.

Not only are preferences—the most visible benefit derived from the peculiar position of developing countries—of doubtful value, but they join with other demands in exercising a damaging effect on industrial countries' attitudes toward trade with developing countries. From these demands astute citizens of an industrial country (the majority of whom are, after all, not economists) would draw the following conclusions:

Imports from developing countries are not so much a mutual benefit as a favor, that is, a form of aid, granted (or owed) to the developing countries.

This "aid" goes to the "wrong" countries (the "dominant" suppliers, as they are called in the case of the Multifibre Arrangement) not to the more deserving.

The "injustice" should be cured by doling out trade opportunities, like aid, to the least successful, while holding back the successful.

The rules that industrial countries are enjoined to obey are not likely to be in their interest, since rapidly growing developing countries claim that they are a hindrance to development, but again a favor owed to developing countries.

In sum, the effect is to undermine the belief that liberal trade is a matter of mutual advantage, or of unilateral advantage to the industrial countries. Rather, the impression is that it is a burden on the industrialized countries. It is not surprising, therefore, that in more difficult times the industrial countries have been less willing to bear such a "burden."

I now turn to the system of trade rules. It is evident that a completely arbitrary distinction between countries has been introduced. Industrial countries "know a hawk from a handsaw" and can see that the difference between Hong Kong and Holland is much smaller than that between Hong Kong and Haiti. In light of the arbitrariness of the distinction between developed and developing countries—an arbitrariness that has meant that developing countries could only be defined by self-designation—it is surprising neither that further categories appear de facto or de jure (such as the category of "countries in transition," against whom discriminatory protection is justified) nor that "graduation" has become an issue of contention.

It is partly because of the arbitrariness of any dividing line between countries that the frequently made proposal that international rules be universal but not uniform is likely in practice to create rather than resolve difficulties. Moreover, these difficulties will grow as the process of ever finer differentiation continues (being aimed at each stage at removing injustices created at the previous one). It should be remembered that the principle of equal treatment before the law is not justified by the proposition that all people are identical; on the contrary, it is justified by the opposite proposition, that differences among people are so many and various that criteria for a just differentiation can never be universally agreed upon. Furthermore, in the absence of such criteria no authority can safely be entrusted with the arbitrary power of differentiation. Exactly the same arguments apply to rules governing the behavior of states.

A difficulty has also been introduced into the liberalization process itself by the GSP (and other preferences). The fruits of trade diversion cannnot be enjoyed if barriers fall more generally. As a result, developing countries became a voice against tariff liberalization during the Tokyo Round of multilateral trade negotiations.

Finally, there are damaging effects on developing countries. Contrary to earlier views, limitless protection is not in the interests of individual developing countries. It is also not true that governments find it any easier in developing countries than in industrial countries to exercise unlimited sovereign discretion wisely and without falling prey to special interests. The release from all external constraints on their policies, however weak, combined with the constant preaching that the ideas embodied in those constraints are damaging, has allowed developing countries to construct restrictive regimes that can be liberalized only with great difficulty and that strangle their own growth.

One of the most damaging licenses for developing countries has been that to construct protectionist preferential trading arrangements. Because of the large element of trade diversion inherent in these schemes, they have proved fragile.[30] Worse, they have proved a diversion from consideration of the need for more comprehensive liberalization. Latin American countries, for example, have put great effort into such schemes but have labored to produce a mouse: In 1979 trade in manufactures within the Latin American Free Trade Area (LAFTA) was $4.7 billion, about a third of the gross manufactured exports of Hong Kong alone.[31]

Assessment of Developing Countries' Demands

Enough has been said to cast doubt on both the premise that equal treatment of unequals is unfair and the demand that rules be universal but not uniform. What these mean in practice is, first, that developing countries are permitted to pursue policies damaging to themselves. As Ian Little has recently put it, "In the trade field . . . [developing countries] beg to be allowed to hurt themselves."[32] In this respect, therefore, the demand for special treatment is similar to a demand by a pedestrian for the "right" to jaywalk and so step under a bus. Second, developing countries obtain a benefit in the form of preferences that appears to be valuable but actually amounts to a particularly inefficient and inequitably distributed form a aid. In the process, they have weakened the commitment of industrial countries to the liberal trading system and so contributed to the pressures that lie behind many of the derogations and failures of the GATT system. Thus, while developing countries are certainly not mainly responsible for the erosion, they have played their part. They have done so, most fundamentally, by their assault on the simple and powerful concept of a body of liberal principles universally applied.

The Role of Developing Countries in Restoring the Open Trading System

Developing countries can make a contribution to a restoration of the open trading system. There are indeed many reasons why they should now be prepared to make such an effort. First, it is no longer possible to ask only for derogations from GATT principles in their favor, in the expectation that the basic framework of liberal trade will be unaffected. At the GATT ministerial meeting of November 1982 it was impossible to agree on more than "to make determined efforts to ensure that trade policies and measures are consistent with GATT principles and rules and to resist protectionist pressures."[33] No more compelling witness to the fragility of the system could be supplied. Second, developing countries are the newcomers and therefore depend most on a liberal trading system that accommodates their growth. Third, developing countries have shown themselves well able to expand manufactured exports, now equal in value to their primary commodity exports (excluding fuel), provided their own trade policies do not tax these exports excessively and there exists reasonably unrestricted market access.[34] Automatic accommodation to their growth (or, in other words, secure market access) is, therefore, their greatest interest in trade negotiations. Fourth, it has proved unnecessary—indeed costly—for them to enjoy limitless freedom to follow import substitution policies. Fifth, the colonial period is now slipping into the past and should no longer be allowed to dominate attitudes. Finally, even if a special status were desirable in itself, it can be achieved only at the price of victimization of the successful. There is little likelihood that industrial countries will grant special privileges to some countries without also victimizing others (or even the same countries in different circumstances).

As Harry Johnson once wrote, "One of the few genuine issues, and the one most subject to obfuscation, is purely and simply that of allowing the developing countries to sell freely what they are good at making."[35]

A Lead by Developing Countries

What is needed is that the developing countries, or as large a group of them as possible, affirm their belief in the value of the open trading system and show their willingness to abide by its disciplines (preferably even if industrial countries fail to do so). This would involve a commitment to replace quantitative restrictions by tariffs and to liberalize tariffs to a substantial extent over a specified period of time, a willingness to abide by GATT articles and codes in essentially the same way as industrial countries (thus accepting a minimum standard of international discipline on commercial policies), an insistence on the applicability of unconditional nondiscrimination in all countries' trade policies, and a willingness to engage in North-South negotiations over such a restoration and over complementary liberalization of industrial countries barriers against them.

The recommended path does not depend on any precisely formulated notion of reciprocity, over which a fruitful discussion of present difficulties can only founder. What is demanded is the sort of commitment that can change the context in which discussions occur, thus breaking the logjam created by present mistrust and the cumulation of past errors.

Objections to Liberalization

Strong objections have been made to these arguments for liberalization by developing countries. The principal point has been that developing countries already import all they can and, with their high level of indebtedness, can certainly not import any more.[36] In order to deal with these arguments, it is useful to distinguish two issues: long-term specialization in international trade and adjustment to liberalization in the short term.

With regard to long-term specialization, it is simply untrue that developing countries already import all they can, if by that it is meant that developing countries cannot export (and, therefore, import) more.[37] Protection against imports is a tax on exports. *Ceteris paribus*, the more protectionist a country, the lower both its exports and imports in relation to gross domestic product (GDP). Since many industrially advanced developing countries are highly protectionist—Brazil, India, and Mexico, for example—and some became still more so after 1973, there is no good reason to suppose that they are unable to increase exports.[38] Thus, after a period of adjustment to the reduction in protection, a perfectly sustainable rise in trade can occur.[39]

The real problem is that of the period of adjustment. Developing countries themselves can do much to facilitate adjustment, largely by ensuring adequate incentives for exports.[40] Nevertheless, with the present recession and the debt problem outside support will be helpful. This should be raised as an international issue. Finance of an adjustment program that will make developing countries more creditworthy is in the interest of both the industrial market economies and the debtor countries.[41] There is a precedent for financial assistance in support of the liberalization of the trade policies of protectionist countries: the Marshall Plan.

Finally, the desired adjustment is possible only if increased exports are accommodated in world markets. Thus, domestic liberalization and strengthening of the liberal trading system go hand in hand, the former helping and at the same time depending on the latter. There is indeed one respect in which they are virtually the same: Concerted liberalization by developing countries will give an automatic increase in access to the world's most dynamic markets, those of one another.

Relation to Optimal Trade Policy

A commitment to liberalization in accordance with GATT principles is, therefore, not against the interests of developing countries, but at the same time it is only a first step toward an efficient trade policy. In view of the starting point of most developing countries, there need be no conflict between the two, but developing countries would be wise to go further than the GATT and not avail themselves of its many loopholes. A useful step might be to incorporate the gains from trade into domestic decisions on emergency protection and countervailing duties, as Michael Finger of the World Bank has recommended.[42]

An Opportunity for Progress

In sum, developing countries have the opportunity to make a commitment that is likely simultaneously to improve the efficiency of their own trade regimes, increase trading opportunities for the whole world as they open their markets, enhance the legitimacy of the liberal trading system in industrial countries, and, one hopes, reduce the barriers of industrial countries against them. That opportunity should be seized.

Issues in International Trade Negotiations

Within the context of the change in policy recommended above, a number of detailed issues in international trade negotiations can be considered. Two of these will be reviewed at some length: safeguard protections and tariffs. Brief comments will then be made on other issues before I turn to the question of tactics.[43]

Selective Safeguards

The Tokyo Declaration, which set the terms of reference for the Tokyo Round negotiations, called on governments to review the operation of article XIX. In doing so they made a concerted effort to negotiate a safeguards code, but it foundered on the European Community's proposal that the code should provide for the imposition of "emergency" protection on a "selective" basis—that is, against imports of a particular product from one or a few countries identified as the cause of "serious injury" to the corresponding domestic industry in the importing country. This proposal encountered determined opposition from the developing countries and from Australia, Canada, and a number of small developed countries. Although the review of article XIX was concluded and thus no amendments were possible, the issue has been kept on the books as unfinished business.

Whether the principle of selective application of emergency protection would have been accepted will not be known; matters never got that far. The negotiators concentrated on the criteria that would determine the "exceptional" circumstances in which selective action might be taken. It was suggested that the dangers of departures from the principle of nondiscrimination could be mitigated by laying down careful restrictions on the use of the privilege. However, agreement could not be reached on clearly defined criteria for what was in effect an escape clause within an escape clause.

The effort to write into GATT law a provision for selective safeguard action might be said to have been an effort to make informal quantitative restrictions formally acceptable within the GATT. This amounts to writing a rule that violates the basic principle of nondiscrimination. Developing countries were absolutely right to resist this proposal as can be seen from inspection of the arguments advanced for it.

The first line of argument was to ask why all exporting countries should suffer from the imposition of emergency protection under article XIX, when the "injury" or "market disruption" is caused by just one or two inordinately competitive suppliers. The argument rests on a belief, entirely inconsistent with the market principles of the GATT, that every producer has a right to be free of irresistible competitors. The economics is also doubtful; if a particular industry suffers from a comparative disadvantage, saving it from the competition of one overseas supplier is unlikely to be enough; the problem will arise again with imports from another supplier. In the case of textiles and clothing, for instance, selective action against Japan led to subsequent problems with imports from Hong Kong, Taiwan, South Korea, and, increasingly, Thailand, the Philippines, and other countries.

The second line of argument acknowledges that "voluntary" export-restraint agreements (VERs) and "orderly" marketing arrangements (OMAs) are undermining the GATT system but suggests that the best way to come to grips with them is to bring them into the legal glare of the GATT. If everybody agrees that VERs and OMAs are the problem, however, why not agree to stop using them? In any case, legalization is neither a sufficient nor a necessary condition for reporting discriminatory trade restrictions.

The developing countries are right to reject selectivity because such legalization of discrimination would be still worse than the present chaos. There are, after all, certain advantages to unofficial VERs. The exporters can capture some of the scarcity rent, and the very illegality of VERs offers them bargaining power. The restricted suppliers have also done well—at least so far—in diversifying into new products and upgrading the quality of their exports. Meanwhile, unrestricted suppliers are given a new export opportunity. Thus, one or two VERs in a sector just are not very effective as a protectionist device in terms of the objectives of the importing country.[44] What is disastrous—and also almost impossible to liberalize—is a comprehensive, global system of bilateral restraints, as in the textile arrangement. The case of textiles shows, however, that it is the proliferation of protection that is threatened by official sanctioning of discrimination, and that such a proliferation is also unlikely to be controlled by the fine words written into any code.[45]

This does not mean that VERs are undesirable. Any discriminatory restraint creates powerful interests opposed to liberalization, not only in the protecting country but also among unrestricted suppliers. It should be remembered, for example, that developing countries have not been averse to being protected from one another in this way. It is in the general interest of developing countries, however, to curb such discrimination and to support proposals for achieving full international notification of VERs and for the creation of a safeguard surveillance committee in the GATT, not only to publicize informal restrictions but also to discuss methods for removal of all quantitative restrictions. Such a position by developing countries would have more force if they were willing to commit themselves to a removal of most of their own quantitative restrictions at the same time.

Tariffs, Tariff Escalation, and Preferences

Developing countries have been concerned about the relatively high level of tariffs against their exports and especially about tariff escalation against the processing of commodities. They have also been pressing for preferential tariffs in their favor by industrial countries as well as for freedom to create preferential trading arrangements among themselves.

A radical solution to the deadlock over tariffs would be to suggest that the cuts negotiated in the Tokyo Round continue until the tariffs reach zero. Developing countries should also accept that the preferential element in the GSP amounts to a form of aid, which will be generously given only to those obviously in need of assistance. They should suggest, therefore, that, so long as tariffs last, the benefits of the GSP be granted, without any of the present restrictions in the various schemes, to all countries that are eligible for IDA credits (except perhaps India and China).[46] In time the tariff cuts would dispose of most of the concern about tariff escalation, leaving only the difficult problem of industries that have been excepted from the tariff cuts, which would require separate negotiation. Alternatively, there could be a negotiation solely about the structure of protection, which aimed at equalizing effective rates of protection. In order to induce such a general lowering of tariffs (or at least their restructuring) the advanced developing countries would accept the immediate loss of GSP privileges and commit themselves to some liberalization of their own barriers to imports.

While reviewing their tariff policy, developing countries should consider whether they would not be much better off if their preferential liberalization with respect to one another, actual and proposed, were instead put on a nondiscriminatory basis.[47] Alternatively, the costs of trade diversion and the consequent fragility of these arrangements could be reduced by negotiating a reduction of the external barriers of the preferential trading arrangements. This is exactly what the European Community did during the Dillon, Kennedy, and Tokyo rounds of Multilateral Trade Negotiations.

Other Issues

There are other issues in which developing countries have a stake.

The codes negotiated during the Tokyo Round have yet to prove their worth. They could, in any case, be only the beginning of a continuous process of consultation and negotiation, which means that everything depends on the implementation of the agreements reached. Since the agreements were signed, a number of difficulties have arisen. There has been considerable disappointment over the number of countries that have become parties to particular agreements. At the same time, some of the agreements, particularly the one on subsidies and countervailing measures, could usefully be clarified and strengthened. In this process, developing countries should reconsider the desirability for them of the exemptions from various disciplines that they won. There is, accordingly, a need for the different GATT codes of conduct on nontariff measures to be reviewed in order to identify problems inhibiting their implementation on the broadest possible basis.

Although the dispute-settlement procedures of the GATT were reviewed during the Tokyo Round negotiations, they need to be further improved in order to enjoy the confidence of signatory countries, chiefly to raise the level of objectivity. In this respect, panels of inquiry appointed to look into disputes should be drawn from a roster of independent experts in whom signatory countries have confidence. Their first task should be to adjudicate on the legal position of the matter in dispute before setting about conciliation between the parties. In addition, the GATT secretariat should be empowered to intitiate inquiries. One issue on which changes cannot be made is that of enforcement of panel findings. The only realistic sanction is a clear finding that a government is in breach of international law.

Special consideration has to be given to the long-standing problems of integrating agriculture and textiles into the world economy by extending the rules of the GATT, and general trade policy, to both sectors, where deeply entrenched policy regimes are in place. In the cases of textiles and clothing the establishment of a safeguard surveillance committee would permit the export restraints imposed on developing countries to be treated as part of the general body of quantitative restrictions to be liberalized, requiring a conscious decision not to renew the MFA (on the understanding that trade liberalization is virtually impossible in an arrangement confined to a single sector).

There are a number of new issues on the table, of which the most important is trade in services. This American priority has been treated with hostility by developing countries, and one can readily understand their concern. It is certainly not the most important problem facing the GATT; nor can one avoid the fear that services could, like the GSP, prove another case of Gresham's Law of negotiations. Nevertheless, the intensity of American interest can prove tactically useful, since developing countries should be able to obtain something in return for a willingness to discuss the issue.

Tactics

It is not possible to discuss tactics in detail, except to note that leadership in the reconsideration of demands that go back for a generation will inevitably depend on a few countries at first. Unanimity will not be achieved. Advanced developing countries must play the central role.

At the same time, all developing countries need to recognize the futility of continuing to propose disciplines for industrial countries that they reject in their own case. They can also usefully consider the leverage that their imports from industrial countries give them. If a number of developing countries can cooperate, they can be a powerful group; in 1979 Indonesia showed such power on its own when it retaliated against the United Kingdom's intention to limit Indonesia's exports of clothing.[48]

Since the negotiations must focus not only on tariffs but also on the liberalization of quantitative restrictions of various kinds, as well as on codes of conduct, standard GATT techniques of reciprocal bargaining are likely to fail. The very different economic sizes of the partners in a North-South negotiation is also likely to prove a difficulty in this regard. Thus, it is important to avoid getting lost in the arid search for precise reciprocity.

What is required is agreement on action in parallel rather than on the basis of a strict *quid pro quo*. Given a common recognition of the errors of the past and of the domestic costs of those errors, each party should commit itself to abandoning some important and politically sensitive restrictions. A historical precedent for such an approach is the liberalization of quantitative restrictions under the program organized by the Organization for European Economic Cooperation (OEEC) in the 1950s.[49] In this program each country committed itself to a progressive increase in the proportion of trade that would be liberated from quantitative restrictions. The lesson of the OEEC program for relations between industrial market economies and developing countries today is that it embodied a mutual commitment to liberalize without the necessity for agreement on equivalent reductions in the rate of protection or on equivalent lists of product categories to be affected. What is needed, then, is a reciprocal commitment that will serve as a lubricant for agreement rather than as a determinant of the form of that agreement.

The Need for an Open World Economy

What is at stake? The argument set out above rests on certain fundamental premises: that trade in millions of commodities among well over 100 countries cannot be "managed" except on the basis of universal, liberal principles followed by at least the governments of major trading nations; that if the rules fail and trade is "managed" on the basis of constant bureaucratic intervention the world economy is likely to fail, just as would a horse whose movements were dictated by a committee of jockeys; and finally that in the process of dividing up the trade "pie" in accordance with what bureaucrats and politicians would consider to be "fair shares," politically weak but economically dynamic newcomers would lose the most. Heedless of the latter danger, however, developing countries have left to industrial countries the responsibility for the order as a whole, demanding only exemptions, privileges, and derogations for themselves. Their demands have worked as a two-edged sword, cutting away at the trunk of the order whose branches they wished to trim.

One is reminded of the myth of Midas, who desired that everything should become gold at his touch and ended by turning to gold even his own food. The developing countries love the idea of liberalism for others but hope to make the liberal system still more golden with privileges and exemptions for themselves. In the process they have threatened to deprive their food of its nourishment.

Historically, the major threat to an open world economy has been posed by the emergence of powerful new economies. That emergence has been associated with opposite reactions. Established powers, on the one hand, have been tempted into devising various schemes of exclusion. Meanwhile, the newcomers have been reluctant to adopt the discipline of the existing order, which they suspect or see to be rigged against their interests. With the established powers no longer committed to an order in which their position is declining in relative terms, and with the new powers resentful of "free trade imperialism" or (more frequently) indifferent to their responsibilities, commercial friction and attendant financial difficulties have contributed to two major collapses in this century.

The problem of the smooth accommodation of newcomers is now as acute as ever. The present group of industrial countries account for no more than a fifth of the world's population. Their share in world economic activity is declining and is likely to continue to do so. New powers will emerge and, indeed, are emerging. The industrial countries should rid themselves of the illusion that it will be possible to sustain liberal trade among themselves while keeping these intrusive newcomers at bay. At the same time the newcomers—the developing countries—should rid themselves of the notion that liberal trade is the obligation of the rich but a luxury for the poor.

If both sides can recognize their common interest in ordered economic relationships, solutions to the outstanding problems of the world economy should not be difficult. If they do not do so, the international economic order will have failed again, but the wreckage of a third breakdown in this century may not even admit of another chance of reconstruction. To choose that, as Lord Keynes remarked in 1945, would indeed be "crazy."

Acknowledgments

Parts of this chapter draw on Kenneth Durham et al., *Words Are Not Enough: a Report on the Perils of Protectionism*, Special Report No.2 (London: Trade Policy Research Centre, 1984). I wish to acknowledge the stimulating comments made by participants at the conference, especially those of Ambassador B. L. Das, Ambassador M. Dubey, Professor Carlos Díaz-Alejandro, Professor Gerhard Fels, Dr. Vijay Kelkar, Professor V. R. Panchamukhi, Dr. Jan Pronk, and Dr. André Sapir. I acknowledge the helpful comments of Dr. Jan Tumlir, director of economic research and analysis at the GATT Secretariat, and of Professor Jagdish N. Bhagwati.

Notes

1. See Richard N. Gardner, *Sterling-Dollar Diplomacy: the Origins and Prospects of Our International Economic Order*, 2d ed. (New York: McGraw-Hill, 1969), chap. 12, esp. pp. 234–235.

2. In 1981 61 percent of world exports and 80 percent of world exports of manufactures came from the industrial market economies. See *International Trade 1981–82* (Geneva: GATT Secretariat, 1982), table A24.

3. For discussions of the EC's trade policies, see Martin Wolf, "The European Community's Trade Policy," in Roy Jenkins (ed.), *Britain and the EEC* (London: Macmillan, 1983); and Jan Tumlir, "Strong and Weak Elements in the Concept of European Integration," in Fritz Machlup, Gerhard Fels, and Hubertus Müller-Groeling (eds.), *Reflections on a Troubled World Economy: Essays in Honour of Herbert Giersch* (London: Macmillan, for the Trade Policy Research Centre, 1983). See also Jan Tumlir, "International Economic Order: Can the Trend be Reversed?" *World Economy* 5 (March 1982): 29–41.

4. See Robert E. Hudec, *The GATT Legal System and World Trade Diplomacy* (New York: Praeger, 1975), p. 208.

5. See Kenneth W. Dam, *The GATT: Law and International Economic Organization* (Chicago: University of Chicago Press, 1970), pp. 225–226.

6. See Independent Commission on International Development Issues, *North-South: A Program for Survival* (Cambridge: MIT Press, 1980), p. 183.

7. For a discussion of the substantive breakdown, see Robert E. Hudec, *Adjudication of International Trade Disputes*, Thames Essay No. 16 (London: Trade Policy Research Centre, 1978), pp. 15–21.

8. For a discussion of the GATT meeting at ministerial level of November 1982, see Lydia Dunn et al., *In the Kingdom of the Blind: A Report on Protectionism and the Asian-Pacific Region*, Special Report No. 3 (London: Trade Policy Research Centre, 1983), chap. 1.

9. Liberalism cannot be defined precisely. In this context what is meant is, first, permitting markets rather than discretionary, administrative intervention to allocate resources and, second, setting protectionist instruments at levels that permit a steady expansion of world trade.

10. The case for free trade, while allowing for other interventions, is set out in a simple manner in W. M. Corden, *Trade Policy and Economic Welfare* (Oxford: Clarendon Press, 1974). This important argument was made in Jagdish Bhagwati and V. K. Ramaswami, "Domestic Distortions, Tariffs and the Theory of Optimum Subsidy," *Journal of Political Economy* 71 (February 1963): 44–50. See also James E. Meade, *Trade and Welfare* (London: Oxford University Press, 1955), and Harry G. Johnson, "Optimal Trade Intervention in the Presence of Domestic Distortions," in Robert E. Baldwin et al., *Trade, Growth and the Balance of Payments: Essays in Honour of Gottfried Haberler* (Chicago: Rand McNally; and Amsterdam: North-Holland, 1965).

11. See Sidney Golt, *Developing Countries in the GATT System*, Thames Essay No. 13 (London: Trade Policy Research Centre 1978), p. 10.

12. These data are from *International Trade 1981–1982* (Geneva: GATT Secretariat, 1982), table A24.

13. For a discussion of such administrative systems of protection, see J. M. Finger, H. K. Hall, and D. R. Nelson, "The Political Economy of Administered Protection," *American Economic Review* 72 (June 1982): 452–466.

14. See *Agreement on Interpretation and Application of Articles VI, XVI, and XXIII of the General Agreement on Tariffs and Trade* (Geneva: GATT Secretariat, 1979), article 14(3).

15. Ibid., article 14(7).

16. For this point, see Alexander J. Yeats, *Trade Barriers Facing Developing Countries* (London: Macmillan, 1979), chap. 4. See also *The Tokyo Round of Multilateral Trade Negotiations*, Supplementary Report by the Director General of the GATT (Geneva: GATT Secretariat, 1980), Annex B.

17. Yeats, table 4.

18. For a fuller discussion of the various derogations from the GATT, see Durham et al., *Words Are Not Enough*.

19. This does not mean that such trade liberalization was not of benefit to developing countries. On this see J. M. Finger, "Effects of the Kennedy Round

Tariff Concessions on the Exports of Developing Countries," *Economic Journal* 86 (March 1976): 87–95.

20. On this see Finger, Hall, and Nelson, "Political Economy."

21. On this see Golt, *Developing Countries*, p. 11; and Hudec, *Adjudication*.

22. See, for example, R. Figueredo, "Multilateral Trade Negotiations," TD/B(XXIII)/SC.I/Misc./ (Geneva: UNCTAD, 1981).

23. See Díaz-Alejandro and Gerald K. Helleiner, *Handmaiden in Distress: World Trade in the 1980s* (co-published by: North-South Institute, Ottawa, Overseas Development Council, Washington, and Overseas Development Institute, London, 1982) p. 15. See also p. 21.

24. See Dam, *GATT*, p. 248.

25. Ibid., chap. 14, esp. p. 237.

26. Ibid., p. 249.

27. On these attitudes, see Karin Kock, *International Trade Policy and the GATT, 1947–1967* (Stockholm: Almqvist & Wiksell, 1969), pp. 223–235.

28. On the GSP see, for example, Robert Baldwin and Tracy Murray, "MFN Tariff Reductions and Developing Country Trade Benefits under the GSP," *Economic Journal* 87 (March 1977): 30–46; Murray, *Trade Preferences for Developing Countries* (New York: John Wiley, 1977); André Sapir, "Trade Benefits under the EEC Generalised System of Preferences," *European Economic Review* 15 (March 1981): 339–355; and Sapir and Lars Lundberg, "The U.S. Generalised System of Preferences and Its Impact" (paper presented at a conference on the Structure and Evolution of Recent U.S. Trade Policy sponsored by the National Bureau of Economic Research and held in Cambridge, Massachusetts, December 3–4, 1982).

29. See Golt, *Developing Countries*, pp. 26–29, for the underlying reasons for these limitations.

30. See Constantine Vaitsos, "Crisis in Regional Economic Cooperation (Integration) Among Developing Countries," *World Development* 6 (June 1978): 719–769. For a discussion of the history of regional cooperation among developing countries in the context of the GATT, see Kock, *International Trade Policy*, pp. 247–260.

31. Data are from *Yearbook of International Trade Statistics 1980* (New York: United Nations, Special Table C).

32. See Ian M. D. Little, *Economic Development: Theory, Policy and International Relations* (New York: Basic Books, for The Twentieth Century Fund, 1982), p. 370.

33. From "Ministerial Declaration," restricted GATT Doc. W 38/4, Geneva, GATT Secretariat, November 29, 1982, 7(i).

34. Apart from the well-known successes, Hong Kong, Singapore, South Korea, and Taiwan, there has been rapid growth of manufactured exports from Brazil

and other countries in Latin America; from other East Asian countries (Malaysia, the Philippines and Thailand); from Sri Lanka; and from Mediterranean countries (Morocco, Tunisia, and, recently, Turkey). India has also achieved substantial progress in the past fifteen years or so. On some of the more recent success stories, see Oli Havrylyshyn and Iradj Alikhani, "Is There Cause for Export Optimism? An Inquiry into the Existence of a Second Generation of Successful Exporters," *Weltwirtschaftliches Archiv* 118 (1982): 651–63.

35. See Harry Johnson, "Commercial Policy: What Is There Left?" *Journal of World Trade Law* 9 (May–June 1975): 346.

36. These arguments were put forward by several participants at the conference in New Delhi.

37. It is perhaps not surprising that this pessimistic view was advanced in New Delhi. As I have observed of Indian trade policy in another context, "The degree of specialization is assumed away as a policy option, but is rather the outcome of the desire for self-sufficiency." See Wolf, *India's Exports* (New York: Oxford University Press, for the World Bank, 1982), p. 58.

38. On the trade policies of newly industrializing countries after the oil shock, see Bela Balassa, "The Newly Industrializing Developing Countries after the Oil Crisis," *Weltwirtschaftliches Archiv* 117 (1981): 142–94, which discusses Argentina, Brazil, Colombia, Chile, India, the Republic of Korea, Mexico, Singapore, Taiwan, Israel, Uruguay, and Yugoslavia.

39. A particularly striking example of the response of exports to import liberalization was provided by Chile in the 1970s. Whatever other problems emerged in the Chilean economy, the growth of nontraditional exports was remarkable. See on this T. G. Congdon, "Apertura Policies in the Cone of Latin America," *World Economy* 5 (September 1982): 140–41.

40. There is a vast literature on the optimal adjustment to liberalization. A concise discussion of the options is in Balassa, "Reforming the System of Incentives in Developing Countries," in *Policy Reform in Developing Countries* (Oxford: Pergamon Press, 1977), esp. pp. 25–26.

41. The issue of official support for transition to outward-looking policy is discussed in Anne O. Krueger, "Loans to Assist the Transition to Outward-looking Policies," *World Economy* 4 (September 1981): 271–281.

42. See J. M. Finger, "Incorporating the Gains from Trade into Policy," *World Economy* 5 (December 1982): 367–377.

43. Another and much fuller discussion of issues raised in this section is in Isaiah Frank, *Trade Policy Issues of Interest to the Third World*, Thames Essay No. 29 (London: Trade Policy Research Centre, 1981).

44. On the ineffectiveness of most protective devices, especially VERs, see Baldwin, *The Inefficacy of Trade Policy*, Essays in International Finance, No. 150 (Princeton: International Finance Section, Department of Economics, Princeton University, 1982).

45. On the evolution of the textile arrangements toward ever greater restrictiveness, see Donald B. Keesing and Martin Wolf, *Textiles Quotas against Developing Countries*, Thames Essay No. 23 (London: Trade Policy Research Centre, 1980), chaps. 2, 3.

46. It is true that the suggested categorization is also arbitrary. If the goal is, however, to ensure that preferences will serve their purported function of stimulating infant exports from the developing countries that need most help, the suggestion seems reasonable. Alternatively, the GSP could be limited to countries with exports of manufactures below a certain level. These are the only sorts of categorization that will lead industrial countries to remove their many restrictions on the use of the GSP, which is desirable if bureaucracy is to be minimized and indeed if the GSP is to be really beneficial for anyone. Nevertheless such *ad hoc* arguments based on political feasibility can never be entirely persuasive. The issue of eligibility for GSP treatment is therefore a vivid example of the difficulty of developing and sustaining a set of clear, generally acceptable and logically compelling rules that are not uniform for all.

47. There is plenty of reason to doubt the value to developing countries of most schemes for preferential liberalization of trade among themselves. A discussion of these issues is in Martin Wolf, *"Fortress Europe" and "Collective Self-reliance"*, Weltwirtschaft und Internationale Beziehungen Sonderdrucke 5 (Hamburg: Deutsches Übersee Institut, 1983). A critical examination of UNCTAD's scheme for a global system of trade preferences among developing countries is in Rolf J. Langhammer, "Problems and Effects of a Developing Country Tariff Concession Round on South-South Trade" (paper presented at a conference on South-South versus South-North Trade: Does the Direction of Developing Country Exports Matter? sponsored by the World Bank under the research project on the Direction of Developing Country Exports and held in Brussels, February 28–March 1, 1983).

48. See Gerard Curzon, "Neo-protectionism, the MFA and the European Community," *World Economy* 4 (September 1981): 261.

49. See Gerard Curzon, *Multilateral Commercial Diplomacy: the General Agreement on Tariffs and Trade and Its Impact on National Commercial Policies and Techniques* (London: Michael Joseph, 1965), pp. 157–165.

10

Rethinking Global Negotiations: Trade

Jere R. Behrman

From the perspective of the early 1980s my assignment to consider global trade policy options for the less-developed economies may seem a bleak task. After several decades of historically high expansion of international trade, recently there has been global stagnation or even a small decline. The major markets in the developed market economy countries have been depressed, with in most cases the highest unemployment rates experienced since the Great Depression.[1] The centrally planned economies likewise have experienced substantial recent declines in their growth. Frictions over economic policies are substantial among the developed countries, with much talk and some action being taken by the United States and the European Community against imports from each other, and more so, from Japan. Talk of the new protectionism is rampant, with recent examples of nontariff barriers (NTBs) and trade disputes among the DCs (the French decree in October 1982 that videotape recorders, mainly imported from Japan, must clear customs at Portiers; increased discussion of local-content restrictions on goods sold; the U.S.-EC disputes on steel and on agricultural exports), some of which spill over to restrict imports from LDCs. In addition, some of the NTBs of the DCs more specifically directed toward the LDCs apparently have been intensified recently, as suggested by the 1981 renegotiation and extension of the Multifiber Agreement (MFA) through 1986. Currency fluctuations have been substantial, with the key yen-dollar competitive edge shifted 70 percent in favor of the former between 1979 and 1982. Mexico, Brazil, Argentina, Chile, Poland, and Yugoslavia, among others, have large debt problems requiring immediate attention.

For such reasons many doubt that discussion of global trade issues has much relevance at this time. At one extreme some are sufficiently pessimistic about the potential benefits to the LDCs from global (or other) discussion on international trade to suggest that the best strategy for most LDCs is to turn inward behind protective barriers or to "delink" the South from the North.[2] Certainly a country may value autarky sufficiently or have a sufficiently dire prognosis of developments in the world economy to make such strategies desirable. However, short of such conditions, the experience of the past few decades suggests that the cost in terms of development and structural change of strong inward orientation or delinking is likely to be considerable. The experience of some of the more outward-oriented[3] LDCs has been extraordinary by historical standards, even during the tumultuous years of the past decade.[4] Of course there is always a problem in social-science research in identifying association from causality, and there are special conditions in the experience of every country. But despite such qualifications I interpret the available studies as strongly supportive of the conclusion that more outward orientation has been important in this experience.[5]

These studies suggest that a more outward orientation is advantageous for a number of reasons. First, more outward-oriented policies induce fewer distortions because the effective exchange rates for exports and imports tend to be similar rather than much higher for the latter as in most inward-oriented regimes. Second, more outward-oriented policies are much less likely to encounter the severe balance-of-payments constraints that are almost inevitable with inward-oriented policies. This generally is the case in part because of the improved export incentives and earnings, as well as reduced need to hold excess inventories for precautionary purposes. Therefore the restraining effects of other bottlenecks, such as infrastructure inadequacies and limited agricultural growth, can be mitigated. Third, under more outward-oriented policies, returns to scale and competition to lessen Leibenstenian X-inefficiency are likely to be more effective than with inward orientation, though direct empirical evidence for these effects is limited.[6] Fourth, outward orientation tends to place certain constraints on policy choices and on policy implementation, which limit inducements to divert scarce resources to directly unproductive profit-seeking activities (DUPs), limit the severity and longevity of policy errors, and generally tend to encourage price rather than quantitative interventions (and avoid the frequently capricious impact of the latter).[7] Fifth, more outward-oriented economies seem to be able to adapt better to the inevitable fluctuations in the world economy and to other external shocks.[8] This seems to be the case because of the development of quicker adjustment capacities in order to be competitive on the world market, greater access to short- and medium-term funding in international capital markets, closer links to capital-surplus countries, and therefore more capacity for handling short-term foreign exchange shortfalls. Sixth, dynamics seems to favor outward orientation since there appear to be important returns to scale and learning by doing regarding the penetration of foreign markets, the location of foreign buyers, the establishment of national goodwill and the satisfaction of foreign quality, labeling, and other critical non-price specifications. In contrast, inward-oriented strategies inevitably eventually become more costly to pursue because of the limits on the size of the domestic market and the related need to introduce production of items in which a country has less and less true comparative advantage, as well as the relative isolation from international technological changes and international pressures for productivity improvements.

A less extreme position than delinking is taken by others who agree that participation in international trade generally increases the options of LDCs but argue that the current overwhelmingly critical issues are not directly related to trade but instead pertain to reinstigating growth in the DCs, buttressing the international financial system, and limiting currency fluctuations.[9] Only when the world economy has moved out of its present malaise, they suggest, will global discussions on international trade have high priority.

I agree that issues other than trade should have high priority currently. But it would not be advisable to give too low priority to trade concerns for at least two reasons. First, the development by the LDCs of new positions for global (or major subgroups) negotiations will take time. Therefore only if consideration of options is active now is there much chance that a consensus will have emerged regarding new options in the trade sphere by the mid-1980s. Second, and perhaps more important, trade policies are not stagnant; they either encourage greater international intercourse or become more restrictive. To emphasize this point, Bergsten and Cline have used the analogy of a bicycle: Either it keeps moving forward or it collapses.[10] The basic problem is political: In a world of nation-states the benefits from restricting imports generally are much more concentrated in politically more powerful producer interest groups (including labor) of the importing nation than are the losses (which are widely dispersed among many users and exporters in the importing country or among exporters from other nations who do not have much of a direct political voice in the importing country).[11] At times a particular nation with a strong free-trade orientation has been sufficiently powerful to lead much of the world toward freer trade despite such interests (examples are Great Britain in the pre–World War I period and the United States in the post–World War II quarter century). However, currently no single nation can play that role. Therefore, unless there is a concerted effort on the part of a number of nations to keep the "bicycle" of free trade moving, the narrow interests of politically powerful production-related groups will lead to greater restrictions, probably reinforced by retaliation. Such an outcome not only might lead to a spiral of deterioration in international trade but might also exacerbate other international interactions, such as those related to financial flows and debts, with a resulting costly reversal of the secular trend toward increased international economic interaction of the post–World War II decades. Therefore in the rest of this chapter I consider some positions that the LDCs might adopt regarding international trade.

Special Treatment for LDCs, the New International Economic Order, and Related Proposals

The General Agreement on Trade and Tariffs (GATT) provides the framework within which most international trade occurs (at least between the LDCs and the DCs). As is well known but is still frequently and perhaps appropriately emphasized, most LDCs were not parties to the establishment of the GATT (though India and some Latin American countries, including Brazil, Chile, and Cuba, were active participants in the postwar negotiations on internationl trade arrangements). The LDCs tend to feel like outsiders to a rich-nation GATT club, though often they are affected by decisions made in that club. Partly in response to this sense, UNCTAD was established to focus on trade and development issues. In global negotiations the UNCTAD secretariat, the Group of 77, and other groups purporting to represent the interest of the LDCs have tended to argue for special treatment of the LDCs and for the creation of institutions to cover dimensions of international trade discussed in the stillborn International Trade Organization (ITO) charter (such as primary commodity agreements and discriminatory preferences for LDCs), but not originally included in the GATT. Many of these proposals were incorporated into the 1974 call for a New International Economic Order (NIEO), which shaped considerably the subsequent discussion about the international economy and the developing countries.

General Themes

The unifying themes in these proposals include producer-oriented mercantilism regarding export markets, doubts about the desirability of free markets, belief in the creation of institutions to improve the nature of international trade from the point of view of LDCs, and a call for special treatment of the LDCs in international markets. Many of these themes were reflected in the words of Manmohan Singh in his 1980 keynote address at the Sixty-third annual conference of the Indian Economic Association:

> The basic philosophy of NIEO is frankly interventionist. It involves interferences with the working of the free market forces both at the national and the international level. . . .
> It is a basic assumption of the NIEO . . . that the trade needs of developing countries cannot be adequately met by adherence to the GATT rules of non-discriminatory multilateral trading system with its emphasis on most favored nation treatment and on reciprocity in trade negotiations. The emphasis in NIEO is on the principle of more favourable treatment on a non-reciprocal basis for the developing countries so as to enhance their access to markets of developed countries and thereby increase their share of world trade. This requires both removal of existing trade barriers as well as positive international action to increase export earnings of developing countries.[12]

Some discussion of these themes is useful. The mercantilism is reflected in the focus on improving export markets for LDC producers. There is relatively little emphasis on LDC users, though some of the concerns about declining and fluctuating terms of trade and the market power of multinational corporations (MNCs) may relate to the position of LDC users. Even in these cases, however, the emphasis is more on the position of LDC economies as a whole than on that of individual users. The concern is more on the availability and the use of national foreign exchange than on the costs to individual users. No emphasis is given, for example, to demands to remove barriers so LDC users, whether consumers or manufacturers, can have better access to low-price Japanese electronics.

The asymmetrical emphasis on export markets for LDC producers as opposed to domestic users of imports is not unlike that on domestic markets for DC producers. In fact, it may in part reflect similar political power of LDC producers in their own domestic markets, which makes it difficult for LDC governments to change their policies in ways that might threaten the strong vested interests in inward-oriented production. There may be some irony in the effort of many LDCs to change the international environment to favor their export producers at the same time they maintain their domestic policies to favor import substitution production over export orientation.

Furthermore, although all producers for export markets are consumers, far from all consumers also are producers for exports, so the asymmetrical emphasis on export markets for producers as opposed to domestic users of imports is likely to make a difference regarding the distribution of benefits. Moreover, LDC exporters tend to be relatively well off within their own societies. The apparent effort of the LDCs to concentrate benefits from new international trade policies among LDC producers for exports while maintaining import barriers therefore may lead to increased internal inequalities.

Of course this is a static concern. Perhaps changes to favor LDC exporters will induce dynamic reactions, for reasons such as mentioned in the introduction, to the benefit of all of society. If so, however, it also would seem desirable for most LDCs to eliminate their own national policy biases against export production in order to accelerate such developments.

Assumptions about the inadequacies of international markets permeate the LDCs' call for changes in international trade regimes. Critiques focus on the distribution of gains from trade, the existence of market power since MNCs and state enterprises are major actors in international markets, and imperfect information.

On both an abstract and an empirical level, many dimensions of these critiques seem well based. Even if most of the problems are assumed away by focusing on static analysis with perfect information, no market power, and no externalities, idealized markets lead to efficiency—but in general not to the optimal distribution of outcomes (unless the initial distribution of assets is just right, which hardly seems the case globally). And even efficiency is not obtained once market power, externalities, uncertainty (given the incompleteness of futures markets), or imperfections in other markets are included in the analysis.

At one level, therefore, it is easy to be sympathetic with the disbelief of many observers when DC policy makers and academics derive strong conclusions and are highly critical of NIEO-type proposals on the bases of extremely simple models. An example is provided by Harry Johnson's severe 1976 criticism of primary-commodity buffer-stock price-stabilization agreements and of UNCTAD economists because "elementary economic analysis" reveals that the UNCTAD proposals would lead either to a reduction in producer revenue or an increase in revenue variability.[13] Even if one grants Johnson his use of simple static supply-and-demand models with no externalities, no market power, and so on, his strong critique depends critically on further simplifying assumptions (for example, linear supply and demand curves with instantaneous adjustments and additive stochastic shifts). Rather than demonstrating the incompetence of UNCTAD economists as Johnson claims, his analysis demonstrated the extent to which special simplifying assumptions may be misleading, no matter how arrogantly the results are presented.

Even if actual markets do not fit simple idealizations and simple models of markets may be misleading, however, markets may provide incentives that shape considerably the behavior of producers and of users. The available accumulated empirical evidence of recent decades, in fact, suggests that the responsiveness to such incentives is substantial, at least in the medium and the long run, in a wide range of human endeavors: supply responses of traditional and modern farmers, investments in human capital, the development of innovations, the energy intensiveness of production, and private agricultural production in some socialist economies. Substitution in production and in use usually seems to be substantial in the longer run if markets create incentives to do so. Therefore policies to improve the functioning of international markets from the point of view of developing countries are more likely to be effective if they recognize and, if possible, use the market responsiveness to market incentives.

Institutions well may help improve the functioning of markets. Most orthodox international economists would claim, for example, that the institution of the GATT has helped on net to improve world international trade in the post–World War II as opposed to the prewar period. The existence of the GATT has helped to protect the diffuse direct interests of users in DCs and the indirect interests of exporters against the national producers' more politically focused interest in restricting access of foreigners to domestic DC markets. Market pressures alone probably would have not balanced off users' and exporters' interests in more international trade against the protectionistic inclinations of DC producers because of the disparities in effective political power among these groups. But the institutionalization of movements toward lessened tariff barriers in the various multilateral trade negotiations (MTNs) of the GATT probably have provided a better, albeit precarious, balance.

In the same vein it is sensible for the LDCs to seek institutional arrangements in which their interests are well represented in the light of disparities, generally to their disadvantage, in economic and political power. For such institutions or institutional changes to be effective, however, they either must increase the effective power of the developing countries themselves or involve the active cooperation of other powerful entities, such as governments of DCs or MNCs. This is all the more important the more the new or changed institutions create market incentives for behavior that counters the attainment of the ends of the institution.

The call for special treatment of the LDCs generally is based on the presumption that the poorer should be treated more favorably in terms of market options and so on than the richer. This is a second-best solution, given that first-best income transfers toward a more equitable world distribution are widely perceived to have been and to be likely to continue to be grossly inadequate. Just as justice demands that equals be treated equally, it also may imply that unequals are treated unequally. Thus, the LDCs have argued for favorable and preferential treatment under international rules, which has been granted *ipso facto* for some time under the GATT.

The call for nonuniform rules is not the same as a call for nonuniversal rules, though sometimes this confusion occurs. As Streeten argues eloquently, universal rules contain no "uneliminable references to individual cases" but do not necessarily imply uniform treatment of different cases.[14] For example, a progressive income tax may be a universal rule, but it does not treat the rich the same as the poor.

The DCs and the centrally planned economies accept the principle and, to a certain extent, the practice of universal rather than uniform rules for their own societies, but they seem less amenable to act on it in the international context, even though global inequalities are large relative to those in their own nations. From the point of view of the LDCs, it obviously would be desirable if greater acceptance of such a principle were to occur in the DCs and CPEs in the longer run, perhaps with concrete manifestations in forms such as an international progressive income tax with revenues redistributed toward the poorer. In the shorter run, however, the LDCs should be careful to exploit what agreement exists regarding their preferential treatment in ways that most aid in their goal attainment and not fall into the trap of advocating special treatment as an end in itself.

Examples of Explicit Policies

I now consider two of the global policies regarding international trade that have been most emphasized by the LDCs in recent years.

International Primary Commodity Market

The commodity problem, as long perceived from the view of LDCs, has two dimensions: destabilizing fluctuations in the world markets, which feed back on the producing LDCs, and deteriorating terms of trade due to lower income elasticities for primary commodities than for manufacturers and to market power in the developed countries, as argued most effectively in Prebisch.[15] Although empirical support for either proposition is weak at best, the call for international primary commodity market regulation long has been high on the list of LDCs' apparent global priorities regarding reform.[16] In part this has been because of the large share of primary commodities in LDC exports: over 90 percent of goods exports in 1960 and over 80 percent twenty years later.[17] Thus, small proportional improvements in the returns to LDCs from these markets would have relatively large impact on their total export earnings.

Catalytic for the call for an NIEO in 1974 in fact was the apparent success of developing-country producers of one of these commodities—petroleum—in raising substantially its international price. Despite the cost in terms of scarce foreign exchange to non-OPEC LDCs (the share of fuels in their import bill more than doubled), euphoria about "commodity power" was widespread in the LDCs. At the heart of the NIEO was a call for an Integrated Commodity Program (ICP) to be developed by the UNCTAD secretariat. After considerable debate and dissension, at UNCTAD IV in Nairobi in 1976 a resolution was approved to establish an ICP.

The UNCTAD ICP focused on international buffer-stock schemes for ten core commodities of particular relevance to LDC exporters, to avoid "excessive fluctuations" and to achieve price levels that would "be renumerative and just to producers and equitable to consumers."[18] The first of these purposes obviously refers to the first dimension of the commodity problem defined above. The second apparently refers to the second dimension, though there was and is considerable ambiguity about what prices are "just to producers and equitable to consumers." (In pre-UNCTAD IV documents there had been considerable discussion of indexation of primary commodity prices to the prices of

LDC imports, but indexation was not mentioned in the resolution in order to lessen opposition from some DCs.) The "integration" in the ICP was to be provided by a $6 billion Common Fund (CF) to help finance the individual international commodity agreements (ICAs). In addition to the establishment of international buffer stocks, the resolution called for a number of other measures, including improved information, enlarged compensatory financing for export shortfalls, improved market access, improved infrastructure, research and development, and "consideration of special measures for commodities whose problems cannot be adequately solved by stocking and which experience a persistent price decline."

The UNCTAD ICP attracted considerable controversy and debate, and even a little analysis of some of its features. Critics charged that price stabilization would reduce producers' revenues or increase variability in those revenues. Some of the same critics, apparently not bothered by consistency, also charged that it would arbitrarily benefit whichever countries or individuals happened to have comparative advantage in the production of the core commodities—not the poorest LDCs or the poorest in the producing countries. Operational difficulties in identifying underlying price trends were emphasized. Criticism was also leveled at the possibility of attempting to change the price level (as opposed to reducing price fluctuations) at the expense of users. Moreover, opposition was strong against some of the proposed additional features (the "second window") and the establishment of another international bureaucracy. Simulations with econometric models which I undertook at the time suggested that there were some possible positive economic gains from the price-stabilization feature that might outweigh the economic costs but that efforts to increase the price levels were likely to bankrupt the agreements fairly quickly.[19]

Negotiations proceeded on the CF at a much slower pace than had been hoped for by its proponents. In June 1980 an agreement was finally reached on a modified and much smaller CF ($400 million) with voluntary financing for the additional "second window" operations. However, ratification has been slow; only 37 countries had ratified the CF by December 1982. The current deadline for full ratification (requiring a minimum of 90 countries accounting for at least two-thirds of the CF's directly contributed capital) is September 30, 1983 (originally it was March 30, 1982). Full ratification by that deadline is far from ensured, and the CF cannot be established and the financial resources committed to it cannot be used until full ratification. An ICA has been established for natural rubber (1979), and ICAs have been renegotiated for cocoa (1980) and tin (1981). The first and third of these reflect the UNCTAD program principle of joint financing by producers and users and contain a provision for negotiation of an association with the CF. Also, the compensatory finance facilities of the IMF have been expanded considerably, as advocated by many proponents of the ICP as a complementary measure but viewed as a preferable alternative by many opponents of the ICP.[20]

All in all, this record with the ICP does not generate much enthusiasm these days. Moreover, recent analysis by Yeats suggests that, for many developing countries, exchange-rate fluctuations have been larger than commodity-price fluctuations in the past decade, and stabilization of dollar prices would have destabilized real terms of trade for a number of countries that are tied into other currency blocks (namely the franc).[21] Even OPEC appears to be in trouble, because of induced expansion of competing energy sources, price-induced reduction of energy intensity in production, and recessionary demand levels. Reports from UNCTAD VI at Belgrade state that even UNCTAD has "disowned" the ICP agreed in Nairobi in 1976.[22] One currently does not hear much about "commodity power." More than a few would agree with Taylor's characterization of the UNCTAD ICP as a "fiasco" and "a resounding failure that had much to do with dragging other more sensible NIEO proposals down."[23]

Was failure inevitable? Taylor seems to suggest that it was, because the second dimension of the commodity problem inevitably would lead to strong downward pressure on the terms of trade for primary commodities that an ICP could not resist. But, as I noted above, empirical evidence for the inevitable decline in the terms of trade for primary commodities hardly seems overwhelming. Nevertheless, I am sure that Taylor is right that a major reason for the failure was the assumption of many in the DCs that the hidden agenda of the UNCTAD ICP was to increase the price levels of these commodities above what they otherwise would have been. I also agree that it is very difficult in most markets to resist long-run market pressures, though if supply and demand elasticities are low enough, as for petroleum in the 1970s, considerable gains may be possible in the short and the medium run.

But that does not necessarily mean that the ICP had to fail. Clearly it is possible to maintain prices above equilibrium levels by policies for considerable periods of time if resources are sufficient and if motivation is strong enough due to income-distribution, political, or supply-security concerns. The DCs, for example, often have followed such policies for their agricultural sectors.[24] However, they did not see the income-distribution, political, or supply-security issues to be sufficiently important to warrant the possibly very large direct costs to them and to users of an ICP that might try to maintain "parity" for the UNCTAD core commodities. And the increasing integration across markets of different types implies that very large resources might be required to protect UNCTAD core commodity markets with price-stabilization schemes from speculative attacks.[25]

Thus, though ICAs probably will come and go in the future as in the past, the current outlook is not bright for the UNCTAD ICP. Even from UNCTAD one hears many rumbles about focusing on processing commodities and expanding compensatory finance instead of emphasizing the ICP and the CF.[26] The 1983 UNCTAD policy paper on commodity issues for UNCTAD VI in Belgrade, for example, claims that the ICP and the CF, if they had been effective, would have attenuated significantly the collapse in primary commodity prices of interest to developing countries between 1980 and 1982, though it is not persuasive regarding the effectiveness of ICAs in such circumstances.[27] It also suggests major changes in the ICP and in the ICAs, specifically the incorporation of supply controls (though without any discussion of how to make such controls effective, nor of demanders' reactions to such controls). Moreover, this policy paper emphasizes expansion of compensatory finance, increased market access, and encouragement of LDC participation in commodity processing and marketing as much as, if not more than, ICP- and ICA-type policies. And, with time and industrialization, primary commodities have become much less important for the LDCs as a group, though they remain very important for a number of individual LDCs.[28]

Generalized System of Preferences (GSP)[29]

At least since the postwar discussions on the ITO charter, the possibility of preferential access to export markets for the LDCs has been discussed. Initially the GATT resisted any modification of the basic principle of reciprocity. The United States was particularly strong in its opposition due to an apparent coalition of DC free traders who feared the violation of the most-favored-nation (MFN) principle of nondiscriminatory treatment and DC protectionists who feared competitive imports from the LDCs.

In the mid-1960s the United States found itself increasingly isolated on this issue and also fearful of being excluded from segmented or regionalized world markets resulting from preferential trading arrangements between the EC and LDCs. Therefore in 1967 the United States changed its position and accepted the principle of preferential tariff treatment toward all LDCs. At UNCTAD II in 1968 this principle was formally established, and in 1971 the contracting parties of GATT agreed to a waiver from the MFN clause of article 1.

Subsequent to UNCTAD II an UNCTAD committe attempted to co-ordinate GSP schemes. Nevertheless, GSPs were drawn up primarily on the national level so that eventually each donor country applied a somewhat different scheme at different times. The EC first introduced its system of preferences in 1971, and many other donor countries followed soon thereafter. The United States, however, delayed its introduction of GSPs until 1976 because of ongoing opposition to the scheme by both free traders and protectionists. Some detail about the U.S. GSP follows for illustrative purposes.

The 1974 U.S. Trade Act, which established the legal bases for the U.S. GSP, reflects the influence of both free traders and protectionists by requiring the president to extend preferences with due regard to (1) their effect on the development of the LDCs and (2) their impact on U.S. producers. It also requires consideration of (3) the extent of other GSPs granted by other donors. In the words of Sapir and Lundberg: "Clearly point (1) is adressed at the free-traders who defend the view that non-discriminating reduction in MFN tariff rates would be more beneficial to these countries (and the world) than the GSP. Point (2), on the other hand, is directed at the protectionists who dread the impact of the scheme on U.S. producers. Finally, point (3) makes clear the fact that the GSP is a political must vis-à-vis the developing countries."[30] These conflicting concerns have resulted in a very complex institution. There are detailed provisions regarding country coverage (including level of development and the extent to which it allows the United States access to its markets and natural resources) and product coverage (with a number of exceptions for "import-sensitive" products like textiles, apparel, watches, electronics, steel, footwear, glass products, and any other items deemed import-sensitive by the president).[31] There are limitations on the GSP pertaining to rules of origin (products must be imported directly from beneficiary LDCs and the sum of materials and value added from the beneficiary LDC must be at least 35 percent of the value of the product) and "competitive needs" (in which a beneficiary LDC loses GSP treatment for a product if its exports to the United States exceed half of the value of U.S. imports of the product or a certain dollar value adjusted annually on the bases of U.S. GNP growth, which was $51 million in 1982).

These exclusions limit considerably the generality of the GSP. For example, Sapir and Lundberg report that for the United States between 1976 and 1981, GSP duty-free imports totaled $34.2 billion as compared to total imports from LDCs of $536.7 billion. For all beneficiary, LDCs with over $100 million of GSP eligible imports, they calculated an average preference margin on total dutiable trade of 1.38 percent in 1979, though with a range from 0.35 percent for Malaysia to 3.66 percent for Israel. In that year the total U.S. tariff revenue forgone was $528 million, the largest four recipients[32] of which were Taiwan (160), Korea (78), Hong Kong (63), and Mexico (45).[33] They note that while the major beneficiaries tend to be relatively well-off LDCs, the incentives as measured by the share of GSP-eligible imports in total imports or by the percentage margin of preferences are not highly associated with per capita income. This limited association and the very limited coverage of the GSP is inconsistent with the avowed emphasis of the United States recently on graduation from the GSP in order to protect better the preferential treatment of the poorer LDCs. Instead it seems motivated substantially by protectionist tendencies.

What can be concluded from this summary of the GSP? On the positive side, from the point of view of global negotiations and the LDCs, international political pressures apparently forced the United States to adopt a policy with explicit preferences for the LDCs that had been long advocated by others but resisted by the United States. Moreover, some LDCs apparently have benefited modestly from the program. On the other hand, GSPs have hardly lived up to the hopes of advocates. The benefits have been small and very concentrated in their distribution. The complexities of the GSPs presumably have discriminated in favor of the better off among the LDCs because of their comparative advantage in acquiring information and satisfying complicated requirements. They also have made it difficult to know the weight being given to protectionist pressures in the process.

Of course, it may be too easy for an academic to be critical of real-world policies, which of necessity often reflect considerable compromise. Perhaps from the point of view of the LDCs the gain from GSPs has been worthwhile in establishing the principle of preferential treatment. Perhaps GSPs will be modified to be less complex and more inclusive.

Perhaps rules consistent with universal progressive preferences will evolve. But I have considerable doubts. The unenthusiastic and limited cooperation of the United States and of some other DCs regarding GSPs has been bought at a price. Rather than assent to a universal progressive principle, there has been grudging acceptance of special treatment and increased complexity in international trade regimes, which tends to work to the advantage of the better off among LDCs and of protectionist elements in the DCs. In my judgment the price probably has not been worth paying.

Strengthening the General and Universal Provisions of the GATT

The GATT was developed and is controlled primarily by the DCs. The LDCs have been on the fringes of the GATT and, within global negotiations, have argued forcibly for special treatment within the GATT framework.

Critical GATT principles, as summarized recently by Díaz-Alejandro and Helleiner, include unconditional nondiscrimination, predictability of market access, and transparency regarding trade barriers.[34] Since the establishment of GATT, the seven MTNs have resulted in a steady (though not without exceptions) movement toward removing tariff (and, to a lesser extent, other) barriers to international trade. This period, as Lewis and many others have noted, also has seen the highest sustained growth of world trade ever recorded.[35] LDCs as a group have participated substantially in this trade expansion and have also attained unprecedented sustained growth for their level of development.[36] There is some controversy over whether trade has been an engine or a handmaiden of this growth. I find the evidence reasonably persuasive that expanded international trade has had an important, and not a minor, role.

Recently, however, there has been growing concern about the "new protectionism" in the DCs. Although tariff barriers have dropped, OMAs and VERs apparently have increased, though the details of many of these arrangements are secret. For the most part these arrangements are outside of the GATT, though the MFA is an important exception to this generalization. They are not subject to open scrutiny by GATT or some other international agency but are administered privately and arbitrarily by the importing countries, often on a bilateral basis. Furthermore the GATT safeguard clause (article 19) is ineffective, and efforts to reformulate it at the Tokyo MTN floundered, in part because of disputes occasioned by the European Community's advocacy of selective safeguards. The concern about the new protectionism has grown to alarm in some quarters, including individuals and institutions generally not thought to occupy the most conservative, pro-market or pro-DC positions.[37] The GATT ministerial meetings of November 1982 did not seem to make major advances, though it may be premature to judge the results since historically many of the most important outcomes of GATT ministerial meetings have been from subsequent study groups.[38]

Hughes and Krueger recently have analyzed the effect of protection in DCs on LDCs' manufactures exports in the 1970s.[39] They note that NTBs often can be ineffective because they are unenforceable, because NTB-constrained suppliers may switch with non-NTB-constrained suppliers to a third market, or because NTB-constrained producers may shift to nonconstrained but similar products and be replaced by non-NTB-constrained producers. They observe that the real average annual growth rate in manufactures exports from LDCs to DCs was 11 percent in the 1970s, that in all major ISIC 2-digit manufactures categories the LDC share in DC imports increased between 1970 and 1980, and that Far Eastern LDC exporters increased their share of total LDC manufactures exports (largely at the expense of Latin America) despite the fact that many NTBs were directed toward the Far Eastern producers. They conclude that LDC supply conditions remain critical to success in foreign trade, that the rate of increase in LDC market shares was sufficient so that "it is difficult to imagine that [they] would have been significantly higher in the absence of any protectionist measures," that "it would appear that the greater welfare losses were to the protecting countries, rather than to the rest of the world."

Hughes and Krueger realize that their results need to be qualified because of the difficulty of controlling for other factors and the partial-equilibrium nature of their analysis. It is also possible that the new protectionism intensified substantially in the 1980s after their sample (for example, with the new MFA and intra-DC NTBs that spill over to LDCs more than offsetting some lessened NTBs, such as for footwear and leather products in the United States in 1981). Despite such qualifications, however, the Hughes and Krueger estimates clearly raise questions about the extent to which the new conventional wisdom regarding the deleterious effects of the new DC protectionism on LDCs exports is valid.

Even if the extent of the new protectionism to date may have been overstated, however, I perceive the threat to be considerable. As Hughes and Krueger note, even in the more optimistic days of 1969, the Burke-Hartke bill with its strict quantitative limits on the levels and rates of growth of all imports into the United States was defeated by a narrow margin. Recently there have been a number of local-content and other protectionist measures debated by major DC governments. In light of the duration of the recent world recession, the probability has not been negligible that a major importer might adopt some such highly protectionist measure and ignite a chain of protectionist reactions. The bicycle may be toppled easily.

Should the LDCs Participate in and Strengthen the GATT?

Several influential commentators recently have called for the LDCs to participate more fully in the GATT and to realize more the advantages to be gained from the basic GATT principles of unconditional non-discrimination, predictability, and transparency. For example, T. N. Srinivasan ended his 1982 Harry G. Johnson Memorial Fund Lecture in this way: "To conclude, the developing countries have a strong interest in an open international trading system. . . . Their commercial diplomacy will be far more rewarding if it is directed towards ensuring such a system than towards special pleading or preferences, while negotiations should go on in other fora towards increasing their voice, and hence their responsibility, in international organizations."[40] A. W. Clausen, president of the World Bank and International Finance Corporation, spoke in a similar vein before the GATT ministerial meeting in November 1982: " . . . all the developing countries have a stake in liberal trade. We hope that more developing countries will join GATT, and the GATT, in turn, will develop mechanisms through which more attention is focused on items of particular concern to the developing countries."[41] Should these statements be viewed as efforts to co-opt the LDCs into putting aside their just demands for special treatment and thereby be exploited more by rapacious DCs and MNCs? Or might it make sense for the LDCs to adopt a global position of further participation in the GATT and support of the GATT basic principles?

I think that there is a strong, though not unqualified, case that the LDCs should accept such advice and follow such a strategy. I say this not because I think that international markets then would become perfect textbook competitive markets but because they probably would be better from the point of view of the LDCs than they would be if the LDCs focus on preferential treatment. If so, then one important gain from the point of view of the LDCs might be the option of the impetus of growth and adjustment from the more-outward orientation, as discussed earlier. Another important gain might be the capacity to balance off better the internal diffuse interests of users and exporters vis-à-vis the entrenched interests of politically powerful, import-substitution producers through internationally coordinated reductions of LDC import barriers. This well might increase efficiency and perhaps equity internally in the LDCs, as well as accelerate the growth in South-South trade (including the important primary commodity component emphasized by Havrylyshyn and Wolf).[42]

Why might international markets be better from the point of view of LDCs if they were to follow such a strategy? There are at least six reasons: Such a strategy would identify with a strong free-trade belief in many DCs and thus gain political support from that important group. The preferential treatment strategy, in contrast, not only loses potential free-trade allies in the DCs but increases the claim for special (and protective) treatment for senile industries, and this is likely to be directed particularly toward the newcomers in the markets, the LDCs. The preferential approach, moreover, may result at most in grudging acceptance by the DCs and therefore long stalemates and quite modest gains of limited duration, as with the UNCTAD ICP and GSPs. If the LDCs and the free trade forces in the DCs form an alliance they probably will be better able to assure adherence to the GATT principles, and the LDC exporters are likely to gain relatively from greater adherence to these principles because their more imperfect information makes predictability and transparency more important to them than to DC producers. With the more open trade, the LDCs would have a larger share of given markets. Moreover, the world economy probably would grow more quickly due to greater gains from international specialization.

Certainly Nirvana will not suddenly appear with the adoption by the LDCs of such a strategy, and there are risks associated with it, depending in part on the quickness of recovery in the DCs. But it seems to be better than continuing the past strategy of advocating special treatment and exceptions.

International Trade Regime That Might be Advocated as Part of
Such a Strategy

Several themes seem noteworthy in considering specific trade policy
positions for the LDCs if such a strategy were adopted.

First, since the LDCs are relatively weak economically, it is desirable
to form coalitions to pursue common ends and to attempt to substitute
institutions and rules for their economic weakness. As noted above,
the most obvious alliance would be with the free-trade interests in
DCs.

Second, as part of the strategy of participating more fully in GATT,
the LDCs probably would have to give up special treatment, such as
GSPs, and reduce their own barriers to imports. As discussed above,
giving up the current GSPs would not be all that costly and probably
would have gains in reducing DC protectionist pressures for special
treatment. Also, reducing their own import barriers probably would
have longer-run advantages regarding efficiency and distribution. But
the transition would be difficult, particularly given current shortages
of foreign exchange in many LDCs. Therefore, a transition period with
explicit scheduled reductions of barriers, presumably coordinated with
other macro and exchange-rate adjustments, might be desirable.[43]

Third, aside from the question of transition, there is the issue of
graduation. In principle, I have no trouble with a universal rule favoring
the poorer countries, particularly as a second-best solution given political
limits on income transfers. However, in practice this may make it much
more difficult for DC governments to resist pleas for special protectionist
treatment from aged industries with low-skilled laborers in poor areas
within their boundaries. The GSPs, for example, may have had this
effect. Therefore, it may be advantageous for the LDCs to accept uniform
rather than universal rules for trade, particularly if this acceptance can
be bargained off for better financial flows or other ends. If there is a
graduation scheme, however, it would seem desirable that it incorporate
lesser preferences for the more advanced LDCs over a continuum and
not a lack of association until some sharp cutoff point, as Sapir and
Lundberg suggest is the case for the current U.S. GSP.[44]

Fourth, just as the LDCs should expect to give up some special
treatment, they should expect to see the elimination of apparent special
discrimination against them. Examples include escalation in tariff structures, the existing higher tariffs on some products that they export than
on other goods,[45] many ongoing NTBs, and perhaps most important

the effective exclusion of temperate agricultural products from GATT principles. Somewhat dated studies by Tims and Valdes, for example, suggest that in the mid-1970s OECD trade barriers in agricultural products cost the LDCs export markets of up to 12 billion 1980 dollars per year.[46] Such a value is at least an order of magnitude greater than estimates of the impact of LDCs of a hypothetical ICP for the UNCTAD ten core commodities.[47]

Fifth, because of the LDCs' information disadvantage, transparency and predictability are of major relevance. This suggests the importance of bringing NTBs under GATT surveillance, with translation of NTBs into temporary tariffs to increase transparency and predictability to the extent possible and with an adequate nondiscriminatory safeguard clause. Article 19 of GATT should be revised to ensure that all NTBs are justified in terms of more explicit criteria with the burden of proof on the importing nations, time-bound, and subject to greater multilateral control and discipline.

Sixth, the above discussion of various policies above (e.g., Hughes and Krueger's study of NTBs) suggests considerable responses to market incentives by various market entities. Therefore, policy should be designed with cognizance of this responsiveness. This generally would seem to mean that more general policies are favored over more specific ones and that price policies are favored over quantitative ones.

If one can judge by the UNCTAD policy papers for UNCTAD VI in Belgrade in 1983, at least some major groups speaking on behalf of the LDCs may be moving in the direction of strengthening the general and universal provisions of the GATT.[48] This support, however, is ambiguous and quite qualified by continued adherence to old and questionable shibboleths regarding matters like ICAs and GSPs. This may be a matter of bargaining strategy; if so, such groups should be careful that they do not unintentionally lose natural allies like the free traders in the DCs by this strategy. But I fear that it is more than a bargaining strategy and that such groups are shackled by previous positions and claims, with the possible result of working unconsciously against the best interests of the LDCs on trade issues. If so, it would be desirable for them to think afresh about the trade-offs between arguing for special treatment and for strengthening the general and universal provisions of the GATT, in which case they might conclude with me that the cost of emphasizing special treatment may be high indeed.

Acknowledgments

I thank conference participants, and particularly Jagdish N. Bhagwati, for helpful comments.

Notes

1. Currently there are increasing signs of recovery, at least in the United States, though concern remains widespread about the possible stillbirth of recovery if inflation accelerates. See, for example, Jonathon Fuerbringer, "President's Forecast Is Revised," *New York Times* (25 March 1983), D1–10 and "The Recovery Game," *Economist* (23 April 1983), 11–12.

2. Among the proponents of delinking or greater protectionism in the LDCs are Samir Amin, Lance Taylor, and the Cambridge Economic Policy Group (CEPC) of the Department of Applied Economics at the University of Cambridge in the United Kingdom. An excellent account of the debate on delinking is provided by Carlos F. Díaz-Alejandro, "Delinking North and South: Unshackled or Unhinged," in Council on Foreign Relations/1980s Project, *Rich and Poor Nations in the World Economy* (New York: McGraw-Hill, 1978). For a recent call (but not much careful empirical analysis) for less dependence on the foreign sector by LDCs, see Lance Taylor, "Back to Basics: Theory for the Rhetoric in the North-South Round," *World Development* 10:4 (April 1982), 327–336.

3. I use the term "more outward-oriented" because for the most part the LDCs with fast-growing exports did not bias their policy regimes in favor of exports over import substitution but merely lessened or removed previous biases against exports and in favor of import subsitution (though in the Republic of Korea and Brazil, there may have been a move to an export bias). See Jagdish N. Bhagwati, *Foreign Trade Regimes and Economic Development: Anatomy and Consequences of Exchange Rate Control Regimes* (Cambridge, Mass.: Ballinger for NBER, 1978), chap. 8, and Anne O. Krueger, *Foreign Trade Regimes and Economic Development: Liberalization Attempts and Consequences* (Cambridge, Mass.: Ballinger for NBER, 1978).

4. For example, average annual percentage per capita real growth rates for 1960 through 1980 (1960 through 1978 for Taiwan) were 7.5 for Singapore, 7.0 for the Republic of Korea, 6.8 for Hong Kong, and 6.6 for Taiwan, the so-called Gang of Four Superexporters. For comparison, the average annual percentage per capita real income growth rates were 1.2 for all low-income countries, 3.8 for all middle-income countries, 3.6 for industrial market economies, 6.3 for high-income oil exporters, and 4.2 for nonmarket industrial economies. In the 1970s as compared to the 1960s, real GDP average annual growth rates declined slightly for Hong Kong (10.0 to 9.3) and for Singapore (8.8 to 8.4) but increased for the Republic of Korea (8.6 to 9.5). Percentage growth rates for 1981 and 1982 are 9.9 and 5.6 for Singapore, 11 and 4 for Hong Kong, 8 and 5 for the Republic of Korea, and 5.5 and 4.2 for Taiwan. See World Bank, *World De-*

velopment Report (New York: Oxford University Press for the World Bank, 1980, 1982), and Steve Lohr, "Protectionism Imperials East Asia's Exports," *New York Times* (9 December 1982), D1, D17.

5. Among the most notable of these studies are the OECD project on industry and trade in developing countries, under the directorship of and summarized by I. M. D. Little, T. Scitovsky, and M. Scott, *Industry and Trade in Some Developing Countries: A Comparative Study* (London: Oxford University Press, 1970); the NBER project on foreign trade regimes and economic development under the directorship of Bhagwati, *Foreign Trade Regimes*, and Krueger, *Foreign Trade Regimes*; a series of World Bank studies under the directorship of Bela Balassa, "Structural Adjustment Policies in Developing Economies." *World Development* 10:1 (January 1982), 23–28, *The Structure of Protection in Developing Countries* (Baltimore and London: Johns Hopkins University Press for the World Bank, 1971), and *Development Strategies in Semi-Industrial Economies* (Baltimore and London: Johns Hopkins University Press for the World Bank, 1982); the Kiel Institute of World Economics project on industrialization policies of semi-industrialized economies under the directorship of Juergen B. Donges, "A Comparative Survey on Industrialization Policies in Fifteen Semi-Industrial Countries," *Weltwirtschaftliches Arciv.* 112 (1976), 626–659; and the NBER project on trade and employment in developing countries under the directorship of Anne O. Krueger with results summarized in Anne O. Krueger, Hal B. Lary, Terry Manson, and Narongchai Akrasanee, eds., *Trade and Employment in Developing Countries, 1: Individual Studies* (Chicago: University of Chicago Press for NBER, 1981), and in Anne O. Krueger, ed. *Trade and Employment in Developing Countries, 2: Factor Supply and Substitution* (Chicago: University of Chicago Press for NBER, 1982). More concise summaries of these and related studies are provided in Jere R. Behrman, "Developing-Country Perspective on Industrial Policies," in F. Gerard Adams and Lawrence R. Klein, eds., *Industrial Policies for Growth and Competitiveness* (Lexington, Mass.: Lexington Books, 1983), 153–186; Jagdish N. Bhagwati and T. N. Srinivasan, "Trade Policy and Development," in Rudiger Dornbusch and Jacob A. Frenkel, eds., *International Economic Policy: Theory and Evidence* (Baltimore: Johns Hopkins University Press, 1978); and Carlos F. Díaz-Alejandro, "Trade Policies and Economic Development," in Peter Kenen, ed., *International Trade and Finance: Frontiers for Research* (Cambridge: Cambridge University Press, 1974), 93–150. Strong reservations are expressed by Taylor, "Back to Basics," and Paul Streeten, "A Cool Look at 'Outward-looking' Strategies for Development," *World Economy* (1982), 159–169, but neither critique is based on scrutiny of the substantial empirical evidence in the studies listed here.

6. See Harvey Leibenstein, *General X-Efficiency Theory and Economic Development* (New York: Oxford University Press, 1978).

7. See Jagdish N. Bhagwati and T. N. Srinivasan, "Revenue Seeking: A Generalization of the Theory of Tariffs," *Journal of Political Economy* 88 (December 1980), 1069–1087, Jagdish N. Bhagwati and T. N. Srinivasan, "The Welfare Consequences of Directly-Unproductive Profit-Seeking (DUP) Activities: Price versus Quantity Distortions," *Journal of International Economics* 13 (August

1982), 33–44, and Jagdish N. Bhagwati, "DUP Activities and Rent-Seeking" (New York: Columbia University, 1983, mimeo.). Bhagwati, *Foreign Trade Regimes*, suggests that costly direct controls "may be significantly less under export promotion because price, distribution and other controls may make little sense to bureaucrats when firms' outputs are mainly addressed to overseas, rather than domestic, markets" (p. 214).

8. See in particular Balassa, "Structural Adjustment Policies," and the references therein.

9. Related proposals to coordinate macro policies, establish new debt relief institutions or facilities, and limit currency fluctuations through target zones for currency movements are frequent. Other chapters in this book consider some of these topics.

10. See Fred C. Bergsten and William R. Cline, *Trade Policy in the 1980's* (Washington, D.C.: Institute for International Economics, 1982).

11. A similar point is expanded on in many dimensions in a provocative recent book by Mancur Olson, *The Rise and Decline of Nations: Economic Growth, Stagflation and Social Rigidity* (New Haven: Yale University Press, 1982).

12. See Manmohan Singh, "New International Economic Order" (New Dehli: Keynote Address at the Indian Economic Association 63d Annual Conference, 26 December 1980), 4, 6–7.

13. Although I have used Johnson's analysis as an example because of his prominence and influence, he was not alone in making such assumptions. Brook, Grilli, and Waelbroeck of the World Bank and McNicol of the U.S. Treasury, for example, also made such assumptions despite the previous demonstration of Newbery, Turnovsky, and others of the sensitivity of the results to the assumptions mentioned. See Harry G. Johnson, "Commodities: Less Developed Countries' Demands and Developed Countries' Response," in Jagdish N. Bhagwati, ed. *The New International Economic Order: The North-South Debate* (Cambridge: MIT Press, 1977), 240–251; E. M. Brook, E. R. Grilli, and J. Waelbroeck, "Commodity Price Stabilization and the Developing Countries: The Problem of Choice" (Washington, D.C.: World Bank Staff Working Paper 262, 1977); David L. McNicol, *Commodity Agreements and Price Stabilization* (Lexington, Mass.: Lexington Books, 1978); David Newbery, "Price Stabilization with Risky Production" (Stanford, Calif.: Economic Working Paper No. 69, 1976); Stephen Turnovsky, "Price Expectations and the Welfare Gains from Price Stabilization," *American Journal of Agricultural Economics* 56 (November 1974), 706–716 and "The Distribution of Welfare Gains from Price Stabilization: A Survey of Some Theoretical Issues," in F. Gerard Adams and Sonia Klein, eds., *Stabilizing World Commodity Markets: Analysis, Practice and Policy* (Lexington, Mass.: Lexington Books, 1978), 119–148. For further discussion of the empirical relevance of these assumptions, see Jere R. Behrman, *International Commodity Agreements: An Evaluation of the UNCTAD Integrated Commodity Programme* (Washington, D.C.: Overseas Development Council, 1977), which is reprinted as "Commodity Agreements" in William R. Cline, ed., *Proposals*

for a New International Economic Order: An Economic Analysis of Effects on Rich and Poor Countries (New York: Praeger for the Overseas Development Council, 1979), 61–153. For provocative discussion of the theory underlying this and other North-South issues, see Gerald K. Helleiner, ed., For Good or Evil: Economic Theory and North-South Negotiations (Toronto and Buffalo: University of Toronto Press, 1982).

14. Paul Streeten, "Approaches to a New International Order," World Development 10:1 (January 1982), 1–18 (esp. p. 4).

15. Raul Prebisch, "Commercial Policy in the Underdeveloped Countries," American Economic Review 49 (1959), 251–273.

16. Fluctuations in the international prices of major commodities exported by the developing countries have been relatively large, but well-specified studies have not found evidence of a substantial impact on producing LDCs' goal attainment, though, of course, in most dimensions they do better when prices are high than when they are low; see F. Gerard Adams and Jere R. Behrman, Commodity Exports and Economic Development: The Commodity Problem and Policy in Developing Countries (Lexington, Mass.: Lexington Books, 1982). Moreover, Jonathon Eaton, "The Allocations of Resources in an Open Economy with Uncertain Terms of Trade," International Economic Review 20:2 (June 1979), 391–403, has shown that uncertainty in the terms of trade may enhance welfare, depending on the flexibility in the economy and attitudes toward risk. Secular movements in the terms of trade are very sensitive to the time period chosen and the indexes and definitions used; see William Loehr and John P. Powelson, Threat to Development: Pitfalls of the NIEO (Boulder, Colo.: Westview Press, 1983). For a pessimistic recent assessment of commodity price stabilization from a theoretical point of view, see David M. G. Newbery and Joseph E. Stiglitz, The Theory of Commodity Price Stabilization: A Study in the Economics of Risk (Oxford: Clarendon Press, 1981).

17. UNCTAD, Handbook of International Trade and Development Statistics (Geneva: UNCTAD, 1979–1981).

18. See UNCTAD, "Resolution of the United Nations Conference of Trade and Development: Integrated Programme for Commodities," Nairobi (30 May 1976), TD/RES/93 (IV). This resolution also is printed as an appendix in Behrman, International Commodity Agreements.

19. Behrman, International Commodity Agreements.

20. A recent review of progress to date with the ICP and various ICAs is provided in UNCTAD, "Review of Progress in the Implementation of the Integrated Programme for Commodities," Geneva: UNCTAD (23 November 1981), TD/B/C.1/223.

21. Alexander J. Yeats, "On the Rationale for International Commodity Price Stabilization Agreements in Periods of Fluctuating Monetary Exchange Rates" (Geneva: UNCTAD, 1983).

22. "Rich Man, Poor Man, Beggar Man at UNCTAD," Economist (11–17 June 1983), 79–80.

23. Taylor, "Back to Basics," p. 328. Robert L. Rothstein, "Commodity Bargaining: The Political Economy of Regime—Creation" (mimeo. 1982), presents a more sympathetic interpretation of UNCTAD's role in the promotion of the ICP, but still faults it with being too inflexible in the light of developments after the mid-1970s.

24. Of course these policies have depended critically on isolating DMEC markets from international markets. A price-raising ICP could not as easily isolate markets of major users, though it might use restrictions of supply for the same purpose or dispose of surpluses in new CPE or LDC markets (but arbitrage would be hard to control).

25. A nice theoretical analysis of speculative attacks is in Stephen W. Salant, "The Vulnerability of Price Stabilization Schemes to Speculative Attacks," *Journal of Political Economy* 91:1 (February 1983), 1–38.

26. Processing primary commodities may or may not be an activity in which LDC producing nations have a comparative advantage (or would have a comparative advantage with less international trade barriers). They have an advantage regarding material costs and perhaps market links and information, but in many cases processing is capital or energy intensive. For discussion of these issues, see F. Gerard Adams and Jere R. Behrman, "The Linkage Effects of Raw Material Processing in Economic Development: A Survey of Modeling and Other Approaches," *Journal of Policy Modeling* 3:3 (1981), 375–397; Michael Roemer, "Resource-Based Industrialization in the Developing Countries: A Survey," *Journal of Development Economics* 6:2 (June 1979), 163–202; and David Wall, "Industrial Processing of Natural Resources," *World Development* 8:4 (April 1980), 303–316.

27. UNCTAD, "Commodity Issues: A Review and Proposals for Further Action" (Geneva: UNCTAD, 1983), TD/273, item 9 of the provisional agenda for UNCTAD VI).

28. By the end of the 1970s, for example, the proportion of total goods exports in non-OPEC LDCs from nonpetroleum exports barely exceeded those from manufacturing. UNCTAD, *Handbook*. However, for many individual LDCs, exports of primary commodities remain much more important than exports of manufactures.

29. This summary draws considerably on the recent useful study by Andre Sapir and Lars Lundberg, "The U.S. Generalized System of Preferences and Its Impact" (Madison: University of Wisconsin, 1982).

30. Ibid.

31. Excluded are communist countries, countries that participate in international cartels, countries that have expropriated U.S. property without adequate compensation, countries that fail to recognize or to enforce arbitral awards to U.S. citizens, and countries that fail to cooperate with the United States in preventing narcotic imports into the United States.

32. Sapir and Lundberg, "U.S. Generalized System," note that in a world of imperfect competition, part of these benefits might have been captured by U.S.

importers or intermediary traders. This point also was emphasized earlier by Rachel McCulloch and José Piñera, "Trade as Aid: The Political Economy of Trade Preferences for Developing Countries," *American Economic Review* 67 (1977), 959–967.

33. Sapir and Lundberg, "U.S. Generalized System," also present more sophisticated analysis of the GSP impact using multivariate regressions, which suggest somewhat smaller effects but the same general patterns. They note that with any methodology, it is difficult to identify the GSP effects from the short available time series given all of the other changes affecting trade flows.

34. Carlos F. Díaz-Alejandro and Gerald K. Helleiner, "Handmaiden in Distress: World Trade in the 1980's," Overseas Development Council, Washington, 1982.

35. W. Arthur Lewis, "The Slowing Down of the Engine of Growth: Nobel Prize in Economic Science Lecture," *American Economic Review* 70 (September 1980), 555–564. The growth rates among the LDCs have varied substantially, with much lower averages for the currently low-income countries than for the currently middle-income countries (see note 4). However, the comparison of relative incomes now with the growth rates in recent decades is not the most interesting comparison since those who grew more quickly as a result now tend to have higher incomes. H. W. Singer and R. A. Mahmood, "Is There a Poverty Trap for Developing Countries? Polarization: Reality or Myth?" *World Development* 10:1 (January 1982), 19–22, make the comparison between initial income levels and recent growth rates and find a much weaker association between growth and ex ante income than usually is presumed to exist on the base of growth and expost income associations.

36. South-South trade figures critically in two recent prominent, more pessimistic assessments of prospects for favorable LDC-DC trade. Lewis, "Slowing Down," advocates explicit measures to encourage South-South trade (such as a huge South custom unions) if there is a longer-run slowdown in DC growth (which Lewis suggests is a possibility) and given the assumption (Lewis might say "fact") that LDC shares in DC imports will not be allowed to grow. But see Helen Hughes and Anne O. Krueger, "Effects of Protection in Developed Countries on Developing Countries' Exports of Manufactures" (Washington, D.C.: World Bank, mimeo., 1982). William R. Cline, "Can the East Asian Model of Development be Generalized?" *World Development* 10:2 (February 1982), 81–90, on the other hand, demonstrates that if all LDCs exported to DCs the proportions of their product that the Gang of Four Superexporters do, the penetration of those markets would be much greater than would be acceptable politically. However, he seems to ignore that if LDCs were more widely outward oriented and lowered their own barriers to trade, the substantially greater LDC exports might be absorbed in significant part in South-South trade.

37. For example, Díaz-Alejandro and Helleiner, "Handmaiden," Bergsten and Cline, *Trade Policy*, and Alec Cairncross et al., *Protectionism, Threat to International Order: The Impact of Developing Countries* (London: Commonwealth Secretariat, 1982).

38. Commitments were undertaken to study services, safeguards, agricultural trade and to strengthen GATT's powers (in the future, parties to disputes will find it more difficult to block GATT rulings that go against them). The DC English popular press evaluated the outcome of these meetings as having avoided disastrous disruptions but not having reversed the growing protectionist sentiments. For example, see "Gatt's Puppet Show," *Economist* (4 December 1982), 13–14; "Making Sense of the Mad Gatters' Tea Party," *Economist* (14 December 1982), 67–70; "Is Free Trade Dead?" *Economist* (25 December 1982), 75–93; Clyde H. Farnsworth, "Fragile Consensus on Trade Reached in 88-Nation Talks," *New York Times* (29 November 1982), 1, D10; Clyde H. Farnsworth, "What U.S. Achieved at Trade Conference," *New York Times* (30 November 1982), D1, D24; Leonard Silk, "GATT Talks: Three Score Cards," *New York Times* (1 December 1982), D2; and Hobart Rowan, "Winner at Geneva: Protectionism," *Philadelphia Inquirer* (1 December 1982), 8C.

39. Hughes and Krueger, "Effects of Protection."

40. T. N. Srinivasan, "Why Developing Countries Should Participate in the GATT System: The Third Harry G. Johnson Memorial Lecture," *World Economy* 5:1 (March 1982), 101–102.

41. A. W. Clausen, "Statement Prepared for Delivery before GATT Ministrial Meeting" (Washington, D.C.: World Bank, 24 November 1982).

42. Oli Havrylyshyn and Martin Wolf, "Trade among Developing Countries: Theory, Policy Issues and Principal Trends" (Washington, D.C.: World Bank Staff Working Paper, No. 479, 1981).

43. The optimal period for such transitions is difficult to know. If they are too long, often political momentum and will may be lost before the transitions are completed. If they are too quick, the cost of the "cold bath" may include practically freezing the patient. The programmed trade liberation with inflationary control effort of Chile under Frei between 1964 and 1969 is an example of the former, and the Pinochét shock treatment in Chile a decade later may be an example of the latter.

44. Sapir and Lundberg, "U.S. Generalized System."

45. After the Tokyo Round tariffs on textiles ranged from 8.6 to 15.1 percent and those for apparel ranged from 12.1 to 21.2 percent for the EC, United States, Canada, and Japan imports, according to Donald B. Keesing and Martin Wolf, *Textile Quotas Against Developing Countries* (London: Trade Policy Research Center, Thames Essay No. 23, 1980).

46. Wouter Tims, "Possible Effects of Trade Liberalization on Trade in Primary Commodities" (Washington, D.C.: World Bank Staff Working Paper No. 1983, 1975); and Alberto Valdes, "Trade Liberalization in Agricultural Commodities and the Potential Foreign Exchange Benefits to Developing Countries" (Washington, D.C.: International Food Policy Research Institute, 1979). These are partial-equilibrium estimates. In addition there may be somewhat opposing general equilibrium effects, as OECD resources move out of agriculture and into manufacturers where they would compete with LDC manufactures imports.

47. Behrman, "Developing Country Perspective."

48. UNCTAD, "Commodity Issues," and "Petroleum, Trade Relations and Structural Adjustment" (Geneva: UNCTAD, 1983, TD/274, Item 10 of the provisional agenda for UNCTAD VI).

III

The Prospects for Other Paths

11

The Soviet Union and the Third World: A Faltering Partnership?

Padma Desai

Soviet participation in the North-South dialogue and negotiations has been consistently negligible. It is a record of acts of omission rather than of commission. However, it is instructive to analyze Soviet arguments for this nonparticipation and to explore Soviet views on alternative approaches to resolving the problems of the South. I undertake this task below. At the same time I examine Soviet capabilities and performance in assisting, and interacting with, the developing countries of the South. I also assess future possibilities.

Soviet Attitudes and Positions on North-South Relations

The generally abstentionist and occasionally rejectionist attitude of the Soviet Union toward the North-South dialogue, in the form in which it has developed in the last two decades in international forums, has been justified in many writings and pronouncements.[1]

Interdependence: Western and Soviet Contrasts

A convenient starting point for discussing Soviet positions is to consider the contrasting analysis of interdependence between North and South by the Brandt Commission. The commission called for converting mutual interests between North and South into creative partnerships. Its report states that "the mutuality of interests can be spelled out clearly in the areas of energy, commodities and trade, food and agriculture, monetary solutions and inflation control, financing of projects and programmes, technological innovations, ground and space communications."[2] The world is an interdependent system, so growth in the South also serves people in the North. In order to quicken Southern growth, it would be necessary to transfer resources from the North.

Clearly the Brandt Commission's view of interdependence is rooted in robust pragmatism. Its notion of shared partnership and of an implied consensus steers clear of the ideological explanations and implications of the vast disparities in the economic wealth and political power between the North and the South and their historical origin.

By contrast, Soviet writers and spokesmen have sharply and emphatically rejected such views, focusing instead on notions of historic responsibility and guilt. The following statement by Soviet permanent representative Yakov Malik to the United Nations is typical: "We shall never accept, in theory or practice, the false division of the world into 'poor' and 'rich' countries or into 'the North' and 'the South' by which the socialist states are put on an equal basis with the developed capitalist countries which have misappropriated so much of the wealth of countries long under their colonial rule. It is for this reason—and I wish to put special emphasis on this—that the Soviet Union bears no responsibility whatsoever for the economic backwardness of the developing countries."[3] This is not the first time that such emphatic rhetoric has come from the Soviet spokesman, nor will it be the last. The significant and rather astonishing point to note is that this rhetoric also happens to be the substantive argument for Soviet nonparticipation in global negotiations.[4]

Furthermore, while there is frequent official acknowledgment of the world as an interlocking system, the areas of shared concern are not those that dominate the Brandt report or the North-South negotiations. In his speech before the Twenty-fifth Party Congress in 1976, for example, Brezhnev referred to arms reduction, management of the resources of the sea and outer space, protection of the environment, and technology as areas of interest on the international scene to Soviet policy makers, but there was no reference to the world trading and financial systems or to commodities and food, nor did he mention the New International Economic Order.

Imperialism and Exploitation versus Mutual Gain and Partnership

Given its pragmatic stance and its stress on mutual gains as the key to building North-South relations, the Brandt Commission naturally rules out confrontation. "Sensible solutions," it reports, "can only result from dialogue and cooperation."[5] As John Ruggie argues more cynically, the ritual of negotiations reflects a process wherein a "hegemonic consensus" emerges, with the dominant party granting concessions that will not endanger the existing power structure.[6]

The Soviet view, however, is much starker and is articulated less elegantly. The South is exploited by the North, and exploitation cannot end with negotiations aimed at working out mutual-gain compromises between unequal partners. Nukhovich writes that "the policy of 'partnership' is, first and foremost, an attempt by imperialism . . . to seek out new opportunities for retaining them [developing countries] within its economic orbit and for expansion by international monopolies."[7] The multinational corporations, in this view, are the key agents of economic exploitation in the present neocolonial phase. They chain the South to the capitalist world, and in the process they also weaken the Southern countries' politically and economically liberating and rewarding ties with countries of the socialist bloc.[8]

Behind the facade of partnership and mutual gains, therefore, lie imperialist designs and a neocolonialist reality. North-South relations arising within this context are therefore vitiated.

The Soviet Union as the South's "Natural" Ally

By contrast, economic relations of the South with the socialist countries are free from this unpleasantness and advance the genuine interests of the South. The Soviet Union is thus the "natural" ally of the South. The radicals should even draw comfort from the fact that, in consequence, the Soviet Union refuses to participate in North-South negotiations that must inevitably reflect Northern designs and interests. They may even look conveniently away from the intruding bourgeois reality that the Soviet Union nonetheless does not embrace radical solutions such as nationalization of MNCs and global debt repudiation.

Consistent with this stance, the Soviet Union has expressed ideological and voting support for many of the South-sponsored resolutions in the United Nations on the New International Economic Order. Thus, the Soviet Union (indeed, the Soviet bloc) supported the Charter of the Economic Rights and Obligations of States, adopted at the Twenty-ninth General Assembly of the United Nations. (The United States, Great Britain, and the Federal Republic of Germany were among the countries voting against it.) The Soviet bloc also reiterated its support for the demand of the South for an NIEO at the Second General Conference of the United Nations Industrial Development Organization (UNIDO) in Lima in 1975 and the Fourth UNCTAD conference in

Nairobi in 1976.[9] Such support is calculated to ensure solidarity with the South in forums where the ethos is known to be in favor of the Third World.

Rejecting Collective Responsibility and Embracing Quid Pro Quo Bilateralism

This support, however, has always been too general to entail genuine concessions on specific demands of the South. Moreover, the Soviet Union has invaribly expressed reservations about concessions, explicit or implicit, on general or specific issues.

In justification, Soviet responsibility for the predicament of the South is vehemently denied. More specifically, the Soviet Union is to be under no obligation to transfer resources to the South or to undertake multilateral obligations that may entail such transfers or economic concessions to the South. Witness the following statement:

The different concepts which have recently emerged, particularly "global interdependence" and "the satisfaction of basic needs," should be treated with attention and caution in the formulation of the new international development strategy. The interpretation of certain circles of the concept of "global interdependence," for instance, is totally unacceptable. In its guise they are trying nothing less than to impose so-called collective responsibility for what happened in the world economy and intensify the exploitation of developing countries. For this reason the term "interdependence" should be replaced by the term "interrelationships."[10]

The implications of such argumentation, which is fairly typical of Soviet pronouncements on the subject, are far reaching and nothing less than cynical. It implies that resources should be, and must be, transferred only if there is a history of past exploitation. The mere fact of affluence therefore is not conceded, as in liberal circles in the North, to be an argument for transferring resources to the poor. The fact of past or current exploitation could indeed be argued as providing a compelling moral argument for transferring resources to the exploited. But its absence surely does not constitute an argument for not undertaking such transfers in a world of haves and have-nots. Our notion of improving the lot of the have-nots must include a modicum of altruistic considerations.

It is not surprising that the Soviet logic has resulted in somewhat self-serving restrictions on the patterns and methods of resource transfer from the Soviet bloc to the South. Automatic transfers of resources (aid, trade, nonreciprocal trade preferences, commodity agreements, compensatory financing, and debt relief) are to be avoided. There must be *quid pro quo* and reciprocity in all these transactions. The general Soviet aid rule seems to be rather blunt: We will not generally help you unless we help ourselves in the process.[11] Furthermore, since collective responsibility for resource transfers is denied, the transfer process, and indeed all other economic relations, must be bilateral. Multilateral negotiations and arrangements are generally to be avoided. *Quid pro quo* bilateralism therefore is the cornerstone of the Soviet approach to the South.

In consequence the Soviet Union has inevitably chosen to opt out of the North-South dialogue (except at the level where no real consequences entail for its policy). It has therefore failed to influence its pace or substance directly. However, does this self-imposed exclusion imply that the Soviet Union has little of economic value to offer to the South?[12]

The Soviet Union and the South: Aid, Technology Transfer, and Trade

The preceding question is important, since by simply providing alternatives in the economic sphere in areas such as aid, trade, and access to technology the Soviet Union may provide the South with the wherewithal to improve its bargaining capacity with respect to the North in these and other areas on the specifics of the North-South dialogue. I shall therefore proceed now to take a close look at past performance and future prospects for Soviet–Third World or East-South interactions in specific fields, starting with foreign aid.

Soviet Aid

Quid pro quo bilateralism in Soviet economic aid is reflected in three major aspects of aid disbursements.[13]. First, substantial economic aid has been given to countries such as China (until the Sino-Soviet rift), Cuba and, Vietnam for strictly ideological and possibly geopolitical reasons. Second, a great amount of economic aid was given to Egypt, India, Turkey, Iran, and Iraq at various times between 1954 and 1979. This was motivated by the declared aim of competing for Third World, neutralist-nation influence, which may have been supplemented by geopolitical reasons. Finally, rather small sums of aid also have been disbursed for strictly economic reasons, along the lines of the Japanese-yen-credit model, essentially to procure raw materials in reciprocation for aid-financed investments. An example is provided by Morocco, where, in a $2 billion deal, the Soviet Union would receive phosphate from Morocco in return for extractive technology and equipment.

The direct nominal value of Soviet aid, however, was never substantial and is now shrinking further. Actual aid disbursement, having risen from an average of $215 million between 1954 and 1970 to $705 million in 1974, stagnated around half a billion dollars in the late 1970s. At its maximum in 1974 it was about 15 percent of comparable U.S. aid flow, but it was around 8 to 11 percent in the late 1970s. According to Franklyn Holzman's estimate, the Soviet Union's net economic aid at its peak in 1964 was 0.1 percent of its GNP. Even for major Third World beneficiaries of Soviet aid, such as India, the Soviet aid program was smaller than that of the United States, having been estimated in terms of aid committed at $2.3 billion for the Soviet Union between 1954 and 1979 and $18.6 billion, in terms of aid disbursed, for the United States between 1954 and 1978.

However, the actual impact of the Soviet program was disproportionately large relative to its value, and the political dividends earned were yet larger. The major reason was that the Soviet Union, in competing for influence in the Third World during the Cold War, could assist developing countries in breaking the ideological and pressure-group constraints that prevented the United States from financing public-sector projects and projects such as steel plants and oil-refining capacities that would compete with major U.S. producers in these industries. The Bokaro steel plant in India could not be financed with U.S. aid because of ideological opposition in the U.S. Congress, and it was picked up by the Soviet Union around 1971.[14] The same dramatic switch occurred in the case of the Aswan Dam in Egypt. In oil exploration, again in India, the Soviet Union and Rumania assisted in exploring oil, which was then refined in public-sector refineries set up with Soviet assistance. The private-sector refineries, which imported their own crude oil, refused to refine public-sector oil in their capacities.

However, the Indian strategy of setting up domestic production capacities with Soviet aid in the drug and pharmaceutical industry to counter the monopoly practices of the Western drug companies did not work as effectively. The Soviet Union even set up a surgical instruments plant, but Indian surgeons preferred to use the finer imports from the United States, Sweden, and Switzerland. At one stage these instruments from the Soviet-aided factory were imported by the Soviet Union, presumably for use by veterinarians.

What then are the prospects of the Soviet Union's extending aid with similar efficacy and impact in the future? Clearly the answer depends on Soviet willingness to extend aid and the Soviet capacity to extend it in useful form. In both respects the answer is somewhat discouraging.

Soviet Willingness to Extend Bilateral Aid

The decline of the Cold War and its replacement with détente until the inauguration of the Reagan administration implied the elimination of the strongest motive for aid to the South. The Soviet Union, no less than the West, is unwilling to pour increasing amounts of aid into the Third World in order to compete for influence. There is an aid fatigue in both the East and the West. In addition, the pressure for domestic absorption of resources is as strong in the Soviet Union today as elsewhere in the developed market economies, fed as it is by military demands and consumerism in the face of substantial economic inefficiency. Furthermore, the Soviet Union has itself become a heavy borrower of funds, along with the Soviet bloc countries, so that its desire to give resources to the developing countries has diminished at the same time that it is dipping into the pool of international capital funds and in effect competing with the developing countries for such funds. Soviet hard-currency debt on a gross basis is currently estimated at about $15 billion. There is, therefore, a double-scissors effect working more to the disadvantage of the developing countries than in earlier years.

Soviet Capacity to Extend Useful Bilateral Aid

I analyze the special aspects of Soviet technology transfer, and the merits and demerits that they enjoy, in the next subsection. Immediately, however, let me note that the special premium that early Soviet aid enjoyed through its customary availability in the form of public-sector, heavy-industry projects is no longer a powerful virtue. The heavy-industry orientation is, in fact, a liability, and the availability of finance for public-sector projects is no longer a major asset.

In the earlier period of aid activity, the Soviet ability to finance and implement projects in heavy industry happily coincided with the pattern of Southern demands for such projects from key developing countries. The happy coincidence has now disappeared. The developing countries' views about optimal developmental strategy have shifted increasingly to a less mechanistic conception that allows for education, population control, agricultural development, and nutrition as against the earlier models that emphasized physical investments. It is difficult, therefore, to think of developing countries now demanding heavy industry to implement such investments. The needs have shifted to other areas, and the Soviet Union is particularly inept at fulfilling these. Imagine, for example, the Soviet Union trying to assist with projects for agricultural development.[15]

Second, while the United States has recently regressed on this matter, the general availability of finance for public-sector projects has increased greatly, partly because multilateral agencies such as the World Bank came to terms long ago with financing public-sector projects and partly because the growth of world capital markets has enabled some developing countries to borrow and finance public-sector investments to a greater degree than before. This diminishes the earlier premium attached to Soviet willingness to undertake such investments in the developing countries.

Key Features of Soviet Technology Transfer

Because Soviet aid has been closely interlinked with projects, and hence with technology transfer, a few words on the key features of such technology transfer are in order. I shall draw on Indian experience for illustrations.

Technology Diffusion
The important element in the process of building up indigenous know-how has consisted in the Indian policy, and the Soviet compliance therein, of inviting and accepting industrial collaboration proposals in the Indian public sector only when these are offered by the foreign partner with complete design documentation. This process has been accompanied by the establishment of research, design, and engineering institutes that now have a reasonable record of technological innovations and adaptations of imported technologies to suit local requirements and conditions. An aspect contributing to such a buildup and diffusion of technology has consisted in the Soviet training of technical manpower, especially in the Soviet-assisted turnkey projects. Though such training programs may not be regarded as massive in terms of the number of people trained, they have certainly been designed to pass on the technical production and managerial tasks to the Indian counterpart.[16] (Soviet

technicians in Egypt during the heyday of Soviet-Egypt collaboration were reported to be high-handed and condescending. Such displays in India have been rare.) Finally, though Soviet technologies are protected by guarantees against disclosure to third parties (especially in private industry), there is no explicit prohibition against the application by a public-sector agency of a given technology package or parts of it in another public-sector plant. In fact, some horizontal transfer of technology does take place.[17] This is in contrast to the practice of multinational corporations (MNCs), which explicitly forbid such horizontal transfer of technology so that identical technologies are repeatedly imported with recurring costs.

Clearly the process of acquiring technology from the Soviet Union tends to promote its effective transfer and diffusion. Its cost, therefore, is correspondingly reduced below what it would otherwise be. But there are other aspects of Soviet technology to consider.

Tying and Financial Arrangements
Soviet technology transfer is further distinguished by the following features.

First, many arrangements with MNCs prohibit exports of items produced under licensing or joint agreements.[18] By contrast, arrangements with the Soviet Union are generally free from such restrictive clauses.

Second, whereas the repayment obligations with MNCs entail use of the foreign-exchange resources of the host country, repayments to the Soviet Union are settled via reverse trade flows from the recipient country. Over time such reverse tying assists the host country in meeting its repayment obligations. Although there is evidence of some diversion of trade from hard-currency areas, there is no evidence of the Soviet Union's having charged higher prices on its exports to, or paid lower prices on its imports from, developing countries.[19] Moreover, trade transactions with the Soviet Union may have supported a developing-country export market that had been sagging (Indian tea and jute) or fluctuating (Ghanaian cocoa).[20]

Third, developing-country recipients occasionally encounter disguised cost elements not explicitly covered by the contractual arrangements in their industrial-technology transactions with MNCs. These arise from the MNCs' practice of pricing their intrafirm transactions in such a manner as to minimize their tax liabilities or circumvent the restrictions on remittances imposed by the developing-country recipient. Thus, wherever such transactions between the parent MNC and the developing-country subsidiary are significant, it pays the parent company to overinvoice imports and/or underinvoice exports so that the pretax profits are understated.[21] There is substantial evidence of high intra-firm trade and of such pricing practices by MNCs, especially in pharmaceuticals.[22] Wherever such practices prevail, the costs of such industrial-technology arrangements in general and of technology transfer in particular with MNCs are higher than the explicit costs mentioned in the underlying contract. Evidently there is no counterpart to such problems in Soviet technology transfer.

Fourth, the industrial-technology arrangements with the Soviet Union result, by contrast with Western aid practices, in higher costs that are attributable to Soviet indifference to the inefficiencies generally endemic to the formulation and implementation of developing-country projects. The inefficiencies in Soviet-aided projects can realistically be argued to be compounded by the absence in the Soviets' own practice and experience of the application of economic norms such as competitive pricing, quality control, and scheduled delivery of items to clients. The viability of a project proposed for technical collaboration by the Soviet Union is customarily assessed by the Soviets exclusively from its technical parameters, without any questions raised, for instance, about whether its location is economic, whether its size is optimal, or its product mix meets marketability tests. By contrast, a potential MNC collaborator or Western aid donor more typically would insist on suitable modifications of some or all these aspects.

In fact one can readily encounter instances of costly and malfunctioning enterprises where these problems can be traced to some shortcoming in the Soviet practices of project conception, planning, and implementation. The most glaring example in India is the Heavy Engineering Corporation (HEC) set up with Czech and Soviet collaboration. It is designed to produce all the equipment for setting up a million-ton steel plant every year. On the basis of strict technological criteria, it is generally described as a first-rate plant. Its physical planning and layout are well designed, and the massive equipment installed in the foundry and the various machine-tool units are of high quality. Furthermore, the various items supplied by HEC to the Bokaro Steel Plant meet the most exacting technological criteria and function normally. However, two specific and related features, both characterizing Soviet aid practices, can be singled out as having contributed to the almost insuperable problems of HEC. The first relates to the massive integrated conception of the plant, which is typically Soviet. This implies that every production task from the rough designing (as per preliminary indications given by the client), to detailed drawings, to the processing of materials and the final manufacturing of an item from start to finish, is carried out by HEC.[23] This in turn implies that the paucity of demand or labor problems or lack of adequate training in one segment or unit of the plant affects the orchestration and functioning of the entire plant.[24] The second problem, compounded by Soviet practice, has been the total absence of any considerations at HEC of competitive pricing and time-bound deliveries of equipment to clients. The entire construction and start-up schedule of the first stage of the Bokaro Steel Plant was delayed and its costs were pushed up as a result of this factor. The HEC, it seems, has not been subjected to the competitive rigors of open or even restricted tendering.[25]

There appear, therefore, to have been both negative and positive aspects to the Soviet practices on technological transfer within their aid programs to date. How does the future then appear in regard to Soviet technological transfer to the South?

Declining Prospects for Soviet Technology Transfer

The future looks less rosy than the past. For one thing, the attractiveness of the Soviet Union as a supplier of technology has diminished as the MNCs' willingness to part with a wide variety of generally more sophisticated and more efficient industrial technologies in the developing country public sector has noticeably increased.

Furthermore, the Soviet Union's success in transferring technology to developing countries has undercut its uniqueness in supplying technologies that may still not be available to them from the MNCs. India today can supply steel-making technology to a developing country that may otherwise be unable to get it from an MNC; the Soviet Union's technological expertise is therefore not quite so necessary now as in the 1950s for breaking bottlenecks. I am reminded of an incident, somewhat ironical, of how the Indian public-sector metallurgy engineering and consulting firm MECON was asked by the government of Nigeria to scrutinize the technical aspects of a Soviet project report for a proposed steel plant in Nigeria and also suggest possible cost reductions. The letter of thanks to the chairman of MECON from the industries minister of Nigeria for its technical and financial recommendations was quite effusive. It is also reported that the Nigerians might seek Indian technical assistance in a MIG factory being built in Nigeria with Soviet assistance if continued Soviet collaboration proved difficult. At the same time, the expertise of other technologically advanced developing countries generally, whether they have been assisted by the Soviet Union or not, has resulted in the availability of intra-South technology. This has diversified the sources of technology transfer to the South and has diminished sharply the special role and opportunity that the Soviet Union had as an alternative source of technology in heavy industry, oil refining, and other areas in the 1950s and 1960s.

Moreover, the Soviet Union is at a disadvantage to MNCs today in the South, since the technologically leading developing countries currently desire accelerated depackaging of technologies. Therefore they will generally consider imports of completely packaged technologies only of the sophisticated variety. The MNCs are better equipped, in terms of their capabilities and their range of experience, to fulfill these requirements. Whereas the Soviet Union has supplied technologies only in the framework of complete plants (which are further integrated in its national production and trade plans), the MNCs have supplied technology through licensing agreements as well. The MNCs can therefore supply technologies to fulfill diverse, well-defined objectives of the developing countries—for example, by undertaking a specific production (well short of turnkey) or processing job. The MNCs are also universally acknowledged sources of sophisticated technologies, so their superiority over the Soviet Union is unquestioned. Indeed, the Soviet Union is itself a large buyer, actual and potential, of advanced technologies.

Southern Trade with the Soviet Union and Other CPEs

If Soviet aid and technical transfer are not likely to be of great importance in the future, what about gains from trade? The prospects here appear equally disappointing.

Southern Exports

If one examines current performance, the actual integration of the Soviet Union in the foreign trade of the South is low. The same is true of the CMEA as a group. The details are given in tables 11.1 through 11.4, where I employ the UN classification of developed market economies (MEs), developing market economies, and CMEA countries, separating out the Soviet Union, however, from the CMEA. Developed MEs correspond to the North, whereas developing MEs correspond to the South and exclude China, Cuba, North Korea, and Vietnam. The CMEA includes the Soviet Union, Bulgaria, Czechoslovakia, East Germany, Hungary, Poland, and Romania. I shall concentrate on Southern exports.

The most striking feature of the observable trade pattern is that developed MEs absorb about 71 percent of Southern exports, whereas the CMEA share has declined from 5 percent in 1965 to 3 percent in 1979 and the Soviet share now stands at 2 percent. The breakdown of these exports in various categories reveals a pattern and trend that should dampen the hopes of those in the South who urge that the developed countries should import more of their manufactured goods (table 11.2). Thus, whereas Southern exports of manufactured items have risen from 10 percent of world exports in 1965 to 15 percent in 1979, the share of developed MEs in total Southern exports has declined from 72 percent to 68 percent and that of the CMEA from 4 percent to 2 percent during the period. The Soviet share has dropped from 2.8 percent in 1970 to 1 percent. The growth in Southern exports of manufactured items is clearly sustained by intra-South trade, which has risen from 21 percent in 1970 to 30 percent in 1979.

The share of Southern exports in world exports of crude materials excluding oil (table 11.3), and food, beverage, and tobacco (table 11.4) has been more or less stagnating around 30 percent. In both cases the relative intake of developed MEs has declined whereas the share of intra-South trade has grown strongly. The CMEA's performance is asymmetrical; their share of crude materials has declined from 9 to 6 percent whereas their share of food, beverage, and tobacco has risen somewhat to a level of 12 percent. The Soviet share of crude material trade has stagnated at 4 percent whereas in food, beverage, and tobacco it has risen from 6 percent to 9 percent.

The main features of the export performance are, thus, discouraging. The North dominates in Southern exports in all categories, but the engine has recently been sluggish. The Soviet bloc is of small and stagnant significance. The relative growth of Southern exports is sustained by intra-South trade. The Soviet Union's share in Southern exports suggests, ironically, a shift in the direction of what radical writers would consider a "colonial" pattern: The relative share of manufactures has been declining and of food, drink, and tobacco has been rising.

However, as with aid and technology transfer, thee is a little more here than meets the eye. Substantial gains from trade do accrue to

Table 11.1
Regional distribution of developing market economy exports (billion U.S. dollars)

	1965	1970	1973	1975	1976	1977	1978	1979
1. Exports of developing MEs	35.9	55.3	109.2	210.9	255.2	288.7	302.4	417.5
2. To developed MEs	25.6	40.0	79.1	148.0	180.6	204.9	214.8	295.7
3. 2 as percent of 1	(71.3)	(72.3)	(72.4)	(70.2)	(71.2)	(71.0)	(71.0)	(70.8)
4. To CMEA	1.9	2.8	4.5	9.1	9.4	10.5	11.5	13.2
5. 4 as percent of 1	(5.3)	(5.1)	(4.1)	(4.3)	(3.7)	(3.6)	(3.8)	(3.2)
6. To Soviet Union	1.1	1.7	2.7	5.7	5.4	6.2	7.0	7.8
7. 6 as percent of 1	(3.1)	(3.1)	(2.5)	(2.7)	(2.1)	(2.1)	(2.3)	(1.9)

Source: *Statistical Yearbook, United Nations* (New York: 1979, 1980, and 1981).

Notes:

All magnitudes are f.o.b.

Developed MEs are the OECD countries. Developing market economies exclude China, Cuba, North Korea, and Vietnam. The CMEA (Council of Mutual Economic Assistance) includes the Soviet Union, Bulgaria, Czechoslovakia, East Germany, Hungary, Poland, and Romania.

"Other Manufactured Goods" include SITC categories 6 and 8.

"Crude Materials" include SITC categories 2 and 4. They exclude fuels, oils, and fats.

"Food, Beverages and Tobacco" include SITC categories 0 and 1.

Table 11.2
Regional distribution of developing market economy exports of other manufactured goods (billion U.S. dollars)

	1965	1970	1973	1975	1976	1977	1978	1979
1. World exports	50.8	90.5	159.4	213.2	240.1	275.2	335.5	412.4
2. Developing ME exports	5.0	10.7	20.8	25.5	34.3	39.2	48.2	63.1
3. 2 as percent of 1	(9.8)	(11.9)	(13.0)	(11.9)	(14.3)	(14.2)	(14.4)	(15.3)
4. Exports of 2 to:								
Developed MEs,	3.6	7.7	15.0	17.0	24.3	26.8	33.5	42.6
percentage share	(72.0)	(74.1)	(72.1)	(66.9)	(70.8)	(68.3)	(69.5)	(67.5)
Developing MEs,	1.2	2.5	4.7	7.3	8.7	11.0	13.4	18.6
percentage share	(24.0)	(21.3)	(22.6)	(28.7)	(25.4)	(28.1)	(27.8)	(29.5)
CMEA,	0.2	0.4	0.7	1.0	0.9	1.1	1.1	1.2
percentage share	(4.0)	(3.7)	(3.4)	(3.9)	(2.6)	(2.8)	(2.3)	(2.9)
Soviet Union,	0.1	0.3	0.6	0.6	0.5	0.6	0.6	0.6
percentage share	(2.0)	(2.8)	(1.9)	(2.3)	(1.5)	(1.5)	(1.2)	(1.0)

Source: Ibid.
Notes: See notes to table 11.1.

Table 11.3
Regional distribution of developing market economy exports of crude materials (billion U.S. dollars)

	1965	1970	1973	1975	1976	1977	1978	1979
1. World exports	23.9	33.1	57.6	65.7	76.0	84.3	93.1	121.4
2. Developing ME exports	7.4	10.1	16.8	18.7	21.9	24.0	26.2	35.2
3. 2 as percent of 1	(31.0)	(30.5)	(29.2)	(28.5)	(28.8)	(28.5)	(28.1)	(29.0)
4. Exports of 2 to:								
Developed MEs,	5.6	7.3	12.0	12.9	15.3	16.0	17.2	23.5
percentage share	(75.7)	(72.3)	(71.4)	(69.8)	(70.7)	(67.2)	(65.6)	(66.8)
Developing MEs,	0.9	1.6	3.0	3.5	4.2	5.3	6.3	8.4
percentage share	(12.2)	(15.8)	(17.9)	(18.8)	(18.9)	(21.5)	(24.0)	(23.9)
CPEs,	0.7	1.0	1.2	1.8	1.9	2.0	1.8	2.2
percentage share	(9.4)	(9.9)	(7.1)	(9.6)	(8.7)	(8.3)	(6.9)	(8.3)
Soviet Union,	0.3	0.6	0.7	0.8	1.0	1.1	0.9	1.2
percentage share	(4.1)	(5.9)	(4.2)	(4.3)	(4.6)	(4.6)	(3.4)	(3.4)

Source: Ibid.
Notes: See notes to table 11.1.

Table 11.4
Regional distribution of developing market economy exports of food, beverage and tobacco (billion U.S. dollars)

	1965	1970	1973	1975	1976	1977	1978	1979
1. World exports	30.5	41.5	77.8	104.0	112.1	126.9	146.3	173.5
2. Exports of developing MEs	10.1	13.4	21.2	29.7	34.4	43.6	45.5	51.5
3. 2 as percent of 1	(33.1)	(32.3)	(27.2)	(28.6)	(30.7)	(34.4)	(31.1)	(29.7)
4. Exports of 2 to:								
Developed MEs,	7.0	9.9	15.1	18.2	22.9	29.8	30.1	33.4
percentage share	(69.3)	(73.5)	(71.2)	(61.6)	(66.3)	(66.6)	(66.2)	(64.9)
Developing MEs,	1.8	2.0	3.8	6.8	6.7	8.0	8.7	13.6
percentage share	(17.8)	(15.9)	(17.9)	(22.9)	(19.5)	(28.6)	(19.1)	(26.4)
CMEA,	1.0	1.3	1.9	4.3	4.2	5.1	6.0	6.2
percentage share	(9.9)	(9.7)	(9.0)	(14.5)	(12.2)	(11.7)	(13.2)	(12.0)
Soviet Union,	0.6	0.8	1.1	3.4	2.9	3.5	4.4	4.6
percentage share	(5.9)	(6.0)	(5.2)	(11.4)	(8.4)	(8.0)	(9.7)	(8.9)

Source: Ibid.
Notes: See notes to table 11.1.

individual trading partners in the South. Soviet purchases of cocoa, tobacco, tea, and jute have at times supported an otherwise sagging market. Debt repayment in reverse trade flows is also an advantage of Soviet-bloc trade, and this should not be minimized in these days of critical debt-management problems. The fear of these trade flows resulting in substantial diversion of hard-currency trade is exaggerated. Recently trade has evolved into implicit and explicit exchanges of Soviet oil for Brazilian soybeans, Argentinian corn and wheat, and Indian rice. In particular, Indo-Soviet trade has diversified substantially over time: manufactured goods, especially textiles, shoes, cosmetics, and light engineering goods, are a major export item from India, and oil has replaced machinery on the Soviet export list. Overall the Soviet Union has replaced the United States as India's major trading partner. This switch is partly the result of the U.S. recession. The advantage of the Soviet market's offering an alternative outlet in these hard times must not be overlooked.

However, simultaneously the Soviet refusal to accept multilateral trade-access obligations implies that considerable reverses in such trade could arise and cause disruption. Therefore, although the EEC may militate against increasing imports and even resorts occasionally to VERs, its protectionism is still heavily constrained by GATT membership and ethos. Soviet economic actions suffer from no such multilateral constraints. That this is not simply a theoretical contention may be borne out by recent Indo-Soviet trade experience. India's exports to the Soviet Union are threatened with a sudden and sharp decline. The correspondent for *India Today* (1983) writes:

From being the brightest spot on a rather gloomy picture of Indian exports, it has become, suddenly, the most alarming part of India's international trade efforts. Till last year, Indian exports to the Soviet Union were booming at an unprecedented rate. . . . Fortunes were made almost overnight by corporations riding on the crest of the boom, and numerous factories representing virtually every major industrial group in the country were set up. They catered, along with hundreds of commodity exporters and traditional industries, to an annual Soviet market for Indian produce which has grown from a modest Rs. 300 crore[26] [crore = 10 million] in the mid-70s to a staggering Rs. 1,800 crore last year, a sixfold increase, perhaps unparalleled in India's export history. . . . But last fortnight it was clear that, for the moment at least, the boom was over . . . the experience of the last six months suggests a drastic curtailment of Soviet buying in India. Cashew nuts, pepper and Virginia tobacco, three high-volume exports for which Russia paid several crore rupees last year, have this year not been purchased at all; orders for Indian cotton textiles, at Rs. 77 crore, are 57.5 percent below last year's record level of Rs. 182 crore; against a bilateral trade plan agreement to buy Rs. 68 crore worth of Indian sewing threads, industrial fabrics and bed linen, there have been no orders placed to date; garment orders dropped 30 percent from a level of Rs. 50 crore last year. High value chemicals and toiletries have been equally hard-hit. Export of soaps, detergents, cosmetics and toiletries, which came down in 1982–83 [April 1–March 31] to roughly Rs. 80 crore from a high of Rs. 108.9 crore in the previous year, have this year dropped almost completely out of the reckoning.

Whether the situation reflects India's diversification away from dependence on Soviet exports of defense hardware and hence an emerging Soviet surplus in trade with India, and possibly a Soviet desire to put pressure on India to shift back to the Soviet Union for such strategic imports, or whether there are simply other economic pressures on the Soviet Union to cut back sharply on imports generally, is difficult to infer without further analysis. What does seem clear is that the Soviet Union's willingness to keep its markets open is not constrained by multilateral economic obligations. This implies a rather serious drawback in the advantages such trade can offer to the Soviet Union's trading partners.

Southern Demands for Access to CPE Markets and the Soviet Response
All this would seem to lend added interest to the observation that at UNCTAD IV the South presented its demands to the Soviet bloc for increased trade via elimination of trade barriers, planned increases in imports from the South on a nonreciprocal basis, the conversion of bilateral balances into hard currencies, and increased financial and technological assistance from the bloc so as to reach the aid target of 1 percent of GNP.[27] The Soviet response was along familiar lines.[28] It emphasized reciprocity of trade concessions: The South must purchase more from the Soviet bloc and eliminate its own barriers. By the time UNCTAD V materialized ten years later, the Soviet position had, if anything, hardened. The conference resolution was criticized in Soviet writings as being "one-sided, protecting only the interests of the developing countries. The socialist countries believe that international measures against protectionist tendencies can be effective only if they are not confined to the interests of one group of countries."[29]

Of course, this hard-line approach reflects the Soviet unwillingness to grant multilateral concessions to all and sundry from the South. However, it also reflects the fact that, like many developing countries with foreign-exchange bottlenecks during the 1950s and 1960s, the Soviet Union carefully husbands its scarce foreign exchange. It uses

Table 11.5
Structure of Soviet imports by major commodity groups, 1970–1980 (percentage)

Commodity Group	1970	1971	1972	1973	1974	1975	1976	1977	1978	1979	1980
Imports, total	100.0	100.0	100.0	100.0	100.0	100.0	100.0	100.0	100.0	100.0	100.0
Machinery and equipment	35.5	34.0	34.6	34.3	32.4	33.9	36.3	38.1	42.0	38.0	33.9
Fuels and electric energy	2.0	2.7	3.0	3.4	3.5	4.0	3.6	3.6	3.7	3.8	3.0
Ores, metals, concentrates	9.6	9.8	8.9	9.9	13.6	11.5	10.8	9.3	9.7	11.2	10.8
Chemicals	5.7	5.4	4.9	4.3	6.3	4.7	4.3	4.4	4.1	4.7	5.3
Wood and wood products	2.1	2.1	1.3	1.6	1.9	2.2	1.8	1.8	1.5	1.5	2.0
Textile fibers and fabrics	4.8	4.5	3.3	3.7	4.1	2.4	2.3	2.6	2.0	1.9	2.2
Foodstuffs	15.8	15.2	18.0	20.2	17.1	28.0	22.8	20.8	19.2	21.9	24.2
Manufactured consumer goods	18.3	20.1	18.6	15.9	14.6	13.0	12.6	12.9	11.8	11.4	12.1
Other	6.2	6.2	6.9	6.7	6.5	5.3	5.5	6.5	6.0	5.6	6.5

Source: *Vneshniaia torgovlia S.S.S.R.*, 1971, 1973, 1975, 1977, 1978, 1980.

credits to import machinery from the West; it spends its hard-currency earnings for food imports, which have been massive recently and can be expected to continue being so;[30] and it uses a shrinking proportion of its overall foreign exchange on imports of manufactures from the developing countries (which in turn often reflect "tied repayments" of earlier Soviet aid, as in Indian exports of manufactures to the Soviet Union). There is little room in all this for granting freer access to the South in Soviet markets.[31] Hence, there is little to the argument that the small ratio of the Soviet share of Southern manufactured-goods exports at 1 percent implies that a great potential for more trade exists. Table 11.5 underlines my argument well; the share of machinery imports (reflecting credits from the West) and food imports in overall Soviet imports has gone up from about 50 percent in the early 1970s to about 60 percent at the end of 1970s, whereas the share of manufactured consumer goods has fallen by over a third to 11–12 percent of the total Soviet import bill.

Conclusion

The implications of my analysis are rather sobering. The Soviet Union is unwilling to participate meaningfully in multilateral endeavors such as the North-South negotiations. The desire of friends such as Willy Brandt and foes such as Ronald Reagan to bring the East into the North-South dialogue and to broaden the negotiations into a truly global effort is therefore doomed to fail. Nor does the Soviet Union appear to be able to play any longer, at least for the foreseeable future, a significant economic (as distinct from political or military) role in the South.[32]

Acknowledgments

My thanks to the participants at the New Delhi Conference on Re-thinking Global Negotiations, January 1983, for helpful comments on the earlier draft of this chapter.

Notes

1. The Soviet Union did vote for the resolution on the NIEO and supported the Charter of the Economic Rights and Obligations of States at the Twenty-ninth United Nations General Assembly. But this support is less than compelling

since few multilateral obligations have ever been accepted by the Soviet Union, if any, in the economic field.

2. *North-South: A Programme for Survival* (1980), p. 20.

3. Cited in Knirsh 1978, p. 106.

4. This argument, while reflecting an ideological position, appears self-serving because it permits the Soviet Union to reject demands for resource transfers. A somewhat comparable example in Western practice would be the contention of Western conservative ideologues that governmental aid, as distinct from private investment flows, is bound to be wasted and therefore should be terminated.

5. *North-South: A Programme for Survival*, p. 22.

6. Ruggie 1982, p. 510.

7. Nukhovich 1977, p. 43.

8. For details, see Obminsky 1977, p. 61.

9. For a discussion of the details see Knirsh 1978, p. 104.

10. For details see Gati 1980, p. 246.

11. This may be generally true also of Western bilateral aid and has certainly been the characteristic increasingly of recent U.S. aid policy.

12. The question of *political* benefits is a distinct one, which this chapter does not address. For example, if I conclude that the economic benefits to the South from the Soviet Union are limited, I do not imply that the political benefits are also small. For example, India has benefited greatly from its relationship with the Soviet Union on political dimensions; Soviet support on international issues such as Kashmir, Goa, and the Bangladesh war was critical. And, perhaps to a greater extent than in Western diplomatic practice, economic and political relationships tend to go together in the Soviet case.

13. The discussion below relies heavily on Desai 1982b.

14. For a detailed account of this complicated project in Indo-Soviet partnership see Desai 1972.

15. I treat at greater length below the problem of Soviet limitations in providing the technologies desired now by developing countries.

16. In Indian steel, heavy engineering, and machine building industries, technology diffusion and its diversification are further aided by the fact that the high-level technical personnel are trained not only in the Soviet Union but also in the United States and West Germany. Most of the Indian Institutes of Technology have also collaboration agreements with their counterparts in the United States and United Kingdom.

17. In 1970 Indian newspapers carried stories of how the visiting Soviet minister Mr. Skachkov expressed displeasure at the Indian steel ministry's policy of

transferring Soviet-trained engineers, intended for the Soviet-aided steel plant at Bhilai, to other public sector steel plants.

18. For extensive details on this point see Stewart 1979, pp. 32–33.

19. In the Indian case, it has been estimated that between 20 and 25 percent of India's exports to centrally planned economies between 1953 and 1967 were diversionary "in the sense that they could have been exported to the hard currency areas" (Datar 1972, p. 182). Also there is some evidence until 1970 of trade switching or reexport by CPEs of their initial purchases from India and Pakistan. "It is accepted in official circles that there is diversion [trade switching] and the range suggested for commodities like tea, coffee, spices, jute goods and grey cotton cloth is between 5 to 10% of India's exports to the East European countries" (Datar 1972, p. 161). Also "some 15% of Pakistan exports to the E.B.C.s [East Bloc countries] is almost certainly switched to Western markets while en route" (Kidron 1972, p. 35).

20. For details, see Nayyar 1977, Datar 1972, and Kidron 1965.

21. The scope for such intrafirm transactions and profits is significant when the subsidiary is a wholly or partially owned affiliate. In licensing agreements where the parent company earns an outright or a continuing royalty (as a proportion of sales), such practices can be presumed to be absent.

22. For details see Stewart 1979, p. 29.

23. By contrast there is considerable specialization and diversification (including dispersal of geographical location and ownership) in heavy machine fabricating capacities in Germany, Japan, the United States, and United Kingdom.

24. In contrast with HEC, Indian public sector enterprises seem to be able to manage these problems as when they occur. Another massive public sector project, Bharat Heavy Electricals Ltd. (BHEL), which manufactures turbines for electricity generation, has had a better and improving record of performance because there is some specialization and even geographical dispersal.

25. The consulting and designing of the further extension of the Bokaro Steel Plant involving the installation of a flat stripmill (where Soviet technology is said to be not the most advanced) will be done jointly by the Metallurgical and Engineering Consultants Ltd. (MECON) and Wean United of the US; furthermore the tenders for equipment will be considered from a number of sources.

26. One rupee approximately equals eleven cents.

27. For details see Gati 1980, pp. 251–252.

28. Details are in United Nations 1976, pp. 147–151.

29. G. Manzhulo and Krasnov 1979, cited by Lawson (n.d., p. 11).

30. See Desai 1981, 1982a, 1983 for detailed analysis and forecasts of these imports.

31. It is remarkable, therefore, that the Soviet methods of dealing with their foreign exchange problems parallel those used by many developing countries

in the postwar period, and concepts such as "foreign-exchange bottlenecks" and "two-gap" analysis are equally applicable to the Soviet situation and predicament. On this, see the extended discussion in Desai and Bhagwati 1979.

32. Evidently this conclusion is compatible with the view that for specific countries such as Vietnam and Cuba the Soviet Union is of critical economic importance.

References

Datar, Asha. 1972. *India's Economic Relations with the USSR and Eastern Europe, 1953–1969*. Cambridge: Cambridge University Press.

Desai, Padma. 1972. *The Bokaro Steel Plant: A Study of Soviet Economic Assistance*. Amsterdam: North-Holland Publishing Company.

————. 1979. "Transfer of Technology from Centrally Planned and Market Economies to Developing Countries." Mimeographed. New York: UN Association of U.S.A.

————. 1981. *Estimates of Soviet Grain Imports in 1980–85: Alternative Approaches*. Washington, D.C.: International Food Policy Research Institute.

————. 1982a. "Soviet Grain and Wheat Import Demands in 1981–85" *American Journal of Agriculture Economics* 64, no. 2 (May).

————. 1982b. "The Soviet Union and Cancun" *Third World Quarterly* 4, no. 3 (July).

————. 1983. *Soviet Livestock Economy, Grain Import Demands and Import Diversification*. New Delhi: Indian Council for International Economic Relations.

————, and Bhagwati, Jagdish. 1979. "Three Alternative Concepts of Foreign Exchange Difficulties in Centrally Planned Economies." *Oxford Economic Papers* (November).

Gati, Tobi Trister. 1980. "The Soviet Union and the North-South Dialogue." *Orbis* 24, no. 1 (January).

Independent Commission on International Development Issues. 1980. *North-South: A Programme for Survival*. London and Sydney: Pan Books.

1983. "Indo-Soviet Trade: Rouble Trouble." *India Today*. May 31.

Kidron, M. 1965. *Foreign Investment in India*. Oxford: Oxford University Press.

Knirsch, Peter. 1978. "The CMEA Attitude to a New Economic Order." *Intereconomics*, no. 516 (May–June).

Lawson, Colin. n.d. "Soviet and Eastern European Responses to the New International Economic Order." Working Paper 0480. University of Bath.

Manzhulo, A., and Krasnov, G. 1979. "International Forum on Trade and Economic Problems: Results of the 5th UNCTAD Session. *Foreign Trade*. no. 9 (September).

Nayyar, D., ed. 1977. *Economic Relations between Socialist Countries and the Third World*. London: Macmillan.

Nukhovich, E. 1977. "Neo-Colonialism under the Banner of 'Partnership.' " *International Affairs*, no. 7 (July).

Obminsky, E. 1977. "Problems of Restructuring Economic Relations." *International Affairs*, no. 1 (January).

Ruggie, J. G. 1982. "A Political Commentary on Cancun." *Third World Quarterly* 4, no. 3 (July).

Stewart, F. 1979. "International Technology Transfer: Issues and Policy Options," Mimeo. Washington, D.C.: Policy Planning and Program Review Department, World Bank.

United Nations. 1976. "Proceedings of the United Nations Conference on Trade and Development, Fourth Session." Joint Statement by the Socialist Countries, Geneva.

12

South-South Economic Cooperation and Global Negotiations

Sanjaya Lall

Most discussions of the New International Economic Order in its various guises have included statements that economic cooperation among developing countries should be promoted. This pious hope seems to be based on one or more of several assumptions: that South-South economic relations are somehow better for development, industrialization, human capital formation, and technological progress than North-South ones;[1] that South-South relations have in some form been held back by the existing structure of the international economy, so that appropriate measures to remove structural barriers would release the productive forces involved and so lead to greater economic growth; that South-South intercourse could—to some unspecified (but it is hoped a large) extent—replace North-South economic relations and so enable the South to achieve greater self-reliance or at least to strike better bargains with the North in future economic negotiations; and that the North was probably doomed to long-term economic stagnation, or in any case would place increasing restrictions on access to its markets and technologies by the South, so that the only feasible way to promote sustained growth in the South would be to rely on intra-South exchange.[2]

The fervor with which the general case for South-South cooperation was propounded seems to have abated in the current harsh and cold economic environment. What is now important for global negotiations, and indeed for national economic policies in the developing countries, is to inject greater realism into the initial sweeping, optimistic declarations of South-South economic cooperation. Even if the value judgment is accepted that such cooperation is in some sense a good thing and should, *ceteris paribus*, be promoted, it is essential to know how far it has gone, what determines its progress, and how much further it can go. Does it offer an alternative to North-South economic transactions? Should it be promoted at the cost of North-South relations? If it is to be promoted, what are the appropriate policies to be adopted? And what role can negotiations of the NIEO-type play in such promotion?

In this chapter I can address only a few of these complex questions. With some exceptions, the peculiar characteristics of South-South economic relations are an underworked field of empirical research so it is difficult to generalize.[3] Rather, I shall concentrate on market-determined South-South trade, technology transactions, and direct foreign investment. Since much of my research has focused on India, the discussion will inevitably have a geographical bias. To the extent that India constitutes something of a special case among the more industrialized Third World countries, this is a limitation.

The Extent of South-South Economic Relations

Trade in Manufactured Goods

The most recent and comprehensive quantitative analysis of South-South trade is that of Havrylyshyn and Wolf (1981), who collected trade data for 1963 through 1977 for a sample of 33 developing countries accounting for nearly two-thirds of exports by the South.[4] Havrylyshyn and Wolf survey total exports by the sample countries as well as manufactured exports and the special category among manufactures of capital goods. They also distinguish between exports by different regions of the South, and they extract data relating to exports and imports by the "newly industrializing countries" (NICs), the most dynamic and important trades in the Third World in the industrial field.

It is difficult to do justice to the various interesting findings of Havrylyshyn and Wolf here, but their conclusions concerning the main trends in South-South trade are worth quoting at length:

Contrary to a widespread impression, there has been no large shift towards trade among developing countries since 1963,[5] at least when the focus is upon non-fuel trade and developing countries are defined exclusive of capital-surplus, oil-exporting countries. The share of non-fuel exports to developing countries, excluding capital-surplus oil exporters was quite stable at between 22 and 23 percent of their total exports, between 1963 and 1973, whereupon it rose to 24 percent in 1975 and 1977. This overall stability gives a misleading impression, however, since at a more disaggregated level there have been opposing and mutually cancelling trends for manufactures and primary commodities.

Manufactured exports were the developing countries' most dynamic export sector in the 1960s and 1970s. The direction of these exports also changed dramatically, the share of developing countries as markets falling from 40 percent in 1963 to 27 percent in 1971 and 25 percent in 1977. In the 1960s and early 1970s it was the industrialized countries that were the main recipients of an increased share of developing countries' manufactured exports. In the later 1970s it was the capital-surplus, oil-exporting countries, whose share rose from 2 percent in 1973 to 7 percent in 1977. Within manufactures capital goods exports have tended to go more to other developing countries at any moment, but the decline in the importance of these markets has been noteworthy, from 66 percent in 1963 to 38 percent of total capital goods exports in 1977. [Havrylyshyn, pp. 81–82]

Havrylyshyn and Wolf use these findings to criticize proponents of South-South trade. Whatever the intrinsic value of such trade (and Havrylyshyn and Wolf have reservations about the dynamic and external benefits of it), the evidence that the North provides the most important and growing market for South's products—in good times and bad—creates a strong presumption that future growth will depend more on the North than on the South. If, on the other hand, the data had shown that intra-South trade was growing in significance, the case for examining its potential benefits would be strengthened.

For the purposes of this chapter, I have collected more up-to-date figures on the extent and content of intra-South manufactured trade. It was not feasible to go into as much regional detail as Havrylyshyn and Wolf, and I concentrated on the period 1973 through 1980, mainly because this is the coverage provided by the source (GATT). The coverage of the GATT data differs from that of Havrylyshyn and Wolf. First, the former include all developing countries, while the latter cover 33 leading exporters; second, the latter count Spain, Portugal, Greece, Turkey, and Yugoslavia as developing countries, while GATT counts these as part of industrialized Western Europe; third, Havrylyshyn and Wolf's category of capital-surplus oil exporters (a subgroup of OPEC) has no counterpart in the GATT data, which simply take the official OPEC group as a category.

These differences in coverage may lead to some divergence in our respective findings, which cannot be corrected for easily. Nevertheless a case can be made that the GATT method of aggregation comes closer to our interest in talking of South-South trade because it covers more developing countries and because it excludes those in Southern Europe (though I would have preferred to see Yugoslavia in the developing country category) and uses a more conventional classification of oil-rich countries. What is more, GATT data go up to 1980 (and for aggregate trade in manufactures, up to 1981) and provide an extremely useful industrial breakdown of the products involved.[6]

Table 12.1 shows the values and percentage distribution by destination of manufactured exports by non-OPEC developing countries. It reveals that the share of the South (OPEC plus other developing countries) in their total exports has risen from 21.8 percent in 1973 (which accords with Havrylyshyn and Wolf) to 28.5 percent in 1980 (and further to 30.3 percent in 1981), which greatly strengthens the rising trend they noted. As for manufactured exports, the trends are the opposite of those described by Havrylyshyn and Wolf: The South claims 28.5 percent in 1973, 36.2 percent in 1980, and 37.3 percent in 1981, while the developed countries decline from 65.2 percent to 58.3 percent and 57.1 percent, respectively. Even more interesting, of the 7.7-percentage-point increase in the share of the South between 1973 and 1980 (and the 8.8-percentage-point increase between 1973 and 1978), the OPEC countries accounted for 3.8 points and the non-oil-exporting developing countries for 3.9 points (between 1973 and 1981, the corresponding figures are 4.1 and 4.7). Thus, in terms of changes in shares, the oil-importing developing countries as a group displaced even OPEC as the most dynamic markets for the South's manufactured products.

Although they do not match the Havrylyshyn-Wolf data precisely, the GATT figures cast grave doubts on the main conclusions Havrylyshyn and Wolf reached. In the past eight years or so sales to other developing countries have been the fastest-growing components of manufactured exports by the South, and this growth is due only in part to the rising share of oil-rich countries. While the total share of the South has not yet reached the 40 percent level of 1963, it is not far short of it; the 37.3 percent achieved in 1981 needs only two years of constant growth at recent levels to bring it to that level.

It is possible that the decline in the share of developed countries owes much to the current recession and the accompanying protectionist measures. Even if this is so, the prospects of continued slow growth in the North and increasing protectionism are real enough to support the argument that South-South trade will continue to rise. It may also be the case that intra-South trade has a momentum of its own, based on distinct features of such trade, and that a resumption of growth in the North will not eat into its share. On the contrary, it is possible that economic recovery in the North will stimulate incomes in the South and increase the demand for the South's products further. But these are all pure speculations, and the evidence does not really support one inference over the other.

Havrylyshyn and Wolf calculated the share of developing countries in their exports of capital goods and found it to decline from 66 percent to 38 percent between 1963 and 1977. The GATT data permit a very rough calculation to be made on similar lines. For engineering products as a whole, the share of the South rises from 36.6 percent to 42.9 percent, while that of the developed countries declines from 61.1 percent to 54.3 percent. If we exclude road motor vehicles and household appliances (though commercial vehicles should be included), we arrive at an approximation to total capital goods: The share of the South in these exports rose from 40.7 percent in 1973 to 43.8 percent in 1980 (OPEC taking 7.5 percent and 10.0 percent, respectively), while that of the developed countries declined from 56.6 percent to 53.5 percent. The lack of exact comparability with Havrylyshyn and Wolf is greater here than with total manufactured exports, but, again, the trends revealed are so different that a serious question about the validity of their generalization is raised.

The GATT data permit us to examine the industrial breakdown of manufactured exports in greater detail. The table shows that between 1973 and 1980 only one major category, chemicals, saw a decline in the share of the South. For the narrower destination of other LDCs, four items witnessed declining shares: chemicals, machinery for specialized industries, road motor vehicles, and clothing. On the other hand, products with substantial rises in shares going to other LDCs were "other semimanufactures" (a rise of 9.3 percentage points), household appliances (8.8 percentage points), and textiles (8.6 percentage points). OPEC pushed up its share (in some cases quite dramatically, as in the case of road motor vehicles) in every category except for office and telecommunication equipment.

There are five product groups in which the share of the South equals or exceeds that of developed countries in 1980: iron and steel, chemicals, machinery for specialized industries, road motor vehicles, and textiles. There are, on the other hand, four groups where the share of the developed countries is over 60 percent: office and telecommunications equipment, household appliances, clothing, and other consumer goods. Of these the first two subgroups of "engineering" are likely to be dominated by offshore processing and assembly activities of multinational corporations (MNCs) from the developed countries. The very high share of the home countries of the MNCs is explained by the

Table 12.1
Destinations of manufactured exports by non-OPEC developing countries, 1973–1980

Product	1973						1980					
	Total value[a]	% DCs	% Socialist	% OPEC	% LDCs	% Total South	Total value[a]	% DCs	% Socialist	% OPEC	% LDCs	% Total South
All exports	68.30	69.8	6.3	3.5	18.3	21.8	253.60	63.1	6.5	6.9	21.6	28.5
Manufactured goods	23.15	65.2	3.0	6.0	22.5	28.5	99.15	58.3	2.8	9.8	26.4	36.2
Iron and steel	0.95	51.6	3.2	15.8	28.4	44.2	4.30	43.0	5.8	19.8	30.2	50.0
Chemicals	1.83	44.2	2.7	6.0	43.2	49.2	9.05	47.0	3.3	9.4	37.6	47.0
Other semimanufactures	3.39	73.5	3.5	4.7	16.8	21.5	11.10	55.9	5.4	10.8	26.1	36.9
Engineering	5.91	61.1	0.7	6.8	29.8	36.6	34.45	54.3	1.0	11.0	31.9	42.9
Machinery for specialized industries	0.81	29.6	1.2	11.1	56.8	67.9	4.20	25.0	1.2	16.7	54.8	71.5
Office, telecommunications	1.28	75.8		3.9	19.5	23.4	8.15	73.6	0.4	2.5	22.1	24.6
Road motor vehicles	0.38	28.9		5.3	63.2	68.5	2.10	28.6		23.8	47.6	71.4
Other machinery and transportation equipment	1.80	55.0	1.1	8.3	32.2	40.5	11.65	49.8	1.5	12.9	34.3	47.2
Household appliances	1.64	79.3	0.6	5.5	14.0	19.5	8.35	62.9	1.2	10.8	22.8	33.6

Textiles	4.05	51.9	7.7	8.6	25.7	34.3	11.50	43.5	7.8	10.0	34.3	44.3
Clothing	3.82	84.6	2.1	3.1	8.1	11.2	14.55	82.5	1.4	6.5	7.9	14.4
Other consumer goods	3.18	75.2	1.6	4.1	14.5	18.6	14.20	69.0	1.4	6.3	17.6	23.9

Source: GATT, International Trade, 1981/82, Geneva, 1982. (Table A24).

Note: Regions: DCs (or developed market economies): all industrialized countries in North America, Western Europe (including Spain, Portugal, Yugoslavia, Greece, and Turkey), and Japan but excluding Australia, New Zealand, and South Africa. Socialist: Eastern Europe, China, North Korea, and Vietnam. OPEC: All members of Organization of Petroleum Exporting Countries. LDCs: All other countries including Israel but excluding Taiwan, Australia, New Zealand, and South Africa. Total South: OPEC plus LDCs. Total: includes Australia, New Zealand, and South Africa but excludes Taiwan.

a. Billions of dollars.

vertically integrated nature of manufacturing, assembly, and selling activities in these industries. Clothing and other consumer goods, by contrast, are probably dominated by local enterprises in the exporting countries, often selling to large buying groups in the developed world and receiving substantial marketing and design assistance from them.

Intra-South trade is relatively significant (over 40 percent of the total) in "heavy," undifferentiated producer goods such as iron, steel, and chemicals, in "light" undifferentiated consumer goods such as textiles, and in relatively complex engineering goods such as machinery for specialized industries, road motor vehicles, and other machinery and transport equipment. Some of these products are highly capital-intensive, though with fairly well-diffused technologies, while others are highly demanding of design and development skills. This raises interesting issues of the determinants and benefits of intra-South trade, which will be addressed below.

The GATT data unfortunately do not permit a countrywise analysis of South-South trade. Other data (surveyed in Lall 1981) suggest, however, that a handful of countries account for the great bulk of South's manufactured exports and so are likely to dominate its exports to other developing countries. Havrylyshyn and Wolf's findings confirm this expectation; the ten leading Third World exporters accounted for over 90 percent of their sample's exports of manufactures and capital goods to other developing countries.[7] They also calculate the share of exports going to the South for different regional groupings of their 33 sample countries. They find that by 1977 Latin America has the highest Southward orientation, with 51 percent of its manufactured exports going to other developing countries, and Asia the lowest (24 percent). Of individual countries of some size in the export scene, Argentina (63 percent), Singapore (44 percent), and Brazil (43 percent) are relatively South-oriented, in contrast to Hong Kong (14 percent) and Korea (15 percent). India comes in the middle range, with 24 percent of its 1977 manufactured exports directed at the South.

Although the sheer weight of the advanced industrial nations in the world economy dictates that their markets will absorb most of South's exports, Havrylyshyn and Wolf point out that the share of the South is larger than may be expected on the basis of its market size. Thus, the share of the developing world in global income is 16 to 18 percent, while its share in the South's exports is much higher—22 to 25 percent according to Havrylyshyn and Wolf and about 30 percent according to GATT data. A comparison of industrial output and exports probably

Table 12.2
Determinants of export performance by Indian industries, 1973–1974 and 1976–1977

Dependent	SCALE	AW	K_FLOW	K_STOCK	TECH 1	TECH 2	MAN	SALES	METAL	CHEM	TESTERS	PROD	R^2
1973–1974													
1. EXP Total	0.448[c] (1.665)	0.212 (0.372)	−0.367[c] (1.461)		0.067 (0.520)		−0.502[a] (2.563)	0.055 (0.379)	0.190[b] (1.701)	−0.018 (0.281)	0.450[a] (3.960)	−0.206[b] (2.117)	0.297
2. EXP Total	0.387[b] (4.724)	0.980[b] (1.713)		−1.245[a] (3.511)		0.089 (0.607)		−0.184[c] (1.483)	0.155[b] (1.733)	0.008 (0.122)	0.286[a] (2.811)	−0.215[b] (2.224)	0.316
3. EXP_DC	−0.043 (0.172)	1.004[c] (1.531)		−1.193[a] (3.039)	−0.081 (0.572)		−0.388[b] (1.783)	0.124 (0.777)	0.205[b] (1.662)	−0.020 (0.275)	0.490[a] (3.908)	−0.174[c] (1.620)	0.326
4. EXP_LDC	0.400[b] (1.820)	0.489 (0.756)		−0.795[a] (2.326)	0.133 (1.073)		−0.481[a] (2.540)	−0.025 (0.181)	0.170[c] (1.585)	0.039 (0.606)	0.327[a] (2.997)	−0.175[b] (1.867)	0.346
1977–1978													
5. EXP Total	0.029 (0.102)	1.171[c] (1.616)		−0.966[b] (2.194)	0.165 (1.246)		−0.469[b] (2.279)	−0.002 (0.012)	0.260[b] (2.178)	−0.032 (0.490)	0.309[a] (2.594)	−0.170[b] (1.690)	0.314
6. EXP_DC	0.317 (0.885)	−0.221 (0.244)		−0.690 (1.252)	0.087 (0.526)		−0.447[b] (1.738)	0.153 (0.841)	0.188 (1.258)	−0.089 (1.076)	0.400[a] (2.689)	−0.130 (1.033)	0.204
7. EXP_LDC	−0.110 (0.376)	1.484[b] (2.00)		−0.956[b] (2.121)	0.167 (1.231)		−0.402[b] (1.905)	−0.045 (0.301)	0.247[b] (2.019)	0.013 (0.188)	0.239[b] (1.958)	−0.182[b] (1.765)	0.304
8. EXP_LDC	−0.028 (0.093)	1.652[b] (2.190)		−0.977[b] (2.075)		0.007 (0.041)		−0.147 (1.106)	0.247[a] (2.423)	0.022 (0.323)	0.152[c] (1.294)	−0.184[b] (1.714)	0.248

Note: t-value in parentheses. Significance levels: a = 1%, b = 5%, c = 10%, using 1 tail test.

shows an even greater Southward "bias." This seems to imply that, whatever constraints may exist on the expansion of intra-South trade, market forces have given developing countries some edge in serving the demands of similar countries. More precise, the more advanced developing countries (the NICs, among which I would include India) have experienced a comparative advantage in selling their products to themselves and to lesser industrialized countries. It is not evident whether this is due to the peculiar nature of the products made by the exporters (which makes them more acceptable to other countries in the South), to their specialization in simple undifferentiated products that they can provide more cheaply than the developed countries, to the "sourcing" strategies of MNCs located in them, to cost advantages based on proximity, or to noneconomic factors such as official promotion of South-South cooperation.

Trade in Technology

In the conventional terminology of the transfer-of-technology literature, "export of technologies" is taken to refer to the following types of transactions: the sale of turnkey plants (in the industrial sector); the sale of engineering and other manufacturing-based consultancy services; the provision of technical know-how and other assets and skills as part of direct investment by foreign enterprises; the sale of such "instruments" as blueprints, patents, drawings, and brand names in formal licensing arrangements; and the sale of pure knowhow (such as troubleshooting, technical assistance, repair, and plant rehabilitation) not in the form of a licensing arrangement.

The export of technology as defined here includes a substantial element of the export of manufactured goods: capital goods involved in turnkey projects and direct investments. Nevertheless, it is worth considering turnkey projects as distinct from trade in capital goods generally, because the sale of a complete industrial plant (which is usually based on designs, equipment, and a diverse collection of engineering and training services by the exporter) may be taken to represent a more advanced and complex technical capability than the sale of individual items of capital goods. This may not be true of every case. Clearly, some capital-goods exports may be based on indigenous design and development, but by and large the ability to design, set up, and commission an entire plant shows local capabilities better than the ability to sell equipment, which may easily be made under foreign license.

The export of manufacturing technology by the more industrialized developing countries has made impressive progress in recent years (Lall 1982a). Enterprises (mostly locally owned) from India, Argentina, Brazil, Mexico, Korea, and Taiwan are setting up turnkey plants in other developing countries, spanning a broad range of activities and technologies. The leader in this activity in the Third World seems to be India, which has (according to my researches as part of a larger World Bank project on technology exports) won well over 200 contracts valued at between $2 billion and $2.5 billion in the past seven or eight years. The main industry involved has been power generation. Some 23 percent of India's projects have involved the design, supply, and erection of power stations, a highly complex, skill-intensive, and technologically demanding activity. Other important industries have been power distribution, cement, textiles, steel mills, machine tools, and sugar, a collection representing both simple, well-diffused technologies and complex, advanced ones. The other NICs are well behind India in this activity and are also more narrowly based in their range of technologies.[8]

The export of consultancy has also grown rapidly, with nearly all the NICs selling detailed engineering, project supervision, feasibility studies, and similar services. There are almost no instances of developing-country firms winning contracts for the sale of basic design services, even though many of them have such design experience at home. Some of the exports have been as subcontractors to developed-country engineering firms, and many have been to supervise or check what construction firms from the developed countries were doing. Comparable figures are not available for the exporters, but India seems to be among the leaders, with about $125 million worth of consultancy exports until early 1982 (about half of which was in the manufacturing sector). A rapidly growing item in this field is the export of computer programming services, which is directed almost entirely at the industrialized world; the rest of the consultancy exports are destined mainly for other developing countries.

Direct investment by Third World enterprises is discussed in a separate subsection below. As for licensing and the sale of knowhow, there is sufficient (but scattered) evidence to indicate that it is a fast-growing area of international activity by many large enterprises in the NICs, with almost all the customers in the Third World. Indian scooters are assembled under license in Taiwan and Indonesia and Indian bicycles in several countries of Asia and Africa. The largest Indian cement firm is running a cement plant in Saudi Arabia. Several Indian textile firms and textile-equipment manufacturers are rehabilitating old plants abroad. Indian brand names for soft drinks and soaps are franchised overseas. It is impossible to collect data on the values of these sales abroad (by their very nature, most of them are small contracts), but in terms of the South-South transfer of technology they are not unimpressive.

This is not, however, to argue that the NICs are substantial exporters of technology in the context of global technology trade. The total value of Third World technology exports in industry is probably smaller than the earnings of one large engineering firm from the United States. The great bulk of technology imported by the developing world comes from the highly industrialized countries. And there are large areas of very sophisticated technology where the developing countries are entirely unable to compete with the traditional technology suppliers. The volume of the South's technology exports is not very substantial yet; it is their emergence and rapid expansion that are of interest.

Developing country enterprises are also emerging as competitive sellers of services in other fields. The major one is civil construction, where South Korea (with over $40 billion of contracts won) is already a major force in the Middle East, followed at some distance by India ($6 billion), Brazil ($3.6 billion), and several other developing countries. Petrobras of Brazil is a large seller of petroleum exploration and related services. Several hotel chains from the NICs have established themselves abroad, as have banks, insurance companies, and traders.[9] The small island economies of Hong Kong and Singapore appear to be particularly active in the export of trading and financial services, as are some of the giant state corporations of Brazil (especially Banco do Brazil). Korean enterprises are also actively involved in natural-resource extraction overseas, emulating the pattern set some decades ago by the Japanese.

The leading role played by India in exports of industrial technology by Third World countries is rather surprising in view of its relatively poor export performance in manufactured goods and in capital goods (Lall 1981, 1982a). Brazil has been the leading Third World exporter of capital goods in recent years and sells a high proportion of these to other developing countries (60 percent in 1977, according to Havrylyshyn and Wolf 1981, p. 79). Korea is also a significant exporter of capital goods (nearly four times larger than India), though only one-fourth of this is directed at other developing countries.

The growth of technology exports by the more industrialized developing countries, mainly to other developing countries, seems to have several interesting implications. First, it offers the buying countries a wider range of choice in their technology purchases. This may mean that they can get cheaper technology better adapted to their needs, or technology sold in a less "packaged" or restricted form than that available from traditional suppliers in the North. Second, it reveals on the part of the exporting countries an impressive (and in many ways unexpected) capability to design, engineer, and construct plants requiring complex technologies. This could be taken as *prima facie* evidence that their sources of comparative advantage are changing rapidly as they develop new skills and enter into innovative activity. In other words, technology exports may be seen as the leading edge of the South's dynamic comparative advantage, and thus they hold important lessons for future South-South cooperation.

On the basis of this rather rosy picture of South-South technology transfer, there would be strong grounds for promoting independent technological development in the industrializing countries, encouraging similar technological strategies in the later-comers, and stimulating intra-South technology transfers as an alternative to North-South transfers. Alas, a closer examination of the nature of technological development and export by the developing countries does not support such a sanguine view. The manner in which Indian technological capabilities have developed, in particular, calls for caution in advocating massive efforts to promote Southern technology as a major alternative to Northern technology.

Direct Foreign Investment

One of the more interesting recent developments on the international investment scene has been the rise of "Third World multinationals."[10] These come mainly from the more industrialized developing countries, and they invest predominantly in other developing countries, though a handful of ventures (mainly in service activities such as export marketing, banking, and restaurants) also go to the developed world. In general terms we are justified in regarding this as a form of intra-South economic relationship, one determined mainly by market forces and representing the transfer of a "package" of industrial technology, managerial skills, investable resources, and occasionally marketing advantages.

Third World MNCs are not, strictly speaking, a new phenomenon. The first recorded instance of a developing-country firm setting up a manufacturing affiliate abroad was in 1890, when Alpargatas, a textile firm in Argentina, invested in Uruguay. In the early part of this century Argentina led industrial development in the Third World, and by World War I its three leading firms were very active overseas in manufacturing, grain trade, finance, and other service activities. With the subsequent drop in Argentina's fortunes, however, these firms grew larger overseas than in the home country or else went bankrupt. They did not herald the coming of Third World MNCs in the normal sense.

The real growth of Third World MNCs began in the late 1960s and picked up momentum in the 1970s. By the early 1980s some 30 developing countries could (according to data collected by the UN Center on TNCs) claim to be the home of some firm with direct investments overseas. The true extent of direct foreign investment by the South is, however, almost impossible to guage. The OPEC capital-surplus countries have invested substantial sums in buying industrial stock, which was essentially a form of portfolio investment and so should be excluded. Some of the largest overseas investors in the South have kept no record of their capital exports. Some investments overseas were made clandestinely to avoid official controls. Some MNCs formally headquartered in developing countries were in fact "expatriate" companies entirely staffed and run by developed-country personnel; their overseas investments are large (e.g., Jardine Matheson of Hong Kong) but can hardly be counted as intra-South transactions. For all these reasons, balance-of-payments data on overseas investments (of the sort used by the UN) by the South can be highly misleading.

A collection of rather patchy data on investments by the NICs gives a more realistic picture. Oil-rich countries aside, the largest single direct investor in the Third World is Hong Kong, with between $1.5 billion and $2.0 billion of direct equity stock overseas, mostly in manufacturing industry. However, a substantial portion of this is held by "expatriate" British firms operating out of the colony, and investment abroad by indigenous Chinese firms is around $600–700 million.[11] These firms invest mainly in neighbouring Southeast Asian countries with significant Chinese populations: Taiwan, Singapore, Malaysia, Indonesia, Thailand, and the Philippines. They are also becoming very active in the newly opened regions of the People's Republic of China. Their tremendous drive overseas, fueled by rising land and labor costs at home and protectionist policies in the developed countries, easily makes Hong Kong the South's largest direct investor overseas in manufacturing.

Hong Kong's foreign investments tend mainly to go into export-oriented ventures in the simpler of manufacturing activities—textiles, standard garments, plastics, consumer electronics, and other light consumer goods. These are the activities that are facing the most competitive pressures from new entrants on international markets. Hong Kong's more sophisticated manufactures (toys, fashion garments, advanced electronics) are kept at home because of their skill, design, and marketing requirements; this is a sort of miniature product cycle within the developing world.[12] Hong Kong MNCs provide mainly managerial and marketing know-how; their basic industrial technology and capital goods come from the advanced countries. There is, in other words, little technology (in the narrow sense) generated and provided by the home country.

The next largest investor overall is Brazil, with some $1 billion of overseas equity stock.[13] There are two noteworthy features of Brazilian overseas involvement. First, a very small amount (about $20 million) goes into manufacturing. This is surprising given Brazil's leadership in industrial activity and heavy manufactured exports in the developing world and repeats the pattern of its relative underrepresentation in the entire field of industrial technology exports. Second, most of it is accounted for by one state-owned firm, Petrobras (other significant but much smaller investors are the civil construction companies). The aggressive foreign investment strategy adopted by this government firm seems to be unique in the Third World.

Singapore is a smaller investor in overall terms than Brazil but a much larger investor in manufacturing industry. Most of its activity occurs in Malaysia, which has such close historical, commercial, and (for the Chinese trading community) ethnic ties that it is almost inappropriate to describe it as foreign at all. Nevertheless, Singaporean enterprises are significant on the Malaysian industrial scene and have also ventured in a smaller way to neighboring countries with ethnic links. It appears on the basis of the tenuous evidence at hand that Singaporean enterprises not only are much less active abroad than their Hong Kong counterparts but also are specialized in more inward-looking manufacturing activity at a comparatively low level of technological sophistication.

Like Hong Kong, Singapore provides little of the basic industrial technology from the home country. It is interesting to speculate why Singapore has not been more active abroad in relation to Hong Kong. After all, the pressure to relocate simpler activities abroad must be greater for Singapore; its wage rates are higher, and land is nearly as scarce. Moreover, its exports reveal a greater degree of technological complexity and sophistication than Hong Kong's: heavy engineering (ships), petrochemicals, and advanced electronics rather than textiles and light consumer goods. The answer probably lies in the relative roles of MNCs from the North in these two economies: Singapore is more dominated by foreign firms than is Hong Kong. If exports are used as an indicator, over 90 percent of Singapore's are accounted for by foreign enterprises, as compared to under 20 percent for Hong Kong. Relocation does take place from Singapore, but much of it is undertaken by the developed-country MNCs based there.

A number of other NICs have invested between $50 million and $100 million each overseas, with manufacturing investments ranging around $30 million to $60 million. These countries include Korea, Taiwan, Mexico, and Argentina. Argentina is probably the leader among these, with affiliates active in food processing, pharmaceuticals, and light engineering. Argentine MNCs are strongly rooted in home-based technology and capital goods, perhaps to a greater degree than the other NICs mentioned. Korea's foreign activity is mainly in export marketing, though it also has some natural-resource-extraction investments.

Outside the middle-income NIC category, but a significant industrial investor overseas, is India, with a capital stock of about $100 million, of which over 80 percent is in manufacturing. Perhaps the most surprising fact about Indian foreign investment is not that it is large in an absolute sense but that in the 1970s net investment abroad far exceeded foreign investment flows into the country. Between 1969 and 1980 the government approved new (gross) foreign investments of about $70 million; in net terms foreign capital flows were significantly negative. (Compare this to a net inflow into Brazil in 1978 alone of $2.2 billion, and the contrast in international economic postures of these two large developing countries really stands out.) Surely it is a paradox that the poorest of the South's industrializing nations has become a net exporter of capital.

This is not the only notable feature of India's foreign investment. Indian MNCs reveal a surprisingly wide range of activities overseas, from simple, traditional ones such as textiles and food processing to large, sophisticated ones such as giant paper and pulp mills (the largest such mill in sub-Saharan Africa is run by Birla), palm-oil fractionation (the world's largest such plant, in Malaysia, is run by Tata), truck assembly, precision tools for electronics industries (Tata in Singapore), rayon, and carbon black. There seem to be two distinct types of Indian MNCs: the conventional type of Third World multinational (small in scale and simple in technology, serving a market ignored by the traditional MNCs from the developed world) and a new breed of investor (specialized in much more advanced activity, deploying large-scale, capital-intensive methods, and in most respects indistinguishable from North MNCs). The earlier Indian investments were dominated by the former, whereas recent investments by some of India's largest business houses are dominated by the latter. Moreover, there is a very high Indian content to the technology transferred. By law most of India's equity contribution is made in the form of capital goods and know-how. Interviews confirm that Indian investors essentially use technologies they have mastered and adapted at home and are able to reproduce from scratch overseas. Their direct investments thus embody some of their technological dynamism, and many large houses have yet to venture abroad.

This is not to argue that Indian or other Third World MNCs are or will be substitutes for the MNCs of the developed world. However, the surge of intra-South direct investments in unexpectedly broad areas of industry does indicate the start of a potentially important form of economic interlinkage. As with other forms of technology exports, we must be aware of its small size at this time. Adding up the bits and pieces of information on the chief foreign investors from the South, we get a total investment stock of under $10 billion—probably less than 2 percent of the total world stock of direct investment. As with other technology exports, the technological dynamism underlying their international production must not raise very high hopes for independent technological development in the South.

The Nature of South-South Economic Relations

Characteristics and Determinants

There is a refrain running through the literature on South-South versus North-South economic relations that the nature of economic transactions between developing countries differs from that of transactions between developed and developing ones.[14] If this is so, there are grounds for considering the special benefits (and costs) arising from the peculiar nature of intra-South relations and for formulating special policies to encourage (or discourage) them.

There are two possible sets of reasons why South-South transactions may differ from North-South ones, both of which concern the more industrialized countries of the South. First, the resource endowments that (in a neo-Heckscher-Ohlin world) determine trading patterns of the NICs with countries of the North would differ from those that determine trade with lesser developed countries of the South. This difference depends only on supply considerations; the dynamic process of physical and human capital accumulation by the NICs shifts their relative position along the spectrum on which all world economies are arrayed. Bhagwati's (1964) analysis had already suggested that, instead of trying to explain a country's aggregate trade pattern along Heckscher-Ohlin lines, it would be more rewarding to explain it differentially: the trade pattern vis-à-vis the aggregate of countries below it in capital-labor endowment and the trade pattern vis-à-vis the aggregate of countries above it in capital-labor endowment. This would imply immediately that the NICs would be exporting physical-plus-human-capital-intensive goods to the South and labor-intensive goods to the North. In the same vein, Balassa's recent "stages approach" to comparative advantage (Balassa 1981, chap. 6) is yet again a neat analytical and empirical demonstration of the possibility that the neo-Heckscher-Ohlin determinants of export performance change as countries become more industrialized. Though Balassa does not test for the characteristics of exports to the North and the South separately, the implication of his findings is clear: The accumulation of physical and human capital leads all exports to become more physical-capital-intensive and more skill-intensive, but those to better-endowed destinations (the North) will embody lower levels of physical and human capital than those to worse-endowed destinations (the South).

Although the empirical evidence on the actual physical capital intensities of NICs' exports to North and South is mixed and unconvincing (especially where cross-section regression analysis of "revealed comparative advantage" is concerned; see in particular Amsden 1980), there is general agreement that the human-capital or skill content of South-South trade is higher than that of South-North exports. The neo-Heckscher-Ohlin explanation of trade patterns is, however, neither theoretically complete nor empirically well tested. It ignores major factors affecting comparative advantage that are widely accepted as of great significance. Its empirical testing has suffered from the use of

U.S. capital-labor coefficients for developing countries, which reduces its relevance.

The second set of reasons for intra-South trade to be different depends on demand considerations and therefore departs from the Heckscher-Ohlin approach altogether. There are two steps in the argument, which is essentially a modified version of Linder's original explanation of the higher incidence of trade between similar rather than different countries. First, demand patterns for imports in the South are different from those in the North. This is not difficult to accept. For consumer goods, sharp differences in income levels will (small elites apart) create markedly different patterns of demand. For producer goods, the pattern of demand for most intermediate products will not differ but that for capital goods may, depending on the scale of operations and the skill endowments of the importer's labor force. Thus, small developing countries with inexperienced workers may tend to opt for capital goods that are of older design, simpler, more rugged, less specialized, and less automated than those provided by the developed countries.[15] Second, these special demands generate in turn a special advantage for South-South trade, for they cannot easily be satisfied by the developed countries. For consumer goods this inability arises partly from the fact that the industries of the developed countries are unfamiliar with the demand characteristics of poorer countries and partly from the high cost of reequipping production units to make slightly different (or older) products for relatively small runs. For capital goods, similarly, older vintages or adapted products are uneconomical to produce because older technologies are forgotten as equipment suppliers and their entire complex of subcontractors tool up for high-volume, new generation products. There are thus good a priori reasons to expect that this combination of demand and supply factors will impart special characteristics to South-South trade.

What do the facts show? A few empirical studies have been published on the differing characteristics of intra-South and South-North manufactured exports. Tyler's (1972) was an early attempt to test only for the skill intensity of Brazil's exports to different destinations. Using U.S. coefficients, Tyler found that skill factors by themselves explained a very small part of Brazil's interindustry variations in export performance but that the skill content of exports to the South was distinctly higher than that of exports to the North.

Krueger (1978) compared the labor content of exports by four developing countries (Chile, Kenya, Thailand, and Uruguay) to developed-country and developing-country markets. In the context of a simple Heckscher-Ohlin-Samuelson trade model, Krueger and associates obtained the expected result that exports to the South were less labor-intensive than those to the North.[16] This set of country studies did not test for the human-capital intensity of trade by destination (though some evidence on five countries was adduced to show that exportables in general were more unskilled-labor-intensive than import-competing industries).

Havrylyshyn and Wolf (1981) extended the Krueger type of calculation to include both human and physical capital for all manufactured exports by the NICs. They worked out these capital intensities for four categories of exports: those of "principal" developed countries (80 percent of exports to the North), those of "secondary" developed countries (60 to 80 percent to the North), those of "principal" developing countries (50 percent or more to the South), and those of "secondary" developing countries (30 to 50 percent to the South). Using Balassa's coefficients derived from U.S. data, they found that South-North exports were much less human-plus-physical-capital-intensive than South-South exports.[17] It was not, however, clear from their initial analysis whether physical or human capital was the predominant factor.[18]

Amsden's (1980) attempt is the most comprehensive in terms of the number of independent variables deployed. She uses not just physical-capital intensity (stock and flow measures) but also two measures of skill (average wage and ratio of technical, scientific, and professional employees), a measure of scale economies, and one of natural resource intensity. For most of the ten countries she analyzes, physical-capital intensity does not turn out to be significant in differentiating the two kinds of exports, but skill intensity does. The other variables also fail to achieve significance.

Amsden focuses on the most significant theoretical drawback of most of the earlier studies: the reliance on an oversimplified analytical model of trade determinants. The modified or original Heckscher-Ohlin model of comparative advantage, which underlies most of these attempts, neglects such important factors as scale economies, technological differences, and even different endowments of different skills. It is often argued that technological determinants play a negligible role in shaping interindustry differences in the comparative advantage of the South. They clearly engage in little R&D and have made few major innovations in terms of product or process breakthroughs. This identification of technological change with major innovations is misleading; much technical progress, even in the advanced world, results from productivity-raising, adaptive, or incremental minor innovations.[19] There is now widespread evidence that enterprises in developing countries undertake considerable minor innovation, partly in the form of production-related engineering activity and partly through the introduction of new products or processes based on R&D.[20] The absolute amount of R&D may be relatively small, but for latecomers on the industrial scene such small investments may yield substantial results in terms of "catching up" or making improvements to known methods.

Although it is plausible that systematic interindustry differences in the propensity to undertake minor innovation can cause differences in export performance, it is very difficult to test this hypothesis in practice. Formal R&D data (even if they exist) do not properly capture the complex of different kinds of effort involved. Neither do conventional measures of skill or crude indices of learning by doing such as the total accumulated value of output. This is unfortunate, since the evidence on technology exports and direct foreign investments by developing countries suggests that these are based heavily on minor innovation. These effects must carry over into manufactured exports, and (if technology exports are any guide) they should stimulate South-South exports more than South-North exports.

In the absence of proper evidence, it is impossible to predict whether export growth based on minor innovation bears any particular relationship to such industrial characteristics as capital intensity, skill intensity, or scale intensity, or to market-structure variables such as concentration and industry or firm size, or to particular forms of government intervention. My research on Indian technology exports (1979, 1982a) shows a wide spread of technological competence in international markets. Labor-intensive industries are present as well as capital-intensive ones and less and more skill-based activities; no clear pattern emerges in relation to traditional trade variables.

The pattern of technology exports by India can be classified into four broad groups:

1. Technologies India cannot provide at all or cannot provide competitively with enterprises from the North. These comprise frontier technologies in industries that are subject to very rapid technological progress (such as advanced electronics), those that are subject to very-large-scale operation (such as some petrochemicals and passenger cars), those that are subject to very expensive and lengthy technological learning (such as several kinds of very complex machinery), and those

that are geared to very sophisticated and rich consumer markets (many modern consumer durables and highly differentiated nondurables). In these industries, Indian enterprises have not imbibed the technology at all or they have done so under conditions that do not enable them to assimilate them properly.

2. Technologies India can provide competitively by conducting substantial R&D at home and supplementing this with periodic injections of imported technology (such as heavy power-generating equipment, machine tools of medium sophistication, various automative products, and chemical plants). The product India provides may be somewhat older or smaller in scale than those provided by developed countries, but other developing countries may desire it for precisely that reason. In light of the scale factor, many Indian technologies (say, in chemical or other process industries) will be indistinguishable from those of the developed countries.

3. Technologies in which India provides highly adapted products or processes, based mainly on indigenous R&D and design change. Indian trucks, certain items of machinery or metal structures, and certain chemical processes (like rayon) are good examples. These technologies usually substitute for rather different and more advanced technologies from the North, and the demand for them arises from the peculiar needs of developing countries.

4. Technologies that are uniquely Indian and do not directly compete with North technologies, such as handicrafts or small-scale industries.

In quantitative terms, categories 2 and 3 predominate over 4, but it is impossible to say which of the first two is the more significant. India's competitive edge sometimes lies in providing technologies identical to those from the North but gaining a cost advantage because of its cheaper engineering manpower. At other times it lies in the adaptations India has made to technologies to make them suitable to conditions in developing countries. I have deliberately included category 1 to emphasize that large areas of modern technology are out of reach for a country like India; the "learning" conditions simply do not exist.

To sum up the technology factor: The neglect of this potentially important influence on developing countries' comparative advantage in trade, while understandable, is a great loss to the explanation of the characteristics of South-South economic relationships. "Learning" and technical excellence are undoubtedly crucial to success in exports to the North also, but it is likely that such learning is different and more limited and has different implications for the economy concerned.

Whether it is better or worse for growth and technological capability is a separate question, which will be addressed later.

Let us consider the scale factor. Much of the neo-technology trade literature suggests that developing countries will face a comparative disadvantage with respect to the North in exporting scale-intensive products (see Hirsch 1977). By the same token, the NICs should have an advantage in exporting scale-intensive products to countries further down the industrialization ladder. There is no evidence to support this hypothesis in the literature at hand, however.

As far as skill composition is concerned, it would appear from the general empirical finding that South-South exports are more skill intensive than South-North exports and that they also involve different kinds of skills. In 1964, Bhagwati suggested that different skills be regarded as different factor inputs. A few attempts have been made to test this empirically, but mainly for the developed countries (see, for example, Baldwin 1979, on the United States). The impact of different skill endowments on South-South trade has yet to be properly investigated.

These considerations bring me to some research I have started, in collaboration with Sharif Mohammad, on the patterns of Indian manufactured exports. This study uses explanatory variables derived from Indian rather than U.S. data. The use of U.S. variables for capital and skill intensity in equations purporting to explain developing countries' export patterns has been a major fault of most earlier studies. The researchers concerned have assumed that the ranking of factor intensities does not change across countries at vastly different income and industrialization levels. We found this assumption suspect. As a preliminary step we selected approximately 30 major commodities of export interest to the NICs and calculated physical-capital, skill, and scale coefficients from U.S., U.K., Brazilian, Indian, and Singaporean census data. The nature of the data permitted only flow measures of physical capital (nonwage value added per employee) and skills (average wages) and a crude indicator of scale (value added per establishment). Nevertheless the results were illuminating. The skill and scale measures were highly correlated across all the different countries, while the measure of physical-capital intensity was highly correlated between Brazil and India, less so between these and Singapore, and not at all between the developed and the developing countries. A number of explanations are possible, but certainly we cannot exclude the strong possibility that different industries display different degrees of adaptability to low-wage conditions. As a result, capital intensities vary sharply but skill and scale intensities do not.[21] Thus, the empirical foundations of many earlier studies are suspect.

We were fortunate in obtaining an extremely detailed occupational breakdown for 1970 of employment in over 80 manufacturing industries in India, published by the Directorate General of Employment and Training. These unpublished data related to private-sector industry (public-sector data are collected for a different year). They were rearranged to yield 17 skill categories we considered economically meaningful. However, since trial runs showed extremely high degrees of multicollinearity between these categories, they were further reduced to the following groups: engineers, architects, and surveyors (TECH 1); all technical workers (TECH 2); all administrative, executive, and managerial workers (MAN); all sales workers (SALES); all metal workers (METAL); all chemical workers (CHEM); testers and packers (TESTERS); and all skilled and unskilled production workers (PROD). All these categories were expressed as percentages of total employment in each industry; they do not cover several other categories of employees, which we considered irrelevant to our analysis of trade-pattern determinants.

The industrial breakdown given by the employment data had to be matched with that given by the industrial census published by the Central Statistical Office. In turn, these sets of data had to be matched with the industrial classifications used in the Indian trade data. In the process of matching we had to drop some observations, and we ended up with a final sample of 71 industries.

The dependent variables measuring industrial export performance were total exports of each industry as a percentage of total industrial exports (EXP_{Total}), exports of each industry to developed countries as a percentage of total industrial exports to developed countries (EXP_{DC}), and exports of each industry to developing countries as a percentage of total industrial exports to developing countries (EXP_{LDC}).[22] These variables were calculated for two periods, each covering two years, to eliminate as far as possible the impact of erratic fluctuations in 1973–1974 and 1977–1978.

Apart from the various skill variables described above, derived from numbers of employees, we used independent variables to capture overall skill differences between industries as measured by the average wage (AW).[23] We also employed two measures of capital intensity: a flow measure, nonwage value added per employee (K_{FLOW}), and a stock measure, total fixed capital per employee (K_{STOCK}). Both measures suffer from well-known deficiencies (see for instance Balassa 1981, chapter 6), but they are the only ones available. As a scale measure we used value added per factory (SCALE), again a very crude proxy but the only one we could calculate given the nature of the census data. (Indian data do not permit the calculation of cost-advantage ratios of large plants over small plants or other measures based on the shares of large and small plants.)

As with other studies, we could not include a measure for technical "learning" or minor innovation (even formal R&D data were not available at this industrial level). However, we hoped that some of the occupational categories, such as technical workers and engineers, metal workers, chemical workers, and testers (who may learn by quality control), might capture these effects, not directly by measuring the technological effort, but very indirectly by showing the relative capabilties of different industries to absorb different kinds of technical learning. Our skill categories cannot be described as measures of human capital in the normal sense.

The objective of the exercise was to identify the major determinants of industrial export performance to different destinations by India, using the standard trade variables (capital intensity, general skill levels, scale economies) as well as the skill profiles of each industry (to see whether specific kinds of skills promoted exports to different destinations). The regressions were run in log-linear form.

Table 12.2 sets out the main results of the regressions for the two periods separately. The various skill-employment variables still suffer from significant multicollinearity (between 0.4 and 0.8), but there is little we could do to avoid this problem. In particular, TECH 1 and TECH 2 are very highly correlated with all the other occupational categories (with PROD coming the lowest with a correlation coefficient of 0.55). Of the other independent variables, SCALE is highly correlated with AW (0.642)—a phenomenon also invariably found in industrial studies in the developed countries—K FLOW (0.631), and K STOCK (0.458). K STOCK is also, not unexpectedly, related to AW (0.501), but the two measures of capital intensity have a correlation coefficient of only 0.356. None of the occupational-skill variables correlate highly with the other independent variables.

The results of the regression analysis are fairly good by the standards of previous such studies; the best equations "explain" about one-third of the variation in the dependent variable. There is no marked difference in the overall performance of the regressions for the two periods.

The results for the individual variables are interesting. Capital intensity—for which we show the results mainly for the stock measure, which invariably performed better—has a negative sign, almost always significant, in all the equations. This is reassuring in general terms—India has a comparative advantage in labor-intensive industries (or, if one accepts more modern product-cycle type of theories, in export of mature "Heckscher-Ohlin goods" where factor costs reassert their significance; see Hirsch 1977)—and it suggests that the measurement of the dependent variable is not too misleading. However, the results do not support the belief that this effect varies significantly according to the destination of exports. In the first period capital intensity does seem a slightly stronger deterrent to exports to DCs, but in the latter period the ranking is reversed.

The general skill variable, AW, shows up as a significant positive influence in a number of equations, but its effect according to destination changes between the two periods. In 1973–1974 it seems to favor DC exports and have no effect on LDC exports, while in 1977–1978 it has a positive and significant effect on LDC exports and none on DC exports. The latter result is more in line with previous findings and may reflect the increased influence of normal workings of comparative advantage on Indian export activity.

Scale factors show significance in the first period, when they have a positive impact on total and LDC exports, but they become insignificant in the second period.

Of the occupational-skill variables, TECH 1 and TECH 2 fail to achieve conventional statistical significance (though TECH 1 almost does in the second period for total and LDC exports). Because of the multicollinearity problems, this may not be very surprising. MAN has a uniformly negative effect, probably signifying that, given the inward orientation of Indian economic policy (Bhagwati and Srinavasan 1975) the better-managed industries exploit the profitable opportunities offered by domestic as opposed to international markets. SALES fails to reach significance (perhaps another indication of the inward-looking protectionist nature of the regime, which has failed to foster effective marketing skills).

Of the two main types of industrial skills, metalworking and chemicals, the former has positive and significant effects but the latter has no significant effects. If my argument is correct, this would suggest that metalworking offers greater scope for minor innovation in a developing country like India than chemicals, which may require much larger-scale, complex, formal R&D. In the first period METAL promotes DC exports marginally more than LDC exports; in the second it does the reverse.

The category of testers and packers has a surprisingly strong statistical effect, always positive. In both periods it seems to promote DC exports more than LDC exports. If this variable catches the effects of quality control, the implications would be that this particular skill strongly promotes international competitiveness and that DC markets are (expectedly) more demanding in this regard than LDC markets.

Finally, the variable PROD, total production workers (including unskilled workers), has significant and negative signs throughout, suggesting that shop-floor experience or skills in general terms do not promote international competitiveness. In the second period the negative effect is slightly stronger for LDC than for DC exports.

These findings can be subjected to many qualifications on the nature of the data and the interpretation of the variables. The most important qualification is that the Indian case is peculiar in many respects. The highly regulated and inward-looking nature of the regime restricts the normal workings of market forces shaping export performance. It is thus difficult to extrapolate from Indian evidence to what may occur in other developing countries. Nevertheless, this case does retain interest, because India is still one of the major industrial producers and exporters in the South and probably its leading exporter of industrial technology. From this exercise, therefore, we may infer that there are some differences in the factors affecting exports to the North and South, but our evidence does not permit simple generalizations. If we concentrate on the second period, we may conclude that exports to the South are more skill- and labor-intensive than exports to the North, and that metalworking skills are particularly conducive to exports to the South. Since the post-1975 period is also the one in which technology exports to the South started in a major way, we may link the two phenomena and argue (in line with previous findings) that the skill content of South-South trade is higher than that of South-North trade but the former is not particularly physical-capital-intensive.

These findings are very tentative; much more empirical work is needed before they are stated with any confidence. In particular we need more information on the nature and role of minor innovation in shaping the comparative advantage of developing countries. Because of the evolutionary (in the Nelson-Winter sense) nature of such technical change, it is likely that in many areas of industrial activity technological effort is endowing individual enterprises with unique assets that they can exploit abroad. In terms of conventional trade theory, it is vital to remember that these assets are composed not of skills or human capital in some broad sense (though they do require the absorptive base of skills) but of specific, consciously directed, problem-solving technological effort. How this can be empirically tested is a difficult problem that cannot be analyzed here.

Benefits and Costs

The benefits of South-South economic relationships are of two types: those arising from the mere extension of international economic activity (increased specialization, greater exploitation of scale economies, diversification of risk, and so on) regardless of the special nature of South-South trade, and those arising from the peculiarities of South-South as opposed to North-South trade. The first are obvious and do not need much discussion. In this section we shall concentrate on the second, and mainly on the exporters rather than the importers.

We have seen that the evidence on the differences between South-South and South-North exports is not wholly conclusive. However, in order to proceed, let us accept that intra-South trade is more skill-intensive and technology-intensive (but not more physical-capital-intensive) than South-North trade.[24] Because of the nature of demand in the South, we also observe the sale of some products and technologies that are based on adaptations and innovations undertaken in the NICs. What can we then infer about the benefits and costs of South-South exchanges?

The benefits arise by providing a larger market for the adapted products and technologies concerned. Thus, South-South trade could enable greater scale economies to be realized, and this may enable greater technological efforts to be undertaken.[25]

As hinted above, however, there may be offsetting costs. I have in mind specifically the brand of technological strategy India has adopted, which has led to a certain amount of technological development but has also resulted in large areas of inefficiency and technological backwardness in Indian industry.[26] The high costs of inefficient import substitution by India are well known (Bhagwati and Desai 1970; Bhagwati and Srinivasan 1975), and its costs in terms of loss of export markets are patently obvious. The fact that as a beneficial by-product of the policy of "self-reliance in everything at all costs" certain technological capabilities have developed and found markets abroad is not necessarily a substantial benefit to the economy. This is so for several reasons. First, it is possible that greater technological learning would have occurred in India had foreign technology and capital been allowed in more freely. Brazil has been a much bigger importer of technology, and as a consequence its industrial sector is far more efficient, a far larger exporter of engineering products to the South, and much more dynamic in its potential for growth. The relationship between technology importation and local technological development is not always negative; after an absorptive base has been established, it tends to be positive. In other words, a persistent policy of local technological development then becomes counterproductive, condemning industry to progressive backwardness. Second, because of this technological strategy, many industries in India have gone for exports to the South as a substitute for exports to the North. The North is and will remain a much larger market, so this has been a growth-inhibiting policy. Moreover, with growth and modernization in the South, the demand for some of India's adapted technologies and products may well decline. Unless India brings itself nearer to international technological frontiers, its independent technological efforts will saddle it with a shrinking market even in the South. Third, markets for adapted products in the South may have been a "soft option" for many exporters, retarding rather than promoting some of the capabilities needed for international competitiveness. For all these reasons, we should be wary of inferring major gains from South-South trade simply because it provides a ready market for technologies developed in the South. I believe that independent technological effort in the South quickly reaches its productive limits and then needs replenishing with injections of modern technologies from the North. If this process takes the industry concerned to world technological frontiers, it will be able to retain and expand its markets in the South. However, in this case, it can also expand its exports to the North, and the two forms of export activity will be complements to, rather than substitutes for, each other; the South will buy larger elements of skill and engineering services, the North more the cheap, skilled labor embodied in the final product. If, on the other hand, the country sticks to "self-reliance," which promotes only minor innovation around obsolete technologies, South-South trade will not be particularly beneficial in the longer term.

The foregoing argument has been strongly Indocentric and may not be relevant to the NICs that have followed a much more open policy to foreign capital and/or technology. For these countries the opportunities offered by South-South trade to develop further their innovative and technological capabilities are surely welcome. The fact that Korean enterprises sell civil construction services on a massive scale in the Middle East has not detracted the same firms from aggressively promoting other exports in the North, and the fact that Brazil has become the South's powerhouse for automobile production and provision of adapted products for assembly in a score of developing countries has not prevented its producers (all multinationals from the North) from using Brazil increasingly as a source of sophisticated components for the North.

To sum up: There is obviously no inherent conflict between exporting highly skilled and technology-intensive products to the South and exporting less technology-intensive products to the North. If one is not sacrificed to the other, South-South trade certainly can promote greater technological and skill development, simply because of the peculiarities of the needs of the South. However, a concentration on the South at the cost of building up international competitiveness in markets of the North may be counterproductive and growth-inhibiting.

South-South versus North-South

As I have argued above, for the exporting countries South-South relationships can serve a valuable purpose if they complement North-South relationships. A similar argument can be made for the general case of South-South trade in relation to North-South trade. For the importing countries of the South, any addition to sources of product or technology exports is an unambiguous benefit. The entry of NICs into such markets not only provides additional competition, it also provides (where relevant) products and technologies that are better adapted to their peculiar needs. As far as direct investment goes, the rise of Third World MNCs provides the package of finance, technology, and management on terms that may be less stringent than those of developed-country MNCs. In particular, Third World MNCs may be more willing to accept minority equity positions and to transfer all their technologies to their affiliates.

The existence of these benefits does not constitute a ground for arguing that South-South can substitute massively for North-South in product or technology trade. It can substitute only insofar as its capabilities have developed to international levels, either independently or as an intermediary between the most advanced technologies and the rather less advanced needs of developing countries. This leaves very large areas of modern industry and technology out of the reach of exporters from the South; the most dynamic, large-scale, and sophisticated technologies needed by the South will continue to be provided by the North.

It is possible that technology sellers from the South will increasingly enter into joint ventures with those from the North to transfer technologies to third countries. There would seem to be a natural division of labor between them in the provision of more routine and labor-intensive detailed engineering, project supervision, and production management services on the one hand and the more high-technology basic design, innovation, internationally integrated production on the other. However, such cooperative ventures have been slow to take off, for reasons that are not immediately obvious.

The basic premise for the argument that North-South and South-South relationships are more complementary than competitive is that the South needs "frontier" technologies in much of manufacturing industry (and in service activities). In most modern industries there is not really a great deal of scope for alternative technologies of much older vintage or much more labor-intensive nature. Exceptions can always be found on the grounds of smaller scales or employment in ancillary activities, but these are indeed exceptions. If this premise is accepted, then the complementary linkages between North and South are clearly established. The South can competitively provide a few adapted technologies in which it is efficient and a few unadapted technologies in which it is cheap; in others it cannot efficiently substitute for the North.

Issues for Negotiation

Where does all this lead us in terms of Global Negotiations? To the extent that the South still needs the North, the most important issues remain in the North-South realm, and so outside the scope of my chapter. However, I have pointed to a number of areas in which beneficial South-South exchange can take place. If these require special measures to promote them, there is an important (if minor) role for South-South economic negotiations.

I have some sympathy for the argument advanced by Havrylyshyn and Wolf that there is not much of a case "to justify a policy specifically aimed at promoting trade among developing countries" (p. 30). To the extent that policies promote export competitiveness in general and so enable industries to capture markets in the North as well as the South, there is obviously a strong argument for liberalization and promotion policies and negotiations. However, there may still be grounds to sponsor special South-South negotiations on the removal of handicaps to intra-South exchanges. After all, there are specific kinds of trade that occur in goods, services, and technologies between countries of the South. The more sophisticated forms of such trade are held back by marketing barriers (lack of established brand names), information gaps (lack of knowledge on the capabilities of other developing countries), institutional gaps (banking, finance), and infrastructural handicaps (shipping and liners' conferences, communications). These barriers cannot be removed simply by trade liberalization. Specific negotiations have to be undertaken—mainly intra-South, but also sometimes involving the North—to ensure that these various gaps are bridged.

My research on technology exports strongly suggests that budding exporters of the Third World have major difficulties in breaking into new foreign markets. Official cooperation can do a great deal to remove some of their handicaps with respect to the established and experienced exporters of the North. This is not an argument for discriminatory trade preferences in favor of the South; as Havrylyshyn and Wolf rightly argue, general liberalization and outward-looking policies are more desirable (and perhaps politically more feasible) than discriminatory, inward-looking policies addressed only to a trading bloc of developing countries. It is an argument, rather, for removing impediments to the entry of new competitors from the South.

By extension, this can also be made an argument to foster "infant" exporters. However, since the protection of infant industries by the South as a whole would necessarily mean that importing as well as exporting countries would share the cost of protection, this is unlikely to be politically feasible. The risk of fostering enterprises that never grow up to competitive international stature is likely to reduce further the chances of such negotiations succeeding. Thus, all the costs of bringing fledgling exporters of goods, services, and technology up to competitive levels will probably have to be borne by their home countries. South-South negotiations can only serve to reduce the extra entry handicaps that they face.

This is not to suggest that such negotiations will be simple or easy. On the contrary, official negotiators will suffer from the same credibility gaps that afflict the parties conducting market transactions. Moreover, the bridging of certain gaps to intra-South economic cooperation will require substantial investments (such as shipping, communications, information gathering, and commercial representation). It is beyond my competence to suggest how best negotiations on such matters can be launched. UNCTAD would be the obvious international forum, but who would provide the financial backup? Could the oil-rich countries of the South be persuaded to invest in such ventures, given their long-term economic viability? Would the importing, lesser industrialized countries see their interests lying in the promotion of alternative suppliers from the South? Would some countries in the North accept that in the long term they would preserve their own trading interests in the South best by entering into collaborative arrangements with its emerging exporters? These are all relevant issues requiring analysis.

Acknowledgments

I am grateful to the conference participants, in particular Andre Sapir and Martin Wolf, for helpful comments.

Notes

1. For a succinct statement of this view see Stewart 1982.

2. See Lewis 1980 and, for a critique, Riedel 1982.

3. In particular, see Amsden 1976, 1980 and Havrylyshyn and Wolf 1981 on South-South trade in manufactured products.

4. This paper is appearing in a forthcoming issue of *European Economic Review*. The authors also refer to papers touching on intra-Third World trade by Helen Hughes and Anne Krueger, both presented to the 1980 IEA Congress in Mexico. Also see Amsden 1980 for 1973 data.

5. The printed text of the Havrylyshyn-Wolf paper gives the year as 1973. This must be a misprint, since the period covered starts at 1963. I have taken the liberty of correcting the date in this quote.

6. Unfortunately the 1981 data are available only for very broad aggregates and so have not been used in table 12.1.

7. In 1977 these countries were, in descending order of importance, Spain, Singapore, Brazil, Korea, Hong Kong, Argentina, India, Yugoslavia, Israel, and Malaysia. This ranking applies to manufactured exports only. See Havrylyshyn and Wolf 1981, table 12.

8. Korea appears to be somewhat unusual in this activity in that its turnkey projects have generally been based on foreign designs and equipment, with

the Korean contractor essentially providing the overall organization and civil construction services. Other turnkey exporters mainly have used their own equipment and design capabilities.

9. Some of these service activities overseas are really intended to serve expatriate communities (banks) or to finance or promote exports from the home country (trading companies) rather than to participate directly in the economic life of the host country.

10. See Wells (forthcoming) and Lall 1982b. I am currently directing a four-country study of multinationals from Argentina, Brazil, Hong Kong, and India, which will be published soon under the title, *The New Multinationals: The Spread of Third World Enterprises* (forthcoming).

11. I am grateful to Professor Edward Chen of Hong Kong University for this information. The estimate is derived partly from interviews with parent companies in Hong Kong and partly by adding up data provided by the main host countries.

12. Based on the analysis of Chen.

13. Information provided by Annibal Villela Consultoria, Rio, Brazil. This figure excludes banking investments abroad by Banco do Brazil, which are also quite significant.

14. See, in particular, Balassa 1981, Krueger 1977, 1978, Baldwin 1979, Tyler 1972, Amsden 1980, Havrylyshyn and Wolf 1981, Díaz-Alejandro 1975, and Stewart 1982.

15. Note that the demand for small-scale, rather older-vintage technologies may also come from large countries that foster fragmented industries aimed at domestic markets, while small countries entering export-oriented operations will opt for large-scale, sophisticated equipment supplied by the developed countries.

16. In a subsequent publication, which became available only recently, Krueger (1983, pp. 108–110) extends this finding to a number of other developing countries.

17. Balassa 1981, chapter 6.

18. However, subsequent work by Havrylyshyn and Wolf, using Indian co-efficients to examine the factor content of the South's exports, shows that South-South exports are both more physical and human capital intensive than South-North exports. The factor content calculation is, of course, heavily weighted by traditional export products and so does not reflect the new sources of comparative advantage of the NICs.

19. For an illuminating historical analysis see Rosenberg 1976.

20. See Lall 1982a.

21. On the different degrees of technological rigidity in different industries, see Forsyth et al. (1980). This important paper strongly supports the possibility

of large changes in factor intensity rankings between developed and developing countries.

22. These measures are not the usual 'revealed comparative advantage' measures (*a la* Balassa), which deflate a particular country's exports by total world exports of that commodity. Both measures would give similar rankings only if the small country assumption were valid for India's exports of the manufactures in question and if the product definitions were close to those used internationally. I am grateful to Andre Sapir for pointing out this limitation of the statistical analysis conducted here.

23. The correlation matrix revealed rather low interrelationships between AW and each of the skill categories, so that we are safe in employing them in the same regressions.

24. Some background data collected by Carl Dahlman of the World Bank for the technology exports project indicate that, of all the NICs, India has had the least recourse to new foreign investment, technology licensing, and capital goods imports in the last two decades.

25. See Havrylyshyn and Wolf 1981, pp. 23–24, for a summary of such arguments.

26. See Lall (forthcoming).

References

Amsden, A. H. 1976. "Trade in Manufactures between developing Countries." *Economic Journal* 86, pp. 778–790.

Amsden, A. H. 1980. "The Industry Characteristics of Intra-Third World Trade in Manufactures." *Economic Development and Cultural Change* 28, pp. 181–219.

Balassa, B., 1981. *The Newly Industrialising Countries in the World Economy.* New York: Pergamon Press.

Baldwin, R. E. 1979. "Determinants of Trade and Foreign Investment: Further Evidence." *Review of Economics and Statistics* 61, pp. 40–48.

Bhagwati, J. N. 1964. "The Pure Theory of International Trade: A Survey." *Economic Journal* 74, pp. 1–84.

Bhagwati, J. N., and Desai, P. 1970. *India: Planning for Industrialization.* London: Oxford University Press.

Bhagwati, J. N., and Srinivasan, T. N. 1978. *Foreign Trade Regimes and Economic Development: India.* New York: National Bureau of Economic Research.

Díaz-Alejandro, C. F. 1976. *Foreign Trade Regimes and Economic Development: Colombia.* New York: National Bureau of Economic Research.

Forsyth, D. J. C., McBain, N., and Solomon, R. F. 1980. "Technical Rigidity and Appropriate Technology in Less Developed Countries." *World Development* 8, pp. 371–398.

Havrylyshyn, O., and Wolf, M. 1981. "Trade among Developing Countries: Theory, Policy Issues and Principal Trends" World Bank Staff Working Paper, No. 479. Washington, D. C.: World Bank.

Hirsch, S. 1977. *Rich Man's, Poor Man's and Every Man's Goods: Aspects of Industrialisation*, Tübingen: J. C. B. Mohr.

Krueger, A. O. 1977. "Growth Distortions and Patterns of Trade Among Many Countries," Princeton Studies in International Finance, No. 40.

———. 1978. "Alternative Trade Strategies and Employment in LDCs," *American Economic Review, Papers and Proceedings* (May), pp. 270–274.

———. 1983. *Trade and Employment in Developing Countries: Synthesis and Conclusions*. Chicago: University of Chicago Press.

Lall, S. 1981. *Developing Countries in the International Economy*. London: Macmillan.

———. 1982a. *Developing Countries as Exporters of Technology: A First Look at the Indian Experience*, London: Macmillan.

———. 1982b. "The Export of Capital from Developing Countries: the Indian Case." In J. Black and J. H. Dunning (eds.), *International Capital Movements*. London: Macmillan.

———. Forthcoming. "India's Technological Capacity: Effects of Trade, Industrial and Science and Technology Policies." In M. Fransman and K. King (eds.), *Indigenous Technological Capability in the Third World*. London: Macmillan.

Lewis, W. A. 1980. "The Slowing Down of the Engine of Growth." *American Economic Review* 70, pp. 555–564.

Riedel, J. 1982. "Trade as the Engine of Growth in Developing Countries, Revisited." Johns Hopkins University, Mimeo.

Rosenberg, N. 1976. *Perspectives on Technology*. London: Cambridge University Press.

Stewart, F. 1982. "Recent Theories of International Trade: Some Implications for the South." Queen Elizabeth House, Oxford, Mimeo.

Tyler, W. G. 1972. "Trade in Manufactures and Labour Skill Content: the Brazilian Case." *Economia Internazionale* 25, pp. 314–334.

Wells, L. T. Forthcoming. *Third World Multinationals*. Cambridge: MIT Press.

Annex: A Statement on North-South Economic Strategy

This statement was drafted by Jagdish N. Bhagwati and Carlos Díaz-Alejandro. It was based on reflections as inspired by the proceedings of the New Delhi Conference, whose papers are selected for publication in this volume. It was signed subsequently by several distinguished economists and political scientists who have made notable contributions to the fields of international economics, development, and North-South issues, as well as by policy makers, both from North and South. It was released before the Nonaligned Summit meeting and along with Brandt Commission's second report made a contribution to the outcome of the summit in favor of a moderate, pragmatic posture. See *India Today*, March 15, 1983, pp. 43–44.

Global Negotiations: Background

1. Global Negotiations at the United Nations have been aimed at review and design of the international economic system, to ensure more equitable outcomes from the international regime for the South and more stable and efficient economic conditions for all nations. These negotiations have made no progress since 1980, when attempts to launch them were initiated.

2. The Global Negotiations were conceived at the Havana Non-aligned meeting in 1979, like the earlier major initiative in favor of the New International Economic Order at the 1973 Non-aligned meeting in Algiers. In each case, the necessary political cohesion was provided by the general sense of solidarity among the Non-aligned nations seeking to play a more important role on the world scene. However, the immediate and critical factor prompting the Southern demands for negotiation was the "oil shock." The sharp increases in oil prices provided, in each instance, the necessary incentive for the North and South to seek a bargain that would include an energy, trade, and development package in exchange for other international economic reforms in areas such as finance and trade.

Why Have They Stalled?

3. A major reason for the Global Negotiations failing to get off the ground is that the energy card currently cannot be played. OPEC is facing difficult times. The North is relaxed about energy, partially justified by the success of conservation efforts since 1973. Therefore, the very factor that legitimated and prompted Global Negotiations, that is, the strength of oil prices, does not exist currently. The North simply does not feel it needs to negotiate, given its disproportionate political strength.

4. Yet another, immediately contextual reason for the failure to launch the Global Negotiations has been the overtly ideological orientation of the early Reagan administration toward Third World issues. These positions have been generally at variance with the political and economic viewpoints advanced by many Southern countries on North-South questions. While the Reagan administration is now more flexible in these matters than at the outset, the fundamentals have not changed yet. In view of the primacy of the United States in the proposed Global Negotiations, since it is the *force majeure* in the world economy, little progress can therefore be expected on these negotiations.

5. More fundamental, and longer-term, reasons also militate against progress on the Global Negotiations. There are deep divisions between the major Northern countries and the leaders of the South on the advisability, in negotiation procedures, of attempting a *"global bargain,"* embracing diverse sectoral issues simultaneously, versus negotiating *sectoral* questions, such as trade and finance, on a "single-issue" basis. The South generally prefers the former; the North generally favors the latter.

6. Closely allied to this asymmetry of preferences in negotiating strategy on global economic issues is the difference in preferences on *where* the negotiations ought to be conducted. The North seeks to negotiate on a sectoral basis at the existing specialized agencies, such as the IMF, GATT, and the World Bank, where the voting procedures are generally weighted and hence generally assign a decisive role to the North. The South prefers action at the United Nations, where the one-nation, one-vote principle is the chief operating procedure, with the South therefore at an advantage.

Need to Rethink Global Negotiations

7. There are therefore both short-term and immediately contextual, as well as medium-term and fundamental, reasons why the Global Negotiations cannot be expected to be launched at present. Energies and efforts directed at launching them cannot reasonably be expected to be successful.

8. Besides, it is important to appreciate that fruitless efforts at launching the unlaunchable are not inexpensive. They absorb high-level diplomatic and bureaucratic talent from the South. They also engender a sense of frustration in the South, a bitterness against the North, a perception of an unrealistic South in the North, and thus create a political environment that cannot be conducive to progress on the substantive issues in North-South relations. This is particularly so in view of the present and foreseeable political weakness of the South vis-à-vis the North. Again there is a noticeable tendency among some segments of Southern leadership, in view of the stalled Global Negotiations, to see and hence pronounce any major North-South or international economic initiative with promise of progress in the right direction for the South and not just the North, as a "diversionary tactic" aimed at destroying Global Negotiations. While this alarmist viewpoint is unpersuasive in view of the North's successful intransigence on the question of launching the Global Negotiations in the first place, it does make it particularly difficult for the G77 nations to seize new and negotiable opportunities.

Temporary Suspension of Global Negotiations: an Immediate Necessity

9. There is a compelling case, therefore, and one increasingly seen as such in academic and policymaking circles in Southern countries, for the South to *suspend* efforts at launching Global Negotiations at the United Nations.

10. Suspending the efforts to launch Global Negotiations can take the form of either formal adjournment or an informal, but concerted and definite, decision to put the launching efforts into a low-key setting with associated diplomatic measures, such as downgrading the personnel in charge.

11. The medium- and long-term question of abandoning Global Negotiations altogether does not need to be addressed at present. Both

the contentious nature of that suggestion and the potential it has for damaging the political cohesion of the South make this more drastic proposal one that must be put on the shelf for now.

Need to Combine Suspension of Global Negotiations with New Initiatives

12. It is imperative for the South's political cohesion and to impart a necessary element of progress to North-South relations that the suspension of efforts to launch Global Negotiations not be undertaken as an isolated measure. It must be combined with a *positive* set of measures that are consistent with, and indeed advance, the aspirations and basic objectives of the South.

13. These aspirations and objectives must include a greater voice in the deliberations concerning global economic problems and their solutions.

Initiating Deliberations on Medium-term Reform

14. In the medium run, this will require hastening the ongoing changes in current global institutions (e.g., the IMF and the World Bank) to allow the developing countries a greater role in policy formulation than was the case at their creation. This can be done while retaining the critical link between "interest" and "voting rights," as argued in a number of studies sympathetic to Southern aspirations for political equity and mindful of Northern concerns for economic efficiency.

15. At the same time, attention will have to be given to ensuring an appropriate and feasible role for the United Nations in global economic management. A compromise proposal that should unify the South and the North is to convert the United Nations, in appropriately modified organs, into a body where a *comprehensive view* of global problems is undertaken periodically, whereas the actual *decisions* on sectoral issues are taken with the aid of this comprehensive view at the specialized agencies.

16. These two medium-run changes require that the operating procedures of the existing specialized agencies be amended still further to ensure greater voice to, and hence loyalty from, their Southern members, consistent with power reflecting interest; whereas the United Nations would house the organ where the comprehensive review of global economic management would be periodically undertaken. This needs

to be supplemented by a serious examination of whether the existing specialized agencies should be added to in order to handle the emerging global economic issues. In this context, the emergence of international migration as a major phenomenon, between the North and South and not merely intra-South and intra-North, and the fragmented and *ad hoc* attention that it receives in different international agencies, if at all, points in the direction of a GATT for Migration to define a consensus on the economic (and political) rights and obligations of member states in regard to their borders and treatment of aliens.

17. We propose that, consistent with the suspension of the Global Negotiations, there should be an agenda for serious deliberations by key members of the South and the North to examine these questions of medium-term reform. There are acceptable and reasonable answers to these questions. Implementation of the proposals that emerge from negotiations concerning them must be treated as part of the renewed business of redesigning the global economic management structure in light of the major political and economic changes in the postwar period, and those impending in the 1980s, that Keynes, White, et al. did not envisage, and hence could not allow for, in their brilliant construction of the postwar international economic regime at Bretton Woods.

An Immediate Opportunity: The World Depression and Debts

18. But there also exists an immediate opportunity to make a concrete move in the direction of more universal global economic deliberations, embracing both North and South, in the current global macroeconomic crisis. This opportunity reflects the genuine mutuality of interests of North and South. It arises from the worrisome world debt situation and its manifold ramifications, which concern several key countries in both groups of nations.

19. It is a cliché, but nonetheless critically important, that all nations must embrace a World Recovery Program. It is hard to find respectable economists or responsible policymakers anywhere today who do not see the urgency of reversing the overkill of global economic activity in the recent fight against inflation. The South can only join in the calls, including the latest from the Brandt commissioners, for bolder and concerted steps to accelerate world recovery.

20. The key opportunity that this crisis paradoxically affords comes because Northern interests are now critically intertwined with Southern imperatives. Debts are a two-way street: the Northern lenders have as

great a stake in the viability of their loans as the Southern borrowers. There are therefore major influential pressure groups in the North that see Southern prosperity, and hence solvency, as vital to their own survival.

21. We need to seize immediately the resulting political opportunity to look at, and deliberate upon, the issues of international money and finance in their broader context, not losing from view therefore the implications for combating protectionism (i.e., the need to keep access to markets open if debts are to be repaid) and the need to direct augmented aid flows to the many distressed Southern nations who cannot borrow from the private markets. The necessity for joint, multilateral deliberations, keeping broader interactions between different sectoral issues in view, evidently exists.

An International Monetary Conference: Seizing the Tentative U.S. Initiative

22. In this context, the recent public pronouncements by Secretary Regan on the advisability of holding an international monetary conference, no matter how tentative, need to be followed up actively by the South and by the important OECD countries that are both politically influential with the United States and have visible interests of their own in the successful organization and outcome of such a conference.

23. The recent negotiations within the IMF for a quota increase, and the decision to expand the General Agreement to Borrow (GAB), are constructive responses to immediate problems and deserve wide endorsement. But they alone are not enough. The international financial system is under acute stress. We must therefore emphasize that, once these measures have been formally agreed to, attention needs to be directed to *further actions* in a comprehensive framework to make the system more resistant to shocks, less susceptible to instability, and more firmly set on a course of global noninflationary growth. Failure to move the system in these directions will have serious consequences, not only for the developed and medium-income developing countries but also for the poorer group of Southern nations whose earnings from exports of primary products have collapsed, creating a cumulative backlog of economic difficulties and potential political unrest. The proposed International Monetary Conference should be able to address the compelling monetary and financial issues that today confront both North and South.

24. In this regard, we suggest that the time is ripe for a substantial expansion and reform of the Compensatory Financing Facility (CFF), now administered by the IMF. The existing facility has proven to be seriously inadequate under the depressed conditions of the 1980s, which witnessed a fall in Southern export earnings unprecedented since the early 1930s. An enhanced CFF could also be restructured so that it moves more forcefully into medium-term, countercyclical finance, without impinging on the more traditional short-term, revolving-fund preoccupations of other IMF lending, which would maintain stricter conditionality.

25. Recent difficulties in the international financial system also demonstrate the need to take a coordinated view of international finance and trade. Toward this end, joint studies should be initiated by the staffs of GATT and the IMF, to quantify the impact of new and old protectionist measures on export earnings, and therefore on debt-servicing capacity. Such studies would clearly highlight the connection between financial and commodity markets, and warn against the damage that protectionist measures could inflict on the viability of the international financial system. Joint GATT-IMF studies could also be extended to explore ways in which gradual Southern trade liberalization could be supported by the international financial community.

26. In addition, both developing and developed countries would be served by consideration anew of the future uses of SDRs and of ways of better management of exchange rate relations.

27. Restructuring and expanding the CFF, initiating joint GATT-IMF studies of the links between trade and finance, and reopening of talks on international monetary reform, are only among the more compelling examples of the concrete actions that the conference endorsed by us ought to immediately address. The conference would provide the forum where these and several other economic and institutional changes of mutual benefit could be considered in a truly multilateral context, against the backdrop of a comprehensive view of the world economy with all its linkages among trade, finance, etc. The opportunity to hold such a conference should not, therefore, be missed.

The 1983 Non-aligned Conference in New Delhi: An Urgent Appeal

28. We urgently appeal therefore to the Non-aligned nations, as they gather in late February through early March 1983 in New Delhi, to embrace our threefold agenda:

i. Temporary suspension of the attempts at launching Global Negotiations.

ii. Simultaneous launching of a constructive, joint North-South program to explore the possible implementation in the medium run of several promising proposals for improved and more equitable global management of the world economy.

iii. An immediate seizing of the opportunity, provided by Secretary Regan's tentative thoughts, to organize and to participate actively in an International Monetary Conference.

29. The 1973 Algiers, and the 1979 Havana, Non-aligned Conferences played a historic role in providing key turning points in Southern postures on North-South relations. The 1983 New Delhi Non-aligned meeting can play a similar, historic role. This will require a bold embracing of new and promising initiatives that reflect substance rather than shadow, reality rather than rhetoric. We have sought to provide the agenda that can serve this end.

The North: Need for Flexibility

30. We would be remiss if we did not equally urge the Northern leadership to be more flexible in its attitudes, less doctrinaire in its ideological assertions, and more mindful of the political aspirations of the South.

31. The agenda that we have proposed here recognizes the North's fears and hesitations, while conforming simultaneously to the South's needs and aspirations.

32. Practicality, not vision, should suffice to embrace it. It would be a sorry reflection on the quality of our leadership, both in the North and in the South, if even practicality were beyond our grasp.

Contributors

Jere R. Behrman is William P. Kenan, Jr., Professor of Economics, co-director of the Center for Analysis of Developing Economies, and associate director of the Joseph H. Lauder Institute for Management and International Studies at the University of Pennsylvania. He is a fellow of the Econometric Society and a past fellow of the Guggenheim, Ford, and Compton foundations. He has written or edited 14 books and about 100 professional papers, largely on development issues, and has consulted widely for international organizations, governments, and research institutions on development.

Jagdish N. Bhagwati is Arthur Lehman Professor of Economics and director of the International Economics Research Center at Columbia University. He was Ford International Professor of Economics at the Massachusetts Institute of Technology and has been professor of international trade at the Delhi School of Economics and Ford Research Professor of Economics at the University of California at Berkeley. He is the founding editor of the *Journal of International Economics*. He has written and edited 25 books on the theory and policy of international trade, North-South issues, aid, international migration, and developmental planning. He is a fellow of the Econometric Society and of the American Academy of Arts and Sciences. He has been a member and a chairman of expert groups at UNCTAD, UNIDO, ECAFE, and several other international agencies.

Albert Bressand has been deputy director of the Institut Français des Relations Internationales since 1980. He was Charge des Missions for economic issues in the policy-planning staff of the French Ministry of Foreign Affairs in 1978–79. He has served as a member of the French delegation to the Eleventh Special Session of the United Nations in

1980 and to the United Nations Conference on New and Renewable Sources of Energy at Nairobi in 1981. He was an advisor to the French president on Euro-Arab-African Relations in 1980–82 and a consultant to the World Bank in 1977. He teaches at the Sorbonne and the Ecole Nationale des Administrations.

Padma Desai is professor of economics at Columbia University. She is a member of the executive committee of the W. Averell Harriman Institute for Advanced Study of the Soviet Union at Columbia and of the visiting committee of the Russian Research Center at Harvard University. Her articles have appeared in the *American Economic Review* and the *Quarterly Journal of Economics*. She edited the volume *Marxism, Central Planning, and Soviet Economy*, and has consulted extensively for international agencies, including the OECD, the ECAFE, the UN, and the FAO.

Carlos Díaz-Alejandro, professor of economics at Yale University, has written extensively on developmental and trade theory and policy and has also made major contributions to the historical study of Latin American economies. A developmental economist, he is also noted for his contributions to policy making. He has served on expert groups at UNCTAD, the World Bank, and several other international agencies, and he was a member of the 1983–84 presidential commission on Central America. His many books include *Foreign Trade Regimes and Economic Development: Colombia, Less Developed Countries and the Post-1971 International Financial System*, and *Handmaiden in Distress: World Trade in the 1980s*. He has served on many editorial boards and is co-editor of the *Journal of Development Economics*.

Muchkund Dubey is a member of the Indian foreign service and a distinguished diplomat in the field of multinational economic issues. He is the permanent representative of India to the United Nations offices in Geneva. Earlier he was India's High Commissioner for Bangladesh. He has been the chairman of the Group of 77 and the rapporteur and chairman of the preparatory committees for drafting the International Development Strategies for the 1970s and 1980s. He has written extensively on international economic issues.

Catherine Gwin was a senior associate at the Carnegie Endowment for International Peace from 1981 through 1983. Before that, she worked at the Council on Foreign Relations as a staff member and then as executive director of the council's 1980s Project. In 1980–81 she served in the U.S. government as North-South Issues Coordinator for the International Development Cooperation Agency. She has authored various articles on international economic cooperation and collaborated on the book *Collective Management: Reform of Global Economic Organizations.*

Sanjaya Lall is a fellow of Green College at Oxford University. He is noted for his extensive contributions to the analysis of multinational corporations and his work on technology transfer. He has also served as honorary director of the Indian Council for Research in International Economic Relations. He has been a consultant to several international agencies, including the World Bank and UNIDO.

John Gerard Ruggie, professor of political science at Columbia University, previously taught at the University of California at Berkeley. His published work concerns aspects of international relations theory, international political economy, and world systemic change. He is the general editor of a series of books on the political economy of international change. He frequently consults for agencies of the United Nations and the United States government.

John W. Sewell, president of the Overseas Development Council, is the author of *The United States and World Development: Agenda 1980,* a co-editor of *Rich Country Interests and Third World Development,* and the co-author of "The Ties that Bind: U.S. Interests in Third World Development."

Martin Wolf is director of studies at the Trade Policy Research Centre in London. He was on the staff of the World Bank in Washington from 1971 to 1981. He is the author of *Adjustment Policies and Problems in Developed Countries* and *India's Exports* and a co-author of *Textile Quotas against Developing Countries.*

I. William Zartman, professor of international politics and director of African studies at the Johns Hopkins School for Advanced International Studies in Washington, is the author of *The Politics of Trade Negotiations* between *Africa and the European Communities* and *The Practical Negotiator* and the editor of *The 50% Solution* and *The Negotiation Process*. He directed the ODC North-South Negotiations Project and is editing the resulting book.

Index